The Business Case for Diversity

4th Edition

Allegiant Media
317 George Street, Suite 420
New Brunswick, NJ 08901-2008

FOURTH EDITION

ISBN 0-972-1112-4-7

DiversityInc

Luke Visconti	Partner and Co-Founder
Foulis Peacock	Partner and Co-Founder
Niraj Kataria	Chairman of the Board
Barbara Frankel	Vice President, Executive Editor
Conrad Ramos	Vice President, Finance and Operations
Kimberly Stewart	Manager, Customer Service

Project Leaders

Barbara Frankel
Elena Maria Lopez
Barbara S. Falk

Editorial

Luke Visconti	Partner and Co-Founder
Barbara Frankel	Vice President, Executive Editor
Oriol R. Gutierrez Jr.	Managing Editor
Yoji Cole	Los Angeles Bureau Chief
C. Stone Brown	Washington, D.C. Bureau Chief
Linda Bean	Deputy Editor
Ruth Zeilberger	Senior Journalist
Angela D. Johnson	Senior Journalist
Elena Maria Lopez	Journalist
Melanie Austria Farmer	Journalist

Web/Marketing

Brian Chambers	Director of Marketing and Web Services
Audrey Taylor	Associate Webmaster
Nneka Keshi	Associate Webmaster
Barbara S. Falk	Circulation Director
Tracy D. Warner-Venzen	Circulation Coordinator
Carolynn L. Johnson	Marketing Manager
Jeffrey Wiggins	Marketing Assistant
Rachelle Pachtman	Public Relations

Sales

Foulis Peacock	Partner and Co-Founder
Kimberly Stewart	Manager, Customer Service
Debby Scheinholtz	Account Manager
Karen Copeland	Sales Administrator
Linda Leonard	Office Administrator

DiversityInc Careers

Carl Braun	President, DiversityInc Careers
Terrence Rice	Recruitment Advertising Account Manager
Patti Yaritz	Recruitment Consultant

Finance

Conrad Ramos	Vice President, Finance and Operations
Margaret Ber	Full-Charge Bookkeeper
Norma Chowdhury	Accounts Receivable

DiversityInc Advertising

Hensley Jemmott	Principal, Account Services
Bill Allen	Principal, Creative Director

DiversityInc Consultants

Luis Munoz	Vice President, General Manager

Table of Contents

Table of Contents

Table of Contents

Table of Contents

INTRODUCTION:

A. Why Is a Business Case Necessary?

Those who still perceive diversity as a "do-the-right-thing" societal goal miss the point. This nation is changing dramatically, and companies that understand the demographic shift must correspondingly shift their customer focus, employee base and management. Convincing leaders of competitive U.S. businesses, as well as educational institutions and government agencies, to include diversity in all their strategic business goals gets easier each year. For those who need statistical proof, we offer the fourth edition of The Business Case for Diversity.

B. New Demographics Tell The Story

Thirty-one percent of the U.S. population in 2000 was comprised of people of color.[1]

Census 2000 was an alarm reverberating throughout corporate America. The data showing the surging population of people of color in this country and, particularly, the rapid growth of the Latino population, resounded through consumer-products companies, financial-services firms and marketing/advertising agencies throughout the nation. Two years since that data was released, the Census Bureau has announced several key updates, most of which confirm the speedy evolution of U.S. demographics but some of which also raise new controversies, such as the issue over which minority group is the largest and why that is important.

Note: Some of the demographic statistics cited here are based on the mid-2001 population estimates by the U.S. Census Bureau and others on the March 2002 Current Population Survey (CPS).

Also, varying demographic studies of the U.S. population show significantly different information. The critical area of controversy, for the Census Bureau as well as others studying the population, is the race of Latinos, who are defined by the Census Bureau as Hispanics. Some Latinos/Hispanics identify as white, others as black, and many as "other" and just about everybody agrees being Latino/Hispanic is an ethnicity, not a race. So how do we best include these "people of color"?

According to Census Bureau demographers, a large number of Latinos put down their race as white, while many others choose "other race" on the census forms. Roberto Ramirez, a Census Bureau demographer, says about 90 percent of those checking off the "other race" category are Latino, and many of them are Puerto Rican. Ramirez says half of Latinos put down "white" as their race on census forms. Therefore, to identify the white population for purposes of this business case, we use the "non-Hispanic white" classification to identify whites.[2]

To identify people of color, we took the total U.S. population and subtracted the non-Hispanic white population. As an alternative, one can compare the white with the non-white population, and subtract "white Hispanics" from the overall white population.

The true strength of the Latino market, as proven by the January 2003 figures released by the U.S. Census Bureau, reinforced the belief of marketers, corporate America and the media that this demographic group will be essential to future success. The revised census data, which estimated the U.S. population for mid-2001, showed the number of Latinos surpassed the number of African Americans for the first time. This total U.S. population estimate was the first released by the bureau since the initial 2000 census report.

The total U.S. population grew to 284.8 million in July 2001, up from 281.4 million in April 2000, an increase of 1.2 percent.

According to the 2001 estimates:

- White non-Hispanics numbered 196.2 million, an increase of 0.3 percent since 2000, representing 68.9 percent of the population.

- African Americans numbered 36.2 million in mid-2001, a 1.5 percent increase since 2000, representing 12.7 percent of the population.

- Latinos numbered 37 million, increasing 4.7 percent since 2000, representing 13 percent of the population.

- Native Americans and Alaska Natives numbered 2.7 million, a 2.3 percent increase since 2000, representing slightly less than 1 percent of the population.

- Asian Americans numbered 11 million, a 3.7 percent increase since 2000, representing 3.9 percent of the population.

According to recently released Census Bureau estimates for March 2002, the African-American population reached 36 million, or 13 percent of the U.S. population.[3] In that same time period, the Asian-American population grew to 12.5 million or 4.4 percent of the overall U.S. population as of March 2002.[4] This is a 13.6 percent increase in the Asian-American population since the July 2001 estimates and an 18 percent increase since Census 2000. In 2002, the Latino population reached 38.8 million, which equals 13.3 percent of the U.S. population.

Growth of Ethnic Populations Between 2000 and 2001

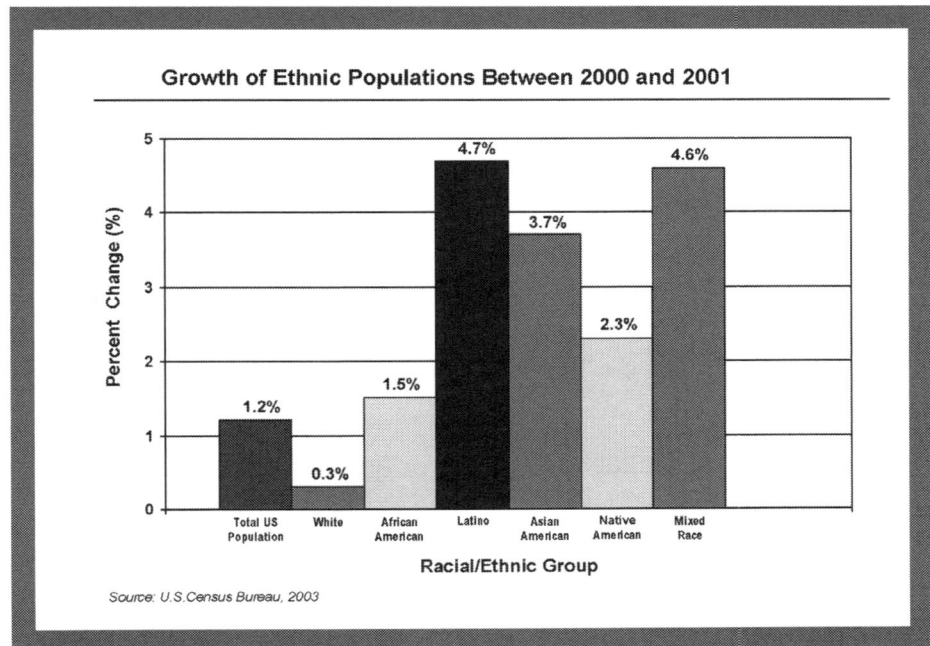

Source: U.S. Census Bureau, 2003

People of mixed race (two or more races) numbered 4.1 million people, a 4.6 percent increase since 2000, representing 1.5 percent of the population. The 2000 census was the first time the U.S. census gave people an option to choose more than one race. Census 2000 researchers created seven race categories from respondents' answers: white, black or African American, American Indian and Alaska Native, Asian, Native Hawaiian and Other Pacific Islander, and some other race. Census 2000 reported that 2.5 percent (5.5 million) of whites were at least one other race, compared with 4.8 percent (1.8 million) of African Americans. About one in three of all people reporting mixed race in Census 2000 were of Latino origin.[5]

Where Biracial People Live

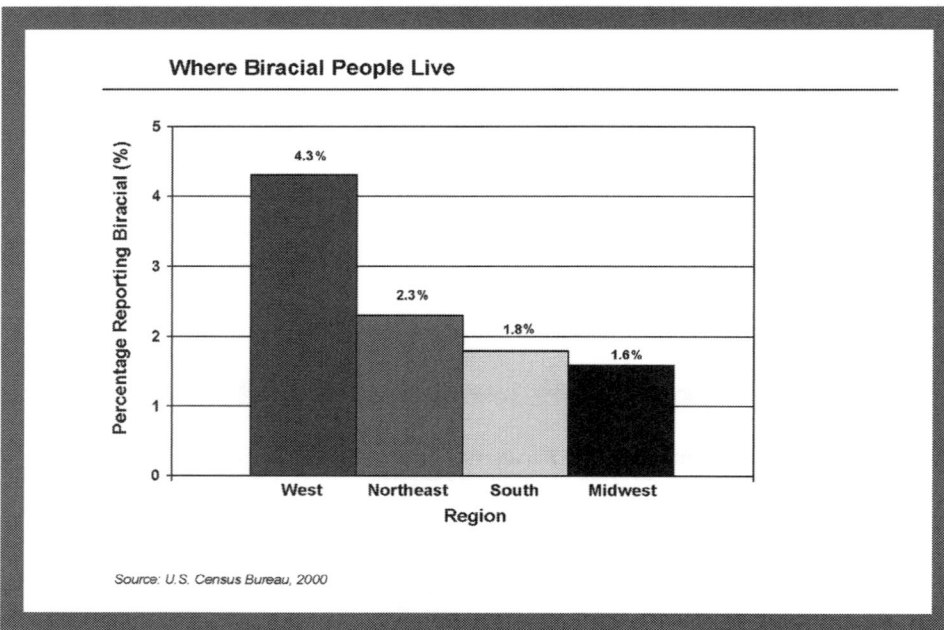

Source: U.S. Census Bureau, 2000

Clearly, the population of the United States is changing dramatically, and these changes are expected to accelerate in the coming decades.

According to Census 2000 statistics: For Americans 70 years and older, there are 5.63 whites for every person of color.

For people younger than age 40 in America, there are 1.72 (non-Hispanic) whites for every person of color.

For people younger than age 10 in America, there are 1.47 (non-Hispanic) whites for every person of color.

The future projections by the Census Bureau make this case even more eloquently. The bureau predicts that:

- By 2010, the U.S. population will be 67.3 percent white; 14.6 percent Latino, 13.3 percent African American; 5.1 percent Asian American/Pacific Islander

- By 2030, the U.S. population will be 60.1 percent white; 19.4 percent Latino, 14.1 percent African American; 7.1 percent Asian American/Pacific Islander

- By 2050, the U.S. population will be 52.8 percent white; 24.3 percent Latino, 14.7 percent African American; 9.3 percent Asian American/Pacific Islander

U.S. Populations by Race and Ethnicity, 2010-2050

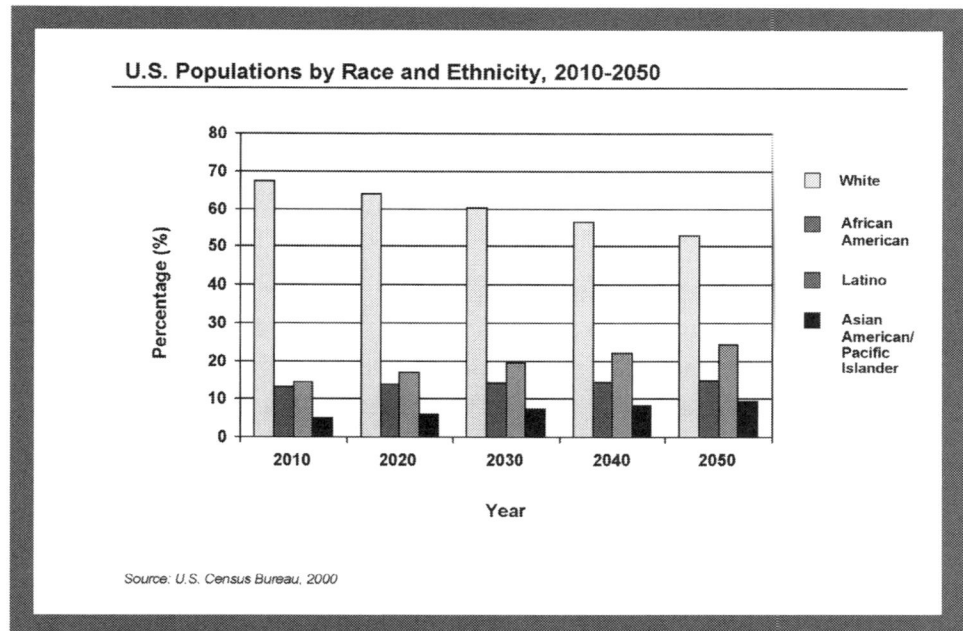

Source: U.S. Census Bureau, 2000

Of the current population, the geographic demographics show an increase of people of mixed race, primarily in the West, where 4.3 percent of all respondents reported more than one race. This compares with 2.3 percent in the Northeast, 1.8 percent in the South and 1.6 percent in the Midwest. California, with 1.6 million claiming biracial heritage, was the only U.S. state with a multiracial population greater than 1 million in 2000.

New York followed California with 590,000 and Texas followed with 515,000. These three states accounted for 40 percent of the nation's total multiracial population.[6]

This number is expected to grow as interracial marriages increase.

According to Census 2000, 7 percent of the 54.5 million married couples in the United States were interracial couples. Another 15 percent of the 4.9 million unmarried heterosexual couples in the country were interracial in 2000.

Western states and states with high multicultural populations have a higher rate of interracial couples, both married and unmarried, according to the census. For example, more than one-third of married couples and one-half of heterosexual unmarried couples in Hawaii were interracial. Alaska, New Mexico and Oklahoma also have high rates on interracial relationships, with New Mexico and Oklahoma having large populations of Native Americans. On the other hand, Maine, New Hampshire and Vermont all have lower percentages of interracial relationships and lower numbers of ethnic and multicultural populations.[7]

1. African Americans

In January 2003, the U.S. Census Bureau released estimates for the population through mid-2001. According to 2001 estimates, 36.2 million African Americans live in the United States, a 1.5 percent increase since Census 2000. In July 2001, African Americans comprised 12.7 percent of the nation's population, up from 12.6 percent in April 2000. The African-American population grew by 700,000 in the 15 months after the census data first was released.

African Americans still tend to be concentrated in the South, as indicated in the April 2003 report by the U.S. Census Bureau. According to census figures, 55.3 percent of African Americans currently live in the South, with 18.1 percent in the Midwest, 18.1 percent in the Northeast and 8.6 percent in the West.[8]

More than 50 percent of African Americans live in urban areas, with 51.5 percent living in a metropolitan area within a city, 36 percent living in a suburban area, and 12.5 percent living in rural areas. This compares with 56.8 percent of whites living in a suburban area, 21.1 percent living in an urban area, and 22.1 percent living in a rural area.[9]

The African-American population also is younger on average than the white population. In 2002, 33 percent of African Americans were younger than 18, compared with 23 percent of whites, according to Census Bureau figures.[10]

The areas with the largest concentration of African Americans are: Gary, Ind.; Birmingham, Ala.; Jackson, Miss.; New Orleans; Baltimore; Atlanta; Memphis; Washington, D.C.; and Richmond, Va.

Where African Americans Live

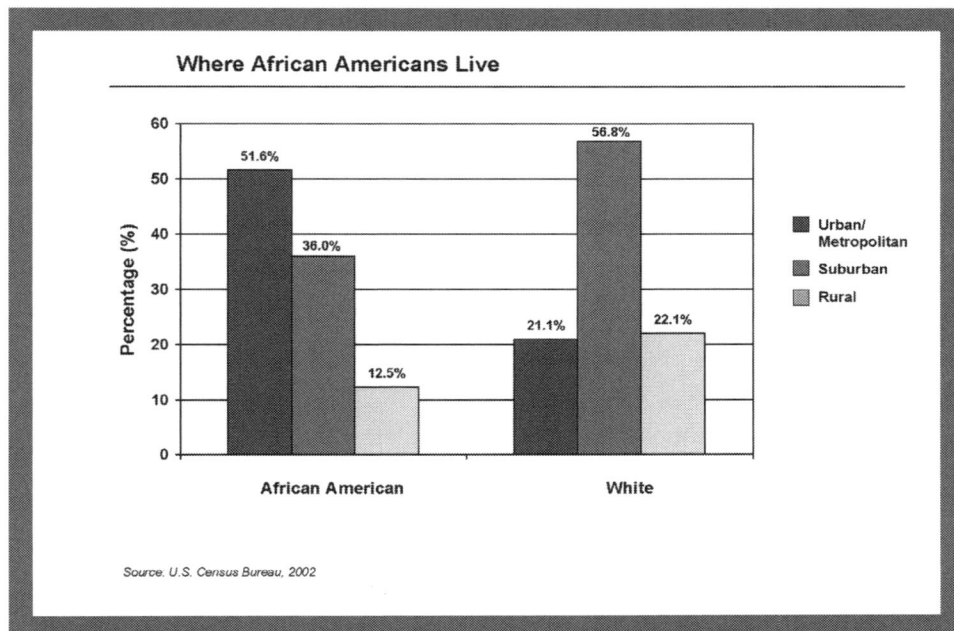

Source: U.S. Census Bureau, 2002

Big cities with large African-American populations are New York, Los Angeles, Chicago, Houston, Philadelphia, Phoenix, San Diego, Dallas, San Antonio and Detroit.

What is the proper term for this group? It all depends on who you are.

The term black or African American refers to people having origins in any of the black racial groups of Africa. Many in the African-American community today use "black" and African American interchangeably. Beginning in the mid to late 1980s, possibly a little bit earlier, people began using the term "African American," says Kenneth W. Goings, department chair of African & African American Studies at Ohio State University. He believes the Census Bureau came up with the designation African American. "I know that once they did, (the Rev.) Jesse Jackson began to use it."[11]

Not all blacks in this country are African American — some come from the Caribbean or from Africa directly.[12] The U.S. Census Bureau records people who live here, whether or not they are citizens.

According to the U.S. Immigration and Naturalization Service, in 2000, 44,731 Africans and 88,198 Caribbeans qualified for green cards, allowing them to live and work legally in the United States.

Thousands more come without documentation. They also immigrate on temporary and seasonal work permits, on student visas, are recruited by corporations on H1B visas for those with special, technical work skills, come as nurses or teachers on H12 visas, or come to visit family, who eventually sponsor them.[13]

The Census Bureau estimates that there are 839,547 Africans in the United States, of whom 557,300 are not naturalized citizens. The Census Bureau also estimates that more than 2.8 million people living in the United States are from the Caribbean, of whom 1.4 million are naturalized citizens. Of these African and Caribbean emigrants, 6.3 percent were folded into the African-American population, according to Census 2000.

Still, most black people living in the United States are African American, so for future purposes in this document, we will use the term African American.

2. Latinos

The federal Office of Management and Budget defines Hispanic or Latino as "a person of Cuban, Mexican, Puerto Rican, South or Central American, or other Spanish culture or origin, regardless of race."

Census Bureau demographer Ramirez says the bureau long has expected that Latinos someday would surpass African Americans because their birth and immigration rates are higher.[14] African Americans accounted for 12.7 percent of the population in 2001 and accounted for 15.3 percent of all births in 2000. Latinos accounted for 13 percent of the population in 2001 but 20.1 percent of all new births in 2000.[15]

By July 2001, the Latino population had increased to 37 million, 13 percent of the entire U.S. population of 284.8 million, according to the U.S. Census Bureau. That's up from 12.5 percent or 35.3 million of the country's 281.4 million residents in April 2000. The U.S. Latino population has increased rapidly in recent years, rising from 6 percent of the population in 1980 to 10 percent in 1995.

Between 2002 and 2020, the population growth of Latinos is expected to be 2.8 percent a year, compared with an annual growth rate of 0.8 percent for the entire U.S. population, according to a study by Global Insight, a Lexington, Mass.,-based research and consulting group. If these projections are correct, this would put the Latino population at 18.9 percent of the U.S. population by 2020.[16]

A principal research associate at the Urban Institute's Population Studies Center, Jeffrey Passel, predicts that in 20 to 50 years, Latinos should account for 25 percent of the population. The Urban Institute is a nonpartisan research institute based in Washington, D.C.[17]

Latino Americans come from a variety of cultural and geographic backgrounds. For example, 62 percent come from Mexico, 14 percent from Central or South America and 12 percent from Puerto Rico, according to the Census Bureau.

In March 2002, 11.5 percent (32.5 million) of the U.S. population was foreign born.[18] In 2002, 52.2 percent of immigrants were from Latin America, 25.5 percent from Asia, 14 percent from Europe and 8.3 percent from other countries.[19]

In 2002, 27.5 percent of Latinos spoke Spanish at home, and 30 percent of them primarily spoke Spanish with little English (8.3 million), according to the Global Insight study. The study projects that 41.7 million Latino people will speak Spanish in their homes by 2020.[20]

Seventy-two percent of foreign-born Latinos are Spanish-dominant, 24 percent are bilingual and 4 percent are English-dominant, according to the Pew Center. This compares with 61 percent of U.S.-born Latinos who are English-dominant, 35 who are percent bilingual, and 4 percent who are Spanish-dominant.[21]

The term Latino appeared on the census form for the first time in 2000. The 1990 and 1980 censuses asked people if they were of Spanish/Hispanic descent and, if so, to choose Mexican, Puerto Rican, Cuban or other Spanish/Hispanic. The 1970 census was the first to include a separate question specifically on Hispanic origin, although it was asked of only a 5 percent sample of U.S. households.

In 2001, 19 percent of all legal immigrants were from Mexico.[22]

More than 7 million emigrants from Mexico moved to the United States between 1990 and 2000, accounting in large part for the surge in the Latino population revealed by Census 2000.

New York City is an excellent microcosm of the changing U.S. Latino population. Puerto Ricans no longer are the city's majority Latino group. The city's approximately 789,000 Puerto Ricans now account for 37 percent of area Latinos, down from 50 percent in 1990. The drop makes New York's Puerto-Rican community the smallest it has been since the 1960s. The decline occurred as emigrants from other South and Central American countries arrived in droves.

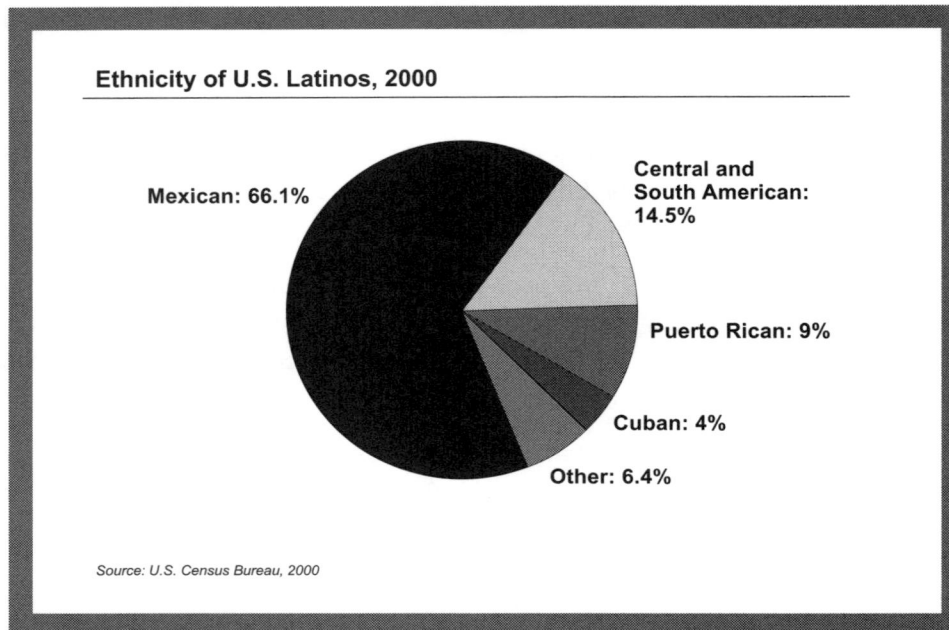

Ethnicity of U.S. Latinos, 2000

Mexican: 66.1%

Central and South American: 14.5%

Puerto Rican: 9%

Cuban: 4%

Other: 6.4%

Source: U.S. Census Bureau, 2000

An influx of Mexicans made the most identifiable impact in the latest census figures. Mexicans have replaced Puerto Ricans as New York City's majority Latino group. Between 1990 and 2000, Mexican population tripled to 187,000 with more than 61 percent of the population living in Brooklyn and Queens. Mexicans comprised almost 9 percent of the city's Latino population in 2000, census data showed, up from 3.5 percent in 1990.

3. Asian Americans

In mid-2001, Asian Americans numbered 11 million, a 3.7 percent increase since Census 2000. Only Latinos (up 4.7 percent) and people of mixed races (up 4.6 percent) increased at a higher rate.[23]

In 2001, 41 percent of all foreigners naturalized in the United States were from Asia.[24]

Asian Americans are the third largest minority group in the United States, according to Census 2000 data. They comprise 3.6 percent of the U.S. population. Data from the U.S. Census Bureau released in March 2002 showed Chinese Americans are the largest ethnicity among Asian Americans, with 2.7 million people, followed by Filipino Americans with 1.8 million people and Asian-Indian Americans with 1.6 million. Vietnamese Americans total 1.1 million and Korean Americans now total 1.07 million. Japanese Americans now rank sixth among all Asian-American subgroups, with 796,000 people. The census reports that all other Asian-American ethnicities equal 1.2 million people.[25]

Additionally, census data showed that Asians were the fastest growing ethnic group in the United States, surging 48 percent between 1990 and 2000. If people who are of partial Asian descent were included, the population increased by 78 percent, compared with an approximate 13 percent increase of the overall U.S. population.

Aside from Chinese Americans, Filipinos and Asian Indians are the next largest Asian group in the United States, at nearly 2 million each, with Asian Indians representing the most rapidly growing segment within the Asian-American population.[26]

A majority of all Asian-American groups (49 percent) live in the Western states, with 75 percent of Asian Americans living in 10 states: California, New York, Hawaii, Texas, New Jersey, Illinois, Washington, Florida, Virginia and Massachusetts. By comparison, only 47 percent of the general population lives in these states.

The Asian-Indian population currently is the sixth-largest ethnic community and third-largest immigrant community — behind Mexicans and Chinese — in the United States.

The surge of immigrants from the Indian subcontinent was fueled by the large number of information-technology professionals entering the country during the 1990s technology boom,[27] according to Peter DeSouza, senior vice president at Admerasia, a New York-based advertising agency specializing in the Asian-American market.

Dave Banerjee, president of the New York-based South-Asian advertising agency 1947 Communications, says South Asians in the United States have an average household income of $67,552, considerably higher than the $45,257 national average. He estimates that, as a whole, the group wields $137 billion in buying power. "It's the most affluent group among any ethnicity in America, by far," Banerjee says.

Ethnicity of Asian Americans, 2002

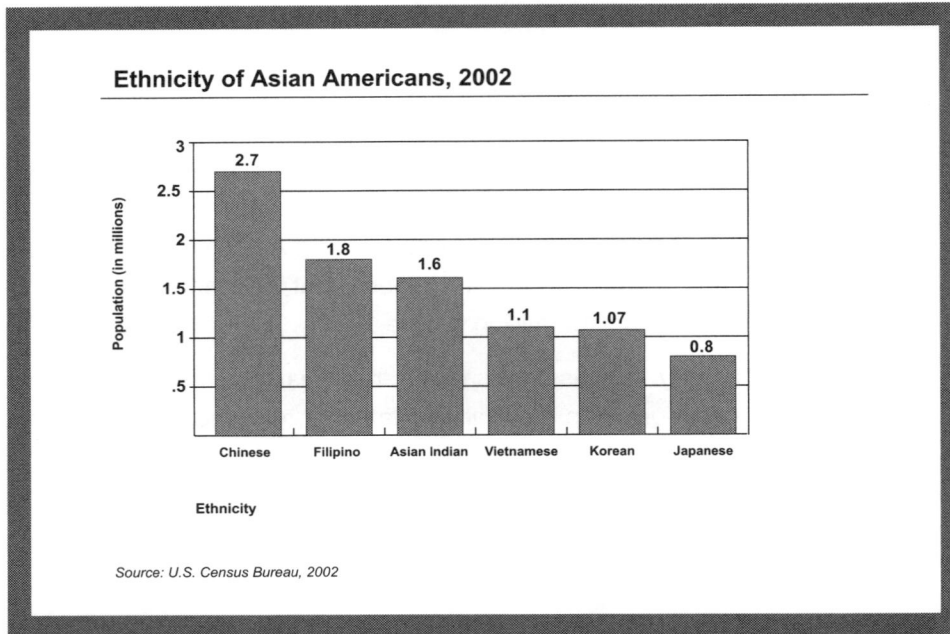

Source: U.S. Census Bureau, 2002

U.S. Census data show that the South-Asian population grew 106 percent to 2.2 million between 1990 and 2000. Much of this growth stemmed from South Asians who came to America in the 1990s on HB-1 visas to work in the technology sector. Banerjee says the dot-com fallout is causing this growth trend to begin to taper off.[28]

4. Gay, Lesbian, Bisexual and Transgender People

Unlike ethnic markets, the gay, lesbian, bisexual and transgender (GLBT) market requires members to identify themselves as part of the group. Therefore, painting an accurate portrait of the exact size of the GLBT market is difficult, although not impossible.

According to data from census 2000, same-sex couples resided in 99.3 percent of all counties across the United States. (Census data did not reveal households that identified as bisexual or transgender.)

Only 0.2 percent of all households identified themselves as a same-sex married couple in the 1990 census, according to the U.S. Census

Bureau. That figure increased to 0.6 percent in the 2000 census.

Washington, D.C.,-based Witeck-Combs Communications and Packaged Facts, a unit of New York-based MarketResearch.com, estimated the size of the GLBT market for "The Gay & Lesbian Market: New Trends, New Opportunities" report in October 2002. The companies derived the size of the GLBT market by benchmarking 6 percent to 7 percent of the total U.S. market as GLBT.

The gay and lesbian population numbers 14.2 million, according to the report, and is expected to reach 15.8 million by 2007, an increase of 10.8 percent. Gay men are estimated to make up 58 percent of this market, with gay men numbering 8.3 million and lesbians numbering about 6 million.[29]

While gay men account for approximately 8 percent of the overall male population, they account for 10 percent to 11 percent of the male population between 18 and 49 years old, according to the report.[30]

According to studies conducted by Witeck-Combs in conjunction with research-firm Harris Interactive, a rough total of 13 million to 14.5 million U.S. residents consistently self-identity as gay, lesbian, bisexual and transgender.

While the count of same-sex unmarried partner households increased in the United States from 145,130 in 1990 to 594,691 in 2000, two surveys of gay, lesbian, bisexual and transgender (GLBT) people show an undercount of between 16 percent and 19 percent of same-sex couples. GLBT people who lived with a same-sex partner on April 1, 2000, could list themselves as "unmarried partners" on the official census form.

The U.S. Census 2000 count of same-sex couples missed at least 100,000 couples, according to a study just released by the Institute for Gay and Lesbian Strategic Studies (IGLSS). The surveys also found that more than two-thirds of the couples not using "unmarried partner" instead listed themselves as "housemates/roommates" on the census forms. When asked why they did not call themselves unmarried partners, respondents reported confidentiality concerns and a lack of fit of census options for their own family configurations. A small group of same-sex couples that referred to themselves as married will be recaptured by the Census Bureau policy of recoding same-sex "husband/wife" couples to unmarried partners.

But the Census Bureau's policy of recoding these couples is "almost deliberately obscuring," says M.V. Lee Badgett, a labor economist and co-author of the IGLSS study. She notes that there are important differences between same-sex couples that marked "unmarried partner" and those that marked "married." Namely, that those who marked married were more likely to have kids and tended to be older.

Perhaps even more significantly, the U.S. Census does not ask any questions about sexual orientation. Same-sex partners were captured unintentionally under the category of "unmarried partner," a question developed out of the Census Bureau's interest in heterosexual unmarried couples, according to Badgett. "That means we know nothing about single (GLBT) people," she said. She estimated that there are at least three or four times as many GLBT people who are not captured by same-sex couple statistics because they are single.

The IGLSS survey asked people in couples to report their census answers after they had registered with the census. It used two sources to survey people in couples: people attending a political rally and people enrolled in a database of online survey respondents.

IGLSS researchers asked individuals if they had been living with a same-sex partner on April 1, 2000, the official census day, and gave respondents who met that criterion a two-page survey to fill out. The team collected surveys from 182 people, 173 of whom lived with same-sex partners and filled out census forms.

In June 2000, Harris Interactive and Witeck-Combs Communications included five questions from the IGLSS survey on their online poll. Out of the 5,458 individuals surveyed, 300 (5.6 percent) identified themselves as gay, lesbian, bisexual or transgender. Of that smaller group, 90 said they had been living with same-sex partners on April 1.

Based on Witeck-Comb's research, 2 percent to 3 percent of those surveyed identified themselves as gay males; 1 percent to 1.5 percent as lesbians; and the remaining 3 percent to 3.5 percent identified themselves as bisexual, making bisexuals the largest subgroup within the GLBT community.

Of the 6.5 percent of Americans who self-identify as GLBT, Witeck-Combs says these people share many of the same characteristics as other Americans (i.e. age, race, socio-economic status), with GLBT people represented across every cross-section of the U.S. population.

The number of gay and lesbian households with children younger than age 18 is on the rise. An October survey by Harris Interactive and Witeck-Combs found that about 20 percent of gay/lesbian households polled have children younger than age 18, compared with 40 percent of heterosexual respondents who say they have children.

There are approximately 3 million to 4 million gay and lesbian people with children (some experts put the figure as high as 6 million people, which includes those who are either not out or do not self-identify as gay or lesbian), according to Michelle Darne, founder and publisher of the bimonthly And Baby magazine. And thanks to a mix of better reproductive technologies and the trend for older gays and lesbians to start families, the number of affluent gay and lesbian families is rising.[31]

In 2000, GLBT activists urged gays and lesbians to check "unmarried partner" rather than "roommates" or "other non-relative" on the 2000 census form to describe their living situations. The end result showed about 600,000 same-sex, unmarried-partner households. In the 1990 census, there were approximately 140,000 same-sex, unmarried-partner households reported. Tavia Simmons, a researcher at the U.S. Census Bureau, says the figures can't be compared because of a change in methodology between the 1990 and 2000 censuses.[32]

Ninety-seven percent of all census tracks identified same-sex couples as heads of households, says Gary Gates, a research associate with the Urban Institute, a Washington, D.C.-based non-partisan policy think-tank specializing in statistical analysis. Tracks are geographic designations the census uses to divide counties into areas that on average include 1,500 households.[33]

Major gay/lesbian cities include Los Angeles, New York City and San Francisco.[34] "This means that gay and lesbian families are in virtually every neighborhood of the country," he says, including those in "very remote and rural communities." Gates notes that the new information gives some context to national and local political debates about gay issues that have so far taken place with "virtually no information about how many [gay] people would be affected."

So far, the U.S. Census Bureau's released counts of GLBT populations have included only gay- and lesbian-couple households, which excludes non-partnered GLBT people. Data material on the number of children living in these homes, income, racial composition, home ownership and other demographics is not yet available.

5. People With Disabilities

For companies considering reaching out to people with disabilities, the facts speak for themselves: According to the U.S. Census Bureau, between 1990 and 2000, the number of Americans with disabilities increased 25 percent, outpacing any other subgroup of the U.S. population. Of the nearly 70 million families in the United States, more than 20 million families have at least one member with a disability. And marketing programs aimed at people with disabilities can reach as many as four out of every 10 consumers.[35]

This population is comprised of people of all ethnic backgrounds, cultures and ages, and represents the largest minority subgroup in the United States. African Americans and Native Americans/Alaska Natives age 5 and older reported the highest disability rates in the 2000 census, each at 24.3 percent. Asian Americans age 5 and older reported the lowest overall disability rates at 16.6 percent, followed by whites (18.3 percent) and Latinos (20.9 percent).[36]

This often-ignored segment totals 49.7 million people, comprising 19.3 percent of the overall population. While 5.8 percent of the population age 5 to 15 has some sort of disability, this number increases to 18.6 percent for the population age 16 to 64 and 41.9 percent of the population age 65 and older.[37]

In 2000, 11.9 percent (21.3 million) of the working-age population, age 16 to 64, had a disability that affected their ability to work.[38]

Additionally, according to research conducted in 2000 by Harris Interactive, on behalf of the National Organization on Disability and Aetna U.S. Healthcare, four out of 10 people with disabilities are online and spend twice the time logged on than their non-disabled counterparts.

6. Immigrants

In March 2002, 11.5 percent (32.5 million) of the U.S. population was foreign born.[39] In 2002, 52.2 percent of immigrants were from Latin America, 25.5 percent from Asia, 14 percent from Europe and 8.3 percent from other countries.[40]

Immigration to the United States by World Region, 2002

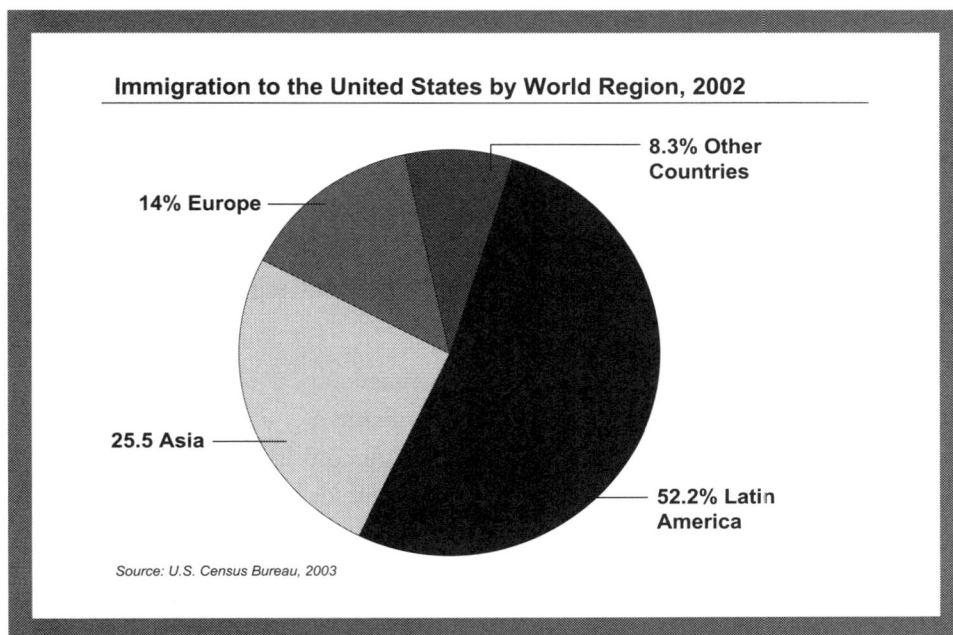

8.3% Other Countries

14% Europe

25.5 Asia

52.2% Latin America

Source: U.S. Census Bureau, 2003

Almost 2 million new legal immigrants arrived in the last two years. In 2001, 1,064,318 foreigners were admitted into the United States for permanent legal immigration. This is an increase of 25 percent from the previous year's 849,807 permanent admissions.[41]

The largest number of immigrants live in the West (38.1 percent), followed by the South (28.2 percent), the Northeast (23.1 percent) and the Midwest (10.6 percent).[42]

Immigrants from Latin America (40.6 percent) and Asia (44.6 percent) are more likely to live in the West.[43]

The foreign-born population in the United States also is more likely to live in cities. In 2002, 43.3 percent of immigrants lived in a city, compared with 27 percent of the native-born population. While the foreign-born and native-born populations had similar chances of living in suburban areas in 2002 (51.1 percent and 52.6 percent respectively), it was less likely for immigrants to be living in rural areas compared with the native-born population, 5.7 percent and 20.4 percent, respectively.[44]

The foreign-born population is twice as likely to be of working age as the native-born population; almost half of the foreign-born population is between age 25 and 44 years old. In 2002, 80.4 percent of the immigrant population was between ages 18 and 64, compared with 59.9 percent of the native-born population. Whereas 27.4 percent of the native-born population was between ages 25 and 44 in 2002, 44.7 percent of immigrants were in that age group.[45]

Almost half of all immigrants arrived in the last dozen years. By 2002, 48.6 percent of all immigrants in the United States arrived since 1990. Another 24.5 percent of the foreign-born population arrived in the 1980s, 14.2 percent in the 1970s and 12.7 percent arriving in the Unites States prior to 1970.[46]

In 2002, 25.5 percent of the foreign-born population had a household of five or more people, compared with 12.5 percent of the native-born population. This number is as high as 38.3 percent for immigrants from Central America and as low as 10.9 percent for Europeans.[47]

Forty percent of the U.S. population growth in the 1990s was based on the 13.2 million immigrants that arrived in that decade. This includes the 7 million births to immigrant women since 1990, 60 percent of U.S. population's growth is attributed to immigrants and their U.S.-born children.[48]

The demographics have changed on immigrants, as well. Latin Americans now account for 52 percent of all new immigrants, compared with 42 percent in 1990 and 31 percent in 1980.[49]

Thirty percent of immigrants are without high-school diplomas, three-and-a-half times the rate of native-born Americans. This increased the overall amount of high-school dropouts by 21 percent in the U.S. since 1990. Fewer than 8 percent of native-born Americans are without a high-school diploma.[50]

The poverty rate for immigrants is 17.6 percent, compared with 10.6 percent for native-born Americans. One in four people in poverty in this country are immigrants.[41]

One-third of immigrants lack health insurance. This is two and a half times the rate of native-born Americans. Immigrants and their native-born children account for 95 percent of the increase in the uninsured population in the United States.[52]

About one in 10 immigrants are self-employed. This is similar to the rate of native-born Americans. [53]

Six states account for 40 percent of the nation's population and 68 percent of the nation's immigration population. These are California (28 percent), New York (12 percent), Florida and Texas (9 percent each), New Jersey (5 percent) and Illinois (4 percent). California alone is home to more than 9 million of the nation's immigrants. Immigrants account for at least half of the population growth over the past decade in Texas, Florida, Arizona, Colorado, Washington, Virginia and Oregon.[54]

The single largest source of immigrants is Mexico. Thirty percent, or 9.7 million, of all immigrants to the United States come from Mexico.[55]

Immigrants comprise 14.6 percent of the nation's full-time work force and 11.5 percent of the total U.S. population.[56]

ADDITIONAL RESOURCES

INTRODUCTION

Brown, C. Stone. "From Negro, Colored, Black to African American –
In Search of An Identity." DiversityInc, 3 February 2003.
http://www.diversityinc.com/members/4394.cfm.

Brown, C. Stone. "New Census Numbers: Latino Population Growing
Even Faster Than Anticipated." DiversityInc, 22 January 2003.
http://www.diversityinc.com/members/4338.cfm.

Camarota, Steven. "Immigrants in the United States – 2002:
A Snapshot of America's Foreign-Born Population." Center for
Immigration Studies. Washington, D.C., November 2002.

Center for Immigration Studies. "Census Releases Immigration
Numbers for Year 2000." Washington, D.C., 4 June 2002.
http://www.cis.org/articles/2002/censuspr.html.

Cheng, Kipp. "Census Shows Chinese Still Largest Asian Group,
Asian Indians on the Rise." DiversityInc, 1 March 2002.
http://www.diversityinc.com/members/2494.cfm.

Cheng, Kipp. "Fast-Growing Asian-Indian Population Is Affluent,
Educated and Ignored." DiversityInc, 14 March 2002.
http://www.diversityinc.com/members/2573.cfm.

Cheng, Kipp. "Gay American Gothic: Rainbow Flag Alongside Pitchfork."
DiversityInc, 22 August 2001.

Cheng, Kipp. "Gay-by Boom: Gay Families Emerge as New,
Affluent Niche Market." DiversityInc, 28 March 2002.
http://www.diversityinc.com/members/2672.cfm.

Cheng, Kipp. "What Marketers Should Know About People
with Disabilities." DiversityInc, 18 April 2002.
http://www.diversityinc.com/members/2761.cfm.

Cole, Yoji. "Are You African, Caribbean or African American?"
DiversityInc, 19 April 2002.
http://www.diversityinc.com/members/2769.cfm.

Cole, Yoji. "Who's White, Who's Black, Who's Brown, Who's Yellow?
Why Do We Care So Much?" DiversityInc, 22 July 2002.
http://www.diversityinc.com/members/3275.cfm.

"Do the Math, Marketers: Biracial Americans Grow in Numbers."
Associated Press, 19 April 2002. [DiversityInc:
http://www.diversityinc.com/members/2772.cfm]

ADDITIONAL RESOURCES

INTRODUCTION

Global Insight. Snapshots of the U.S. Hispanic Market, Lexington, Mass., April 2003.

Johnson, Angela D. "Asian Indians: Upscale Marketers Ignore This Prime Consumer Segment." DiversityInc, 15 April 2003. *http://www.diversityinc.com/members/4786.cfm*.

Johnson, Angela D. "Reaching People of Color is the Key to Future Business Success." DiversityInc, 11 April 2003. *http://www.diversityinc.com/members/4771.cfm*.

Pew Hispanic Center and Kaiser Family Foundation. 2002 National Survey of Latinos. Washington, D.C., December 2002.

"Unmarried Couples More Likely to be of Mixed Race." Associated Press, 14 March 2003. [DiversityInc: *http://www.diversityinc.com/members/4605.cfm*]

U.S. Census Bureau, The Black Population in the United States: March 2002 (Current Population Reports, Series P20-541). Washington, D.C., March 2003.

U.S. Census Bureau. Disability Status: 2000 (Census 2000 Brief, C2KBR-17). Washington, D.C., March 2003.

U.S. Census Bureau. The Foreign-Born Population in the United States: March 2002 (Current Population Reports, Series P20-539). Washington, D.C., February 2003.

U.S. Census Bureau. Statistical Abstract of the United States: 2002. Washington, D.C., 2002.

U.S. Department of Justice, Immigration and Naturalization Service. 2001 Statistical Yearbook of the Immigration and Naturalization Service. Washington, D.C., February 2003.

Witeck-Combs Communications, Inc. and Packaged Facts, The Gay and Lesbian Market, New Trends, New Opportunities. 3rd edition, New York, October 2002.

How Do Most Americans Perceive Corporate Diversity? They're Confused, Poll Finds

By Barbara Frankel

October 25, 2002   *© 2003 DiversityInc.com*

How do most Americans perceive the value and success of corporate diversity initiatives? They believe their own companies care about the subject but that U.S. business as a whole still discriminates against people of color, gays and lesbians, people with disabilities and older workers. And they're not yet convinced that a diverse workforce means a more profitable business.

These are among the key findings of a unique nationwide survey released Thursday. The Diversity Survey, a project of PricewaterhouseCoopers (PwC), was designed to increase both public and corporate awareness of workplace diversity. The first survey of its kind, the poll of 1,930 Americans was unveiled at PwC's Eighth Annual Chief Diversity Officer Summit, held in Washington, D.C., Wednesday and Thursday.

"While we can take heart because most Americans believe that their companies are committed to an inclusive workforce, this survey makes it clear that a great deal of work remains unfinished regarding matters of diversity," said Toni L. Riccardi, chief diversity officer of PwC. "The fact that older and disabled workers, [and] gays and lesbians face a tougher road to career advancement is alarming. We've got a long ways to go before we can realize the American dream of a workplace which truly affords equal opportunity for all employees."

The survey was conducted by NFO WorldGroup, a Greenwich, Conn.-based market-research company, using a sample of its U.S. consumer panel of 5,000 adults, which the company said reflects the key demographics of the United States. The response rate for the mail-in survey was 69 percent, with a margin of error of plus or minus 2.5 percent.

Of those surveyed, 68 percent said their company or organization seemed wholly committed to diversity, which the survey defined solely from a workforce perspective as "having employees of different races, cultures and backgrounds." Interestingly, Latinos most strongly believed their organizations were wholly committed to diversity (71 percent), compared with 60 percent of African-American respondents, 65 percent of Asian-American respondents and 68 percent of white respondents.

How Do Most Americans Perceive Corporate Diversity?
They're Confused, Poll Finds (cont'd.)

Conversely, African Americans surveyed were twice as likely as whites to believe that African Americans face job discrimination. Sixty-four percent of African Americans said African-American men face more discrimination and 61 percent said African-American women face more discrimination, compared with 24 percent of white respondents who said African-American men were the victims of discrimination and 28 percent of white respondents who said African-American women faced bias on the job. Both African-American and Latino respondents said gays and lesbians faced discrimination in the workplace.

The survey found younger Americans, defined as those less than 30 years old, saw bias in the workplace, especially among African-American women, Asian-American women and workers with disabilities. But, said Michael J. Weiss, a demographer and author of the survey, "there's a general unanimity among demographics groups that older workers face the most barriers to advancement. With the oldest members of the Baby Boom generation – the nation's largest population group – now 56 years old, that finding could foreshadow problems for companies in the future."

The survey asked if respondents believed U.S. employers with long histories of recruiting and advancing minorities have the best reputations as diversity-friendly employers, and 60 percent of respondents agreed. But African Americans more frequently cited the need for having managers accountable for promoting people of color. And older respondents preferred more traditional corporate programs, such as mentoring.

What's the best way for people of color to advance? The respondents overwhelmingly (60 percent) believed significant management or operations experience was crucial. That was followed by 35 percent of respondents who said mentoring was a key to advancement. Twenty-eight percent cited holding managers accountable for minority promotions, while 28 percent also cited inclusion in informal networks of communication.

When asked if a diverse workforce translates into higher revenues, 56 percent of respondents expressed uncertainty and only 32 percent unequivocally said yes. The racial breakdown was interesting. Forty-five percent of African Americans, 39 percent of Latinos and 33 percent of Asian Americans surveyed saw the link between diversity and profits, but only 30 percent of whites surveyed agreed. Education was a factor, too, with 40 percent of those with post-graduate degrees noting the connection, 34 percent with college degrees, and only 23 percent with high-school degrees.

How Do Most Americans Perceive Corporate Diversity? They're Confused, Poll Finds (cont'd.)

"It's time for corporate leadership to step up with more meaningful efforts to level the playing field," said Weiss.

The survey's release was the leading event at the PwC program, which also included a panel entitled "Diversity in International Focus," moderated by DiversityInc.com Executive Editor Barbara Frankel. The panel featured Barbara Pope, assistant secretary, Office of Civil Rights, U.S. Department of State; Janet Portzer, director of diversity, GlaxoSmithKline; and Rita Rochelle, producer, Voice of America.

Cari M. Dominguez, chair of the U.S. Equal Employment Opportunity Commission, spoke to the audience of more than 200 national corporate-diversity leaders Wednesday night, saying "Our mandate [at the EEOC] is much narrower than corporate America's. Our mission is to enforce the laws. Our world cannot exist without yours, and yours can't without the EEOC."

At a panel entitled "How Organizations Are Stretching to Deal With Diversity Effectively," Rosanna Durruthy, vice president, global human resources development, Vivendi Universal, said, "In a time of great crisis, the issue is not about diversity but on which of your core assets to keep." Discussing her company's reorganization, Durruthy said diversity initiatives are becoming local to each operating unit as opposed to corporatewide.

Reaching People of Color is The Key to Future Business Success

By Angela D. Johnson

April 11, 2003   *© 2003 DiversityInc.com*

Demystifying the multicultural market and identifying the best ways to reach these consumers was the focus of American Demographics' "How to Succeed in Multicultural Marketing" seminar Thursday in New York. A select group of demographers and marketers provided an audience of more than 200 with insights into this growing and often complex business segment.

Panelists in the first session, "The Multibillion Dollar Multicultural Market: Growing Opportunity in Tight Economic Times," agreed that people of color are driving population growth in several demographic categories, including the youth market and families with children. Jeffrey Passell, principal research associate at the Population Studies Center of the Urban Institute, attributed much of the country's population growth to increases in the Latino and Asian American populations. He predicted that in 20 to 50 years, Latinos should account for 25 percent of the population, while Asian Americans should comprise 10 percent.

Jeffrey Humphreys, director of Economic Forecasting at the Selig Center for Economic Growth at the University of Georgia, urged marketers to look beyond the population numbers to examine which categories rank highest for spending by people of color. He said Latinos outspend others on food, telecommunications services, furniture, children's apparel, footwear and transportation, while African Americans direct a great deal of money toward personal-care products, children's clothing and telecommunications services.

At roughly 4 percent of the population, Asian Americans often are ignored by marketers. During a session titled "Speaking Their Language," Bill Imada, chief executive officer of the IW Group, an advertising agency based in Los Angeles specializing in the Asian-American market, noted that some companies are quick to execute detailed marketing efforts in foreign countries without examining the potential of this domestic market. He relayed the story of a food manufacturer that had a trilingual marketing campaign in Belgium. Imada explained to an executive at that company that the purchasing power of Asian Americans in the United States is greater than that of several European countries, including Belgium, Norway, Ireland, Finland and Portugal. The company soon became a client.

Reaching People of Color is The Key to Future Business Success (cont'd.)

But despite the evidence of the market's growing size and buying power, some companies that currently are industry leaders fail to see the advantage of targeting people of color, said Raiford Cockfield, vice president of market development at IBM, headquartered in Armonk, N.Y. Cockfield warned that these companies would have to change their strategies to remain on top. He drove home his point by citing the companies that appeared on the Fortune 500 list when it began in 1965, as an example of what can happen if businesses fail to change with the times. As early as 1985, only 14 companies on the original list still were in existence.

During a luncheon keynote address, Jeffrey Yang, chief executive officer of New York-based marketing company Factor, Inc. and founder of the now defunct aMagazine, reinforced the idea that is it imperative for companies to change their approach to marketing.

"Today, if you're speaking to everyone the same way, you're speaking to no one at all," he said. "In this day and age, the phrase multicultural marketing is redundant. It's like talking about cold ice or wet water. What began as a buzzword is now a basic fact of doing business."

Introduction

New Numbers on African Americans: Education, Jobs, Marriage

By C. Stone Brown

April 28, 2003   *© 2003 DiversityInc.com*

About 80 percent of African Americans have earned at least a high-school diploma and 65 percent are in the labor force, according to a report released Friday by the Commerce Department's Census Bureau. African-American women participated in the labor force at a slightly higher rate, 62 percent, than white women, 60 percent.

"It dispels a myth," said Tony Allen, executive director of the Metropolitan Wilmington (Del.) Urban League. "It strikes me as a dual reality that supports a strong assertion that African-American women work and are successful in that regard, and two, it flies in the face of the myth that they all are welfare recipients and have an aversion to work."

The report was the first released by the Census Bureau on African-American data since census 2000. It was announced at the Black Mayors Annual Conference in Houston, Texas.

The report, "The Black Population in the United States: March 2002," presents tabulations on such characteristics as geography, age distribution, marital status, family type and size, educational attainment, labor force participation, occupation, income and poverty.

Census Bureau Director C. Louis Kincannon said, "This report is being released to coincide with the gathering in Houston this week of the nation's African-American mayors. It is the first look since Census 2000 at the demographic and socioeconomic state of blacks in America. We hope it will be the subject of much serious discussion by the mayors."

The report also showed that African-American women age 25 and older were more likely than their male counterparts to have earned at least a bachelor's degree, 18 percent versus 16 percent.

Allen said he wasn't surprised that more African-American women were attaining their bachelor's degrees than men because of what he termed "significant pitfalls" for African-American men. He said one of the factors is the criminal-justice system disproportionately impacting the African-American men. The census

New Numbers on African Americans: Education, Jobs, Marriage (cont'd.)

data also noted that for African-American men, the most common job category was operator, fabricator and laborer, in which 28 percent were employed.

About 19 percent of African-American men worked in three other occupational categories: technical, sales and administrative support jobs; service occupations; and managerial and professional specialty jobs. However, among African-American women, 36 percent worked in technical, sales and administrative support jobs and about 27 percent in managerial and professional specialty jobs and in service occupations.

In marriage and in the size of families, African Americans were in stark contrast to whites, according to the report. Forty-eight percent of all African-American families were married-couples; for non-Latino white families, the corresponding figure was 82 percent. In addition, African Americans were less likely than non-Latino whites to be currently married, 35 percent compared with 57 percent.

Who Counts as Black? Who Counts as Hispanic? Clearing Up the Census

By. C. Stone Brown

January 31, 2003   © 2003 DiversityInc.com

Ever since the first U.S. census was taken in 1790. African Americans held the distinction of having the largest non-white population in the United States. Last week, when the U.S. Census Bureau released estimated figures as of July 2002, it marked the first time African Americans surrendered this distinction to the Hispanic population – or did they?

The Census Bureau estimated that the nation now has 36.2 million African Americans, compared with 37 million Hispanics. The confusion occurred because the 2000 census marked the first time U.S. citizens could check off one or more races on the census questionnaire. For instance, a U.S. resident with both African-American and white parents could check off black and white or a white person also could check off Native American if he or she had some Native American ancestry.

This option was added to the census questionnaire after the Office of Management and Budget issued a directive in 1993 to account for the growing diverse population. Adults who had inter-racial parents wanted to more accurately identify their heritage, said Claudette Bennett, chief of Racial Statistics for the U.S. Census Bureau. "This came about because of the growth in the number of inter-racial unions and the numbers of children in those unions … individuals were saying they were no longer a single race and they needed to be able to identify."

Prior to the 2000 census, the offspring of inter-racial couples only could select a single race, such as white, African American, Native American, etc. "Hispanic" isn't considered a race on the census questionnaire. U.S. residents who consider themselves Hispanic have the option of selecting their origin, as white, black, etc.

The chairperson for the U. S. Census Bureau Advisory Committee, Robert Hill, doesn't entirely agree with the new options on the 2000 census questionnaire. Hill, who is African American, said the headlines reporting the Hispanic population out numbering the African-American population isn't entirely accurate.

Hill, who holds a Ph. D. in sociology from Columbia University, said he spoke out because it's part of the function of his appointed position as chair of the

Who Counts as Black? Who Counts as Hispanic? Clearing Up the Census (cont'd.)

Advisory Committee. "We are supposed to communicate information out to the community; when certain things aren't correct, we're supposed to communicate that to our constituency," said Hill.

"The 36.2 million African Americans cited in the media represented individuals who checked only one box on the census form," said Hill. "Most of the news stories omitted 1.5 million African Americans who checked off two or more races."

Bennett said Hill is correct. "There are basically two ways of looking at the information on race. One can look at individuals who report race alone, and race with any combination."

What puzzles Hill most is why there is an inconsistency when comparing African Americans with Hispanics. Hill said the only time the combined numbers aren't used is when they're compared with the Hispanic population. "They use the [combined] numbers for apportionment…the total numbers they use in all of their population numbers, only when they want to compare it to Hispanics that they then get blind-sided," he said.

Jose Chapa, who sits on the Hispanic Census Advisory Committee, also questioned whether the Census Bureau got it right. "I would say, because of the ambiguity of the race question, it's possible that the census announcement was premature. It's really a question of judgment and interpretation, but it's certainly arguable that the Hispanic population may not have exceeded the size of the black population on July 1, 2001, for which the estimate was reported," said Chapa, who is Latino.

Chapa, a professor and director of Latino Studies at Indiana University, attributed the confusion to the 2000 census. "This is an issue that has been created by the change in the race question on the census. In the 2000 census, the respondents choose more than one race."

Gwendolyn E. Holmes, who sits on the African American Census Committee, conceded the Census Bureau has some work cut out for it. "We are still looking at and having concerns with the number of boxes being checked, because there are so many boxes," she said. Holmes predicted every group's numbers would shrink. "I have some Indian in me… if I mark African American, that's going to decrease on the Indian side."

Who Counts as Black? Who Counts as Hispanic? Clearing Up the Census (cont'd.)

Whatever one marks Hill just wants the census to get it counted properly. Geographic areas, such as states and cities that are undercounted are less likely to get resources in heath, housing, and jobs that they need, he said, regardless of race or ethnicity. "If you're undercounting people, there are government resources that won't accrue to people based upon an incomplete count...there are $200 billion allocated based upon census figures, if you have an undercounted community, they get less of those funds."

Who's White, Who's Black, Who's Brown, Who's Yellow? Why Do We Care So Much?

By Yoji Cole

July 22, 2002   *© 2003 DiversityInc.com*

Raquel Welch, who established her sex symbol status with films such as "One Million Years B.C." (1966), as a bleached blond, made headlines recently when she came out.

Welch, who now stars as Aunt Dora in the critically acclaimed PBS television series about a Mexican-American family in East Los Angeles, "American Family," didn't step out of the proverbial gay closet but emerged from the one next to it: The race/ethnicity closet. Welch, 62, admitted, after 40 years in Hollywood and a body of work that spans the gamut of white female characters, that she is half Latina.

Her four-decade journey of ethnic ambiguity is analogous to the nation's evolving understanding and acceptance of race and ethnicity, especially following Census 2000's revelation that the United States is well on its way to becoming a majority-minority nation where people of color make up most of the population.

Mixed heritage is also an increasing phenomenon as a greater number of people produce children who claim allegiance to more than one racial/ethnic group. But can they? And, when is a person's blood link to a particular race too diluted for that person to claim it as his or her identity?

These questions become more than sociological quagmires when placed in the arena of supplier diversity, where a company's assertion that it is "minority-owned" legitimizes a parent company's claims that it is making inroads with diverse vendors.

The number of businesses owned by people of color is increasing, according the U.S. Census Bureau, which indicates that in 1997, the most recent year for which figures are available, 3.04 million people of color owned businesses, up from the 1992 number of 2.15 million. In total, Census 2000 estimated there are 81.9 million African Americans, Asian Americans and Latinos living in the United States.

The National Minority Supplier Development Council (NMSDC), which has a membership of 15,000 businesses owned by people of color, contends that those figures are grossly underestimated.

Who's White, Who's Black, Who's Brown, Who's Yellow? Why Do We Care So Much? (cont'd.)

"The problem with the survey is that it is conducted every five years and then it takes two years for the numbers to be crunched," said Steve Sims, spokesperson for the NMSDC. "Given the growth of minority business, the study should be conducted annually." According to DiversityInc.com's Business Case for Diversity, between 1992 and 1997, the number of women- and minority-owned business enterprises increased by 150 percent, with WMBEs generating $495 billion in collective annual revenue as of 1997, the most recent data available. As efforts to reach emerging market yield a desire for racially diverse suppliers and executives, an increasing number of people come out, like Welch. It's incumbent upon organizations, such as the NMSDC, to ensure that its member organizations are truly owned by people of color.

To be distinguished as a business owned by a person of color, the NMSDC requires owners to produce legal documentation that will attest to their racial status, such as a birth certificate or immigration papers. If they don't have either, they must provide the birth certificates of at least one parent or other appropriate documentation, Sims said. He added that if only one parent is half of a race other than white, then at least one grandparent must be a non-mixed person of color for an owner to qualify.

Owners who claim American Indian heritage must belong to a tribal registry.

"The burden is always on the applicants for them to prove they come from the ethnic group they claim," Sims said.

The nation as a whole has come a long way from the 1940s, when Welch's father emigrated from Bolivia. Census 2000 marked the first time the nation's demographers allowed people to check off more than one box to indicate racial heritage. Before Welch was born and during her childhood, census demographers, who knocked on front doors across the nation, took a good look at the people living inside the home and then checked off their racial heritage, said Andrew Hacker, professor of political science at City University of New York and author of "Two Nations: Black and White, Separate, Hostile, Unequal."

In Welch's case, the nation's hostility toward ethnic immigrants directly affected the manner in which she was reared. Her father tried to assimilate at all costs and even banned Spanish in the home.

"My father came to this country in the '30s and like many in his generation, [he] wanted to eradicate all the signs of being different, of being Latino, of speaking the language or speaking English with an accent," Welch said in a PBS publicity interview for "American Family." "The idea was to fit in and be American first.

Who's White, Who's Black, Who's Brown, Who's Yellow?
Why Do We Care So Much? (cont'd.)

And although there are many good things to be said about that, because we all are Americans here in this country, I do think that men of my father's generation and maybe the women, too, maybe sort of lost a piece of themselves in doing that."

Welch's father's effort to blend in is not a unique experience, said Debbie Giunta, director of the Center for Cultural Fluency and a professor in the Education Department at Los Angeles-based Mount St. Mary's College.

Giunta, who also teaches adult-education courses, had a 40-year-old mother as a student who was so offended when called a disparaging term for a Latina at the age of 8 that she decided not to identify as Mexican any longer.

"From that day on, she made up her mind she wasn't going to be Mexican American," said Giunta. "She said she put baby powder on her skin to try to lighten it, dated only white guys, married a white guy and hasn't brought up her two [teen-age] boys to be very Mexican. Europeans moved here [at the turn of the century] and changed their surnames so they didn't sound so Polish, Jewish, Greek or Italian."

Census 2000 demographers, when researching the answers to the race question on the long form, created six race categories from respondents' answers: white, black or African American, American Indian and Alaska Native, Asian, Native Hawaiian and Other Pacific Islander, and some other race.

The admonition of the significant numbers of multiracial individuals, like Welch's struggle with identifying as Latina early in her career, is analogous to the change in the times.

Now, actor Vin Diesel can package himself as the nation's first multiracial action star. Diesel, who is best known for his gravely voice, double-digit sized biceps and roles in movies such as "Boiler Room" (2000), "The Fast and the Furious" (2001) and the soon-to-be-released "XXX" (2002), can play with the mystique of being multiracial and not cast an allegiance with any particular race.

"I feel 100 percent multicultural. And that's it," said Diesel, 35, in an interview with the magazine Gentleman's Quarterly. "It's a unique way to think, but it's the right way to think, because otherwise you're going to have an ever-growing population of kids checking off twenty different boxes to describe who they are. Why pigeon hole people?"

According to Census 2000, 6.8 million people in America identified themselves as multiracial, one of the more famous being Tiger Woods.

Who's White, Who's Black, Who's Brown, Who's Yellow?
Why Do We Care So Much? (cont'd.)

Hacker said he believes the 6.8 million to be a low number and that many people who are half African American and another race identified only as African American because society has pigeon holed them.

The Diesels of the world, who claim more than one race, are a small number, Hacker said and points to the multiracial singer Mariah Carey as an example.

"Society decided who she is," said Hacker, of the singer who identifies more as African American than anything else". In my view, there are only two races in this country: people of European origin and people of African origin – those are races."

It is true that Hacker's point of view doesn't stand up to the U.S. Census bureau's definitions but, being a political scientist, he contended that other races attempt to identify themselves as close to being white as possible and so on his political spectrum only two races exist.

"The white population isn't having enough kids, while the black population is and the Hispanic population is even more," said Hacker. "[So] the white population is beginning to set some people up on deck as probationary whites. That's why we don't call the Chinese or Koreans the yellow race anymore – they're on deck as probationary whites and you notice how they all take Anglo first names."

To further prove his point, Hacker said a greater number of whites marry Chinese and Koreans than they do African Americans. According to the U.S. Census, of the populations that mixed their races, the white and African-American populations had the lowest percentages of respondents who reported more than one race.

And, according to 1990 census figures, there were 465,332 Asian Americans and Pacific Islanders who married whites and only 206,374 African Americans who married whites. Similar figures from Census 2000 were not available.

Census 2000 did report that, "of the 216.9 million respondents who reported white alone or in combination, 2.5 percent, or 5.5 million, reported white as well as at least one other race. Similarly, of the 36.4 million individuals who reported African American or Black alone or in combination, 4.8 percent, or 1.8 million, reported Black or African American as well as at least one other race." Of all people who reported more than one race in Census 2000, about one in three was of Latino origin.

Identifying oneself as a certain race is usually dependant on socialization and life experience, said Giunta.

People who are mixed with African American, but claim it as their sole race,

Who's White, Who's Black, Who's Brown, Who's Yellow? Why Do We Care So Much? (cont'd.)

probably do so because the traits of an African American – curly hair, dark skin etc. – are not so easy to hide, Giunta said.

"We're so quick to put people in boxes," Giunta said. "It feels as though there are culture police around all the time."

But along with a greater understanding of race and its manifestations comes a broader understanding of what it is to be white, Giunta said.

Americans realized the nation's immense diversity, following the terrorist attacks in September, when Muslim Americans came out of the woodwork to proclaim their allegiance to the United States. Since, the nation has been slowly recognizing that to be an American is not to be white and white people have learned that as well, Giunta said.

"Now white people are beginning to get that 'white' is one of many," Giunta said.

Still, multiracial people of color, who don't have the platform of movie stardom that enables them to rise above society's need to identify, are often forced to prove their allegiance to a race, Giunta said.

"Are you Mexican? How do you prove that? Do you wear the Cholo [a common name for a Mexican American in Los Angeles] clothing? Or, do you speak the [Spanish] language? It takes a while to develop the intellectual ability to see people as more nuanced," Giunta said. "It'll take time for us to see ourselves in that way."

Are You African, Caribbean or African American?

By Yoji Cole

April 19, 2002   *© 2003 DiversityInc.com*

As African and Caribbean immigrants enter corporate America, their acculturation provides insight into how U.S. race relations create sociopolitical groups within different races.

These immigrants, like those who came to the United States in past generations from other countries, struggle between preserving their ethnic culture and the dual forces that tug them between assimilation with whites and, separately, with African Americans.

"If you're black and living in America you will always be faced with your twoness – you cannot escape your blackness just as you cannot escape your Americanness. And it's a constant struggle with and between those," said the famed African-American writer W.E.B. Dubois in "The Souls of Black Folks."

African Americans wrestle with that twoness daily, as indicated by the adjective "African," while immigrants from Africa and the Caribbean arrive with nary an understanding of what it is to be a dark-skinned person in a predominantly white world.

"I didn't know anything about race and how it works in the United States before I came here," said Yodit Alemu, who is originally from Ethiopia.

Going the legal route to get to the United States is a long, arduous process for Africans, so those who make the cut usually are well educated and from their countries' middle or higher classes, said Moradewun Adejunmobi, assistant professor of African and African-American Studies at the University of California, Davis.

According to the Immigration and Naturalization Service, in 2000, 44,731 Africans qualified for green cards and 88,198 Caribbeans. Thousands more come without documentation. They also immigrate on temporary and seasonal work permits, on student visas, are recruited by corporations on H1B visas for those with special, technologic work skills, come as a nurse or teacher on H12 visas, or come to visit family, who eventually sponsor them.

Are You African, Caribbean or African American? (cont'd.)

The U.S. Census Bureau estimates that there are 839,547 Africans in the United States, of whom 557,300 are not naturalized citizens. The Census Bureau also estimates that more than 2.8 million people living in the United States are from the Caribbean, of whom 1.4 million are naturalized citizens. Of these African and the Caribbean immigrants, 6.3 percent were folded into the African-American population, according to Census 2000.

For Alemu, 22, who settled in Washington, D.C. with her family when she was 11, the different races in the area were novel. She wasn't used to the diversity and thought it simply exciting at first. That changed in high school, when she noticed that the African-American students didn't sit with the white students during lunch, she said.

"I realized then how color difference makes problems," Alemu said, her slight Ethiopian lilt still present at the end of her sentences. "African Americans assumed I didn't understand and couldn't relate, while whites thought I was unique."

Alemu's circumstances in high school play themselves out in corporate settings as well. African Americans and whites have had hundreds of years to thread their relationships into the tapestry that is American culture.

African and Caribbean individuals bring with them the similar skin color as African Americans, but a different attitude. Caribbean immigrants from Trinidad, Grenada or Barbados have quasi-British accents, while African immigrants from Ethiopia, such as Alemu, or those from Nigeria, often may be more worldly.

Africans and Caribbeans see race relations in a more positive light, or often do not focus on the differences between the races because they come from countries where they are the majority of the population. People who share their color are rich, poor, and middle class and are the dictators, the presidents, the prime ministers as well as the maids and the janitors.

"These [African and Caribbean immigrants] are coming from societies in which they've always been the majority," said Ransford Palmer, professor of economics at Howard University and author of "U.S.-Caribbean Relations" and "Pilgrims From the Sun: West Indian Migration to America (Twayne's Immigrant Heritage of America)."

"[In the Caribbean] they've run their own governments since the 1950s and they've generally been in charge of the public sector and the politics of the area," Palmer said.

Are You African, Caribbean or African American? (cont'd.)

Nancy Wilson, 34, who moved to the United States from Trinidad in 1990, said that white colleagues at her Maryland state agency and bosses are usually very interested in her background and home country when they hear her accent. African Americans are usually used to the sound of the Caribbean and African accents because they live in the same neighborhoods. "White Americans treat us differently because of our connections with Britain," Wilson said. "They hear our speech and mannerisms as more proper and in some ways, I think we're more tolerated."

Adejunmobi, who said most legal immigrants from Africa come to the United States with college degrees and find high paying jobs in corporate America, experienced the same dynamic.

African-American co-workers sometimes develop an animosity toward their Caribbean and/or African colleagues because the immigrants are gaining favor with the white executives for being unique, Adejunmobi and Palmer said. African Americans also might experience frustration because they suspect their African and Caribbean colleagues are being duped by a system that in the end will see color first and their accent or education after that.

"It often might be easier for [Africans] to make friends with white Americans [before African Americans]," said Adejunmobi.

White Americans who make friends with an African or Caribbean coworker would be the type of person who is interested in the immigrant worker's country of origin. The white colleague is probably knowledgeable of the politics of the region, or has vacationed in a Caribbean island and can discern between Jamaica and Haiti or Nigeria and Senegal.

"Africans are often exasperated by the fact that there seems to be a mythical Africa that exists for African Americans but very little concrete knowledge," said Adejunmobi. "So, the kind of white American who would make friends with an African would tend to have more of a concrete knowledge of the reality that the specific African is coming from and that forms a basis for some kind of communication and discussion."

African and Caribbean immigrants come to the United States to prosper, as most immigrants have. They lack the understanding of why an African-American colleague may warn of a racial undertone that could pervade and undermine interracial friendships.

According to a Gallup poll conducted in May 2001, 66 percent of African Americans said race relations would always be a problem in this country.

Are You African, Caribbean or African American? (cont'd.)

Another Gallup poll conducted last June indicated that the areas in which African Americans tend to be least satisfied, and are far less satisfied than the white majority, include personal safety and one's job.

Palmer said Africans and Caribbeans are less likely to see a racial joke as warranting a response.

"The ability is a characteristic of immigrants," said Palmer whose country of origin is Jamaica. "You come to this country and your goal is to be as successful as you can. You try not to let things throw you off track."

So the immigrant will refrain from looking at an incident of racism as an epidemic and see it as an isolated incident.

Adejunmobi said the African and Caribbean immigrant may not be ignoring racism but just be ignorant of its subtle forms. They may expect it to rear up in the form of a burning cross, a dragging death, or brutal beating and not realize that it could be found in a joke that makes reference to an African American eating watermelon, or being a thief.

Immigrants are made aware of racism when they attempt to climb the corporate ladder that provides institutional power, said Adejunmobi.

"Most African immigrants tend to underestimate the significance of race in the United States," said Adejunmobi, who was born in Nigeria. "Generally speaking, the longer immigrants stay, the more they experience race as an important thing and many times in corporate settings that happens when they apply for positions that would give them institutional power and they're continually passed over [for colleagues who are less qualified]."

It is at that point in the African and Caribbean immigrants' American lives that they tend to befriend African Americans in a corporate setting, Adejunmobi said.

"Eventually, you find that African immigrants who have been here for a long time – five to 10 years – when they are discussing what's happened to them professionally, economically, politically, you'll find that more and more race becomes one of the categories that explains why certain things are the way that they are," Adejunmobi said.

From Negro, Colored, Black to African American – In Search of An Identity

By. C. Stone Brown

February 03, 2003   © 2003 DiversityInc.com

In one of his stage routines, comedian Richard Pryor once said that when a black American would refer to another black American as an "African," fights would break out. The same was true during different periods of American history with the terms Negro, colored and black. At one time or another, all of these terms were held in contempt by the descendants of slaves, who now refer to each other as African-American, the hyphen symbolically bridging them back to Africa. Today, the descendants of slaves embrace "African" American as the designation that best expresses not only their past, but also, their hope for the future. Why the numerous designations over the course of three centuries?

The changing designations are central to the celebration of Black History Month, according to James Newton, chair of African Studies Department at the University of Delaware. "In 1976, you started seeing Negro History week to Black History Week…to Black History Month, and embracing of the black presence in American society, says Newton. "You'll see it…in February, corporations, churches, all kinds of people embracing Carter G. Woodson's Black History Month concept…from Tom Joyner, McDonald's, to major corporations throughout the nation all begin to celebrate the major contributions by blacks in American society."

The journey to "African American" has been a 300-plus-year odyssey that started with Negro, colored, black and finally, African American. "It actually started from the time we were taken as slaves", says Joe Madison, national Black Talk Radio host.

"There were many slaves who maintained their identity as best they could, they fought and struggled to maintain their heritage and cultural identity with Africa," he says.

However, Madison says, the terrorization of Africans took its toll over time. "Hundreds of years of branding, lynching, ignorance and beating our history out of us, both physically and mentally, took that history and culture and identity away."

From Negro, Colored, Black to African American –
In Search of An Identity (cont'd.)

The word Africa still is repugnant to many people, says Madison. "There are folks who are still unaware of what that word means. For too many people, Africa is a country as oppose to a continent."

What Madison believes changed the opinion of the term "Africa" is when blacks began to define their existence. "For three quarters of our existence as black people in this country we were defined by others. We then developed a sense of consciousness and self-worth primarily due to Black History that allowed us to define ourselves. In essence, it allowed us to do what people have done for themselves since the existence of time," Madison says.

Kenneth W. Goings, department chair of African & African American Studies at Ohio State University, is young enough to remember being identified as "black" to be insulting. "I'm 51, I could remember in junior high school if someone called you 'black' you'd be ready to fight. It was associated with all these kind of evil and nasty things."

Those "evil" and "nasty" things Goings is referring to were embedded into American culture, according to Newton. "Part of the American media expression… Africa began to be connected with savagery, and viewed as the 'Dark Continent'…we were viewed as people who were less civilized.

Goings agrees. "I think the whole notion of Africa as a 'Dark Continent' meant that any people that came from there were clearly outside the realm of civilization. And because people knew so little, academics, historians, anthropologist could basically say whatever they wanted and not be challenged."

African Americans found a way to make terms that were imposed on them, such as "Negro and colored" palatable until "black" and "African" came along, says Goings.

"Colored" was a designation that the black middle class embraced. 'Negro' was a word that was becoming outdated to African Americans, and they wanted to reject that, particularly because of the lower case 'N.' "Instead of totally abandoning "Negro" African Americans chose to capitalize the "n" in Negro, in the 1920 and 1930s, he said.

Newton gives some of the credit to mainstream African American organizations and artists. "The NAACP and others started to capitalize the "n" on Negro and the "C" on colored," he says.

Newton remembers the book "The New Negro" authored by Alaine Locke, a philosopher and the first African-American Rhodes scholar. "The implication

From Negro, Colored, Black to African American –
In Search of An Identity (cont'd.)

was that we were 'new' Negroes because we were looking at the world from an African view. We began to take on the heritage of Africa. We were no longer in the shadow of slavery." Once this shadow was removed, it made it possible for "black" and "African" to be embraced.

The usage of the term "black" came at a seminal point in American history, according to Newton. He believes that "black" came to prominence in the American and African-American cultural mainstream when sociologist Kenneth B. Clark, conducted what now is simply referred to as the "Doll Study."

The Clark "Doll Study", conducted for the NAACP, consisted of elementary-age black school children being shown four identical dolls, two black and two white. They would then be asked to identify them racially and to indicate which doll was best, which was nice, which was bad, and which they would prefer. These tests were administered to children throughout the country and they clearly showed that a majority of the children rejected the black doll and expressed a preference for the white doll. Clark's study was used to win the 1954 decision Brown v. Board of Education, which declared school segregation unconstitutional.

"When Kenneth B. Clark did the doll study, whereby blacks had to determine which doll do you like…they kept consistently picking the white doll. This was a process of segregation; it made black people have a negative self-concept…and this self-concept, needed to be rejected."

Madison remembers studying the Clark Study in college. " What the Clarke experiment showed was the personal aspect of cultural conditioning…the external aspect of that cultural conditioning that the standard of beauty was white…black was considered inferior even as it related to beauty."

"This is one of the classic cases where they brought it before the Supreme Court…segregation was doing a disservice not only to black America but whites as well. This really was a critical time for blacks to begin dealing with their own identity. You started seeing people begin to embrace Africa…beginning to look at 'black'," says Newton.

The transition from Negro to black wasn't a smooth transition, says Goings. "There were strong fights over what to use, Negro or black. Calling yourself black, meant you wanted freedom, now." The term "Negro" he says was more associated with the Rev. Martin Luther King Jr. and getting freedom through peaceful means.

"It was a generational transition. It really happened with younger people who saw Dr. King as someone not as in touch with African Americans as they

From Negro, Colored, Black to African American –
In Search of An Identity (cont'd.)

thought. Indeed, the term "black" came to prominence coinciding with the rise of Malcolm X and the phrase "Black is Beautiful." This was a period when African Americans asserted their identity. It was OK to where an "Afro" or "Natural" hairstyle. Straightening combs and bleaching creams, the products that provided a false identity were generally discarded.

Many in the African-American community today use "black" and "African" American interchangeably. "For my generation, we are probably in the mixing bowl of that usage," says Monte Evans, 31, Producer for WOL-AM in Washington, D.C. "My generation says I'm 'black American and I'm an 'African American.' We haven't really come through any one struggle…my generation really doesn't have any claim to one particular name."

Beginning in the mid to late 1980s maybe a little bit earlier, people began using the term "African American," Goings says. He believes the Census Bureau came up with the designation African American. "I know that once they did, (the Rev.) Jesse Jackson began to use it."

Madison says Black History Month is a time for African Americans to reflect on who they really are. "We've always sought our own self-identity, our history is replete with individuals who have tried to maintain a self-identity. And we have struggled trying to find that identity."

Introduction

New Census Numbers: Latino Population Growing Even Faster Than Anticipated

By C. Stone Brown

January 22, 2003   *© 2003 DiversityInc.com*

The excitement over the booming Latino consumer market won't be receding anytime soon, thanks to Tuesday's newly released U.S. Census Bureau figures.

The new data, the first released since the initial 2000 census report that caused a national marketing flurry, showed the Latino population has increased by an estimated 1.7 million people, a 4.7 percent increase.

The estimates, based on information collected in July 2001, are the Census Bureau's first statistics on race and ethnicity since results from the 2000 census were released two years ago. In an Associated Press report, Census Bureau demographer Roberto Ramirez said it has long been expected that Latino someday would surpass blacks because their birth and immigration rates are higher.

"And the trend shows it will clearly be increasing more in the future," Ramirez said. Latinos now comprise nearly 13 percent of the U.S. population, which grew to 284.8 million in July 2001. That's up from 12.5 percent or 35.3 million of the country's 281.4 million residents in April 2000. African Americans make up 12.7 percent of the nation's population, up from 12.6 percent in April 2000. The African-American population grew by 700,000 in the 15 months after the census was released.

These new figures certainly will impact how businesses market their products and services to the ever-increasing Latino market, which is estimated to be $580 billion in spending power this year, according to the Selig Center for Economic Growth at the University of Georgia.

And smart companies understand that. Ana Compain-Romero, spokesperson for Illinois-based State Farm Insurance, said her company spent $9 million in advertising targeting the Latino community in 2002. "This is actually up from $7 million in 2001," said Compain-Romero.

Indeed, as the Latino population blossoms, so will its economic clout. Latino disposable income nationwide has grown 160 percent since 1990, according to the Selig Center.

New Census Numbers: Latino Population Growing Even Faster Than Anticipated (cont'd.)

The U.S. Latino population has increased rapidly in recent years, rising from 6 percent of the population in 1980 to 10 percent in 1995. Projections from the Census Bureau indicate that the trend will continue for the next several years.

The Census Bureau uses the term "Hispanic" instead of "Latino," although the community appears split on preferred usage. According to research conducted by the Monthly Labor Review, a publication of the Bureau of Labor Statistics, the term "Hispanic" encompasses persons from many different cultural backgrounds. Hispanic Americans come from a variety of cultural and geographic backgrounds. For example, 62 percent come from Mexico, 14 percent from Central or South America and 12 percent from Puerto Rico.

Given the nuances of intra-cultural differences among Latinos, it can be challenging to businesses to pinpoint their buying habits. What's appealing to the large Cuban-American population in Miami may be very different than what's appealing to the Southern California Hispanic community, says Compain-Romero. "This is the ultimate challenge, you want to remain respectful, and speak to the 'general' Hispanic community in your marketing efforts."

Census Shows Chinese Still Largest Asian Group, Asian Indians on the Rise

By Kipp Cheng

March 01, 2002   *© 2003 DiversityInc.com*

New data from the U.S. Census Bureau released Monday showed Chinese Americans comprising more than 20 percent of the 11.9 million people who identified themselves as Asian in Census 2000. Totaling 2.7 million people, Chinese Americans continue to represent the largest Asian group in the United States.

Additionally, census data showed that Asians were the fastest growing ethnic group in the United States, surging 48 percent between 1990 and 2000. If people who are of partial Asian descent were included, the population increased by 78 percent, compared to a 13 percent increase of the total U.S. population.

The census data is a clear indicator that the Asian-American market is becoming a formidable one, according to Wanla Cheng, principal at Asia Link Consulting, "Marketers targeting these consumers should continue and those not yet doing so need to take a serious look at implementing strategic marketing plans," she said.

"What's interesting about the data is that it shows growth in addition to immigration," Cheng said. "While immigration continues to be a dynamic pipeline for the Asian-American community, there's an opportunity for marketers to reach out to all Asians in the United States."

Cheng said developing marketing communications initiatives aimed at Chinese Americans should be "a top priority" because of their huge numbers within the Asian-American population. "If marketers have budget priorities," Cheng said, "Chinese consumers should be the first segment to target, and then it's a question of targeting other in-language segments."

Aside from Chinese Americans, Filipinos and Asian Indians are the next largest Asian groups in the United States, at nearly 2 million each, with Asian Indians representing the fastest growing segment within the Asian-American population.

The surge of immigrants from the Indian subcontinent was fueled by the large number of information-technology professionals entering the country during the 1990s technology boom, according to Peter DeSouza, senior vice president of strategic marketing, planning and business development at Admerasia, a New

Census Shows Chinese Still Largest Asian Group, Asian Indians on the Rise (cont'd.)

York-based advertising agency.

DeSouza said the current surge of Asian-Indian immigration is the third wave since the 1960s, when a tremendous "brain drain" occurred in India following the loosening of U.S. immigration policies coupled with the limited number of professional jobs in India.

A majority of all Asian-American groups (49 percent) live in the Western states, with 75 percent of Asian Americans living in 10 states: California, New York, Hawaii, Texas, New Jersey, Illinois, Washington, Florida, Virginia and Massachusetts. Only 47 percent of the general population live in these states.

While Asian Americans still trail behind Latino and African Americans in number, the group's attractive demographic profile, including high rate of education and high median income, should make marketers take a more serious look, said Cheng.

"Marketers need to do a full-court press if they want to reach this growing audience now and in the year to come," Cheng said. "They can't just do one thing, they have to approach it on all fronts."

Fast-Growing Asian-Indian Population Is Affluent, Educated and Ignored

By Kipp Cheng

March 14, 2002   *© 2003 DiversityInc.com*

Asian Indians are the fastest-growing segment among all Asian groups in the United States, now totaling nearly 2 million people, according to the U.S. Census Bureau. Additionally, the Asian-Indian population currently is the sixth-largest ethnic community and third-largest immigrant community – behind Mexicans and Chinese – in the United States.

A recent survey conducted by Simmons Market Research for India Abroad – a 31-year-old U.S.-based English-language newspaper with an audited weekly circulation of 65,000 – found that Asian Indians are the most affluent ethnic group in the country, with the highest level of education and highest level of home ownership.

The India Abroad study found that its readers have an average annual household income of more than $170,000 (compared to a median annual household income of $41,000 in the general population, according to the U.S. Census Bureau). Additionally, India Abroad readers reported an average net worth of $1.3 million.

With more than $88 billion in combined spending power, Asian Indians are a highly desirable market. So why have marketers been so slow to specifically target this group?

"Multicultural-marketing initiatives occur in trends," said Ron Mann, U.S. director of sales and marketing at Rediff International, a Mumbai, India-based media and communications company. "First, it was about reaching out to Latinos, then African Americans and then Asians in language. Asian Indians are the last group for marketers to tap."

Part of the reason why Asian Indians have not been targeted in the same way that other ethnic Asian groups have been is because unlike Chinese or Korean immigrants, for example, Asian Indians tend to arrive in this country with English fluency.

"Asian Indians are a kind of invisible minority," said Peter DeSouza, senior vice president of strategic marketing, planning and business development at

Fast-Growing Asian-Indian Population Is Affluent, Educated and Ignored (cont'd.)

Admerasia. "This is not a group that stands out because it [speaks] a different language or looks different."

Because of the group's proficiency with English, DeSouza said marketers have believed that Asian Indians were being reached via mainstream media. While that's true, to a certain extent, DeSouza said marketing-communications messages have not yet specifically targeted Asian Indians, and doing so would require only minor tweaks in the messages to accommodate Asian-Indian sensibilities.

"There's truth in both approaches," said DeSouza. "It's not that all mainstream-media ads do not work because they do not feature [Asian Indians]. But there's a mindset difference. Consumers know when an ad is or is not crafted to speak to them."

But addressing this group can be a challenge because of the diversity among Asian Indians, who may be Hindu, Catholic, Muslim or Buddhist, among other religions, and bring with them various regional differences.

"That diversity and complexity can be seen in Asian Indians in the United States as well," said DeSouza. "However, despite the differences, there is something quintessentially Indian. It's not in the external; it's in the internal. It's in the mindset and beliefs that are shared." DeSouza said it's possible for marketers to reach Asian Indians by emphasizing value and a shared focus on family.

Another reason why marketers have not targeted Asian Indians is because as a group they tend to assimilate into American society more quickly than other ethnic groups, said Mann. Therefore, high-end marketers that want to reach Asian Indians are already able to reach them via upscale, mainstream media.

While high-net-worth Asian Indians can be reached in media such as The Wall Street Journal, DeSouza said marketers should include targeted programs aimed at Asian Indians in Asian-Indian media outlets because the cost-per-thousands (CPMs) – the general pricing metric for media buying – is significantly cheaper than mainstream media. For example, in the United States, there are nearly a dozen broadcast networks aimed at Asian Indians.

Historically, there have been three waves of immigration from India, according to DeSouza. The first saw the arrival of professionals such as doctors and engineers from India in the 1960s when immigration laws in the United States loosened. Shortly thereafter, a second wave of relatives came. The most recent wave of immigration from India brought IT professionals during the dot-com boom of the early- and mid-1990s. In recent years four out of 10 start-up companies in

Fast-Growing Asian-Indian Population Is Affluent, Educated and Ignored (cont'd.)

Silicon Valley alone were built by Asian-Indian entrepreneurs, according to research conducted by Rediff International.

The huge numbers of Asian Indians in high-skill, professional jobs account for the unusually high-income levels, according to Mann.

"Like other Asian groups, Asian Indians come to this country with a strong entrepreneurial edge," said Mann. "The difference is that rather than opening markets or delis, Indians tend to start companies, such as tech firms or import businesses."

Nearly 50 percent of all H-1B work visas (or those given to workers with skills in "specialty occupations," according to the U.S. Labor Department) are issued to Asian Indians each year, adding 250,000 Asians Indians to the U.S. Indian population annually. And because of their English fluency, Asian Indians do not move into enclaves that predominantly include other Asian Indians. Korean and Chinese immigrants, and many others with language barriers, tend to seek out those of similar national origin when they move to the United States.

The combination of English-language fluency and relatively inexpensive operating costs have encouraged businesses to base back-end functions such as customer service and customer relationship management (CRM) operations in India.

"You need to look at the cost-cutting trends in business," Mann said. "What's happened is … companies have shifted their CRM and tech support operations to India not only because it's cheaper, but because they can hire an educated staff that's fluent in English."

Asian Indians: Upscale Marketers Ignore This Prime Consumer Segment

By Angela D. Johnson

April 15, 2003   *© 2003 DiversityInc.com*

They love luxury cars, have a penchant for designer clothing, and consider cruises almost a right of passage, yet marketers of these goods and services have failed to take note of Asian Indians and other South-Asian immigrants, including people from Bangladesh, Pakistan, Sri Lanka and Nepal. (Asian Indians make up 88 percent this group, according to the U.S. Census Bureau.)

"There is a very strong business case for the South-Asian market," said Tariq Khan, vice president of multicultural marketing for MetLife, a New York-based insurance company. "They have among the highest income and highest education. Their growth is among the highest, also."

An increasing number of businesses have set their sights on Asian-American consumers. However, MetLife is one of the few companies, most which are limited to the financial-services and telecommunications industries, which specifically target the South-Asian segment of this group.

Dave Banerjee, president of the New York-based South Asian advertising agency 1947 Communications, said South Asians have an average household income of $67,552, considerably higher than the $45,257 national average. He estimates that, as a whole, the group wields $137 billion in buying power. "It's the most affluent group among any ethnicity in America, by far."

U.S. Census data show that between 1990 and 2000, the South-Asian population grew 106 percent to 2.2 million. Much of this growth stemmed from South Asians who came to America in the 1990s on HB-1 visas to work in the technology sector. Banerjee said the dot-com fallout is causing this growth trend to begin to taper off.

Neeta Bhasin, president and chief executive officer of ASB Communications, a full-service communications agency in New York, said the South-Asian population was severely undercounted in the latest census. The 2000 Census didn't offer a specific box for South Asians of Pakistani, Bangladeshi, Sri Lankan or Nepalese decent to acknowledge their race. Some may have selected "Other Asian" without denoting their country of origin. Based on this, Bhasin estimates

57

Asian Indians: Upscale Marketers Ignore This Prime Consumer Segment (cont'd.)

the South Asian population in the United States to be around 3.5 million.

Despite the small size, South Asians' high household income makes the segment an ideal target for marketers of upscale products such as luxury cars and homes.

"If you're talking about Colgate, I'd say our market is not the market," said Bhasin. "But if you're talking about education, real estate ... we are the one."

"I don't see why brands like Ethan Allen wouldn't advertise or Saks Fifth Avenue," said Banerjee. "Any upscale brand should advertise because the ROI [return on investment] is incredible …. The cost of entry for any brand in this market is probably the lowest because the media cost is minuscule compared to any other market, even compared to the Chinese market or the Korean market."

For example, the cost of a full-page ad in the Chicago edition of the weekly India Tribune is $1,800, significantly lower (and assumedly more effective) than a full-page ad in the Chicago Tribune.

South Asians are prime consumers of luxury cars.

"When we come from India, we have one dream," said Bhasin, "to own a Mercedes-Benz."

Travel also is important to this market. "If you haven't been on cruises then you don't belong in [the South-Asian] society," said Bhasin. She added that Disney World often is the first place South Asians want to take their children.

So what's keeping upscale marketers from courting these consumers?

"I would say lack of knowledge, lack of education," said Bhasin. "[Companies] have to have an open mind to listen and understand about this market."

Bhasin said that before the establishment of agencies specializing in the South-Asian market, little research was available about these consumers. Arti Caprihan, marketing manager of the Montvale, N.J.-based Western Union said the challenge now is getting detailed data about segments within the South Asian population.

Marketers also may be intimidated by the idea of addressing a market that has more than 30 different languages and 300-plus dialects. The realization that most South Asians are fluent in English may ease their apprehension, but experts warn against approaching this group in English.

"That will never ever work in this market," Banerjee said. "In fact it can potentially harm a brand. A lot of things that we see on general network television, some of them are culturally not even acceptable by South Asians."

Asian Indians: Upscale Marketers Ignore This Prime Consumer Segment (cont'd.)

"You do not have to have creative in 10 different languages," said Bhasin.

Advertising featuring English dialogue interspersed with some South Asian words – or what Banerjee calls "Hinglish," a mixture of English and Hindi – is most effective.

For companies looking to enter the Asian-Indian market, experts recommend using cultural touch points such as education, family, and future security. "We believe in family values," said Bhasin. "Anything that has to do with family connects you better."

"South Asians are a little crazy about investments," added Banerjee. "They are in some ways very insecure about the future .... Their lives revolve around financial planning."

MetLife's current television advertising campaign plays into the importance of saving and education. Western Union's latest TV commercial taps into the South Asians love of family and the game of cricket to promote its wire transfer service.

There is no silver bullet for penetrating the South-Asian market. To reach these affluent consumers marketers must use a strategic mix of television, print, and radio advertising, as well as grassroots marketing such as participating in community events including the Indian Independence Day and Divali celebrations.

Banerjee said those who have made an effort to reach the South Asian market have found success. "The most important thing [about the South Asian market] is who ever has advertised in this market has never left this market," said Banerjee.

"That says something."

Newest Census Data on Gay, Lesbian Couples

By The Associated Press

May 15, 2003 *© 2003 DiversityInc.com*

Gay and lesbian couples are slightly better educated than married people and earn similar paychecks but aren't as likely to own their homes, according to a study of Census Bureau data released Tuesday.

More than 35 percent of people living with same-sex partners had a college degree in 2000 compared with 28 percent of married people and 19 percent of opposite-sex unmarried partners, said the analysis commissioned and released Tuesday by Human Rights Campaign, an advocacy group for gay, lesbian, bisexual and transgender people.

Median wages earned by gay and lesbian couples were equal to married people — about $32,000, $8,000 more than for opposite-sex unmarried partners. About 64 percent of homosexual couples owned their homes, compared with 78 percent of married partners and 41 percent of heterosexual unmarried couples.

The data were culled from detailed 2000 census data released for 15 states so far. The Human Rights Campaign study includes data from California, New York and Texas — the states with the greatest number of same-sex unmarried partner homes. Also covered was Vermont, which three years ago passed the nation's first civil union law recognizing gay and lesbian "domestic partnerships."

Human Rights Campaign strategist David Smith said the study shows homosexual couples are "a mirror image of the majority of families in the country" who should have the same benefits and protections.

The 2000 census was the first in which the bureau extensively analyzed data for unmarried partners, regardless of sexual orientation.

A question on the census asked "How is this person related?" For people living together who were unrelated, options included "Roomer, boarder," "Housemate, roommate," "unmarried partner" and "foster child."

Gay rights groups considered a person living with someone of the same sex who checked off unmarried partner to be homosexual.

Newest Census Data on Gay, Lesbian Couples (cont'd.)

The Census Bureau does not ask about a person's sexuality and is required by law to keep answers confidential.

Data released two years ago revealed there were 594,000 households headed by same-sex partners — about 1 percent of the nearly 60 million households in the United States led by couples. The vast majority of those homes — over 54 million — are led by married people. Differences in homeownership may arise because same-sex couples, especially gays, tend to cluster more in cities, where home prices are more expensive and rental units are more plentiful, said Gary Gates, a demographer from the Urban Institute who did the analysis. For instance, the median property value for a gay couple that owned a home was over $162,000, $25,000 more than the median for lesbian and married couples, and $50,000 more than for opposite sex partners.

Lesbian couples are more likely to have children than gays and are concentrated more in suburbs, where housing is cheaper, Gates said.

About 8 percent of lesbian partners said they had prior military service, compared with 1 percent of women who are married or who are in unmarried partnerships. About 14 percent of gay men had served in the military, about the same as for men in unmarried partnerships but half the rate of married men.

Other states covered in the report were Alabama, Florida, Illinois, Kansas, Maryland, Nebraska, New Jersey, Ohio, Oklahoma, Rhode Island and Wyoming.

Where Have All the Gay Couples Gone? Census Missed More Than 100,000, Study Finds

By Ruth Zeilberger

March 11, 2003   © *2003 DiversityInc.com*

The U.S. Census 2000 count of same-sex couples missed at least 100,000 couples, according to a study just released by the Institute for Gay and Lesbian Strategic Studies (IGLSS).

While the count of same-sex unmarried partner households increased in the United States from 145,130 in 1990 to 594,691 in 2000, two surveys of gay, lesbian, bisexual and transgender (GLBT) people show an undercount of between 16 percent and 19 percent of same-sex couples. GLBT people who lived with a same-sex partner on April 1, 2000, could list themselves as "unmarried partners" on the official census form. IGLSS surveyed individuals in same-sex couples about their census responses at the Millennium March for gay equal rights. A second survey asked similar questions of online respondents to a Harris Interactive/ Witeck-Combs survey.

The surveys also found that more than two-thirds of the couples not using "unmarried partner" instead listed themselves as "housemates/ roommates" on the census forms. When asked why they did not call themselves unmarried partners, respondents reported confidentiality concerns and a lack of fit of census options for their own family configurations. A small group of same-sex couples that referred to themselves as married will be recaptured by the Census Bureau policy of recoding same-sex "husband/wife" couples to unmarried partners.

But the Census Bureau's policy of recoding these couples is "almost deliberately obscuring," said Lee Badgett, co-author of the IGLSS study. She noted that there are important differences between same-sex couples that marked "unmarried partner" and those that marked "married". Namely, that those who marked married were more likely to have kids and tended to be older.

Perhaps even more significantly, the U.S. Census does not ask any questions about sexual orientation. Same-sex partners were captured unintentionally under the category of "unmarried partner," a question developed out of the Census Bureau's interest in different-sex couples, according to Badgett. "That means we know nothing about single (GLBT) people," she said. She estimated that there are at least three or four times as many GLBT people who are not captured by same-sex couple statistics because they are single.

Where Have All the Gay Couples Gone? Census Missed More Than 100,000, Study Finds (cont'd.)

The IGLSS survey asked people in couples to report their census answers after the fact. It used two sources to survey people in couples: people attending a political rally and people enrolled in a database of online survey respondents.

The 2000 Millennium March drew an estimated 325,000 GLBT and heterosexual people to Washington D.C. on April 30, 2000, according to the IGLSS. After the main part of the march had reached its destination, the research team approached individuals who were waiting in line to enter the adjoining street festival, who were sitting in the mall, and who were in the area designated for families. Researchers asked individuals if they had been living with a same-sex partner on April 1, 2000, the official census day, and gave respondents who met that criterion a two-page survey to fill out. The team collected surveys from 182 people, a 173 of whom lived with a same-sex partner and filled out a census form.

The group of GLBT people attending the march was not representative of all GLBT people in the United States, according to IGLSS. For instance, the need to pay travel and lodging expenses in an expensive city would suggest that attendees probably had a higher average income than the average GLBT person, according to IGLSS. It also seems reasonable to expect that the people attending the march were more politically active or at least more politically aware than those not attending, according to IGLSS. This tilting of the survey respondents toward politically active or aware people means that this group also was more likely to know the significance of the "unmarried partner" option on the census and might have been more likely to use that designation than the average same-sex couple.

"The people we surveyed were politically aware and were more likely to know about and use the 'unmarried partner' option," said Marc Rogers, one of the authors of the report, in a statement. "They're a best-case scenario, meaning the actual undercount is likely to be far higher."

In June 2000, Harris Interactive and Witeck-Combs Communications included five questions from the IGLSS survey on their online poll. Out of the 5,458 individuals surveyed, 300 (5.6 percent) identified themselves as gay, lesbian, bisexual or transgender. Of that smaller group, 90 said they had been living with a same-sex partner on April 1. The people in the online poll probably are more representative of the GLBT community than the marchers, according to IGLSS, but it also is likely that GLBT Internet users are different than those who do not use the Internet. Research suggests that Internet users have higher levels of income and education, according to IGLSS, which is likely to be true for GLBT online respondents as well. The online respondents also might be more comfortable with surveys and have fewer confidentiality concerns about the census than would the typical gay person.

Where Have All the Gay Couples Gone? Census Missed More Than 100,000, Study Finds (cont'd.)

In the Millennium March sample, 13 percent of the couples did not use the "unmarried partner" designation on the census, while 19 percent of those surveyed online did not use the "unmarried partner" designation.

The IGLSS suggests the following changes in future census questions and publicity efforts for more accurate future counts:

Future censuses should change the way the "unmarried partner" option is presented, explaining the term and including it with the family relationships. The census form lists the option "unmarried partner" without explanation, which may be part of the undercount problem if the term is unfamiliar to some couples.

Furthermore, the option is listed as referring to people "not related to Person 1," which may be considered insulting or inappropriate by same-sex couples. The structure of the census does not allow all GLBT families to document their family configurations.

Public-education campaigns are effective in increasing accurate census responses. Seeing a campaign increases the probability that a couple will check the unmarried partner box.

E-mail campaigns within the gay community appear to be capable of reaching many GLBT people. The e-mail campaign may be particularly effective for people who may not be on organizations' target lists, which substantially increases the reach of email as a public education tool.

Education campaigns, especially those using non-GLBT mainstream media, may be more effective for influencing the responses of couples who are not so active in the GLBT community. The Census Bureau's own marketing efforts have the potential to reach far more people than a campaign based on pro-bono advertisements in GLBT publications, and the bureau should educate people about the use of the "unmarried partner" term and about confidentiality of data.

The Census Bureau should conduct research on how couples decide to answer relationship questions. For instance, what characteristics of relationships, such as longevity of relationship, cohabitation, or age of partners, influences which couples check "unmarried partner"? Also, the Census Bureau should investigate ways of capturing unmarried partner couples when one member is not the household's reference person.

The U.S Census Bureau will release a report this week describing the 594,691 same-sex couples in the 50 states and the District of Columbia.

Gay-by Boom: Gay Families Emerge As New, Affluent Niche Market

By Kipp Cheng

March 28, 2002   *© 2003 DiversityInc.com*

The number of gay and lesbian households with children under age 18 is on the rise and major marketers should take note of this affluent and fast-growing community. Between 1990 and 2000, the number of self-identified gays and lesbians who reported having children rose more than threefold, from 148,000 families to more than 600,000 families, according to data from the U.S. Census Bureau.

"And that's grossly undercounting," said Michelle Darne, founder and publisher of And Baby, a New York-based magazine aimed at gay and lesbian families. "The U.S. Census figures are useful, but the numbers skew much lower than they actually are."

According to Darne, there are approximately 3 million to 4 million gay and lesbian people with children (some experts put the figure as high as 6 million people, which includes those who are either not out or do not self-identify as gay or lesbian). And thanks to a mix of better reproductive technologies and the fact that older gays and lesbians are starting to have families, the number of affluent gay and lesbian families is rapidly rising.

"There is a baby boom happening in the gay and lesbian community," said Angeline Acain, publisher of New York-based Gay Parent magazine. "And it's been going on for about 20 years now and it's not losing steam."

But while lesbian parents outnumber gay parents by nearly 3 to 1, "The 'gay-by' boom now includes more and more gay men having children," said Stuart Miller, CEO of Growing Generations, a Los Angeles-based surrogacy agency that helps a predominantly gay clientele.

The so-called "gay-by" boom has created a tremendous opportunity for marketers looking to tap into this affluent market. Gay, lesbian, bisexual and transgender (GLBT) consumers share a collective spending power of $450 billion, according to research from PlanetOut Partners, a San Francisco-based media company serving the GLBT community. Additionally, gays and lesbians are twice as likely as the general population to have annual household incomes of more than $250,000 and to have graduated from college.

Gay-by Boom: Gay Families Emerge As New, Affluent Niche Market (cont'd.)

Of the 16.5 million people who identify as gay or lesbian, nearly 13 reported having at least one child under age 18 living at home, according to the 2001 Gay/Lesbian Consumer Online Census, which was conducted by the OpusComm Group and the S.I Newhouse School at Syracuse University. (Among gay and lesbian African Americans, 40 percent of African-American lesbians reported having children and 18 percent of African-American gay men said they had children, according to a recent study from the National Gay and Lesbian Task Force.)

By comparison, U.S. Census data indicates 29 percent of all U.S. households have a child under age 18 living at home.

Acain said many gays and lesbians have had children in the past, but the 2000 U.S. Census report was the first time that their numbers of been counted with as much relative precision.

Now that the market of gay and lesbian families has begun to emerge, the challenge for marketers is effectively addressing the group. There are a handful of publications targeted specifically at gay and lesbian parents, including the bi-monthly Gay Parent magazine – which Acain said has a press run of 10,000 and is distributed for free at gay and lesbian centers – and And Baby – which is the first glossy magazine to address this group and comes out six times a year. Darne said And Baby has an unaudited circulation of 100,000.

"I would say that the basic issues of being a parent are the same, whether you're gay or straight," Acain said. "However, for gay families, there's a dual coming out process. Not only are the parents coming out as gay or lesbian, the children are coming out [about their parents] to their teachers and friends."

Marketers, then, need to be sensitive to the issues that are specific to children who are being raised by two fathers or two mothers.

"The mainstream parenting media, for example, tends to focus on mothers," said Miller. "Parenting has traditionally been very female-focused. Marketers who want to reach gay families might adjust their messages to include images of fathers as the primary caregiver."

And what exactly does a gay or lesbian parent look like? That question was answered succinctly during a highly publicized interview on ABC's "Primetime" when talk-show host Rosie O'Donnell said, "I am that [lesbian] parent."

Gay-by Boom: Gay Families Emerge As New, Affluent Niche Market (cont'd.)

A survey following O'Donnell's disclosure showed that a majority of her fans – who are mostly women, mostly straight and between the ages of 35 and 44 – were accepting of her as a lesbian parent. According to a snapshot survey by Witeck-Combs/Harris Interactive, 73 percent of those asked said O'Donnell's sexual orientation made no difference in their opinion of the talk-show host.

"I think it's great what Rosie did," Darne said. "Middle America needs an icon to see what a gay parent looks like. For marketers and a lot of people who haven't seen or been exposed to this market, when I've spent time with them, then they get it. They start to see what I'm talking about."

Introduction

What Marketers Should Know About People With Disabilities

By Kipp Cheng

April 18, 2002   *© 2003 DiversityInc.com*

What often-ignored market segment is 54 million people strong, maintains an aggregate income that now exceeds $1 trillion and boasts $220 billion in discretionary spending power? The group is comprised of people of all ethnic backgrounds, cultures and ages, and represents the largest minority subgroup in the United States.

It's people with disabilities, rarely the focus of major marketers.

"Disability is an uncomfortable topic for people," said Carmen Jones, president of The Solutions Marketing Group (SMG), an Arlington, Va.-based marketing-consulting firm that helps companies target consumers with disabilities. "People like to push it aside. But once you start answering their questions, people will say, 'You helped me understand things better.' And that's the first step."

For companies considering reaching out to people with disabilities, the facts speak for themselves: According to the U.S. Census Bureau, between 1990 and 2000, the number of Americans with disabilities increased 25 percent, outpacing any other subgroup of the U.S. population. Of the nearly 70 million families in the United States, more than 20 million families have at least one member with a disability. And marketing programs aimed at people with disabilities can reach as many as four out of every 10 consumers.

Additionally, according to research conducted in 2000 by Harris Interactive, on behalf of the National Organization on Disability and Aetna U.S. Healthcare, four out of 10 people with disabilities are online and spend twice the time logged on than their non-disabled counterparts.

Jones said while there is no specific data indicating the distribution of people with disabilities in this country, there is a higher concentration of people with disabilities in urban areas – where the infrastructure for public transportation is more widespread – as well as in some cities, where people with hearing impairment, for example, tend to live. Denver is an example of a city that has a high population of people with mobility impairment, Jones added.

New, Untapped Revenue

The popular perception that most people with disabilities rarely leave their homes is untrue, Jones said. According to research conducted by the SMG, people with

What Marketers Should Know About People With Disabilities (cont'd.)

disabilities spent more than $81 billion on travel in 1995. This figure excludes the expenditure of their families, friends and escorts. The data highlights an opportunity for travel-services companies, still reeling from Sept. 11 fallout, to reach out to a new market and address an underserved consumer base.

Another example of companies that have been slow to address people with disabilities is the food-service industry. At a recent focus group of people with disabilities held by the SMG, participants reported to eating out between two and 30 times a month.

"It was an eye-opening finding for all of us," Jones said.

The process of educating companies about the market of people with disabilities, though, is ongoing. Jones said companies should promote that they are complying with the U.S. Americans with Disabilities (ADA) law, even if the compliance is mandated by the government. By publicizing that a company supports accessibility to all people, regardless of their physical abilities, the message consumers perceive is that the subgroup of people with disabilities are welcomed and that the company is a friendly, caring organization.

According to a report from the General Accounting Office, since the implementation of the access provisions of the ADA 10 years ago, the hotel and hospitality industry has experienced a 12 percent increase in revenue, attributable, in part, to consumers with disabilities.

Jones added that companies that have been insensitive to workers and consumers with disabilities in the past should be especially vigilant about establishing programs that support people with disabilities because they are under closer scrutiny by the public than companies that have a track record of support.

"If there are vulnerabilities within a corporation, if there have been any lawsuits, people need to be aware of that, and [the company] needs to try to right that wrong and understand the nature of the offense," Jones said.

Developing Programs

"How I advise clients is to think about their marketing efforts in two phases," Jones said. "First, targeting the 'mainstream' disabled market, which captures the most people. Then they should go after specific niches within the market."

Jones said it's vital for companies to assess whether their marketing message is telling the proper story about a commitment to reaching people with disabilities. Typically, Jones added, expressing the specific needs for assistance in service industries is different from consumer packaged goods, which do not necessarily require a distinct message between the general market and the people-with-disabilities market.

What Marketers Should Know About People With Disabilities (cont'd.)

"You don't need Braille on the side of a cereal box to reach the visually impaired," Jones said.

What's more important than accommodating message delivery is articulating the unique selling propositions of a product or service for a niche market that's very different from the market as a whole.

People with hearing impairments, for example, do not view themselves in the same way as other people with disabilities, Jones said. "It's a delicate balancing act of understanding the culture of each subgroup or niche, and working doggedly to be all encompassing [in a marketing effort.] A marketer doesn't want to do anything that would jeopardize a company's credibility."

Jones cited Nike as an example of a company that blundered in a marketing effort, which featured language that was insensitive about people with mobility impairment. After Nike came under fire, the athletic-shoe and apparel maker made an apology that was viewed as patronizing, which exacerbated the problem.

"[Nike] will do what's politically correct, of course, especially since [golfer] Casey Martin is a Nike endorsed athlete," said Jones. (Martin has Klippel-Trenaunay-Webber Syndrome, a rare circulatory disorder that has made his right leg extremely weak.)

Jones said developing marketing communications programs aimed at people with disabilities is not simply "putting a person with a wheelchair in the background of a commercial. It's a larger commitment. It starts with the leadership and trickles down. Someone from the marketing department can't execute a project without support from the top."

Additionally, marketers need to be creative when thinking about marketing plans. "Don't only use the obvious ways to reach people with disabilities," Jones said. "The disability publications don't have a wide enough reach." Instead, marketers should develop campaigns that integrate a message that includes people with disabilities.

"Corporations haven't yet made the connection between the [disability] market and profit. They still think of people with disabilities as a charity," Jones said. "It's OK to write a check, that's cool. But let's make a communication bridge that's built on more than just dollars."

Introduction

Unmarried Couples More Likely to Be of Mixed Race

By The Associated Press

March 14, 2003   *© 2003 DiversityInc.com*

Unmarried couples – whether same-sex or opposite-sex – are far more likely than married couples to mix race or ethnicity, Census Bureau data shows.

About 7 percent of the nation's 54.5 million married couples are mixed racially or ethnically, compared with about 15 percent of the 4.9 million unmarried heterosexual couples. The percentage is only slightly lower for the nation's nearly 600,000 same-sex couples.

Deva Kyle, an African-American law student who lives with her white boyfriend, said people in interracial relationships tend to be more liberal so are more apt to share a home without being married.

Kyle, 24, of Alexandria, Va., has no plans to marry her boyfriend of five years. She said they plan a "commitment ceremony" that is not legally binding but still makes a statement for family and friends.

"Marriage has a lot of patriarchal underpinnings that I have a lot of problems with," she said.

Dorion Solot, executive director of the Boston-based Alternatives to Marriage Project, said Kyle is an example of a growing number of people who don't see race as an inhibiting factor to a relationship.

"What was once the talk of gossipmongers is now the new normal," she said. "The younger generation expects to live together before marriage, and doesn't see race as a barrier to love."

The census report summarizes unmarried partner data initially released two years ago by state, race and age. The 2000 head count was the first in which the bureau extensively analyzed unmarried partner data.

Specifically, a question on the census asked "How is this person related?" For people living together who were unrelated, options included "Roomer, boarder," "Housemate, roommate," "unmarried partner" and "foster child."

Unmarried Couples More Likely to Be of Mixed Race (cont'd.)

By state, Utah had one of the lowest percentages of homes headed by unmarried couples, about 5 percent of all coupled households. Alabama and Arkansas were also among the lowest states.

Alaska, Nevada and Vermont each had over 12.5 percent of their coupled households led by unmarried partners, among the highest in the country.

Totaling heterosexual and homosexual couples, the census found 5.5 million households headed by unmarried partners nationwide, just over 5 percent of the country's 105.5 million homes, while married couples head just over 50 percent.

Interracial relationships – regardless of marital status – tended to occur more often in the West and states with higher minority populations, said Martin O'Connell, head of the bureau's family statistics branch.

It occurred most often in Hawaii, where over one-third of married couples were interracial, along with over one-half of opposite-sex unmarried couples. Interracial couples comprised less than one-half of gay and lesbian partnerships.

Rates were also high in Alaska, New Mexico and Oklahoma. The latter two have large populations of Native Americans.

Conversely, the New England states of Maine, New Hampshire and Vermont, which have low minority populations, also have lower percentages of interracial relationships.

Vermont in 2000 passed the first law granting homosexual couples virtually all the state rights and responsibilities afforded to married couples. Among homosexual partners in Vermont, just over 1 in 20 were between people of different races or ethnicity.

David Smith, spokesman for the gay rights advocacy group Human Rights Campaign, called the report "groundbreaking" since the government hadn't issued such a detailed report on homosexual relationships before.

Smith believes homosexual couples are undercounted, regardless of race or ethnic background. He said some people, fearing discrimination, may not have admitted on the census form that they are in a same-sex relationship.

Federal law mandates all answers to the census remain confidential.

The 1990 census form was the first to offer an "unmarried partner" checkoff. It found 3.2 million total unmarried partners, less than 5 percent of whom were the same sex. That data cannot be directly compared with 2000 because of differences in its collection and analysis.

Do the Math, Marketers: Biracial Americans Grow in Number

By The Associated Press

April 19, 2002   *© 2003 DiversityInc.com*

The bride is white, the groom is black, and they stand on a layer of moist cake and rich icing.

Lately, Monique Allen's interracial couple figurines have been topping more wedding cakes, a subtle sign of America's increasing diversity. She runs one of a growing number of businesses trying to cash in on that diversity, although several entrepreneurs said marketing to multiracial Americans and mixed-race couples remains an unproven proposition.

"Most people are so surprised when they first hear about it," Allen said of the figurines, which she sells through her Web-based business. She draws on personal experience: Allen is black and her husband is white.

"It's a fertile target audience," said Allen, from New Castle, Del. "You have so many different opportunities with race and ethnicity."

Nearly 7 million Americans took advantage of the first opportunity to check off more than one race on their 2000 census forms. More than 40 percent of those who did so were younger than 18, proof that the American populace will be even more diverse in decades to come.

Some larger businesses see that as a signal to start broadening their messages now. For instance, toy maker Mattel has introduced a multiracial Barbie, which the company says could be viewed as a "mix of cultures in one doll."

Other, mostly smaller companies have started offering products tailored specifically to interracial couples or mixed-race Americans.

"The fact that Census 2000 was the very first time that this nation identified with more than one race is huge," said Matt Kelley, publisher of Mavin, a Seattle-based magazine targeted at young, multiracial adults. "All of a sudden, we have this new group of people that is very attractive to advertisers," Kelley said.

But it's a group that is also a bit mysterious to businesses, simply because no demographic data was collected on the multiracial population before 2000, said

Do the Math, Marketers: Biracial Americans Grow in Number (cont'd.)

Tom Spencer, a vice president at the San Diego-based marketing company Claritas Inc.

For instance, information about how much these families earn, or how much schooling they have had, is not yet available from the Census Bureau. That data from the 2000 census is scheduled to be released later this year.

Businesses already have that demographic data for African Americans, Latinos and other minority groups from previous census surveys; with multiracial Americans, analysts are starting from scratch.

So far, basic demographic information gathered in the 2000 head count has been released, including age, family makeup and homeownership. The bureau also is reporting state-by-state figures that cover specific Latino and Asian subgroups, American-Indain tribes and multirace combinations.

Businesses interested in developing broader markets will probably have quite a challenge. State-by-state figures can vary widely. In Nevada, for instance, less than 1 percent of the 751,000 households in 2000 were headed by someone whose background is white and Asian. While the median age of all Rhode Island residents was 36.7, it was 24.8 for people of black and Native Hawaiian and Pacific Islander descent.

Kelley said an informal survey of his magazine's readership yielded results that may foreshadow what future Census 2000 releases may show — most live in urban, affluent areas and are well-educated.

Tracy Jackson started her Web-based business after the birth of her first child in 1991. She is white and her husband is African American. She began selling what she called "multicultural gifts that reflect the diversity of America" after being dissatisfied with what was on the shelves at traditional brick-and-mortar stores.

"The face of America is changing," Jackson said. "Children are children, period, but having biracial children for me, it was something that made my heart sensitive to see."

For the most part, though, mainstream businesses have ignored the multiracial population and the country's diversity in general, said Ramona Douglass, spokeswoman for the Association of Multiethnic Americans.

"At this point, advertisers are busy just trying to figure out how to talk to minorities in general," said Beth Barnes, an advertising professor at Syracuse University.

Immigration Said to Keep Pace With 1990s

By The Associated Press

November 27, 2002   *© 2003 DiversityInc.com*

Legal and illegal immigration into the United States so far this decade has kept pace with the surging rates of the 1990s, with nearly one-third of the new immigrants arriving from Mexico, a private analysis released Tuesday revealed. More than 3.3 million new immigrants entered the country between January 2000 and March 2002 as the nation's foreign-born population swelled to more than 33 million, according to a report from the Center for Immigration Studies, a research group that supports some limits on immigration.

Researchers remain divided over how the souring economy and the Sept. 11, 2001, terrorist attacks affected immigration. The report's author, Steven Camarota, said his analysis of Census Bureau data showed little evidence of an immigration slowdown.

"There's such a huge queue of people in line on legal immigration, that even if some people dropped out, there's still a tremendous number waiting to get in," Camarota said. Even during a recession, the economy is better in America than in most of the countries from which new immigrants come, he added.

Roberto Suro, director of the Pew Hispanic Center, cautioned against using the data as a barometer of any post-Sept. 11 immigration trends since the study stopped at March 2002, just six months after the terrorist attacks.

Typically though, Suro said, there is a short-term response in immigration rates to dramatic events and then "the underlying trend reasserts itself – trends tied to economic factors and family reunification."

Among the findings by Camarota:

The number of foreign-born residents increased about 1.1 million a year between 1990 and 2000, to 31.1 million.

Adding to that number the 3.3 million new immigrants this decade through March, then subtracting the 1.3 million immigrants who either died or left the country during the same period, gives the number of immigrants as of March 2002 – 33.1 million.

That total includes an estimated 8 million to 9 million illegal immigrants, with

Immigration Said to Keep Pace With 1990s (cont'd.)

roughly 1 million to 1.5 million entering during the first two-plus years of this decade.

Of all immigrants who arrived since 2000, about 1 million were from Mexico and 88,000 were from the Middle East.

Some evidence points to small declines in the number of student and employment visas granted to immigrants from Middle Eastern countries since Sept. 11, in large part due to crackdowns after the attacks, said Jim Zogby, president of the Arab-American Institute.

Other potential immigrants may be hesitant to come to the United States amid reports of increasing discrimination against Arab-Americans, Zogby said. The FBI on Monday said Muslims and people who are or appear to be of Middle Eastern descent were reported as victims of hate crimes more often last year than ever before.

The mission statement for Camarota's group calls for "fewer immigrants but a warmer welcome for those admitted." According to Camarota, that could be accomplished by better policing the nation's borders and punishing employers who hire illegals, along with maintaining stricter guidelines over who gets visas.

Angela Kelley, deputy director of the pro-immigrant National Immigration Forum, said problems with the current system existed long before the fallout from Sept. 11.

Since security was heightened, U.S. Border Patrol arrests have dropped to their lowest level in more than a decade.

That may be a sign that immigrants are electing to take a more treacherous route or more drastic measures to enter the country, Kelley said.

Kelley favors an overhaul of the immigration system to allow more undocumented workers to gain legal status, an issue being discussed this week in Mexico City between Bush administration officials and Mexican President Vicente Fox.

Part I - Diversity 101: The Basics

A. What Is Diversity?

Diversity can be defined in many ways, including embracing those with different viewpoints and those from disparate backgrounds. For purposes of making the business case for diversity, however, we define diversity in measurable human capital, specifically in groups of people that have not been part of the majority. Those groups include: African Americans, Latinos, Asian Americans, Native Americans, people with disabilities, and gay, lesbian, bisexual and transgender (GLBT) people.

B. Why Do Companies Care About This?

Companies support diversity initiatives for two reasons — reward and punishment. The reward clearly is in the form of a current competitive edge and strong future business prospects with growing communities. Increasingly, diversity initiatives deliver a definitive return on investment and can offer measured financial proof of success.

Based on the changing U.S. demographics, managers realize that having people of color, GLBT people and people with disabilities in visible and important places in the company is the best way to reach new customers and secure relationships with emerging-market communities. And they've quickly learned, with new numbers reinforcing that lesson on an almost daily basis, that if they don't reach out to those customers, they won't be in business much longer.

C. Costs of Ignoring Diversity

What's the punishment? Lack of business and, of course, the specter of lawsuits. Job-discrimination complaints filed against private companies with the Equal Employment Opportunity Commission (EEOC) increased by 4.5 percent in FY 2002, with the EEOC reporting more than 84,000 discrimination filings. This is the highest level in seven years. Although the number of age-discrimination cases has been growing, there also has been a growing awareness among employees of color, women, GLBT people and people with disabilities that this avenue is available to them.

Interestingly, the highest growth in bias complaints last year was in religious discrimination (21 percent), age discrimination (14.5 percent increase), and national-origin bias (13 percent).

An EEOC survey of discrimination lawsuits settled between 1997 and 2001 found the average settlement was $264,000. The cost, however, can be much higher. In 1998, Mitsubishi Motors settled a sex-discrimination case for $34 million. And earlier this year, the California Public Employee's Retirement System settled an age-discrimination case for $250 million, the largest settlement the EEOC has recorded.

ADDITIONAL RESOURCES

PART I - DIVERSITY 101: THE BASICS

U.S. Equal Employment Opportunity Commission (EEOC)
1801 L Street, N.W., Washington, D.C. 20507 (202) 663-4900
http://www.eeoc.gov

Diversity 101: A Primer for Beginners

By Barbara Frankel

March 18, 2002   *© 2003 DiversityInc.com*

D o you wonder what the big deal is about diversity? Is everyone afraid of lawsuits, or are there other reasons this subject keeps coming up in memos, meetings and messages from the CEO? Is this stuff for real?

Are you someone who believes in the idea of diversity, as in "We're all equal, we all have something unique to contribute" but you don't really have a clue how to advance beyond altruistic rhetoric and really make it happen at your company?

Have you just been appointed to your corporation's diversity council or committee or, even scarier, been put in charge of diversity initiatives? Are you trying to sound good but actually clueless about what to do?

If you see yourself in any of these descriptions, or just want some basic information, welcome to Diversity 101. This is a primer of basic corporate diversity tenets - clear advice from the experts and the staff at DiversityInc.com. If you're a long-time reader of this site, this may seem simple and obvious to you. Make sure someone at your corporation who needs the ABC's of diversity reads it, but also make sure he or she has his own premium subscription. Sharing content is a violation of our copyright.

Lesson #1: Why Does My Company Care About Diversity?

(or Why Should My Company Care About Diversity?)

A. Demographics

This statistic says it best:

Among Americans age 70 and up, there are 5.3 white people for every person of color - a ratio of roughly 5-to-1. For Americans below 40, however, that ratio is 2-to-1. And among children under 10 years, the ratio is 1.5-to-1.

There are many more where this came from, all in Census 2000 (see Census Premium Section, DiversityInc.com for more details).

The population of the United States is rapidly changing. Census 2000 brought that home to companies everywhere, particularly the astonishing news that the Latino population soon would become the largest minority group in the country

Diversity 101: A Primer for Beginners (cont'd.)

and that people of color already are a majority in California and soon will be in several other states.

More and more, top managers began to think, "We need to get a piece of that pie before it's too late." Their interest in diversity was born, along with a realization that having people of color in visible and important places in the corporate world is the best way to reach these new customers.

B. Fear of Lawsuits

Job-discrimination complaints filed against private companies with the Equal Employment Opportunity Commission (EEOC) increased by 1.2 percent last year to 80,840, their highest level in six years. While the faltering economy certainly was a factor (particularly in the growing number of age-discrimination cases), there also has been a growing awareness among employees of color, women, gays/lesbians and people with disabilities that this avenue is available to them.

After seeing the Coca-Cola settlement of $192.5 million for African-American employees who charged racial discrimination, many corporations want to be proactive and avoid problems before they start. They often start by naming someone, usually a person in human resources, to head their diversity efforts, or by forming a diversity council.

Lesson #2: I'm Now In Charge of Diversity. What Do I Do First?

A. Read DiversityInc.com

DiversityInc.com is the best and only source of managerial-level content on this subject. Most of your questions can be answered by doing a search of the site or checking the various departments, particularly Diversity Management. And if you have any questions that we haven't yet addressed, please send them to info@diversityinc.com.

B. Get Support from the CEO and Top Management

One of the easiest ways for diversity to become a cul-de-sac in a corporation is for it to serve as window dressing and nothing else. Before agreeing to have anything to do with your company's diversity initiative, be positive that your superiors, particularly the CEO, are on board and enthusiastic.

Just remember, as demonstrated in Malignant Neglect: When Diversity Director Means Dead End, "there are hundreds of other organizations - either by design or through malignant neglect - that have relegated diversity to the bottom of the human-resources heap. Even the strongest mission statement can't fool employees into thinking that a company is serious about diversity when the corporate

Diversity 101: A Primer for Beginners (cont'd.)

diversity director labors alone in a basement office with no staff, no budget and no real impact on day-to-day operations."

C. Push Hard to Make Diversity a Key Business Imperative That's Integrated Throughout the Company

Effective diversity directors are involved in all areas of a company. They have power over executive bonuses (which in the best companies are tied to diversity initiatives), and they are respected and trusted. As discussed during DiversityInc.com's plenary session at the Rainbow/PUSH Wall Street Project conference in January, if diversity isn't positioned throughout the company as a business strategy - not a frivolity - the white men who have been in power will decide these programs are a waste of time.

D. Don't Waste A Lot of Time on Festivals and Luncheons

While there's nothing wrong with honoring Black History Month or your employees' native cultures, these feel-good events take time, budget and effort away from real diversity initiatives that matter. Spend your resources, whatever they are, pushing for strategic diversity initiatives that further your company's business mission and help your firm gain a solid foothold in multicultural communities. That will ensure your success far more than a costume party or a luncheon.

D. Work with Employee Affinity Groups

Employee groups are a good way to reach employees. Use these groups strategically to advance the business initiative and listen to what they know about their respective multicultural audiences. You set the agenda - the business imperative - but listen to their ideas.

Lesson #3: How Do I Demonstrate I'm Doing This Right?

A. Measure, Measure and Measure

From the start, make sure tools are in place to measure and document everything you are doing. For example, monitor representation and percentage changes, along with promotions, salaries and complaints. Monitor supplier-diversity initiatives, including percentage changes and dollar amounts. Check whether new customers in multicultural communities are signing on since your diversity initiatives began. Prove your case, once and for all, to senior management.

B. Improve the Web Site and Mission Statement

Have an immediate impact by changing your corporate Web site to support diver-

---

Diversity 101: A Primer for Beginners (cont'd.)

sity and ensure the company's mission statement accurately reflects the new commitment. These two areas are critical means of communication. By making sure they reflect the company's commitment, you will also prove your own worth.

C. Promote Yourself and Your Diversity Mission At All Times

Don't be shy. Don't be hesitant. You are the voice for the future of your company and you have to make yourself and your mission heard everywhere. Go to as many meetings as you can, particularly those focused on the company's core business strategies. Make this diversity initiative an imperative for everyone.

Consumers Value Diversity When Deciding Where to Spend

By Kipp Cheng

October 14, 2002   *© 2003 DiversityInc.com*

When it comes to fostering workforce diversity, a growing number of companies have realized the bottom-line benefits of recruiting and retaining a multiethnic and multicultural employee base. After all, a diverse group of workers helps corporate America better tap into emerging markets by giving companies the kinds of competitive insights and knowledge only insiders can provide.

So it's surprising to note that some companies – even the most diversity-conscious and culturally competent ones – continue to fail to effectively communicate to consumers, especially those from emerging markets, a commitment to diversity and inclusion.

This failure of a corporation to express its internal values of diversity to the marketplace could cost corporate America millions, if not billions, in potential revenue. According to a new report from research firms Harris Interactive and Witeck-Combs, consumers from emerging markets, notably gay, lesbian, bisexual and transgender (GLBT) consumers, actively consider companies' internal diversity policies when selecting a company for business plans or when making purchasing decisions.

Additionally, the study concluded that consumers in emerging markets are positively impacted when dealing with sales staffs and/or company representatives that reflect the ethnicity or culture of the customers.

"Most consumers believe that people are not going to discriminate against their own kind," said Jake Stafford, a marketing strategist at Washington, D.C.-based Witeck-Combs, who worked on the survey. "In most cases, people were somewhat positively or very positively impacted rather than negatively impacted when dealing with people who were like them."

Although the study focused primarily on consumers in the GLBT market, Stafford said there was evidence that consumers of color were also positively impacted by doing business with companies that had clearly stated diversity policies, employed a diverse workforce and developed inclusive marketing programs.

Consumers Value Diversity When Deciding Where to Spend (cont'd.)

Stafford said the sample size of non-GLBT consumers of color in the study was too small to produce scientific results, however, anecdotally there appeared to be a correspondence between how GLBT consumers felt about dealing with "out" salespeople and how African Americans, in particular, preferred to deal with African-American salespeople. (The ethnic sample of non-GLBT Latinos, Asian Americans/Pacific Islanders and Native Americans did not show the same strong preferences for interaction with those of the same race.)

The survey was fielded through both telephone and Internet responses between Sept. 24 and Oct. 2, with more than 2,000 respondents. The sample was weighted to reflect the age, gender, ethnic and income distribution of the overall U.S. population.

When those respondents who self-identified as gay, lesbian, bisexual or transgender were asked if they chose to do business with companies with recognized commitments to diversity, 75 percent said they somewhat agreed or strongly agreed. By contrast, 38 percent of self-identified heterosexuals said they somewhat agreed or strongly agreed to the statement.

"The heterosexual numbers are interesting because as a group they seem almost apathetic about a company's diversity commitment," said Stafford. "They don't seem to care one way or the other. Almost half said it's not a factor in their decision to purchase a company's products or services."

Stafford said both the GLBT and heterosexual samples were comprised of respondents of all races and backgrounds.

When GLBT respondents were asked about the impact of interacting with an "out" salesperson or company representative, a majority said it would somewhat positively or very positively impacted their decision to purchase. This was especially true for legal, financial and health-care services companies; 56 percent of GLBT respondents said they would be very positively or somewhat positively impacted when dealing with out representatives working in these industries.

"Unless you live in a gay ghetto, the fact is that most GLBT people live in a straight world," said Stafford. "Therefore, you still have to receive your legal, financial and health-care services in a predominately straight world. That's just how the world is."

With all other factors being equal – such as price, quality, value and function – Stafford said GLBT consumers are inclined to be more positively impacted by GLBT vendors, especially when it comes to products or services where sexual orientation might be a sensitive issue. For example, gay and lesbian couples look-

Consumers Value Diversity When Deciding Where to Spend (cont'd.)

ing to purchase homes have special needs with it comes to financial services, and GLBT people have specific health-care issues that their straight counterparts may not, such as domestic-partner benefits.

The survey found GLBT consumers were slightly less choosy when it came to selecting vendors for every-day purchases, such as groceries and drugstore goods. However, despite slightly smaller percentages (43 percent), Stafford said GLBT consumers overall tend to be highly aware of companies' diversity initiatives and actively seek to support companies that have inclusive policies in place and avoid those that don't.

"The important thing to note is GLBT consumers tend to be more open-minded than their straight counterparts. If they know they are dealing with someone who understands, especially in purchases that are a little bit more sensitive, where someone's sexual orientation can help with the relationship, then [GLBT] consumers have more confidence and comfort in the transaction," said Stafford.

The report was released on Oct. 10, the eve of National Coming Out Day 2002, an annual event when GLBT people are encouraged to be open and honest about their sexual orientation to friends and family. The findings, Stafford added, highlight why companies such as American Airlines, Coors Brewing Company and IBM have designated GLBT employees to spearhead strategies to expand market share among GLBT consumers.

But what about companies that have solid diversity policies in place that are unknown to consumers?

"Of course, that's always the challenge for some companies," said Stafford. "Because of some companies' unfounded fear of backlash, they don't want to promote the fact that they have these diversity policies."

However, by closeting diversity initiatives, corporations are missing out on reaching new customers.

"Perceptions of fairness and openness consistently matter to GLBT consumers," said Wesley Combs, president of Witeck-Combs Communications. "Clearly, any company that chooses to motivate and make its GLBT employees visible will stand to gain a great deal in terms of support from GLBT consumers. It's a logical matter to match a company's employee diversity policies with the needs and expectations of its diverse customers."

Meetings and Malcontents: Why Some Diversity Councils Don't Work

By Linda Bean

March 04, 2002   *© 2003 DiversityInc.com*

Here's a quick exercise aimed at determining the likely success of your internal corporate diversity council. Just finish the following sentence, choosing from the list below the answer that most accurately describes your company's council.

"Our diversity council ... "

A. Provides the food for our monthly ethnic celebrations. Yum.

B. Seems to attract all the malcontents.

C. Should pay much, much more attention to my African-American/Latino/Gay/Lesbian/Transgendered/Native American/Asian-Pacific Islander/Women's/White Male issues and much less attention to everyone else's.

D. Should hold longer/shorter, more frequent/less frequent meetings.

E. What council?

F. Is focused on the company's bottom line and is responsible for developing strategies that will leverage diversity's benefits throughout the organization.

Any answer except the last one signals trouble for a diversity council. At the same time, companies frequently offer up the existence of a council as proof of the corporate commitment to diversity - even if the council's mission is poorly defined or non-existent.

"There's almost an assumption that there will be a diversity council," said Terrence Simmons, CEO and managing partners at Simmons and Associates, New Hope, Pa. "It's a common practice so people just assume there's going to be a council."

"If you are going to have a good council, then you are going to have to have a good strategy," said Edward Hubbard, who owns the Petaluma, Calif., consulting firm of Hubbard & Hubbard. "Otherwise, it doesn't do people any good."

Too often, corporate diversity councils are formed when management throws a group of unhappy employees together and directs them to come up with a plan.

Meetings and Malcontents: Why Some Diversity Councils Don't Work (cont'd.)

Hubbard isn't necessarily opposed to bringing all the malcontents together "if those people will have some power to make change occur."

"If you are just putting people in a no-harm, no-foul situation, that doesn't do them any good," he added.

The most effective diversity councils share two key elements: top managers actively lead them and the council's goals are strictly aligned with corporate business objectives.

"If you want to have a buy-in from the standpoint of management, you have to make that management understands that there is something in it for them," Hubbard said. Otherwise, the process will be as futile "as pushing rope."

"Nothing happens unless executives are willing to make something happen," Simmons echoed.

Siemens Information and Communications Networks (ICN), Boca Raton, Fla., is a case in point. Siemens ICN, which employs 6,000 people in the United States, unit builds integrated voice and data networks. It is a subsidiary of Siemans AG, Europe's largest electronics and electrical engineering firm and one of the world's leading mobile phone handset makers. Al Baker, vice president of product management for Siemens ICN, also leads the company's internal diversity council.

"I'm not a paid human-resources person or a paid diversity director," said Baker, who is African American. "I run a global business unit for Siemens."

Baker is an alumni of AT&T and Lucent, where, he said, diversity awareness had been woven into the corporate fabric for decades. But Siemens, perhaps because of its European leadership, came late to an awareness of diversity issues in the United States. Four years age, Siemens formed an overall U.S. diversity council. And Fred Fromm - then CEO of Siemens ICN - set about developing a separate diversity council for his organization.

"This came about for two reasons," Baker said. "We were selling to companies that were made up of people of diverse backgrounds and gender. For us to come to the table and not be able to match that diversity ... that is a problem."

Second, he said, the economy was booming and managers at all levels recognized that it "was hard to find the right people."

Participation in the Siemens diversity council was by invitation only, and those invited had clearly been selected because they brought "a diversity of back-

Meetings and Malcontents: Why Some Diversity Councils Don't Work (cont'd.)

ground" to the table, Baker said. The council's members almost immediately hired a consultant to help them establish their mission and goals. "We came up with an early mission statement and an early vision statement. They were totally revamped ... but our mission, basically, was to take a hard look at the make up of ICN and move it forward."

The council's first objective was to educate its line executives about the strategic business value of diversity. With the assistance of the consultant, the council put together a pilot program, tested it in several locations and then rolled it out at Siemens ICN locations nationwide.

Producing the pilot program required considerable "time and attention ... close to eight months," Baker said. "We recognized (that diversity awareness training) can bring up a lot of emotions, and we didn't want these to be sessions where people come and bring all their emotional baggage and spew it out on the floor."

Instead, the diversity council wanted to assure that every element of the program served a strategic business objective. To accomplish that end, the council established subteams to examine specific issues. "Are there any parts of the hiring process that make it easier or harder for a manager to look at diverse candidates? What methods were we using for recruiting? What about retention. Nobody wants to stay if they don't thing they have future," Baker said.

The council work is still in the early stages, Baker said, "but we are getting the word out that Siemens is beginning to develop a culture that cares about this."

At Siemens ICN, the diversity council was formed at the direction of the company CEO and it has a budget that allows it to hire the expertise it requires.

Most important, the council is structured to assure that every diversity initiative is linked to a strategic business goal.

As a diversity council matures, it's important for the executive leadership to consider all the roles the council might play within the organization, Simmons said.

For example, a council can serve as a good tool for two-way communication - bringing information about the corporate climate to executive leaders and sharing information about diversity strategies with the rank and file.

A council that includes human resources expertise could help line managers articulate their diversity goals for the year and evaluate diversity plans, examine succession planning and explore mentoring. Each of those elements requires different skills - "small teams that would have be very carefully chosen,' Simmons added.

Meetings and Malcontents: Why Some Diversity Councils Don't Work (cont'd.)

The council shouldn't be some sort of umbrella over corporate affinity groups, Simmons said, but it could work with race- and gender-based groups to leverage their contributions to business-related goals.

"Diversity is a change-process within an organization," Simmons said. "If it is not focused on business results, then I don't think it is a legitimate activity."

When 'Diversity Director' Means 'Dead End' – Malignant Neglect: Mistakes You Don't Know You're Making

By Linda Bean

January 15, 2002   © *2003 DiversityInc.com*

When a public road disappears into a cornfield or landfill, municipal officials are usually good enough to post a big yellow sign, warning drivers of the impending dead end.

But when the career path of a woman or person of color leads to a corporate diversity post, top executives don't generally caution candidates that they are headed for a professional cul-de-sac.

It's up to the candidates to read the road ahead, said Los Angeles management consultant Sondra Theiderman. Otherwise, "they will be giving little cultural lunches with different kinds of foods each month and that's as far as it is going to go."

"It can become a dead end in companies where diversity is viewed as a program - the flavor of the day or month or year," said Clay Osborne, vice president of global diversity and workforce development at vision-care giant Bausch & Lomb. "Is it a program or an overall process that links diversity to business success?"

To be fair, some companies understand that human-resources functions, including diversity management, are crucial to the bottom line. Those companies accord diversity directors the same respect - and demand the same kind of accountability - that line executives receive.

But there are hundreds of other organizations - either by design or through malignant neglect - that have relegated diversity to the bottom of the human-resources heap.

Even the strongest corporate mission statement can't fool employees into thinking that a company is serious about diversity when the corporate diversity director labors alone in a basement office with no staff, no budget, and no real impact on day-to-day operations.

When 'Diversity Director' Means 'Dead End' – Malignant Neglect: Mistakes You Don't Know You're Making (cont'd.)

And once employees have gotten that message, management will have a tough time undoing the damage. After all, who wants to work for a company that makes it clear diversity - of opinion, gender, race and sexual orientation - doesn't count?

As for diversity directors, "it's a case-by-case kind of a thing," said Theiderman. "It can be a career dead end, but it isn't always. There are people who have made wonderful careers" by accepting a diversity assignment.

"A piece of it, too, is what you make of it," echoed Anita Rowe, a partner at the Los Angeles consulting firm of Gardenswartz & Rowe. "Part of the power of making it work or not lies within (the candidate). If you think it is going to be a dead-end job, it will be. We do create a reality that validates what we think is going to happen."

Before a candidate accepts a diversity position, it's important - and not always easy - to assess the offer, clarify expectations, and examine the implications of saying no.

Why me? The first thing a candidate needs to do is determine why he or she was approached in the first place. That's easy enough when a company's diversity practices are well-established and mentoring and career-development activities are routine. Within those organizations, it's likely that candidates for all promotions are identified as part of the corporate succession plan and groomed for new opportunities.

But in companies where "diversity" is erroneously defined as racial representation or lawsuit-prevention, it may be more difficult to establish the motive behind a diversity job offer.

Is the job just a lateral move into corporate limbo - a subtle statement that it's time for the candidate to send out new resumes? Has management denigrated or ignored diversity in the past? Is there a bias lawsuit pending? Could the offer signal a change in corporate culture or is it just an exercise in tokenism?

Management consultant Cornelia Gamlem frames the last question like this: "Are they asking me just because I'm a person of color or because I'm a woman?"

"Just because you are a member of a particular group doesn't mean you have the competencies - or the interest - to do a particular job," added Gamlem, principal in GEMS Group Ltd., Herndon, Va.

Check the chart: Rowe would advise any candidate for a diversity director's post to take a good look at the company's internal structure.

When 'Diversity Director' Means 'Dead End' – Malignant Neglect: Mistakes You Don't Know You're Making (cont'd.)

In some organizations, the diversity director answers to the vice president of human resources. In others, the executive responsible for diversity reports directly to the CEO.

"You have to be really clear," Rowe said. "Diversity is about culture change. Find out where the commitment really lies. Ask questions: 'To whom will I report? What kind of support will I have? What happens when I meet with resistance?' "

"And believe me," Rowe cautioned, "there will be resistance."

It is sometimes difficult for an employee to ask tough questions when presented with what appears to be the flattering offer of a promotion, Theiderman said. Her advice? "Don't be seduced by a title."

Just Say No: Candidates also need to evaluate the risk of turning down a job that has been presented - even falsely - as a promotion.

Theiderman advised candidates to focus discussions about the position as business-strategy sessions and turn the company's attention to the benefits of diversity.

"If you approach it like a business (decision)," Theiderman said, "there is less risk of there being negative consequences if you say no."

Meanwhile Osborne, at Rochester, N.Y.-based Bausch & Lomb, suggested a short list of key questions that could help a job candidate judge the offer:

Is there a commitment from senior management? "The whole 'walk the talk' thing."

Is the diversity role viewed as a key position in the organization?

Is there funding? "You can tell how much support there is by how it's funded."

"I would also find out what opportunity there is for me to move to other key positions of responsibility - positions with profit-and-loss responsibility," Osborne said. "Is there an opportunity to rotate through other roles - not only to get the experience, but to understand the linkages between those roles and the diversity goals and objectives?"

Osborne, a 10-year veteran of Bausch & Lomb, has the standard human-resources responsibilities - recruiting, succession management, employee relations and equal employment opportunity compliance.

But - because he says the company understands the business case for diversity - he is also responsible for leveraging diversity into creativity. "Diversity used to be a choice. Now, it's a fact," he said.

When 'Diversity Director' Means 'Dead End' – Malignant Neglect: Mistakes You Don't Know You're Making (cont'd.)

Bausch & Lomb operates in a global marketplace against an increasingly "diverse group of competitors" Osborne said. "Our consumers are more diverse. Our workforce is more diverse."

The company has a broad definition of diversity that recognizes differences and similarities of thought and belief, as well as race, ethnicity, gender and sexual orientation. That definition supports the company's emphasis on creativity. And leveraging diversity to produce creative solutions is "probably the most profound issue," he faces, Osborne said.

"Creativity and innovation. We need to become more nimble, more creative. The more diversity of thought you have, the more that diversity allows you to be innovative and creative," he said.

"Leveraging diversity makes your company more successful and more profitable," he said. "And if you can't do that, you will fail."

Limiting Discrimination Lawsuits: EEOC Launches New Mediation Program

By Linda Bean

April 28, 2003   *© 2003 DiversityInc.com*

The Equal Employment Opportunity Commission (EEOC) is joining forces with nine state and local fair-employment agencies to expand the use of voluntary mediation to resolve employment-discrimination complaints.

The pilot program is aimed at reducing the time and cost involved in mediating a dispute and represents an expansion of the EEOC's existing mediation programs.

The agency's new partners are state civil-rights agencies in Alaska, Florida, Indiana, Iowa, Ohio, New Mexico and South Carolina, as well as municipal agencies in Kansas City and New York City.

"This pilot program strengthens our partnership with (fair employment-practices agencies) and builds on our mutual goal of eradicating discrimination in the workplaces of America," EEOC Chair Cari Dominguez said in a statement.

The EEOC launched a nationwide mediation program under the Clinton administration in 1999. Since then, the agency has conducted 44,000 mediation sessions, resolved 29,000 charges, and obtained $400 million in compensation for employees. On average, it takes 86 days to resolve a complaint through mediation, compared with years if a case goes to trial.

"The more recent average for mediation is even lower than that – 82 days, as of the end of fiscal year 2002," said David Grinberg, EEOC spokesperson.

"Litigation is time-consuming and a lengthy process," Grinberg said. "And mediation is more fair. The two sides themselves craft the resolution, rather than an agreement handed down to them."

Both the employee and employer have to agree to mediation. The mediation sessions are paid for by the EEOC and employers aren't required to admit any wrongdoing, even if an agreement is reached. Further, the charging party can have an attorney present.

"Sometimes, it is just a matter of getting both parties to sit down in a room and talk the issue through with a neutral third party," said Grinberg.

Dominguez has made mediation the centerpiece of her five-point plan to improve

Limiting Discrimination Lawsuits: EEOC Launches New Mediation Program (cont'd.)

efficiency at the EEOC.

The new pilot program comes on the heels of a "referral back" mediation pilot program for private employers. Through that program, discrimination complaints filed with the EEOC are "referred back" to the employer's internal-dispute resolution program. The EEOC also has formal agreements to mediate with 200 local employers and "a handful of national employers," Grinberg said. Those companies have agreed in advance to submit all employment disputes to mediation.

Mediation is a voluntary process, Grinberg said, and complaining parties are not required to submit their dispute to mediation.

From an employer's perspective, mediation is far cheaper than litigation, said Samantha Halem, an attorney with the Center for Mediation and Dispute Resolution, based in Wellesley, Mass.

"I think there is certain amount of feeling that you've been heard, which you may never feel if never you never get to trial. It is very empowering," she said.

Mediation particularly is valuable when both parties would like the employment relationship to continue, she said. "It is invaluable. Litigation destroys relationship."

According to a five-year study of lawsuits filed by the EEOC, 91 percent of federal employment-discrimination lawsuits filed by the agency between Oct. 1, 1996 and Sept. 30, 2001 were resolved successfully through consent decrees, settlement agreements and favorable court orders.

The study shows the EEOC's success rate in trials is 60.24 percent - compared with a success rate of 26.8 percent for private plaintiffs in workplace-bias suits - and the agency's success rate is 80 percent in the appeal of trials - compared with a 16 percent rate of success for private attorneys.

Part I - Diversity 101: The Basics

Job-Discrimination Cases Hit 7-Year High

By The Associated Press

February 07, 2003   *© 2003 DiversityInc.com*

Federal job-discrimination complaints filed by workers against private employers jumped more than 4 percent in 2002 to the highest level in seven years.

The Equal Employment Opportunity Commission said Thursday that complaints increased to 84,442 during the 2002 budget year, up from 80,840 the previous year.

Complaints in 2002 reached the highest level since 1995, when 87,529 were filed.

The poor economy, an aging and multinational workforce and backlash from the 2001 terrorist attacks likely contributed to the increase, said EEOC Chairwoman Cari M. Dominguez. She noted the large increases in allegations of religious, age and national origin discrimination.

Religious complaints increased 21 percent, age complaints were up 14.5 percent and national origin complaints rise 13 percent.

The rise in age-discrimination complaints "continues to be troublesome for us, because with baby boomers getting into the 50-plus category, it's cause for concern that employers have not yet gotten their arms around this issue," Dominguez said.

"It's very costly – in terms of settlement and the loss of human talent."

Allegations of race and gender discrimination accounted for a majority of the complaints, at 35 percent and 30 percent respectively.

The industries generating the most complaints were retail, food services and manufacturing.

The commission resolved 95,222 cases last year, a 5 percent increase from 2001. A record $310.5 million in monetary benefits for complainants was recovered.

EEOC Offers 'Plain English' Anti-Bias Guide

By The Associated Press

December 05, 2002   © *2003 DiversityInc.com*

Complaints of discrimination based on national origin have risen 20 percent over the last eight years, the Equal Employment Opportunity Commission (EEOC) said Tuesday.

The agency attributed the rise to hostility to Muslims and Middle Easterners after the Sept. 11 attacks, increasing numbers of immigrants in the labor force and other population changes.

"Most people think about race and gender discrimination — national origin discrimination doesn't come to mind, but it's having a greater impact on the workplace," EEOC spokesperson David Grinberg said as the agency announced its Web site's new user-friendly explanation of how discrimination law works.

The Sept. 11 reaction has also caused problems for Sikhs, Asians and Arabs.

Between Sept. 11, 2001, and November of this year, 688 charges have been filed by people of these national origins and others alleging Sept. 11 backlash discrimination — some relating to religion.

The EEOC filed a lawsuit on behalf of a Muslim employee of a car rental company who said she was fired for covering her head with a scarf during the holy month of Ramadan a couple of months after the Sept. 11 attacks. The company had not objected when she wore the scarf during Ramadan the previous two years. The three lawsuits were all filed Sept. 30.

Of the roughly 84,000 total charges filed to the EEOC during the fiscal year that ended Sept. 30, about 11 percent, or 9,052, allege discrimination on the basis of national origin. That's up roughly 20 percent from 1994, when 7,414, or 8 percent, of total cases filed dealt with national origin bias, the EEOC said.

Commission officials said the 9,052 charges filed in the last fiscal year likely represents only the tip of the iceberg, that a lot of discrimination may be unreported because many fear retaliation or are not aware of the law. To help educate employers about their responsibilities and employees about their rights, the commission has posted on the Internet a plain language explanation and a fact sheet.

EEOC Offers 'Plain English' Anti-Bias Guide (cont'd.)

Randy Johnson, vice president for labor policy at the U.S. Chamber of Commerce, welcomed the changes.

"EEO laws, as interpreted by the courts, have become extremely convoluted and difficult to understand," Johnson said. "We've always believed if the government's going to impose obligations on employers, it ought to spend some money on explaining what they are in plain English."

Part II - Corporate Governance:

Human Capital: How to Get and Keep Good People

A. Recruitment

Recruitment is critical to having a diverse work force and having multicultural leaders of an organization, all of which are vital to attracting the increasing number of multicultural consumers in the United States.

How to reach talented diverse people, from beginners to experienced professionals, is a challenge for many companies, especially those in industries that haven't been attuned to the benefits of diversity.

1. Benefits & Costs

Attracting the best and brightest employees during a recession can be a double-edge sword for both companies and job seekers. With national unemployment rates up, (4.8 percent in 2001 and 5.8 percent in 2002; to 6 percent in April 2003) corporations can choose from a larger pool of potentially qualified job applicants, making it an employer's market. Meanwhile, the recent economic downturn has put more multicultural talent in the job market, giving corporate America a critical opportunity to recruit these workers before more diversity-savvy companies recruit them.

With the glut of qualified workers and a decrease in new jobs, however, finding the right people for the right jobs has become increasingly difficult.

Cities such as New York City, still experiencing some post-Sept. 11 aftershocks, and San Francisco, where the fallout of failed dot-coms continues to ripple through the Bay Area economy, are ripe with opportunity for corporations seeking talented, diverse employees.

The good news is that corporations can take advantage of the economic downturn by recruiting from a diverse talent pool. After all, top talent with diverse backgrounds brings a wider perspective and deeper connection to emerging markets.

"Minority applicants bring a broader picture because they are connected to a broader range of people,"[57] says Herminia Ibarra, a professor at Harvard Business School. "They have to keep two different networks."

A commitment to diversity in the work force must come from the top. Increasingly, corporate executives realize that a diversity commitment must be visible both internally and externally, especially at the executive level.

Shirley Harrison, vice president of diversity for New York-based Altria, says she has noticed over the past few years that shareholders tend to ask more questions related to a corporation's diversity programs, recruitment and retention efforts. From current employees to prospective ones and those who opt for retirement, it's about maintaining the humanity throughout the relationship,[58] she says.

Harrison emphasizes that recruiters must remember to put their best faces forward since they represent the company to job applicants, who also are consumers.

"How you approach anybody in the recruitment outreach process is critical because employee prospects are also our consumers," Harrison says. "You want them to remain consumers."

Diversity-conscious companies have found that drawing from a larger and more diverse candidate pool via the Internet results in savings beyond the costs of employee acquisition. Online recruiting of diverse workers also benefits companies with overall savings in employee retention, since online job seekers are typically better informed about the companies to which they are applying for jobs.

Searching for jobs online makes sense in a world where vast majorities — more than 90 percent — of large, U.S. companies are recruiting via the Internet, according to the Harvard Business Review.[59]

According to a survey conducted in 2000 by the Society for Human Resource Management (SHRM), 96 percent of job seekers apply for career positions online. SHRM believes that percentage will continue to rise.[60]

Peter Cappelli, the George W. Taylor Professor of Management at the Wharton School of Business, University of Pennsylvania, estimates that, on any given Monday, at least 4 million job seekers search the Web, while thousands of corporate recruiters scour job boards.

Consider this: Studies show that people of color from all socioeconomic backgrounds are clicking online at a greater rate proportionately than whites, suggesting that for a company to reach the greatest number of Internet-savvy and educated African Americans, Latinos, Asian Americans, or other ethnic minorities, companies must post their job openings electronically — or lose out on the cream of the crop.

The first step to developing a successful strategy to attract top-tier multicultural talent can be as simple as declaring an intention to seek out a diverse work force and then executing on that promise. Word of mouth goes a long way and having a pro-diversity reputation — whether it's a company known as an employer of choice for people of color, women and gays/lesbians — will greatly facilitate reaching out to and attracting diverse job applicants.

Studies show that solid reputations invariably yield positive bottom-line results, while poor reputations can hinder financial returns.

A Pennsylvania State University study found that companies with the highest marks on Fortune magazine's reputation survey had an average annual return of 22.2 percent increase, including dividends, which far outperformed the Standard & Poor's 500, which had a 16.3 percent return during the same period. Companies with the lowest reputation ranking had a negative return of -1.7 percent.

The Penn State study, conducted from 1983 to 1997, also found that corporate reputations — good and bad — tend to endure over time, with many companies remaining in either the top or bottom 10 of the survey for many years.

"Employees are the major stakeholder group," says Barbara Burton, president of the Burton Company, a San Diego-based consultant firm focused on corporate social responsibility. "If humanity is not at the crux of these businesses even in these tough times, their corporate reputation will suffer, and ultimately their bottom line will be affected."

When asked how much they thought American corporations could be trusted to look out for the interests of their employees, respondents to a January 2002 Gallup poll indicated that for the most part they expected a company to keep their interests in mind. Forty-one percent of respondents said they held "a fair amount" of trust in corporate America, while 35 percent said they held "only a little" amount of trust in corporate America.

Antoinette Malveaux, president/CEO of the National Black MBA

Association, (NBMBAA), says today's job recruits understand that developing a career is up to them.[61] This understanding, while good for the proactive recruit, is bad for the company because many times employees leave after a few years at a job. As a result, "more companies are engendering trust in their recruitment process because they're clearer about their needs," Malveaux says.

Most companies recruiting these days are honest in their tactics, Malveaux says. "Companies are coming with real jobs, prepared to hire and are extending offers."

In the past, the success or failure of corporate-diversity initiatives was measured using "soft" data, such as whether or not a given workplace fostered diversity through "ethnic" lunch days. Today, that sort of diversity awareness clearly is deficient when compared with the hard metrics that support a business case for diversity.

While measurements such as the percentage increase of multicultural employees or the total number of diverse executives can shed light on certain aspects of a company's diversity commitment, there is a growing science developing to gauge the actual bottom-line contribution of diversity.[62]

While tools and approaches to measuring diversity may vary widely, even the most modest corporate-diversity program should be measured and judged against its contribution to the bottom line, says Ed Hubbard of Petaluma, Calif.-based Hubbard & Hubbard.

Hubbard & Hubbard uses detailed tools to help diversity directors gauge the impact of their programs on business objectives, such as increasing sales or market share — a process Hubbard calls "calculating the diversity return on investment." Linking diversity to business objectives "is how you begin to convince people that diversity makes sense," Hubbard says.

Consider, for example, a company where the corporate culture isn't particularly welcoming to women or people of color — a place where employees spend at least some portion of the workday thinking about how, or whether or not, they fit in. A company with 5,000 employees who earn $12 an hour and spend 25 percent of the workday worried about corporate-culture issues will lose $120,000 a day in productivity, Hubbard says. Over the course of a year, assuming 260 work days, the company would lose $31.2 million.

If the lack of a comprehensive diversity process is responsible for only 40 percent of that loss, then the total is $14.04 million. And even if the company is only 85 percent certain that diversity issues are responsible for that loss, the total still tops $11 million.

If any other business unit — sales, for example — was responsible for an $11 million loss, "a head would roll," he adds.

The key to developing a strong measurement program is building what Hubbard calls a "financial performance mind-set" that requires integrating diversity with other critical business strategies that are measured on a regular basis.

Some companies, Hubbard notes, are "still grappling with their definition of diversity.[63] They confuse diversity with affirmative action, and that, in many cases, is one of the first barriers to get beyond."

Consider that the average cost-per-hire for a salaried employee was estimated at $6,000 in 2000. Total costs, including recruiting fees, salaries, overhead and applicant travel expenses, exceeded $10,000, representing a steady 5 percent increase per year since 1990. These figures vary greatly by industry, with the most significant costs noted in the utilities, pharmaceutical and media industries.[64]

2. Work-Force Demographics

a. African Americans

African Americans comprised 12 percent or 25.4 million of the 216.8 million members of the U.S. labor force in 2002, according to the Census Bureau.[65] African Americans are projected to be 12.7 percent of the labor force by 2010.[66] In 2002, African-American men had a lower labor-force participation rate (68 percent) than white men (73 percent), and African-American men had a higher unemployment rate (11 percent) than white men (5 percent), according to Census Bureau figures. African-American women had higher labor-force participation rates (62 percent) than white women (60 percent) in 2002.[67]

While similar amounts of African-American and white men were employed in technical, sales and administrative-support positions (20 percent) in 2002, only 18 percent of African-American men were in managerial compared with 33 percent of white men. A higher percentage of white men (19 percent) worked in precision production, craft and repair jobs in comparison to African-American men (14 percent). African-American men were twice as likely to work in service occupations (19 percent) or work as operators, fabricators or laborers (28 percent) than white men. In 2002, 8 percent of white men worked in service occupations and 16 percent worked as operators, fabricators or laborers.[68]

In 2002, 26 percent of African-American women were in managerial or professional positions, according to the Census Bureau. This compares with 37 percent of white women in those positions in 2002. Thirty-six percent of African-American women and 40 percent of white women held technical, sales and administrative-support jobs in 2002. African-American women were almost twice as likely than white women to hold service positions or work as operators, fabricators and laborers. Fifteen percent of white women worked in service occupations, compared with 27 percent of African-American women. And 9 percent of African-American women worked as operators, fabricators or laborers, compared with 5 percent of white women.[69]

As of March 2002, 79 percent of African Americans had high-school diplomas, with 17 percent having bachelor's degrees, according to the U.S. Census Bureau. Eighteen percent of African-American women had bachelor's degrees, compared with 16 percent of African-American men.

b. Latinos

Latinos were 11.1 percent of the labor force in 2001 and are projected to be 13.3 percent of the labor force by 2010. Latinos had an overall labor force participation rate of 68.1 percent in 2001 and are expected to reach 69 percent in 2010. Latino men had a 79.8 percent participation rate in 2001, with Latina women having a 56.8 percent participation rate in that year. The participation rate of Latino men is expected to go down slightly by 2010 to 79 percent, while the participation rate for Latina women is expected to increase to 59.4 percent by 2010.[70]

Only 14 percent of Latino workers were employed in managerial or professional positions in 2000, the U.S. Census Bureau reported.

According to Census 2000, only 57 percent of Latinos in this country are likely to have high-school diplomas and 27.3 percent of Latinos have less than ninth-grade educations. (This latter figure compares with 4.2 percent of whites with below a ninth-grade education.) In 2000, 10.6 percent of Latinos had bachelor's degrees, compared with 28.1 percent of whites.[71]

c. Asian Americans

Asian Americans had a 67 percent participation rate in the labor force in 2002: 75 percent for Asian-American men and 59 percent for Asian-American women.[72]

Asian-American men were more likely to be employed in managerial and professional positions (41 percent), compared to white men (33.4 percent) in 2002. In the same year, 37.2 percent of Asian-American women were employed in those same occupational groups, compared to 36.9 percent of white women. White women (40.2 percent) were more likely to be employed in technical, sales and administrative support positions than Asian-American women (33.5 percent) in 2002. Half the percentages of Asian-American men (9.4 percent) were employed in precision production, craft and repair than white men (18.6 percent).[73]

While Asian Americans are more likely to have earned college degrees than the white population, they also more likely than whites to have less than a ninth-grade education. In 2002, 87 percent of the Asian-American population had at least high-school diplomas, compared with 89 percent of whites. Seven percent of Asian Americans had less than a ninth-grade education, compared with 4 percent of whites. In 2002, 5 percent of Asian-American men and 10 percent of Asian-American women had less than a ninth-grade education.[74]

d. Gay, Lesbian, Bisexual and Transgender People

One challenge of interpreting census data for the GLBT community, according to Gary Gates, a researcher in the Population Studies Center at the Urban Institute, is that the U.S. Census does not ask respondents about sexual orientation. Therefore, while census data can provide some insights into the GLBT community, particularly information about same-sex partner households, it otherwise does not effectively characterize many components of the GLBT community.[75] Therefore, to acquire an overview of GLBTs in the work force and education, private surveys often are conducted.

According to a Kaiser Family Foundation survey conducted in November 2001, self-identifying lesbians, gays and bisexuals had higher levels of college degrees (34 percent) compared to the general population (17 percent) taking part in the survey. The survey also showed that 25 percent of GLBT respondents had a post-graduate education compared to 8 percent of the general population surveyed.[76]

The Kaiser Family Foundation also estimates that between 11 percent and 12 percent of the GLBT population is self-employed. This compares with a 6 percent self-employment rate of the overall employed population, according to the Bureau of Labor Statistics.[77]

e. People With Disabilities

According to Census Bureau statistics, 11.9 percent of the working adult population in the United States (ages 16 to 64) had a condition that affected their ability to work in 2000. This percentage is slightly higher for men (13 percent) than for women (10.9 percent).[78] The labor-force participation rate for men with disabilities ages 16 to 64 was 60.1 percent in 2000, compared with a 79.9 percent participation rate for men without disabilities. For working-age women, the rates were 67.3 percent for those without disabilities and 51.4 percent for those with disabilities in 2000. In 2000, 10.4 million men and 8.2 million women with disabilities were part of the work force.[79]

Fifty-four percent of people with disabilities either are working or looking for work, according to the online disability community iCan.[80]

One-third of people ages 18 to 64 with disabilities are working, but two-thirds of the unemployed population with disabilities would prefer to be working, according to a National Organization on Disability/Harris Interactive poll. The poll showed that 82 percent of the working-age population without disabilities is employed.

f. Women

Women of all races had a participation rate of 60.1 percent in 2001 and are projected to reach a 62.2 percent participation rate by 2010.[81]

Eighty-four percent of both men and women age 25 and older were likely to have completed their high-school educations. While women (26 percent) were more likely to have completed associate's degrees or some college compared with men (24 percent), 29 percent of men were more likely to have completed bachelor's degrees, compared with 25 percent of women.[82]

Seventy-nine percent of the 18 million people working in administrative-support positions were women in 2002. Ninety-one percent of the 14 million people working in precision production, craft and repair occupations were men in 2002. Fifty-nine percent of men worked in four occupational groups: 18 percent in precision production, craft and repair; 16 percent in executive, administrators and managerial; 14 percent in professional specialty; and 11 percent in sales. Seventy-three percent of women worked in four occupational groups: 23 percent in administrative support and clerical; 19 percent in professional specialty; 17 percent in service; and 15 percent in executive, administrators and managerial.[83]

3. Layoff Demographics

While labor-force participation rates have more than doubled for women in the last 50 years, they have decreased for men. In 1955, 35.7 percent of all women participated in the labor force, compared with 85.4 percent of men. In 2002, 59.9 percent of women participated in the labor force, compared with 73.9 percent of men.

Unemployment rates for people of color, especially African-Americans, have been double that of white workers since unemployment statistics were first charted in the 1930s. While the unemployment rate for all workers was 4.4 percent in 1955, people of color had an unemployment rate of 8.7 percent while white workers had an unemployment rate of 3.9 percent. In 2002, whites had an unemployment rate of 5.1 percent while African Americans had a 10.3 percent unemployment rate.[84]

A study of the 50 Top Companies for Diversity found that 29 (58 percent) had layoffs in 2002. DiversityInc asked them to break down the people laid off by ethnicity/race.

Here are the findings: Of the 29 companies, the average percentage of African Americans laid off was 13.7 percent, slightly more than the 12.7 percentage of African Americans in the U.S. population. The average percentage of Latinos laid off was 8.1 percent, much smaller than the 13 percent reported for the U.S. population. The average percentage of Asian Americans laid off was 7.1, almost double the 3.9 percent reported for the U.S. population by the U.S. Census Bureau.

4. Best Practices: Successful Recruitment Strategies From Top Companies

There is a war for talent and anyone who intends to win it better realize two things: First, that it is a global war and, second, that if you restrict your search for talent in any way – by race, gender, national origin, sexual orientation or any other factor – you will be giving your competitors the edge they need to put you out of business.

–William G. Parrett, President and Managing Partner, Deloitte & Touche

There are several reasons why Deloitte & Touche, the New York-based accounting giant, was No. 1 in this year's DiversityInc Top 10 Companies for Recruitment & Retention. Along with the other nine on the list – Freddie Mac, Aetna, Altria, Merck, Fleet Boston, Citigroup, Pitney Bowes, Marriott and JPMorgan Chase – Deloitte puts an emphasis on recruiting programs aimed at schools, professional organizations and targeted media that reach diversity candidates. Deloitte also measures its recruitment successes and failures to understand what's working and makes sure its recruiters, in all facets of the organization, communicate with each other and make diversity recruiting a priority.

A study of this year's Top 10 Companies for Recruitment & Retention reveals they measure and put emphasis on reaching numerical goals. Of new hires at these top 10 in 2002, 34 percent were people of color. Virtually all the top 10 companies look for diverse employees on Web career sites, in newspaper classified sections, at job fairs, at colleges and universities, and at professional associations. Fifty percent of these companies said they actively recruit GLBT employees and 50 percent said they actively recruit people with disabilities.

Word of mouth, or reputation, particularly is important to diversity candidates. Henry Hernandez, executive director, Global Diversity Leadership, at Stamford, Conn.-based Pitney Bowes, says top candidates seek the company out because of its diversity reputation, often without knowing exactly what Pitney Bowes does (integrated mail and document management solutions.)

And building strong, long-term relationships with schools and professional organizations is critical to both reputation and as a pipeline for diverse recruits of a high caliber. DiversityInc's survey of top companies for diversity recruitment found they recommended these organizations: INROADS, National Black MBA Association, Consortium for Graduate Study in Management, the National Society of Hispanic MBAs, Society of Women Engineers, Society of Hispanic Professional Engineers, National Society of Black Engineers, National Association of Black Accountants, Association of Latino Professionals in Finance and Accounting, Hispanic Business Student Association, Black Business Student Association, Gay & Lesbian MBA, and The Urban League.

Additional Resources

PART II - CORPORATE GOVERNANCE

Bean, Linda. "Counting Heads? Measuring Diversity Requires More Than Simple Math," DiversityInc, 30 November 2001.
http://www.diversityinc.com/public/1837.cfm

Cheng, Kipp. "More Than Numbers: Adequate GLBT Stats Still Elusive, Problematic." DiversityInc, 16 September 2002.
http://www.diversityinc.com/members/3528.cfm.

Cole, Yoji. "How Do Corporations Build Trust? Recruitment and Retention," DiversityInc, 18 March 2002.
http://www.diversityinc.com/members/2590.cfm

Cole, Yoji. "Playing the Race Card: For Job Applicants of Color, Racial Network Is An Advantage," DiversityInc, 20 February 2002.
http://www.diversityinc.com/members/2409.cfm

Consortium for Graduate Study in Management, 5585 Pershing, Suite 240, St. Louis, MO63112-4621. *http://www.cgsm.org/contact.asp*

Economic Report of the President. GAO Printing Office, Washington, D.C., February 2003.

Employment Management Association (a professional-emphasis group of the SHRM), Society for Human Resource Management (SHRM), 1800 Duke Street, Alexandria, Virginia 22314.
http://www.shrm.org/ema/index.asp

Heidi van Arnem Disability Consumer Research Report. iCan, Spring 2002.

Ph.D. Project, KPMG Foundation, 3 Chestnut Ridge Road, Montvale, NJ 07645. *http://www.phdproject.com/*

"A Report Card on Diversity," Harvard Business Review, January-February 1999.

Report from the Society for Human Resource Management (SHRM)

Society for Human Resource Management (SHRM), 1800 Duke Street, Alexandria, Virginia 22314. *http://www.shrm.org/*

U.S. Census Bureau. 1997 Economic Census: Survey of Minority-Owned Business Enterprises (EC97CS-7). Washington, D.C., July 2001.

ADDITIONAL RESOURCES

PART II - CORPORATE GOVERNANCE

U.S. Census Bureau. The Asian and Pacific Islander Population in the United States: March 2002 (Current Population Reports, P20-540). Washington, D.C., May 2003.

U.S. Census Bureau. The Black Population in the United States: March 2002 (Current Population Reports, Series P20-541). Washington, D.C., March 2003.

U.S. Census Bureau. Disability Status: 2000 (Census 2000 Brief, C2KBR-17). Washington, D.C., March 2003.

U.S. Census Bureau. The Hispanic Population in the United States: March 2000. (Current Population Reports, P20-535). Washington, D.C., March 2001.

U.S. Census Bureau. Statistical Abstract of the United States: 2002. Washington, D.C., 2002.

U.S. Census Bureau. Women and Men in the United States, March 2002 (Current Population Reports, P20-544). Washington, D.C., March 2003.

Witeck-Combs Communications, Inc. and Packaged Facts. The Gay and Lesbian Market, New Trends, New Opportunities, 3rd edition. New York, October 2002.

B. Retention

One of the common complaints is that people of color and women often leave to start their own businesses. The Census Bureau reports that between 1992 and 1997, the number of women- and minority-owned businesses increased by 150 percent.[85]

Is there any way to stop budding entrepreneurs? Not really, the top companies say, but successful retention/promotion programs will keep them on staff or tied to the company as long as possible.

1. Benefits & Costs

Corporations that have successfully recruited top, diverse talent frequently are faced with the additional challenge of retaining these valuable and highly sought-after employees. Stellar multicultural employees bring insight and access into emerging markets that might otherwise be inaccessible to most corporations. This is why it's crucial for competitive companies to implement plans and strategies to retain their best and brightest diverse employees.

Retention, however, is not simply about fulfilling mandates or vague policies of a multicultural headcount. Employee turnover has serious fiscal implications that often are not immediately apparent — until it's too late.

Ernst & Young, whose employee base mirrors today's diversified labor pool, reports that its commitment to diversity has saved the company millions in recruitment and retention costs since 1997. Twenty-one percent of Ernst & Young's work force and 20 percent of its professional and management-level employees are people of color, says Leslie Jones, the firm's director of ethnicity diversity initiatives.

The company has not relied on guesswork to calculate the benefits of fostering a diverse work force. To determine the impact of its diversity commitment on the bottom line, Ernst & Young's Office of Workforce Retention has devised a formula to calculate the costs associated with replacing a seasoned employee.

"Every time we lose 10 professionals, it costs us about $1.2 million," says Jim Freer, Ernst & Young America's vice chair of human resources. "That's a huge impact on our bottom line, and it gives staying power a whole new importance."[86]

In general, losing a single employee costs companies as much as four times that employee's annual salary. The costs include paying temporary hires to fill a position, advertising costs to find a qualified replacement and the time spent training a new worker. Multiply that figure by a high rate of turnover, and the potentially huge financial toll on corporations is clear.

Federated Department Stores, on the other hand, does not directly identify retention and career development as the most essential elements of diversity employment. But the retail-store conglomerate certainly has created more of an opportunity to focus on these elements.

"Given that retail is a relatively high-turnover business, Federated will always concentrate on recruitment and community relationships. However, retention is an area we give equal attention to. When we hire new employees, we want them to feel comfortable and stay," says Ann Lazarus, the company's operations vice president for diversity and vendor development. "Interestingly, we've found that our turnover of multiethnic, multiracial individuals is lower than the population as a whole. This was not true five years ago."[87]

An essential part of attracting and retaining qualified, diverse talent is fostering a work environment that doesn't simply give lip service to awareness of diversity, but actually integrates cultural competency at every level of business. For top diverse talent, seeing people of color at the higher echelons of the corporate structure conveys to multicultural employees that diversity is valued.

But corporate America has a long way to go before there are many executive mentors of color. There aren't very many to go around. According to the EEOC, in 2001, the last year for which figures are available, African Americans accounted for 6.5 percent, Latinos 4.7 percent and Asian Americans 3.4 percent of the officials and managers in corporate America, whereas whites accounted for 85.1 percent. Women accounted for 34 percent of the officials and managers in corporate America in 2001. The percentages of professionals who were African American and Latino were 6.9 percent and 4 percent, respectively, compared with 80.2 percent for whites. In 2002, Asian Americans made up 8.5 percent of the professional population, while women made up 51.4 percent.[88]

An organization's culture either can encourage inclusion and workforce diversity or perpetuate bias, prejudice and discrimination. For an organization to become truly inclusive, executives must evaluate the practice of their policies and commit to providing resources to educate employees on how to think about diversity. Executives must walk and talk the diversity shuffle.

Corporations that create an all-inclusive work environment and work with the most diverse group of suppliers can capture the attention of the widest variety of customers. Company executives must inject the notion of diversity into the marrow of the business.

The traditional norms of doing business are rapidly changing, along with the changing demographics that comprise the current and future work force.

The types of clothes employees wear, the types of jokes employees tell, the rigor with which employees approach their work, the types of pictures employees place on desks and in cubicles, all of these thing suggest a culture that needs to be respected and taken into account.

Diversity should permeate all facets of cultural behavior in the work-place. "Once diversity becomes a part of your business process, it no longer becomes something you have to think about," says Malcolm Berkley, a spokesperson for United Parcel Service. "Like brushing your teeth — it's just something that you do."[89]

To ensure that the proverbial glass ceiling is shattered at their respective organizations, corporate leaders have to change the norms of the officials and managers beneath them to ensure that day-to-day business etiquette invites employees of all hues, genders, abilities and sexual orientations to the corporate party.

2. Promotion

Korn/Ferry International, a Los Angeles-based executive search firm, did an extensive study of retaining and promoting employees and managers of color in 2002. The study found that corporations believe skills training is 98 percent effective and managerial training is 95 percent effective in retaining managers of color. But there's a clear gap in what corporations believe and what managers believe those actual managers say skills training is 70 percent effective and managerial training is 70 percent effective.

Corporations stress these factors - reward programs (43 percent), bonuses (29 percent) and pay increases (26 percent) as incentives. Corporations say reward/recognition programs are most effective, with 77 percent advocating those, while 66 percent advocate bonuses and 58 percent advocate pay increases as the means of keeping valued employees of color. Next on their lists – awareness training (54 percent), educational and diversity workshops (54 percent), external conferences and seminars (54 percent), affinity or networking groups (49 percent), diversity councils (49 percent) and mentoring (46 percent).

Employees of color rate as most effective: (69 percent) skills training; (69 percent) managerial training; (89 percent) reimbursement for educational costs; (86 percent) work and family benefits; (85 percent) commitment of senior management; (66 percent) making diversity an integral part of business strategy; (22 percent) establishing a critical mass of minority employees; (9 percent) historic commitment to diversity; (9 percent) openness to cultural change; (9 percent) financial support for diversity-related programs.

A critical best practice used by several top companies is to set up a program to identify and work with people of color and women who have potential. At Verizon, for example, the company implemented the Development Leadership Initiative, which focuses on Latino managers. In 2000, Verizon's senior leadership was 2.5 percent Latino, with only six Latino vice presidents and 84 Latino directors. The most recent count shows the senior leadership now is more than 5 percent Latino with 16 vice presidents and 97 directors.

At Altria, an advancement-planning process identifies employees with leadership qualities and sets an agenda for them, including executive "shepherds" who are knowledgeable about the employees. They monitor them and keep records of their progression through the company.

In their 1999 book "Breaking Through: The Making of Minority Executives in Corporate America," Harvard Business School Professors David Thomas and John Gabarro, who studied 20 executives and three corporations, said career trajectories for executives of color are different than those of white executive. "Early career development in critical," they write. "In the early years, in terms of job assignments and opportunities for development, minority executives had few but large promotions and a moderate rate to reach middle management. They reported frequent instances of added responsibility without promotions that are stretch assignments and several eye-opening experiences."

Both mentoring programs (formal and informal) and employee-affinity groups are crucial for nurturing talent, providing role models and allowing managers to air concerns. Harvard Professors Thomas and Gabarro write that extreme competence can compensate for the absence of strong social networks but "experience also suggests that demonstrating competence was not enough for minorities to succeed; they also had to gain organizational credibility. Credibility depends on a manager's reputation for successful performance, integrity and impact on the core business."

According to a 2002 Catalyst survey on women of color, 57 percent of the women surveyed were promoted at least once in the three-year period and their average salaries rose from $81,300 in 1998 to $111,700 in 2001.[90]

A total of 919 women of color completed the mail-in survey in 1998. Of the 734 contacted for the follow-up survey in 2001, 268 responded, a 37 percent response rate. The survey pool was 59 percent African American, 21 percent Asian American, and 19 percent Latina.[91]

A 1997 Society of Human Resource Management (SHRM) study found that "Managers at all levels commented that when it comes to recognition and rewards, business results – not diversity results – are what matter."

Many corporations favor inside candidates, even these days. It's a good way to improve retention. At Hyatt Hotels, for example, promoting from within is the company's practice. About 37 percent of the company's management were people of color, and 70 percent of the managers were promoted from within. Breaking down its managerial force, the company reported 14 percent were African American, 10 percent were Latino and 8 percent were Asian American in 2002.

3. Mentoring

Mentoring dramatically impacts both retention and ability to move up. The SHRM study found that strong mentoring relationships, particularly within the first five years of employment, significantly reduce turnover rate and improve the rate of promotions.

Is there a benefit to having a formal mentoring program? Yes, in that an infrastructure exists, which facilitates these arrangements. No, because the best mentoring programs are successful personal relationships and an organization can't always engineer that.

At SC Johnson, there is a unique mentoring program called "mentoring up," which seeks to pair employees of color and women with executives – be they white or of color – and flip the relationship so that employees mentor executives.

"Employees operate as mentors and executives act as mentees," says Maria Campbell, director of diversity for Racine, Wis.-based SC Johnson. "The employee and the executive are both learning and they're both winning."

SC Johnson has between 30 and 40 vice presidents who have gone through the program, Campbell says, which is a volunteer effort that begins with a pilot phase in which the executives are educated on being open to the issues that employees of color and women face. To help ensure that middle managers of color and women don't waste away in the middle expanse, SC Johnson created an offshoot of the mentoring up program – an executive shadow program. The program pairs middle managers with senior executives so the managers can learn the ropes in preparation for their eventual promotion.

4. Domestic-Partner Benefits, Non-Discrimination Policies

There is no federal legislation prohibiting job discrimination on grounds of sexual orientation. A bill called the Employment Non-Discrimination Act would make it illegal to discriminate based on real or perceived sexual orientation. The bill first was introduced in Congress on June 23, 1994 and never has been passed, although in 1996 it came within one vote of passing the Senate. It would prohibit employers with more than 15 workers from using an individual's sexual orientation as the basis for employment decisions such as hiring, firing, promotions or compensation.

An executive order singed in May 1998 by former President Clinton prohibits discrimination based on sexual orientation in the federal civilian work force.

Fourteen states, the District of Columbia and 142 cities and counties ban anti-gay discrimination in private workplaces as well as public-sector jobs. Nine states ban discrimination in the public sector by executive order. Twelve states, the District of Columbia and 159 local governments provide health insurance benefits to their employees' domestic partners.[92]

According to a 2001 survey by Harris Interactive/Witeck Combs, 72 percent of gay, lesbian, bisexual and transgender consumers feel it is important for companies that advertise to the GLBT community to "Demonstrate effective corporate citizenship" by supporting the community's causes. Another Harris Interactive survey found that 57 percent of GLBT people, when deciding where to open a financial-services account, think it's important the company has a policy banning discrimination against gay people.

According to the Washington, D.C.-based Human Rights Campaign Foundation's WorkNet Project, the number of employers that provide domestic-partner health-insurance benefits has increased from 2,856 employers in August 1999 to 5,791 in June 2003.

A survey released in November 2001 by Hewitt Associates, a benefits-consulting firm, found that the number of companies that offer domestic-partner benefits has doubled since 1997. Nearly 90 percent of companies offering the benefits began to do so in the past five years, and 31 percent of those that did not yet provide the benefits indicated they were considering doing so within the next three years. Hewitt surveyed the nation's 570 largest employers.

The trend toward offering domestic-partner benefits occurs mostly in the Fortune 500 companies. The number of Fortune 500 companies offering these benefits has more than tripled in the past five years, from 61 in 1998 to 194 in 2003.[93]

A survey by market-research firm Opinion Research Corp., found that 71 percent of major corporations cited the increased visibility of the company's diversity commitment as the No. 1 reason for adopting the benefits. Fifty-three percent cited retention of employees and 47 percent mentioned improved relations with gay and lesbian markets.

As of June 2003, HRS WorkNet found that 316 or 63 percent of Fortune 500 companies include sexual orientation in their non-discrimination policies.

According to the Human Rights Campaign, common steps gay-friendly employers take are:

- Adopting a written non-discrimination policy that covers sexual orientation and, sometimes, gender identity, that is in the employee handbook and is widely publicized to all employees.

- Implementing a benefits program that treats employees' domestic partners equal to marked spouses, including provision of health insurance, pension and retirement benefits, life insurance, bereavement leave and family leave.

- Recognizing and supporting an LGBT employee-resource group.

- Providing diversity awareness education for all employees that addresses sexual orientation and gender-identity issues.

- Respectful and appropriate marketing and advertising to GLBT consumers and/or investors.

- Charitable support for LGBT and HIV/AIDS community organizations.

- Respect for employees' right to bargain collectively to obtain anti-discrimination protections and equal benefits.

- Endorsement of the Employment Non-Discrimination Act

5. Best Practices: Successful Retention Strategies from Top Companies

A look again at this year's Top 10 Companies for Recruitment & Retention – Deloitte & Touche, Freddie Mac, Aetna, Altria, Merck, FleetBoston, Citigroup, Pitney Bowes, Marriott and JPMorgan Chase – shows both the numerical proof and the methods of strong retention efforts. Besides making work/life successful for the companies and the employees, they also provide clear paths for advancement for people of color and women.

The 10 companies averaged 19 percent people of color in management positions, and 45 percent women in management positions. Of their top 50 highest-paid employees, an average of 9 percent were people of color and an average of 13 percent were women. Ninety percent of these companies offered formal mentoring programs and 90 percent had succession planning. Eighty percent offered domestic-partner benefits and 70 percent had nondiscrimination policies that included sexual orientation.

Work/life was demonstrably important to them. Ninety percent offered employees the ability to work at home and/or telecommute; 90 percent offered dependent-care assistance, including child-care assistance; 70 percent offered adoption assistance; 60 percent offered cafeteria-style benefits plans, allowing employees to choose benefits from a menu; and 50 percent offered on-site child care.

What are some benchmark numbers for promoting people of color and women into management positions?

According to the Equal Employment Opportunity Commission (2000 data), of managers in U.S. private companies, 33.8 percent are women and 14.4 percent are people of color. Of that 14.4 percent, 6.4 percent are African American, 4.5 percent are Latino and 3.1 percent Asian American. By gender, of all managers, 28.1 percent are white women, 3 percent are African-American women, 1.6 percent are Latino women and 1.1 percent are Asian-American women.

Since women of color who hold top jobs in their organizations are rare, it is more difficult to track a large number who are in corporate management. Currently, women of color comprise a mere 1.3 percent of corporate officers in 400 of the Fortune 500 companies, according to the 2000 Catalyst Census of women corporate officers and top earners.

An EEOC study undertaken for DiversityInc. found that there was wide variety by industry in the number of legal complaints filed by women and people color asserting that they did not receive promotions they were due. This data is all from July 1, 2000 to June 30, 2001. In the communications industry, for example, there were 160 such allegations, with 5.1 percent resulting in a promotion eventually being received. But in the automobile industry, there were only 28 such complaints, with a success rate of only 1.7 percent. And among banks and financial institutions, there were 46 such complaints during this time period, with a 2.4 percent success rate.

ADDITIONAL RESOURCES

PART II - CORPORATE GOVERNANCE

Cole, Yoji. "Whole Culture: What Companies Leading in Diversity Are Thinking," DiversityInc, 29 January 2002.
http://www.diversityinc.com/public/2266.cfm

"Diversity-Savvy Companies Prioritizing Retention," DiversityInc, 28 January 2002.

"Employee Satisfaction Comes First For Big Five Accounting Firm," DiversityInc, 18 January 2001.

Human Rights Campaign (HRC), 1640 Rhode Island Ave., N.W., Washington, D.C. 20036-3278. *www.hrc.org*

U.S. Equal Employment Opportunity Commission (EEOC), "Occupational Employment in Private Industry by Race/Ethnic Group/Sex, and by Industry, United States, 2001,"Job Patterns For Minorities And Women In Private Industry, *http://www.eeoc.gov/stats/jobpat/2001/national.html*

Women of Color in Corporate Management: Three Years Later. Catalyst. New York, 2002. *http://www.catalystwomen.org*

3. Management

A corporation focused on developing trust among its employees, investors and customers must clearly communicate its commitment to the community and the populations with which it does business. That commitment to diversity must be backed by the top and given the time to blossom, even if it doesn't yield a profit right away.

And it can't just be a feel-good diversity initiative that provides employees with tamales for lunch or a quiz on famous African-American leaders during Black History Month.

For a diversity initiative to create and nurture a sense of trust, it must receive engaged support from the CEO and a company's senior officials and be an evolving program that empowers employees.

A company's ability to be trusted is linked to corporate transparency — its ability to share openly with the public. The most important antidote to problems with trust is to ensure that employees and other stakeholders feel that their needs are being heard and addressed.

With the slow economy and threats of violence, this is a time in corporate America ripe for feelings of mistrust to fester and create divisions among staff.

"When there's insecurity in the environment for any reason, it particularly shows up along diversity lines, especially among people who are not in the dominant roles," says Howard Ross of Cook Ross, a Silver Spring, Md., diversity consultancy. "That's one of the reasons we see race crimes increase during times of economic crisis. When people feel immediately threatened, they turn inward and to other people like themselves, rather than people who are different from them."

So it's vital at this time for corporate leadership to take the reigns and communicate trustworthiness to all members of a company's stakeholders — employees, customers, investors, vendors — and embracing diversity is one facet of that trust.

Diversity directors are those usually charged, within a corporation, of setting up and/or implementing diversity initiatives.

More often than not, they report to the head of human resources, which can be, but is not always, a side department in a corporation, not considered essential or urgent to the company's survival.

In a few of the most progressive companies, such as PricewaterhouseCoopers, Agilent Technologies, Bank of America, Ernst & Young and Chubb Family of Companies, diversity directors report directly to the CEO or have one direct report between themselves and the CEO. Why is this important? It shows the top manager of the company is directly responsible for the success of integrating diversity into every aspect of the business, particularly those in the revenue stream.

But what if the diversity director's job is pigeonholed in a corner of human resources or worse, partitioned off, all by itself?[94] "It can become a dead end in companies where diversity is viewed as a program — the flavor of the day or month or year," says Clay Osborne, vice president of global diversity and workforce development at Bausch & Lomb. "Is it a program or an overall process that links diversity to business success?"

To be fair, some companies understand that human-resources functions, including diversity management, are crucial to the bottom line. Those companies accord diversity directors the same respect — and demand the same kind of accountability — that line executives receive.

Even the strongest corporate mission statement can't fool employees into thinking that a company is serious about diversity when the corporate diversity director labors alone in a basement office with no staff, no budget and no real impact on day-to-day operations.

And once employees have received that message, management will have a tough time undoing the damage. After all, who wants to work for a company that makes it clear that diversity — of opinion, gender, race and sexual orientation — doesn't count?

But in companies in which diversity erroneously is defined as racial representation or lawsuit-prevention, it may be more difficult to establish the motive behind a diversity director's position. What does an effective diversity director do?[95] He or she understands the corporate leadership's mission and is able to implement diversity in the strategic, bottom-line daily business decisions.

"It is a job in which you're marketing a product and you're trying to make sure it is in every office of the organization," says Carolyn Pemberton, director of diversity for banking conglomerate ABN AMRO North America. "You have to show how that product will affect revenue — how diversity should be part of the fabric of the business, as well as the fabric of how people relate internally and externally to their customers."

The most effective diversity directors weave their initiatives into a company's fabric through their knowledge, salesmanship and awareness of interpersonal issues. They simultaneously are advocates and business leaders, and they are respected for their views and contributions to the company's core business goals and values.

Benjamin Reese, assistant vice president for cross-cultural relations in the Office of Institutional Equity at Duke University, Durham, N.C., lists three attributes that an effective diversity director will champion: Orientation to a company's skills and enhancement development. Diversity directors need to understand that to increase the cross-cultural competency of the staff they need to focus on managing conflicts that often involve issues of people's differences.

In this way, diversity will be linked to the company's business sense. Historically, diversity has been and still is tied to issues of fairness and equity. But in today's competitive work environment, highlighting the link between diversity and business acumen is critical.

Diversity directors need to understand the differences and similarities between racial, cultural, ethnic and sexual orientation. Diversity directors who are stuck in an outdated paradigm of whites and blacks don't understand some of the differences that new immigrants bring to the work environment.

1. Management Demographics

According to the EEOC, in 2001, the last year for which figures are available, African Americans accounted for 6.5 percent, Latinos 4.7 percent and Asian Americans 3.4 percent of the officials and managers in corporate America, whereas whites accounted for 85.1 percent. Women accounted for 34 percent of the officials and managers in corporate America in 2001. The percentages of professionals who were African American and Latino were 6.9 percent and 4 percent, respectively, compared with 80.2 percent for whites. In 2002, Asian Americans made up 8.5 percent of the professional population, while women made up 51.4 percent.[96]

2. Board of Directors' Demographics

Interestingly, when asked if they'd like to see their boards more diverse, board directors of Fortune 1000 companies surveyed by Korn/Ferry said yes, but the response was far from overwhelming: 93 percent of Fortune 1000 companies had a least one woman, while 57.9 percent had an African American, 18.5 percent had a Latino, 10.7 percent had an Asian American on the board and 6.2 percent had another person of color.

African Americans went from 3 percent to 5 percent of board representation from 1992 to 2000. Women went from 8.3 percent of Fortune 500 board representation in 1993 to 12.4 percent in 2000.

When asked which groups they are giving special consideration, they replied this way:

Women	50.0%
African Americans	46.1%
Latinos	42.8%
Asian Americans	25.5%
Others	2.0%

Perhaps this is the last really strong good old boys' club, a highly selective organization that is made up of the same guys, virtually all the time. To be invited in, you have to look, talk and sound the same. In a recent USA Today article, James Kristie, editor of Directors & Boards magazine, said, "Getting on a board is like being invited into a secret club. There's a collegiality that's required, so you aren't going to be invited in unless you've demonstrated that you can work within the system and the club. No one wants a wild card."

About 1,800 Fortune 1000 Directors resign each year but that number could go up because of current scrutiny about boards and efforts to limit the number of board seats individuals can hold.

At the largest companies, consultants report they can earn as much as $115,000 a year per board. And most payment is in stock or cash. Time spent on boards is now 15.3 hours a month on average, up 17 percent in the past year, Korn/Ferry reports.

Joseph Anderson, CEO and chairman of Chivas Industries in Michigan, is an African American who sits on the boards of Quaker

Chemical and Arvin Meritor. He told DiversityInc that "Most of the traditional board members are white males. Because of that, those boards can typically fall into groupthink in terms of their view of the world."

Why are the same people on all the boards?

Because it's easier to keep picking the same brand names than to develop new talent. And it's flattering and lucrative to people to keep getting named to boards. But it also has an undesirable effect in that it stifles diversity. Five women, five Latinos, five African Americans, five Asians, each have different views on subjects. If the same Asian, African American, Latino or woman is on all the boards, that diversity won't happen.

3. CEO Commitment

Diversity doesn't succeed without an imperative from the CEO and consistent follow-up, including strong support from those directly under the CEO. If employees know the initiatives are merely lip service, they will treat them that way, with a nod, a wink and a laugh. The message has to be clear, and it has to be reinforced. This is essential to the success of the company. Take it seriously.

The companies with the most successful diversity efforts all have orders from the CEO that this must be a top priority for everyone. And most of these corporations directly tie the compensation of the CEO and upper management to the success of diversity initiatives. They also have metrics in place to examine whether units and operating companies, down to the lowest level, are implementing and following up on their diversity initiatives and what results they are producing.

Two questions a consumer or job seeker should ask about a company are: Does the CEO incorporate diversity into the company's strategic business plan or goals?

4. Lines of Command

It takes roughly 15 years to ascend the corporate ladder to the executive ranks, says Judith Bardwick, a management consultant and professor of psychiatry at the University of California, San Diego. That period certainly can be longer for those joining many-faceted multinational corporations, or shorter at a high-tech start-up.

Each year, Sara Lee's senior human-resources team meets with senior leaders from the company's business units to examine the career possibilities for more than 100 high-performers – executives who are in the pipeline for promotions and new assignments. "We report on the diversity demographics for each of the divisions," says Lois Huggins, Sara Lee's vice president organization development and diversity. "It is an all-encompassing talent-management discussion."

The company now has a process to identify 75 "future leaders" – employees who are one rung below the high-performers on the Sara Lee ladder.

JPMorgan Chase tracks vice presidents based on race/gender, below level of managing director and senior vice presidents. This identifies the next rung of executives.

Corporate leaders of color, such as Franklin Raines of Fannie Mae, Ken Chenault of American Express, Stanley O'Neal of Merrill Lynch and Richard Parsons of AOL Time Warner, had to assimilate — learn the language, manners of dress, intellectual and entertainment interests of the existing, and typically white, managers — to succeed.

While they reign over their companies now, they have not held power positions long enough to imbue their philosophies of business throughout their organizations. Thus, succession planning is key to bringing people of color into top roles in corporations.

George Gamble, executive director for the Institute for Diversity and Cross-Cultural Management, University of Texas, views most succession plans with a jaundiced eye. The role of diversity in succession planning is still relatively new, Gamble says, and to date it hasn't produced an appreciable increase in the number of women and people of color in executive posts.[41]

Gamble contends that a proper plan reflects the racial makeup of the work force. If 40 percent of all employees are people of color, then 40 percent of all executive candidates should be people of color as well, he says. "But that poses a problem, no question about it. [White employees] are going to look at it as being unfair."

Corporate leaders can short-circuit that discontent if they make a strong business case for diversity in succession planning, Gamble says. "They have to make sure the message is communicated that this is in the best interests of the company."

5. Best Practices: Successful Leadership Strategies from Top Companies

An examination of this year's Top 50 Companies for Diversity found 50 percent of the companies on the list received the highest point values for their CEO's commitment to diversity.

How did they do that? Their CEOs were involved directly both in implementing and supporting diversity throughout the organization, particularly as a business strategy. In most cases, the CEOs signed off on bonuses for senior executives tied to diversity and were involved in assessing diversity metrics. The CEOs often had strong vision/mission statements emphasizing diversity as a core company value. In several cases, the diversity director or lead diversity person reported directly to the CEO.

Here are some of the Top Companies statements on how their CEOs demonstrate support for diversity initiatives:

Aetna: [CEO John Rowe] chairs a special committee on Diversity & Minority Health Disparities; includes diversity metrics in compensation/bonus for senior executives; incorporates diversity in Aetna Values developed by CEO; makes diversity presentations for board of directors; makes speeches including support for diversity; holds executive forums, including diversity focus; corporate vision statement incorporates diversity; employee handbook reinforces diversity; CEO's annual message incorporates diversity; diverse cultural celebrations are acknowledged

American Express: Commitment to diversity begins at the top. Ken Chenault, chairman and CEO, actively supports the company's many diversity initiatives. He regularly speaks both internally and externally about the importance of diversity and how we –- as a global company with global customers served by a talented group of employees of various nationalities, races and experiences –- must strive to make diversity an integral part of our workplace.

BellSouth: Chairman and CEO Duane Ackerman chairs our Diversity Council. In 2001, BellSouth's Diversity Council created the position of chief diversity officer. This officer reports directly to Mr. Ackerman.

Darden Restaurants: CEO Joe R. Lee believes the greatest legacy a successful company can provide for future business leaders is an unwavering commitment to diversity and ethical conduct. For this reason, diversity initiatives are integrated throughout Darden Restaurants. Our company's diversity is communicated internally through speeches, e-mails and voice-mails from the company's CEO. Diversity also is communicated through officer meetings, seminars, employee meetings and holiday celebrations. Executives and middle management (directors and above) are required to attend a diversity immersion experience.

Eastman Kodak: Chairman and CEO Daniel Carp established the tone for leading Kodak's initiatives for diversity and inclusion well before becoming CEO. As president and chief operating officer, he co-created the CEO Diversity Award in 1998.

JPMorgan Chase: [Chairman and CEO William B. Harrison Jr.] is chairman of our corporate diversity council; hosts regular Diversity Town Hall meetings with employees in our major sites around the world; holds diversity planning sessions with each business executive; executives held accountable for diversity progress using diversity standards and a diversity scorecard; participates in our reverse diversity mentoring program; reports on our diversity progress to our board of directors.

Marriott: [President and CEO Christopher Nassetta]: Frequent public and internal comments and statements reiterating Marriott's commitment to diversity; presentation of work-force diversity reports semi-annually to the board of directors; requirement that corporate executives reporting directly to the CEO prepare and present plans to increase diversity in their business; membership on the board of trustees of the National Urban League.

Merck: [Chairman, President and CEO Raymond Gilmartin]: Formal letter of support; endorsement of the creation of a diversity worldwide business-strategy team and the approval of their subsequent recommendations to the company; diversity presentation to the board of directors; five points on corporate objectives dedicated to diversity and tied to bonuses.

Pitney Bowes: Our CEO [Michael Critelli] is chairman of the National Urban League and is a board member of catalyst. Our CEO and board of directors evaluate each business unit's diversity strategic plans. [Also cited] creation of business diversity group and linking diversity objects to management compensation

PricewaterhouseCoopers: [CEO Samuel DiPiazza]: Ongoing and regular series of communications from CEO to partners and staff supporting diversity and diversity initiatives; appointed chief diversity officer as member of CEO management team; CEO's management team provides strategic and financial support for diversity and diversity initiatives around minority recruiting/retention; mentoring and mentoring partnerships program; achievement and measurement of diversity goals/metrics through diversity index and diversity assessment; CEO presence in media and other external forums promoting diversity initiatives.

Safeco: Chairman and CEO Michael McGavick is also Safeco's chief diversity officer. He established a corporate diversity advisory group that recommended a corporate diversity vision and strategy. The strategy will contribute to profitable growth ...; hired a leader, corporate diversity initiatives, to implement the diversity strategy and align/leverage our efforts across all business organizations; expects all employees to attend mandatory diversity training; requires his senior leadership team to hire for all openings from diverse applicant pools; articulates four foundational strategies for Safeco, one of which is "invest in people" and reiterates the need to employ individuals who are able to sell to a diverse customer base.

Seagate Technology: CEO Steve Luczo had the corporate diversity department established at his request in 2000. To optimize success, he ensured that the newly formed division had adequate staff and financial resources. When tough economic times ensued right after the department was established, Luczo ensured that the diversity budget was not cut, even when other departments were facing financial and people cuts.

United Technologies: Chairman and CEO George David has designated work-force diversity as a strategic initiative. He has a personal message on diversity (also on United Technology's Internet and Intranet Web sites): "We remain totally committed to diversity within our workforce and to opportunities for advancement for all. I expect our entire team, advised by our diversity councils and staff, to embrace these practices and values."

ADDITIONAL RESOURCES

PART II - CORPORATE GOVERNANCE

"Benched: Lack of Succession Planning Sidelines Talented People of Color," DiversityInc, 7 January 2002.

"How to Make an Impact as a diversity Director: Affect the revenue Stream," DiversityInc, 24 January 2002.

Korn/Ferry International, 1800 Century Park East, Suite 900, Los Angeles, CA 90067.
http://www.kornferry.com/Library/Process.asp?P=Home

"Occupational Employment in Private Industry by Race/Ethnic Group/Sex, and by Industry, United States, 2001," EEOC Web Site, *http://www.eeoc.gov/stats/jobpat/2001/national.html*

"When Diversity Director Means 'Dead End' – Malignant Neglect: Mistakes You Don't Know You're Making," DiversityInc, 15 January 2002.

U.S. Equal Employment Opportunity Commission (EEOC), "Occupational Employment in Private Industry by Race/Ethnic Group/Sex, and by Industry, United States, 2001,"Job Patterns For Minorities And Women In Private Industry, *http://www.eeoc.gov/stats/jobpat/2001/national.html*

Science, Engineering Jobs Await Latinos but Education Lags

By Yoji Cole

© *2003 DiversityInc.com*

June 02, 2003

While the proportion of degrees awarded to Latino students has increased over the decade, a new study from Educational Testing Service (ETS) reports that increasing the number of Latino students in college and university science and engineering schools is necessary to keep pace with population projections.

The ETS report said that as the number of Latino children increases, to maintain proportional representation and take advantage of opportunities in the science and engineering fields, the number of Latinos earning degrees in those fields will have to increase.

The percentage of Latino students who graduated with degrees in science and engineering increased from 1991 to 2000, from 4.5 percent to 7.2 percent of bachelor's degrees, 3.1 percent to 5.2 percent of master's degrees, and 3.2 percent to 4.1 percent of doctorate degrees, according to the ETS study.

Even though the increase is encouraging, the ETS study warned that it does not keep pace with the growth projections for Latino youth. Latinos are expected to make up 61 percent of the 18-to-24-year-old population through 2015, according to the Census Bureau.

"This means that very large increases in the numbers of Hispanics earning degrees are required just to maintain the same proportions," said Paul E. Barton, author of the ETS report. "You want to increase beyond these percentages, which means you have to work a whole lot harder, first to stay even and then to get ahead."

As the Baby-Boom generation ages into its senior years, there will be an increase in demand for scientists and engineers and substantial room for expanding employment of Latinos in such occupations. Employment projections through 2010 indicate that the engineering field will experience a 9 percent growth for engineers, with 452,000 job openings; 69 percent growth for computer specialists, with 2.2 million job openings; 6 percent growth for mathematical scientists, with 26,000 job openings; and 18 percent growth for physical scientists, with 124,000 job openings, according to the ETS report.

Science, Engineering Jobs Await Latinos but Education Lags (cont'd.)

A pipeline of educational proficiency in math and science must be established to adequately prepare elementary-school youth in general and especially elementary-school Latino youth for the academically demanding fields, said Barton.

"Only 4 percent of Latino 12th graders reach the 'proficient' level in mathematics as defined by the National Assessment of Educational Progress (NAEP) – students below this level are not likely candidates for science and engineering," Barton reported.

Nationally, the overall high-school graduation rate has hovered around 70 percent for the last three decades, according to the ETS report. The high-school dropout rate for 16- to 24-year-old Latinos decreased slightly from an average of 32.5 percent during 1972-1975 to 28.1 percent during 1996-2000, according to the U.S. Department of Education. The improvement was partly caused by a gradually declining non-completion rate for females, dropping from 33.8 percent to 25.2 percent, while the rate for males changed very little from the beginning of the period to the end, according to the ETS.

Additional statistics from the Department of Education indicate that 18-to 29-year-old Latinos have a non-completion rate of 44 percent when excluding the Graduate Equivalency Diploma. The non-completion rate for all 18-to-29-year-olds when excluding the GED is 18 percent respectively.

Latino immigration is also a factor in the population's dropout rate. Immigrants bring varying degrees of education with them. In the period from 1970 to 2000, the native-born Latino high-school completion rate rose from 40 percent to 60 percent. Nevertheless, the net result is that almost three in 10 Latinos have no high-school diploma, and while there is improvement for women, there is little change over this three-decade period for men, according to the ETS.

To see improvement, Barton says, there must be greater effort made to educate Latino youth from elementary through college so as to keep them actively involved in the educational system. About half of 25-to-29-year-old Latinos, who have some college education, did not complete their associate's or bachelor's degrees, according to the ETS.

"It's a matter of getting better teaching in science and math throughout elementary school," Barton said. "We're talking about getting people in the top ranks of education to be prepared to pursue a career as a scientist or engineer."

FBI's Fight Against Terror Fuels Agency's New Diversity Recruiting Drive

By Linda Bean

© 2003 DiversityInc.com

March 19, 2003

The FBI has $1 million to spend on recruiting ads this fiscal year. The agency intends to use the entire amount to find "skilled diverse recruits," said Robert Cromwell, chief of the agency's applicant-processing section.

The agency's urgent push to bring new agents of color and linguists on board comes with a seismic shift in responsibilities. Before the attacks of Sept. 11, counter-terrorism was just one of many FBI areas of investigation.

"Now, it is our No. 1 focus," Cromwell said.

Since Sept. 11, the Federal Bureau of Investigation (FBI) has hired more than 400 people who speak Arabic languages, bringing the total to more than 1,100 employees fluent in Middle-Eastern languages.

As the nation prepares for war and the potential threat of increased domestic terrorism, building a diverse workforce has become a mission-critical issue.

"For us to be successful, we need to reflect the diversity of the customer pool – suspects, witnesses, victims. We need to be able to communicate," he said.

The agency's budget – recently approved by Congress – contains roughly $1 million for advertising to potential recruits. By the end of September, the close of the fiscal year, the FBI will have spent that money on reaching Arabic speakers, African Americans, Asian Americans, Latinos and women, as well as agents and linguists fluent in dozens of languages and dialects.

"If we did no advertising whatsoever," Cromwell said, "we would get all the white males we need."

The agency's employment statistics bear that out. The agency has 11,570 agents. Of those, 9,651 are white and 9,480 are men.

Women and people of color make up less than 17 percent of the agent ranks. The FBI has 2,090 women agents, 857 Latino agents, 643 African Americans and 49 Native Americans.

There's broader racial and gender representation among the 15,731 professional

FBI's Fight Against Terror Fuels Agency's New Diversity Recruiting Drive (cont'd.)

and support employees. Among those employees, 10,582 are women and 5,149 are men. Nearly 11,000 are white; 3,440 are African American; 854 are Latino; 374 are Asian American; and 85 are Native American.

Before Sept. 11, each of the agency's 56 field offices established its own recruiting priorities, based on data that highlighted the prevalence of certain crimes. Recruiting lacked a unified focus.

Now, "we are taking a very active role in trying to recruit people who speak the languages we need – Arabic dialects, several dialects of Chinese and Spanish," said Cromwell. Cromwell added that there is no specific data on the number of Arab-American agents because they are counted as white.

Since the start of fiscal year 2002, the FBI has hired about 175 Arab linguists and is seeking at least 70 more. The agency has hired 32 people who speak various dialects of Chinese; seven who speak Hebrew; 10 who speak Pashto; four who speak Turkish; 11 who speak Urdu; and 40 who speak Farsi. The agency's capacity to process Arabic-language information has increased 200 percent, Cromwell said.

"Before Sept. 11, we were basically broadcasting across the spectrum. Now, we've taken a different tack and we've attacked this with some zeal," Cromwell said. "We are doing things we haven't done before."

The agency directs all potential recruits to its recently established Web-based process, which lists the critical skills the agency is seeking.

Applicants complete the online paperwork, which is filtered to reject candidates who don't meet basic criteria. The applications are downloaded by ZIP code and transmitted to a field office near the applicant's home for additional screening, Cromwell said.

Applicants who survive the screening are called into the field office for a test. If they pass the test, they are invited back for an interview with three FBI officials. If the interview is successful, they are given a conditional offer of employment and must then pass a lie-detector test, a physical and a background check.

The process, from start to finish, takes about six months.

Meanwhile, individual field offices are monitored to assure that they are screening and interviewing applicants in a fair manner.

"We have a quality-control system in place," Cromwell said. "We look at what information is being downloaded and who is being tested. We ask why one appli-

FBI's Fight Against Terror Fuels Agency's New Diversity Recruiting Drive (cont'd.)

cant was accepted and why another was rejected."

In the aftermath of Sept. 11, the FBI faced heavy criticism for gaps in intelligence-sharing and a dearth of federal agents fluent in Middle-Eastern languages. That lack was particularly troubling, given that the agency had been aware of extremist activity at some mosques since the 1993 bombing of the World Trade Center. Boxes of Arabic-language documents and audiotapes gathered during that investigation were stored without ever translating the contents.

"Ignorance," Colonel David Hunt, U.S. Army, retired, told DiversityInc on the first anniversary of Sept. 11. "That is criminal behavior on the part of our government agencies."

"There were only two Arab speakers in the FBI a year ago," said Hunt, who now runs D.A.R. Inc., an international security-consulting firm. "There aren't enough women in the spy business or the police business. It's all white males … and I don't need white males. I need Arabs."

The agency, which has been sued several times by agents of color – most recently in New York – also is seeking more African-American recruits.

Agents from the New York field office have alleged that a supervisor was so driven by racial animus that he interfered with the investigation into a Sept. 11 lead.

The FBI has launched new partnership with the National Association for Equal Opportunity in Higher Education (NAFEO), a consortium of African-American colleges and universities. The agency is also working with Edventure Partners, a Berkeley, Calif., company that established marketing programs at universities on behalf of corporate and government clients.

The FBI is sponsoring marketing classes at some African-American colleges, Cromwell said. The students develop and implement plans to market the FBI both on and off campus. "We give them a budget," Cromwell said.

The agency is also working with Bernard Hodes, a New York-based staffing and communications company, to develop a broad media-placement plan.

According to Bernard Hodes, planned media include the Arabic-language Al-Ahram; ATA Chronicle, a publication of the American Translator's Association; LinguistList.org, a resource for academic linguists; direct e-mail; language-specific newspapers and magazines; urban radio stations; and neighborhood billboards.

Cromwell has firsthand experience with diversity as a law-enforcement tool. As

FBI's Fight Against Terror Fuels Agency's New Diversity Recruiting Drive (cont'd.)

the assistant special agent in charge of the Jackson, Miss. field office, he helped investigate the brutal murder of a woman and her children.

Local police believed her husband, a casino employee who was unemotional and impassive at the crime scene, was responsible.

"But the Biloxi police didn't speak Vietnamese and he hardly spoke English," Cromwell said. "We brought in an agent, a native speaker, and we learned very quickly that he had been hounded by a gang that wanted him to do something illegal at the casino."

The man's apparent lack of emotion was the response his culture dictated, Cromwell added.

Cromwell wants all those within the agent ranks to develop and understanding of cultural nuances.

"Basically, we are trying to get the point across that a diverse organization is good for the FBI. It is good for our bottom line," he said. "We are trying to educate our managers as to the tremendous value of a diverse organization."

Are Women's Colleges Still Necessary? And Are They Still Viable?

By Melanie Austria Farmer

© *2003 DiversityInc.com*

March 06, 2003

Now burdened with the dual effects of the sour economy and intense competition, women's colleges constantly are addressing the changing face of higher education while working to overcome longtime challenges linked to being small, liberal-arts, private institutions and maintaining their single-sex mandate.

"In some ways, we are a product of our own success," said Carmen Ambar, who is dean of Douglass College, the woman's college of Rutgers University in New Brunswick, N.J. "We've been very successful in helping women achieve leadership roles in various areas. Some people may question what's the use anymore. But, I think that the time has not come where we can abandon women's colleges as an important option for women."

Ambar added that while there has been definite progress for women in leadership roles, barriers remain, specifically in non-traditional fields, such as science and engineering. Women's colleges are key in helping them advance in these career fields, she said.

Notable graduates of women's institutions include Sen. Hilary Rodham Clinton, former U.S. Secretary of the State Madeline Albright, and Geraldine Ferraro, who was the first woman U.S. vice presidential candidate. Proponents of an all-women's education have said that what sets women's colleges apart is that they are dedicated to the advancement and support of women. Women's colleges have a reputation for creating women leaders, are well regarded for their efforts in ethnic diversity, and pay close attention to the benefits of mentorship, especially in fortifying ties with new graduates and alumnae.

There is limited research available about women's colleges. But, according to the Women's College Coalition (WCC), there are about 140,000 students currently attending women's colleges. On a broader scale, the National Center for Education Statistics (NCES) reported as of fall 2000 a total of 13.2 million students enrolled at U.S.-based undergraduate institutions. Of that figure, women represented the dominant group at 7.4 million. The WCC, a Washington, D.C.-based group that represents 68 women's colleges in the U.S. and Canada, said

Are Women's Colleges Still Necessary? And Are They Still Viable? (cont'd.)

average applications for the class of 2002-03 at women's colleges increased by 10 percent.

Meanwhile, turning applicants to enrolled students has been a challenge for many women's colleges.

Juliette Landphair, the interim dean at Westhampton College, which is the women's college of University of Richmond in Virginia, said the future of women's colleges is not a rosy one and that for the most part, young women are not immediately seeing the value in a single-sex institution that others have in the past. Landphair said the generation of women who attended women's colleges benefited from the women's movement and that now, high school seniors generally are not relating to the benefits that women's colleges continue to tout.

"They don't have the historical perspective," said Landphair. They view being "separate from men as inequality, and don't see that [the experience] really can strengthen you."

Ambar agreed that this idea has gotten lost in the shuffle, and it has become even tougher for women's colleges to sell their longstanding tradition and benefits to today's young women.

Young women "are not seeing the benefits immediately," said Ambar. "We have to work harder to establish that benefit with young women. They don't see it as quickly as their mothers did."

Jadwiga Sebrechts, president of the WCC, said for women's colleges, size matters.

"Small institutions have to be extremely creative and nimble to try to prove they have a full spectrum offering that, frankly, students expect," said Sebrechts.

Sebrechts argued that similar challenges face women's colleges and small, coed institutions that fit the same profile. In order to overcome some of these hurdles, a number of women's colleges have either partnered with bigger schools to expand their course offerings or opened their doors to male students in an attempt to boost admissions. Some colleges that have not been able to address the financial pressures have had to shut down altogether.

Carol T. Christ, president of Smith College in Northampton, Mass., acknowledged that the landscape for women's colleges has changed and that women's colleges have been responding to competitive challenges, but for Smith, it's a different story. Smith's longstanding tradition of investment on the part of alumnae and its generous endowment allows the college to maintain its staying power. Smith, which is part of the "Seven Sisters" circle that includes Barnard, Bryn

Are Women's Colleges Still Necessary? And Are They Still Viable? (cont'd.)

Mawr, Mount Holyoke, Radcliffe, and Wellesley College, has seen a 10 percent increase in applicants this year. Vassar, which was also a part of this elite group, has since turned coed.

"I know that some colleges feel that they have to go coed to remain economically viable, but this is not Smith's sense of itself," said Christ. "There's a healthy market for women's education that we serve and I think we make a set of commitments, along with other women's colleges," to address the needs of this particular market.

Citing financial difficulties, Trinity College of Vermont closed its doors in September of 2000. Marymount College, a Roman Catholic women's college in Tarrytown, N.Y., is on the path to merge completely with coeducational institution Fordham University. Emmanuel College in Boston recently turned coed and since has reported a large increase in admissions. According to the WCC, nine out of 10 women's colleges have cross-registration with other colleges and universities.

"The decision to become coeducational was the result of extensive research and deliberation," said Molly Honan, a spokesperson for Emmanuel. "Based on our data, only 2 percent of women would even consider applying to a single-sex college."

Shortly after opening its doors to men, Emmanuel welcomed its largest incoming class in 30 years, and 30 percent of the Class of 2005 are male students. Since the decision to become coed, applications have tripled and enrollment has doubled, said Honan.

The course ahead for women's colleges is a hazy one. In the near-term, most institutions face a bumpy road, but proponents remain hopeful.

"The future is bright but it's a future that is certainly going to require innovation and reinvention," said Ambar.

"We've passed the time of skepticism of women's colleges," said Christ. "Those women's colleges that are strong as institutions will continue to strive."

Limiting Discrimination Lawsuits: EEOC Launches New Mediation Program

By Linda Bean

© 2003 DiversityInc.com

April 28, 2003

The Equal Employment Opportunity Commission (EEOC) is joining forces with nine state and local fair-employment agencies to expand the use of voluntary mediation to resolve employment-discrimination complaints.

The pilot program is aimed at reducing the time and cost involved in mediating a dispute and represents an expansion of the EEOC's existing mediation programs.

The agency's new partners are state civil-rights agencies in Alaska, Florida, Indiana, Iowa, Ohio, New Mexico and South Carolina, as well as municipal agencies in Kansas City and New York City.

"This pilot program strengthens our partnership with (fair employment-practices agencies) and builds on our mutual goal of eradicating discrimination in the workplaces of America," EEOC Chair Cari Dominguez said in a statement.

The EEOC launched a nationwide mediation program under the Clinton administration in 1999. Since then, the agency has conducted 44,000 mediation sessions, resolved 29,000 charges, and obtained $400 million in compensation for employees. On average, it takes 86 days to resolve a complaint through mediation, compared with years if a case goes to trial.

"The more recent average for mediation is even lower than that – 82 days, as of the end of fiscal year 2002," said David Grinberg, EEOC spokesperson.

"Litigation is time-consuming and a lengthy process," Grinberg said. "And mediation is more fair. The two sides themselves craft the resolution, rather than an agreement handed down to them."

Both the employee and employer have to agree to mediation. The mediation sessions are paid for by the EEOC and employers aren't required to admit any wrongdoing, even if an agreement is reached. Further, the charging party can have an attorney present.

"Sometimes, it is just a matter of getting both parties to sit down in a room and talk the issue through with a neutral third party," said Grinberg.

Dominguez has made mediation the centerpiece of her five-point plan to improve

Limiting Discrimination Lawsuits: EEOC Launches New Mediation Program (cont'd.)

efficiency at the EEOC.

The new pilot program comes on the heels of a "referral back" mediation pilot program for private employers. Through that program, discrimination complaints filed with the EEOC are "referred back" to the employer's internal-dispute resolution program. The EEOC also has formal agreements to mediate with 200 local employers and "a handful of national employers," Grinberg said. Those companies have agreed in advance to submit all employment disputes to mediation.

Mediation is a voluntary process, Grinberg said, and complaining parties are not required to submit their dispute to mediation.

From an employer's perspective, mediation is far cheaper than litigation, said Samantha Halem, an attorney with the Center for Mediation and Dispute Resolution, based in Wellesley, Mass.

"I think there is a certain amount of feeling that you've been heard, which you may never feel if never you never get to trial. It is very empowering," she said.

Mediation particularly is valuable when both parties would like the employment relationship to continue, she said. "It is invaluable. Litigation destroys relationship."

According to a five-year study of lawsuits filed by the EEOC, 91 percent of federal employment-discrimination lawsuits filed by the agency between Oct. 1, 1996 and Sept. 30, 2001 were resolved successfully through consent decrees, settlement agreements and favorable court orders.

The study shows the EEOC's success rate in trials is 60.24 percent - compared with a success rate of 26.8 percent for private plaintiffs in workplace-bias suits - and the agency's success rate is 80 percent in the appeal of trials - compared with a 16 percent rate of success for private attorneys.

Malignant Neglect: Failure to Tend To Diversity Issues Signals Broader Management Lapse

By Linda Bean

January 30, 2002

© 2003 DiversityInc.com

Since Kmart filed for bankruptcy last week, experts from across the retail spectrum have reached a common conclusion: Kmart doesn't know who its customers are.

The Troy, Mich.-based discount retailer filed for bankruptcy protection last week and the announcement ended weeks of speculation about the fragile state of Kmart's finances. The company has secured $2 billion in debtor-in-possession financing, allowing its 2,114 stores to remain open in the short-term.

"Kmart … could not afford to build simply on volume and cost-cutting," said Ken Smikle, publisher of Chicago-based Target Market News, which tracks the African-American marketplace. "Every company has to carve out a solid position with the customer bases that are growing and all of those are ethnic customers."

Kmart's apparent inattention to diversity didn't drive the No. 2 discount retailer into bankruptcy court, but the company's failure to capitalize on multicultural markets it once controlled is indicative of its broader failures to execute sound retail strategies.

"I think that all retailers increasingly have to look at diversity and certainly ethnic diversity is one of the prisms you have to use," said Kevin Murphy an analyst with Stamford, Conn., based Gartner Group. "I think Kmart in particular among the discounters … has an opportunity because of the location of their stores. They have a much bigger presence in the cities than Wal-Mart or Target."

Bentonville, Ark.-based Wal-Mart Stores Inc., and Target Corp., the Minneapolis-based parent of Target discount stores, have been squeezing Kmart for years, even though the Troy, Mich.-based Kmart had a huge head start on its rivals.

In late 1963, for example, Wal-Mart had one store. Kmart parent S.S. Kresge Co., meanwhile, had 53 stores and posted $83 million in sales. Now, Wal-Mart is seen as consistently cheaper than Kmart. Target has cornered the market on cheap, stylish chic.

Since the bankruptcy filing, analysts have repeatedly warned that Kmart has to

Malignant Neglect: Failure to Tend To Diversity Issues Signals Broader Management Lapse (cont'd.)

develop a distinct identity - something beyond the company's current "authority for what Moms value."

Finding a successful mix of products and building a solid customer base clearly requires a strong awareness of diversity issues - the cultural awareness that helps companies identify and serve key markets.

Kmart's dismal circumstances raise three critical diversity questions: Does the company know who its customers are? Does Kmart have the talent, tools and skills to provide those shoppers with goods they want to buy? And finally, will other corporate leaders recognize that a flawed diversity strategy often signals other lapses in corporate governance?

It may be too soon to answer those questions, and the company didn't respond to requests for information. Still, the time is right to examine some of Kmart's strengths and weaknesses through a diversity lens.

Location: Kmart - which began as S.S. Kresge Co. in Detroit 1899 - has deep urban roots. Michael Porter, a retail analyst for Morningstar, the Chicago-based financial firm, considers Kmart's continued urban presence as a strength. Kmart, for example, operates two stores on Manhattan, including one that serves the tens of thousands of commuters who use Penn Station every day.

"It's one of the few things that differentiates them at this point," Porter said. "This is something they are probably stronger at than (Wal-Mart and Target).

In the 1960s and 1970s, Kmart made a point of putting stores "where the people were," Porter said. "Then they ran out of places. They needed to go out in the suburbs and build stores. That worked for awhile, but the mighty Wal-Mart pretty much won that battle."

The discounter could survive as a "much smaller" exclusively urban chain - perhaps 1,000 stores - although that's not the route Porter expects the company to take. "I don't see them going strictly for the cities," he said, "but I don't think they are going to bail on the cities."

Cynthia Cohen, a Miami retail strategist, sees the company's urban experience as a plus, as well.

"They have for years been operating in very Hispanic areas, very black areas, very Asian areas," Cohen said. Cohen doesn't believe the company's troubles are rooted in "an inattentiveness to diversity" - if diversity is defined as race. Instead, she said, "it's an issue of an aging retailer, trying to re-invent itself."

Malignant Neglect: Failure to Tend To Diversity Issues Signals Broader Management Lapse (cont'd.)

Now, as Gartner's Murphy noted, Kmart has the opportunity to reinvent itself as a company that courts multicultural consumers.

"There is a huge opportunity there for someone who knows how to capitalize on it," he said. "By trying to be big and compete with the other guys, they quite naturally excluded other avenues they might have pursued. If they scale back … it could open their eyes to other opportunities."

Leadership: Maybe James Adamson - former CEO at Advantica Restaurants - will provide diversity guidance. Advantica is the parent company to the Denny's restaurant chain and Adamson is known as a turnaround specialist for troubled companies.

Denny's troubles certainly could be said to have centered on a failure to appreciate diversity. The company hit the headlines when African-American Secret Service agents were treated poorly in one of its restaurants. In 1994, the company lost two class-action lawsuits, and was forced to pay $54 million in damages. Adamson joined Advantica after the lawsuits. In his book about the Denny's saga, he wrote: "We learned the language of inclusion because we were forced to learn it; and then we learned to walk our talk to survive." Still, Kmart's board of directors is primarily white and male. Willie B. Davis, president of All Pro Broadcasting, Inc., is African American. Lilyan Affinito, former chairman of the board of Maxxam Group, is female.

The executive leadership team is mostly white and male, as well. Randy Allen, a former Deloitte & Touche executive and the company's top diversity official, is the sole female. Valeria Stokes, an African-American woman, the company's former vice president for human resources, corporate, left her position last year during one of the company's frequent restructuring programs. Stokes, who declined to comment for this story, had been in charge of Kmart's diversity programs.

Its not clear how many Kmart employees are women or people of color, since the company doesn't post those numbers.

Wal-Mart's Web site, by contrast, claims that the company is the nation's largest employer of African Americans and Latinos, with 125,000 and 74,000 employees, respectively.

Target Corp. - which includes two department store chains, as well as the discount retail group - goes a step farther and breaks its corporation-wide employment numbers out by race, gender and position.

Nearly 70 percent of the company's employees are women, including 53 percent

Malignant Neglect: Failure to Tend To Diversity Issues
Signals Broader Management Lapse (cont'd.)

of all managers, 59 percent of all professionals and 75 percent of sales employees. Some 33 percent of all employees are people of color, including 18 percent of all managers, 16 percent of all professionals and 35 percent of all sales workers. The company notes on its Web site that is employs more women and people of color than the U.S. retail industry overall.

Web sites: Target's Web site, in fact, offers more information about diversity than sites maintained by either Wal-Mart or Kmart. Kmart's online diversity presence is the weakest of the three discount chains.

A recent Web site survey by DiversityInc.com indicated that much of corporate America is failing to effectively communicate diversity efforts through their Web sites, which are often the first interface with customers, job seekers and investors.

Target's diversity information is included under the "careers" heading on the corporate home page. The company defines its diversity policy, lists its diversity initiatives and offers its employment numbers in detail.

Wal-Mart's diversity message is contained in its career section, accessible from the corporate homepage, as well. The company offers less information about employment than Target and more than Kmart.

Kmart's Web presence - Bluelight.com - doesn't include any diversity information, with the exception of some outdate press releases that relate to specific community events and personnel announcements.

Malignant Neglect: Why 'We're Doing The Best We Can' Just Doesn't Cut It Anymore

By Linda Bean

January 14, 2002

© 2003 DiversityInc.com

When a company representative earnestly declares "we're doing the best we can" to promote diversity in the workplace, a careful listener reaches for the nearest diversity-decoding device.

That statement could be taken at face value as a positive indicator of corporate commitment: "We recognize and value diversity; we work toward firm and measurable goals and we seek to integrate diversity practices throughout the organization."

Or it could be recognized for what it often is - encrypted notice that the company deliberately intends to fail. Once deciphered, it sounds more like:

- "We're doing the best we can, given that our CEO dismisses diversity as political correctness run amok and won't authorize a budget that goes beyond monthly heritage 'celebrations' and lawsuit-prevention programs."

- "We're doing the best we can, given that we only recruit from the top 10 percent of the same schools our CEO and president attended."

- "We're doing the best we can, given that no one here sees any need to reach multiethnic consumers or work with multiethnic suppliers. Listen, we're already making money. Why do we need them?"

In matters of diversity, there's no such thing as benign neglect. The failure to tend to diversity issues - differences and similarities of thought and opinion, as well as race, gender and sexual orientation - diminishes employees and ultimately damages the communities from which businesses draw their consumers.

How does a company reverse years - or sometimes decades - of neglect? There aren't any easy answers to that question, but there are good answers - answers that mindful leaders might want to consider the next time they hear someone in the organization suggest "we're doing the best we can."

Re-examine corporate leadership: Mission statements and training programs won't further diversity unless they're supported by a demonstrable commitment from the top. If the leadership consists of white males surrounded by other white

Malignant Neglect: Why 'We're Doing The Best We Can' Just Doesn't Cut It Anymore (cont'd.)

males, for example, it's tough to convince the multi-cultural rank and file that diversity is a priority.

A. David Brown, who heads the diversity practice at executive recruiter Whitehead Mann, works with some companies that "have a history of inclusion and want to see that continue."

Brown also works with what he describes as "rural, Southern companies where the majority of the workers are black or Hispanic and the executive ranks are typically all white males."

"More and more companies are finding that they can't continue to do business that way and they come to us for help," Brown said.

Companies also come to Whitehead Mann, Brown said, in a bid to forestall race-based discrimination lawsuits.

"They want to beat the sheriff. They don't want the same kind of problems that Coca-Cola had or Texaco had or Denny's had and it's finally dawned on them that if they are going to compete in a global arena, the executive ranks are going to have to reflect … the customer base," he added. "They are going to have to be inclusive, and develop a perspective that goes beyond the traditional Anglo, insulated culture of leadership."

Rethink recruiting: Jim Sandman, a lawyer and partner at Washington, D.C.-based Arnold & Porter, would encourage law firms - or any business entity - to rethink recruiting.

Sandman is impatient with firms that insist they can only the hire top students from the best schools. "There are a million reasons that people attend the law schools they attend," Sandman said. "It's naïve to think that all the good ones are at the top 10 schools."

At the same time, he recognizes that any shift in recruiting practices might produce hostility from at least some employees.

"As a practical matter, it can be difficult. It's a deviation from the past … that in any institution might be perceived as a change in standards," Sandman said. "But that is only a transition, a temporary situation. It will pass once you can begin to demonstrate that successful (employees) can fit different profiles."

Educate or train? The transition period Sandman described can be managed - with foresight and good information - in the same way that any other predictable business event is handled. Good information is critical, however, and - in diversi-

Malignant Neglect: Why 'We're Doing The Best We Can' Just Doesn't Cut It Anymore (cont'd.)

ty work - what constitutes "good" is often at issue.

Some companies focus on "awareness" programs aimed at increasing employee understanding of the issues that might get their employer sued - sexual harassment, racial discrimination and sexual-orientation bias. Awareness training is the bottom rung of the diversity education ladder and it is sometimes dismissed by diversity professionals because of its potential to generate a backlash.

"If it tells people how to act, it is an act," said Lani Roberts, an ethics professor and diversity expert at the University of Oregon in Portland. A company "can require people to act a certain on the job, but this doesn't necessarily do anything to alter how people think about the other human beings with whom they share communities," she added.

It takes more work, but makes better sense to offer a multifaceted diversity education, diversity practitioners contend. That includes defining unacceptable behavior and codifying the consequences, reinforcing the alignment between business goals and diversity practices, and providing employees with the skills they need to work through on-the-job conflict.

"Education is far preferable to training," Roberts added.

Know your customers: Victor Ornelas, who runs Ornelas & Associates, a Dallas advertising agency, recently pitched a new business prospect that has operations throughout the Southwest and Texas, home to dense concentrations of Latino residents.

"We showed them that one-third of their customers are Latino," Ornelas said, "… and they were stunned."

Stunned? The U.S. Census Bureau released its 2000 information in March, announcing a nearly 60 percent increase in the U.S. Latino population. For days, news coverage of the Census revolved around the implications of that population surge.

"We can present the numbers are all day long - Jose was the number one name for newborn boys last year in Texas, salsa outsells ketchup - just to show (corporate leaders) the influence that Latino culture," Ornelas said. "But they don't embrace it."

In Ornelas' experience, "most key decision-makers are non-ethnic and they do not have personal relationships with many ethnic people in their lives. They don't feel a kinship with ethnic communities," Ornelas said.

Malignant Neglect: Why 'We're Doing The Best We Can' Just Doesn't Cut It Anymore (cont'd.)

There are, of course, exceptions. Anheuser-Busch Cos, Inc., the Budweiser brewer, has taken a series of ads originally produced by Ornelas for Latino television outlets and moved them to general-market circulation, a strong success for the Ornelas agency.

But for the most part, he said, corporate leaders "have a great fear of change. And then there is the whole relationship piece."

Invest in communities: Dorothy Brothers runs the supplier-diversity program for Bank of America, the third-largest bank in the country behind Citigroup and J.P. Morgan. The bank has 4,500 retail branches in 21 states and claims market-share leadership in California, Florida and Texas and a vendor-development program that is well-regarded by other supplier diversity experts.

"The one thing that has made our program a success is strong leadership at the top, starting with the chairman and CEO," Brothers said. "I have not seen a company have a successful supplier-diversity initiative and achieve continued success that didn't have that level of support."

By year's end, Brothers said, the company will have spent $400 million with women- and minority-owned businesses - roughly 7 percent of the total procurement budget. Brothers said she expects supplier-diversity spending to climb to 15 percent of procurement spending by 2004.

"We know that small businesses and women-owned businesses are creating the lion's share of new businesses. Bottom line - if we don't support that growth, we won't have the consumer base we need to support our products," Brothers said.

Multicultural Marketers Focus on ROI, Buy-In From the Top

By Kipp Cheng

© 2003 DiversityInc.com

November 05, 2002

What do Sears, Jaguar, Gatorade and Doritos have in common? At first blush, probably little, but look further and you'll see that they are among a growing number of major national advertisers that have started to recognize the importance of reaching out to emerging markets via multicultural-marketing efforts.

Television commercials for these brands – along with TV spots for companies such as Johnson & Johnson, H&R Block and AT&T – were highlighted during an opening presentation at the Association of National Advertisers' Fourth Annual Multicultural Marketing Conference in San Francisco.

The conference kicked off Sunday with an immersion tour of San Francisco's Chinatown, sponsored by the Asian-American Advertising Federation (3AF), followed by a dinner reception and Casino night at the Four Seasons Hotel, where the conference was held.

Jim Speros, chief marketing officer at Ernst & Young and chair of ANA's Multicultural Marketing Committee, welcomed more than 150 attendees to Monday's plenary sessions. Speros said working in multicultural marketing has evolved from simply a matter of recognizing the business imperative for reaching out to African-American, Latino and Asian-American consumers, as well as gay and lesbian consumers, to getting down to the business of conducting relevant and insightful research on emerging markets and establishing return on investment for these efforts.

Multicultural marketing is about "marketing to everyone, as the new American consumer is increasingly multicultural," Speros said.

John Sarsen, president and CEO at the ANA, said panelists for the various sessions – who represented some of the most progressive advertisers and agencies in the country – provided "thoughtful and highly useful insights on the hows and the ROIs for marketing to specific emerging-market segments."

"As specific populations in this country have reach critical mass," Sarsen said, "it's not the mainstream that has assimilated these groups, these emerging groups

Multicultural Marketers Focus on ROI, Buy-In From the Top (cont'd.)

have profoundly changed the mass market."

Speros added that it was time for marketers to move beyond statistics and demographics and move toward understanding the culture and value of emerging markets.

During Monday's first general session, titled "Selling Multicultural Marketing Internally," Gigi Dixon, director of emerging markets at Wachovia, and Ford Motor Company's Connie Fontaine, discussed the importance of having buy-in from top management in order to achieve company-wide support for diversity initiatives.

Dixon said Atlanta-based Wachovia's approach to diversity was "strategic not tactical," meaning multicultural-marketing and recruitment efforts at the financial services firm are tied to business imperatives, rather than in response to "soft" human-resources issues. Plus, Dixon added, to see the true benefits of diversity, companies must be prepared for long-term commitments, not quick fixes or one-shot solutions.

Dixon presented Wachovia's approach to prompting internal buy-in for diversity initiatives: assessment, enlightenment, and engagement and execution. She admitted that previous diversity efforts with the company were "fragmented" among the company's various units but going forward, Wachovia planned a more holistic approach to diversity initiatives.

Fontaine said "getting it right the first time" is critical to the success of diversity initiatives in marketing. Companies that dabbled in multicultural marketing and then quickly backed off "reeked of insincerity to emerging marketing," she added.

She stressed that getting senior management to sign on with diversity initiatives requires an education process. Even within highly competent organizations, Fontaine said, there are some people who "get it" and others who do not.

"Don't bore people with numbers," she added. At the same time, she utilized several graphs and charts from DiversityInc.com's "Business Case for Diversity" to underscore the value of putting demographic information in a marketing context.

Pie charts that simply illustrate the ethnic breakdown of the United States offer little information, she said, but a chart that showed the ratio of people of color to white people is extremely useful in making the case to those who didn't yet understand the business imperative for reaching out to emerging markets.

"If you show a senior manager that there is one white child for every one-and-a-

Multicultural Marketers Focus on ROI, Buy-In From the Top (cont'd.)

half children of color, people will get it," Fontaine said.

The second general session centered on measuring return on investment. In this new age of corporate accountability, measuring effectiveness is critical "as budgets are scrutinized like never before," said panel moderator Laurel Wentz, international and multicultural editor at Advertising Age. The issue of return on investment in multicultural marketing is debated with great passion among those working in the sector, which is often held to a higher standard than the general market," she added.

Roberto Garcia, director of Masterfoods Hispanic Market Group, said the key to understanding return on investment is collecting accurate data on consumer behavior. In the case of Latino consumers and their consumption of Masterfoods brands such as M&Ms, Garcia said data could be extrapolated based on selling patterns in smaller, local markets such as neighborhood bodegas, to see that Latino consumers were brand loyal and high consumers for products such as chocolate candies.

"In some industries that sell direct to consumers, it's easier to derive consumer data," Garcia said, adding that sales estimates for the Latino market were based on sales audits within certain markets and creating models based on population projections.

Ed Miller of Verizon, who also presented during the ROI panel, said there's little room for guesswork, given the scrutiny that multicultural marketers face from upper management.

"There is only enough grace given to being new at this," Miller said. "There's plenty of learning [in the data], but often it raises more questions than it provide answers. But it's what allows us to have the jobs that we have."

The afternoon session featured a presentation from Stephanie Blackwood and Arthur Korant, co-founders of Double Platinum, a marketing agency that specializes in the gay and lesbian market. Korant presented a case study for the Toronto launch of Crest Whitestripes to the gay market. Meanwhile, Blackwood presented facts and figures about the gay, lesbian, bisexual or transgender (GLBT) market, including the numbers (17 million to 25 million Americans identify as GLBT; GLBT spending power – at $450 billion – is second only to African-American consumers) and the characteristics that define the group.

Finally, Barbara Bacci Mirque, vice president at the ANA, revealed the results of a survey conducted by the ANA of its membership to find out how multicultural marketing factored into overall marketing spending. While an overwhelming

Multicultural Marketers Focus on ROI, Buy-In From the Top (cont'd.)

majority of respondents said they either currently participate or plan to participate in multicultural-marketing efforts on behalf of their products or services, Bacci Mirque said the greatest concern for ANA members was whether using boutique or multicultural agencies would thwart efficiency and produce less-than-stellar creative work.

The ANA Multicultural Marketing Conference wraps up Tuesday with sessions on avoiding common mistakes in multicultural marketing and future trends in diversity marketing initiatives.

More Than Numbers: Adequate GLBT Stats Still Elusive, Problematic

By Kipp Cheng

© *2003 DiversityInc.com*

September 16, 2002

Marketers, economists and social-science researchers gathered on Saturday at this year's National Lesbian and Gay Journalists Association (NLGJA) convention in Philadelphia to discuss the best route to uncover the whole truth about the gay, lesbian, bisexual and transgender (GLBT) community. The panel discussion was titled "Gay Demographics: The Rocky Road to Research," and at odds were different camps of marketers and researchers, and their respective methodologies and the results of their work.

On the panel – held at the Loews Philadelphia Hotel – were the pre-eminent experts in the field of GLBT market and social-science research: Lee Badgett, professor of economics at University of Massachusetts; John Bremer, research analyst at Harris Interactive; Amy Falkner, professor of media studies at Syracuse University; Jeff Garber, president of OpusComm Group, a marketing firm specializing in the GLBT market; Gary Gates, a researcher in the Population Studies Center at the Urban Institute, and Kipp Cheng, deputy editor of DiversityInc.com. The panelists were convened by Bob Witeck, CEO of research and marketing firm Witeck-Combs and national board member of NLGJA.

Panel moderator Kim Mills, education director at the Human Rights Campaign, opened the discussion by saying that statistics about the GLBT community are difficult to come by, but discerning the difference between good and poorly acquired findings is critical to effectively report on the GLBT community. Mills said few journalists covering issues of concern to the GLBT community are properly trained to interpret the findings in research, resulting in media coverage that "misleads the audience, or worse, skews data simply to sell widgets."

"These are not simple questions with simple answers," Mills said. "You need to be suspicious of researchers with answers that come too quickly."

Mills emphasized that good statistics were critical to fairness and accuracy. She added that misrepresentative data that paints the GLBT market as an affluent minority "can and will be used against us," particularly by the conservative right.

One challenge of interpreting data from primary sources, such as census data, according to Gates, is that the U.S. Census does not ask respondents about sexual

More Than Numbers: Adequate GLBT Stats Still Elusive, Problematic (cont'd.)

orientation. Therefore, while census data can provide some insights into the GLBT community, particularly information about same-sex partner households, it otherwise does not effectively characterize many components of the GLBT community, notably single GLBT people, for example.

Still, Gates said census data continues to be valid because of its large sample size and detailed information.

Badgett presented the work she has done over more than 10 years that debunks the myth of GLBT – especially gay male – wealth in the United States. Calling herself an idealist and a realist, Badgett said there's an incredible dependence on data, although "there's not a whole lot of data to work with."

A critical point for journalists and marketers to understand, according to Badgett, is that "all data is not created equal."

"Comprehensive data about the LGBT community will not emerge from market-research studies," Badgett said, adding that the first step toward gathering representative data is to increase funding in social-science and economic research.

Garber and Falkner presented the findings of the GL Census, a joint venture of Syracuse University, OpusComm Group and GSociety. Falkner said the results of the study were not projectible to reflect the larger GLBT community and the sample for the study was not randomly selected. These points caused the greatest amount of concern from panelists and audience members.

Falkner said it's virtually impossible to effectively gather a random sample of GLBT people given the climate of homophobia in this country. By using the Internet to survey respondents, which the GL Census does, respondents can answer anonymously and without fear of discrimination.

"Are there biases in this approach?" Falkner asked. "Of course. But we're offering a convenience sample." This convenience sample, Falkner said, allows marketers to gain insight into the GLBT market based on the more than 6,000 respondents in the GL Census.

Audience member Katherine Sender, professor of media studies at the University of Pennsylvania's Annenberg School of Communications, questioned the value of unprojectible data, leading to a heated discussion among the panelists about which data sets were statistically valid and which should be viewed with caution. "We invite controversy," said Garber, "because it's a controversial topic we're looking at."

According to the University of California, Davis, Web site, researchers some-

More Than Numbers: Adequate GLBT Stats Still Elusive, Problematic (cont'd.)

times use a convenience sample – also known as a nonprobability sample – because all individuals within a given population may not be available for study.

"The closet is obviously a problem," said Witeck, adding that research about the GLBT market that's weighted against a general market sample – as the data from Harris Interactive and Witeck-Combs does – paints a more complete picture because "GLBT consumers may not always have on their GLBT lenses when they are making their purchasing decisions."

"There are similarities and differences between GLBT and general consumers," said Witeck. "We're looking to find out what the differences – and similarities – are between these groups."

Cheng said the difficulty for many journalists – who are not necessarily trained as researchers or statisticians – is sorting through reports that frequently offer contradictory findings. "Is there a tip sheet, in terms of how to interpret results, that the panels can recommend?" Cheng asked.

Bremer said asking basic questions, such as the source of the research and how the study was conducted is a critical first step. Beyond that, Bremer cautioned that sampling a small group delivers information only about that selected group, and therefore cannot be used to effectively measure or characterize the larger GLBT market.

Badgett said the differences in research approaches and styles ultimately is not a matter of comparing apples and oranges, but it's more accurately described as the difference between comparing apples from different orchards. She added that in the realm of research, there is a continuum of "good" and "not-so-good" data, and journalists need to do a better job at asking questions about the source and the results of all research.

"All research is different," Garber said. "But do we need to tear each other down? After all, we are all after the same goal."

Mills concluded the panel by saying that GLBT journalists have a responsibility to fairly and accurately report on research, but it's critical for journalists to consider the social implications of reporting on unrepresentative research rather than focusing solely on the business implications.

Part II: Corporate Governance

Diversity on Boards of Directors Adds Credibility

By Yoji Cole

May 21, 2003

© *2003 DiversityInc.com*

There is an upside to the corporate scandals and economic downturn: They've stirred interest in diversifying corporate boards as one of many means of creating improved accountability, responsibility and infusing corporate boards with different forms of thought.

At least that's what a Deloitte & Touche survey found. The survey found that 58 percent of the directors at 209 Fortune 1000 companies agreed that a diverse corporate board is important.

The findings were presented at, "Diversifying the American Board," a session organized by Deloitte & Touche, held Tuesday at the Four Seasons Hotel in New York City. The audience included approximately 125 executives, most of whom were vice presidents or higher at Fortune 1000 companies, and many of whom serve on boards of middle-market companies and nonprofits, said Mai Browne, manager national marketing and communications for Deloitte & Touche.

In the current economic environment, corporate boards are taking their fiduciary responsibility very seriously, said Martin Somelofske, national practice leader of the Compensation Consulting Group of Deloitte & Touche.

Somelofske, along with Donna Stettler, senior manger in the executive-compensation practice of Deloitte & Touche, presented their findings on trends in executive and director compensation before turning the podium over to three female executives who sit on corporate boards.

Trends that are affecting executive and director compensation include: forcing CEOs to get shareholder approval of their compensation plans; prohibiting the CEO from being a member of the company's compensation committee; and creating equity ownership of a CEO's stock options that create holding periods when stock could not be sold, said Somelofske and Stettler.

Stettler added that companies are selling high-level perks, such as executive apartments, and decreasing their numbers of corporate jets and moving such perquisites toward pensions. Her research also revealed that 78 percent of 209 Fortune 1000 corporate boards featured at least one female member, while 68

Diversity on Boards of Directors Adds Credibility (cont'd.)

percent of 209 Fortune 1000 corporate boards featured at least one person of color.

While the diversity of boards still is practically nonexistent, more executive-search firms are being used to find qualified diverse candidates and some search firms are making such searches a specialty, Stettler said.

Following Somelofske and Stettler's presentation was a panel of three female corporate executives who sit on corporate boards. The panel consisted of Martha Clark Goss, chief financial officer of Blaqwell, Rosina Dixon, a member of a variety of corporate boards, including those of Church & Dwight, and Shirley Young, president Shirley Young Associates, and a senior adviser to General Motors Asia Pacific.

After being appointed to a board seat, the new member should ask to be briefed on key issues, said Goss.

"If you have to ask, ask and make it happen," Goss said.

The lack of racial and gender diversity is part and parcel of the lack of diversity of thought, which, in the long run, creates problems with governance, so asking questions is important, said Young.

"You have to stick your nose up and ask the questions no one wants to ask," agreed Goss. "I ask those questions because if I don't know the answer someone else probably doesn't know as well."

As Jobless Rates Rise for People of Color, Smart Companies Recruit

By Elena Maria Lopez

© 2003 DiversityInc.com

March 13, 2003

The February unemployment numbers released last week were grim, particularly the rates for African Americans and Latinos. But several corporations known as diversity leaders say it's even more imperative in tough economic times to recruit, hire and retain people of color, even when layoffs are occurring.

More than 308,000 workers lost their jobs in February, putting the unemployment rate at 5.8 percent, with 8.5 million Americans unemployed, according to the Bureau of Labor Statistics (BLS). In January, the rate was 5.7 percent while in April of 2000, for comparison, it was 3.8 percent.

February recorded the highest number of job losses since the two months following the Sept. 11, 2001 terrorist attacks, according to the BLS.

Unemployment can be caused by a variety of factors, including involuntary job loss. The Bureau of Labor Statistics does not break down job loss specifically by race for the monthly figures. But the overall monthly figures for unemployment for February show significantly higher overall unemployment in people of color. Whites had an unemployment rate of 5 percent in February, while the rate for African Americans was double that at 10.5 percent. Asian Americans and Latinos also had higher unemployment rates at 6 percent and 7.7 percent, respectively.

People of color also were unemployed longer than whites, exhausting their state unemployment benefits more, the BLS said. The February jobless report showed 12.8 percent of whites were unemployed for at least six months, while 15.4 percent of Native Americans or Alaska Natives, 17.8 percent of Latinos, 18.8 percent of Asian and Pacific Islanders, and 19.5 percent of African Americans were unemployed for that length of time.

Latino unemployment rates only have been broken out since 1973 so there's not that much comparison, but African-American unemployment has a history of being two to two-and-a-half times that of whites over the last 50 years, according to the Economic Report of the President released in February.

"African Americans tend to be a bit younger and younger people have larger

As Jobless Rates Rise for People of Color, Smart Companies Recruit (cont'd.)

numbers of unemployed," said Harvard University Labor Economics Professor Richard Freeman. This historical disparity in unemployment rates was based on African Americans' limited access to training and education, as well as "some residual discrimination," he said. "Connectedness" is another key component, said Freeman, where finding jobs happens because of what "your network of friends and family could get you."

Of the 1.61 million people who filed for unemployment based on what the federal government terms an "extended mass layoff" in 2001, 14 percent were African American and 19 percent Latino, the BLS reported. These are layoffs of 50 or more employees in a company for a minimum period of a month. The total civilian labor force is 12 percent African American and 11 percent Latino.

With these numbers in mind, how does a diversity-conscious corporation continue to recruit and retain talented people of color? The answer, leaders of three of these companies said, is to keep focusing on hiring, even in tough times.

"I think you would be hard-pressed to find anyone within Deloitte &Touche to say 'You can take your eye off the ball around talent in bad times,' because that would be so incredibly short-sighted," said Redia Anderson, national partner for the Diversity & Inclusion Initiative at the giant accounting firm headquartered in New York. "Bad times don't last, and you still need to have that talent."

Stamford, Conn.-based Pitney Bowes conducts prelayoff audits to avoid "any particular group being severely impacted by reductions," said Henry Hernandez, executive director for Global Diversity Leadership.

Pitney Bowes, Deloitte & Touche and Rochester, N.Y.-based Eastman Kodak all experienced layoffs recently, but new people still must be hired and they should be diverse, said May Snowden, Kodak's chief diversity officer.

Before instituting a layoff, Eastman Kodak offers early retirement for senior employees, said Snowden. "The people who are closest to retirement within five years to 10 years are really white males," said Snowden, "because when you go back 30 years, 40 years, who was really being hired at that point?" Many of these senior employees choose to retire early, she said, opening the door for people of all backgrounds to move up in the company.

Kodak is one of the 68 corporations that filed an amicus curiae or "friend-of-the-court" brief in support of the University of Michigan in two affirmative-action cases now before the U.S. Supreme Court. The corporate interest in this case is directly relevant to the diversity-conscious corporations' continued interest in recruiting diverse people.

As Jobless Rates Rise for People of Color, Smart Companies Recruit (cont'd.)

General Motors, which filed its own brief in support of the university and has been a leader in the affirmative-action court battle, has said in its court documents that a ruling prohibiting the consideration of race and ethnicity in admissions' decisions dramatically would reduce the diversity at the nation's top universities. This then would deprive future leaders of "the interracial and multicultural interactions in an academic setting that are so integral to their acquisition of cross-cultural skills" and "reduce racial and ethnic diversity in the pool of employment candidates from which the nation's businesses can draw their future leaders," GM's briefs stated.

Of the Detroit, Mich.-based automobile manufacturer's annual new hires, annual averages of 500 are university students and 5 percent to 10 percent of those are from the University of Michigan, according to GM.

Rod Gillum, vice president of diversity and corporate relations for General Motors, told DiversityInc Feb. 12: "The most obvious example of our involvement in our communities was the brief we filed in support of the University of Michigan. It showed that we believe in affirmative action in higher education, and that we would support that belief with deeds, not words. Most companies wouldn't jump out and do that."

And once a company develops good sources to hire good talent, you don't just give that up in bad times, said Snowden.

"This is definitely is the kind of environment that differentiates those that are truly committed to diversity and those that are doing it just for the sake of doing it," said Hernandez. Diversity is a way for companies to differentiate themselves, said Hernandez. "That doesn't mean that we can't be operating frugally or will not be held accountable for keeping our costs in check."

Deloitte & Touche views diversity staffing as a long-term plan. "What our clients are paying for is really the diversity of our talent, whether they be linguistic, gender-based or ethnic or religious or just thinking styles," said Anderson. "So being able to attract the best talent into the firm is still always a priority for us ... regardless of the economic times."

Part III: Corporate Communications

A. External

1. Benefits & Costs

A corporate mission statement in today's marketplace that articulates a company's proactive stance on diversity not only is a courtesy to shareholders, employees and customers, it's an absolute necessity. Given the increasing diversity of the American work force and the multicultural-consumer base, companies that express a commitment to work-force and supplier diversity will attract the most talented multicultural employees and gain the greatest number of investors and customers.

In the past, a typical corporate mission statement was brief, to the point and primarily addressed increasing shareholder value. But after weathering a recession, a terrorist attack on the nation's financial center and the collapse of various former Wall Street darlings, corporate America now needs to consider more than just shareholder value. After all, Enron and Global Crossing both were committed to increasing shareholder value — even if the companies defined "shareholder" as a select group of people in the know.

A corporation should be using its mission statement to develop trust among its varied constituency of employees, customers and investors. Indeed, a company must communicate diversity in its mission to all of its corporate stakeholders, not simply its shareholders.

The task of creating a corporate mission statement frequently falls to corporate-communications professionals, who are responsible for crafting the company's mission statement as well as most other forms of external and internal communications, including press releases, Web-site content and company newsletters.

Companies can differentiate their diversity-conscious business practices in their mission statements from the business practices of less culturally competent — and less competitive — companies with subtle shifts in language,[98] according to Laura Moseley, vice president at Caponigro Public Relations in Detroit. "After the Enron debacle, I think all people are looking for words like 'integrity' and 'accountability' within any statement," Moseley says.

"Add to that Sept. 11 and the actual declaration of a recession — although they say it's over now — and we have the beginnings of a major public-relations problem that could grow into a crisis in corporate leadership the likes of which we haven't seen in 20 years."[99]

A corporate mission statement, then, is vital to laying the foundation to restore and enhance trust among all corporate stakeholders.

2. Advertising

The biggest push since Census 2000 came out has been to market to Latinos.

Advertisers still spend most of their Latino ad dollars, about $2.4 billion in 2001, on Spanish-language media. To encourage them, Univision plans to start five new cable channels devoted to music, movies and lifestyle by the end of this year, and is spending $3 billion to buy radio group Hispanic Broadcasting Corp. In some U.S. cities, the leading radio stations are Spanish-language, and there's a fast-growing Spanish-language Internet radio network called Batanga.

Advertising Age, a trade publication for the advertising industry, reported that ad spending across all industries targeted toward Latinos was estimated at $2.1 billion (10 percent of all spending) in 2000, the most recent figures available. Advertising Age pegged overall spending on the African-American market at $1.5 billion (5.5 percent) and spending on the Asian-American market at $363 million (1.5 percent) in 2000. Overall ad spending in 2000 was $216.4 billion, according to Robert J. Coen's Universal McCann U.S. Volume Report.

"Multicultural marketing and advertising is a key priority for ANA members who have been putting enormous effort into all elements of multicultural marketing. They want and need all the messages they communicate to be comfortably multicultural," John J. Sarsen Jr., former president and CEO of the Association of National Advertisers, said last year.

Corporations are missing a big chunk of the Latino market as a result of inadequate advertising budgets, according to the Association of Hispanic Advertising Agencies (AHAA), and a recent report aims to serve as a guide toward maximizing the potential of the Latino buying power.

Last year, AHAA released "Missed Opportunities: Vast Corporate Underspending in the U.S. Hispanic Market." The study concluded that for maximum effectiveness, corporations should be allocating a minimum of 8 percent of their total national marketing budgets to the Spanish-dominant and bilingual markets. It also revealed that among the top 50 leading Latino advertisers, current spending targeting Latinos across all categories is approximately 3.2 percent of national budgets – well below the 8 percent recommended threshold.

The AHAA released recommendations on how to set appropriate spending targets based on media usage, consumption data and population data. Latinos, for example, over-index in consumption of most food categories, requiring resource allocations much more than the actual representation of Spanish-dominant and bilingual households. To reach Spanish-dominant and bilingual households across top Latino markets commensurate with existing household food-consumption budgets, the AHAA concluded that instant-coffee and yogurt companies, for example, should direct about $1 out of every $3 in marketing resources.

The Latino market's current size, formation of larger households, heavy concentration in the top, youngest, trendsetting markets in the United States, accompanied by their speedy wealth creation and high consumerism, are at odds with the neglect of investment in most categories, concluded the AHAA.

Changes in demographics and spending power explain why companies are spending more money to reach these multicultural markets. For example, Bloomington, Ill.,-based State Farm Insurance increased its Latino-targeted advertising budget from $7 million in 2001 to $9 million in 2002, according to spokesperson Ana Compain-Romero.

Allstate Insurance Co. began its push into the Latino market in 1996 by spending $60 million on Latino-targeted advertising for the five years leading to 2001. The payoff has been substantial, according to Raymond Celaya, assistant vice president of Emerging Markets at Allstate, who says that the company's business with Latino customers increased from $1 billion in 1995 to more than $2.1 billion in 2001.

The Northbrook, Ill.,-based insurance firm hoped to duplicate the success it had with Latino consumers by expanding efforts to attract African-American and Asian-American consumers in 2003. Orlando, Fla.,-based Darden Restaurants changed its Olive Garden chain's general-marketing advertising slogan, "When you're here, you're family," to attract Latino customers. The effort, which began in 2002, was expected to increase Olive Garden's marketing budget between 5 percent and 10 percent in 2003, says Greg Watson, vice president of brand marketing for Olive Garden Restaurants.

Ford Motor Co. has made the greatest inroads into the multicultural automobile market with advertising and community partnerships focused on Latinos. In the past five years, Ford has increased sales in the Latino market by 50 percent. Registrations among Latino customers in 2001 surpassed the year before by more than 2,000 vehicles. Indeed, since 1996, Ford registrations to Latinos have increased by 74.2 percent, says Michael Wright, multicultural-marketing manager for Ford Division. In addition to Ford cars and trucks, Ford also manufactures brands such as Aston Martin, Jaguar, Lincoln, Mercury and Volvo, each with its own multicultural-marketing effort.

A strong Latino consumer market explains why NBC and parent company General Electric acquired the second-largest U.S. Spanish-language television network, Telemundo, in April 2002. Telemundo claims to reach 91 percent of the U.S. Latino market through 14 stations and more than 30 affiliates, with a distribution to more than 425 cable systems in 115 television markets.

3. Web Sites

Since the fall of 2001, DiversityInc has critiqued the corporate Web sites of the nation's largest corporations. Some Web sites have done top-notch jobs at conveying the importance and bottom-line benefits of fostering workplace- and supplier-diversity initiatives, while others have faltered.

The mixed results serve as an accurate reflection of the state of diversity programs and initiatives in U.S. business today. Although communicating a commitment to diversity may or may not represent actual follow-through on diversity programs, it's clear that companies that care about diversity also herald their achievements via their communications and marketing programs. And there's no denying that a corporate Web site is a vital communications platform for any business, disseminating information to a wide and varied constituency.

These are the criteria used:

1. Is there a link to diversity or diversity-related information on the homepage?

2. Is there a link to diversity or diversity-related information within

one click of the homepage?

3. Does a simple search for the keyword "diversity" yield relevant results?

4. Is the diversity information up to date?

5. Does the site utilize multicultural images?

6. Does the site offer diversity information in its career area?

7. Does the site offer information for diverse suppliers?

8. Does the site highlight company activities that impact diverse communities?

While mounting evidence has shown that competitive corporations have steadily increased their commitments to diversity, many top companies still are failing to communicate diversity policies and initiatives effectively on their corporate Web sites. This communications breakdown has a potentially devastating effect, since Web sites are most often the first — and sometimes the only — interface between a company and its potential customers, job seekers and investors.[100]

"Web sites are very 21st century and represent an increasingly important way people interact with a company," says Ed Rutland, executive vice president of Atlanta-based Matlock & Associates. "Corporate sites should give visitors an idea of exactly how diversity-friendly a company might be.[101]

It's just like walking into the lobby of the corporate headquarters. People of color will be looking for certain visual clues to tell them they're welcome."

Rutland identifies several visual clues from the brick-and-mortar world that carry over onto the Web, which he phrases in a series of questions that should be addressed on a corporate Web site: Are there people of color in management positions? Is the company doing anything to recruit people of color? Is the company doing anything to retain and advance people of color via employee affinity groups or mentoring programs? From a social responsibility perspective, how is the company addressing the needs of communities of color? What opportunities are available for diverse suppliers?

This list of must-have information falls into three main categories: diversity in employment, diversity in community outreach and supplier diversity. The key to communicating a commitment to these ideals is presenting the information in a timely, accessible and plainly written manner.

"With most sites, if you click around looking for diversity information, your fingers will get tired," says Marie Johnson, Washington, D.C.,-based Fannie Mae's vice president, Office of Diversity, Health and Work Life Initiatives. Johnson says making it easy for site visitors to find information about diversity should be the top priority. This means offering links to diversity-related information on a company's homepage or at least within one click from the homepage.

Additionally, the links must be labeled in such a way that site visitors can discern easily the intention or content behind the link. Lastly, diversity-related information should be up-to-date and relevant – otherwise, diversity will come across as being of secondary importance.

"On Fannie Mae's site," Johnson says, "one click will take you to diversity information. This is important because at companies that rely on the Internet, there's always a fight over who gets icon space. [That] diversity is right there [means] … it's up there with our top corporate initiatives."[102]

Web-usability experts caution developers of corporate Web sites from burying diversity-related information too deep into their sites or confining diversity information to specific sections, such as the typical pigeonholes of "corporate social responsibility" and "careers."

Integrating a diversity message throughout a corporate Web site most effectively conveys a company's true commitment. Like a well-trained and diversity-conscious customer-service representative, those who create and manage Web sites require proper training in order to communicate diversity messages effectively. The proper forethought in the application of technology requires the same degree of vigilance applied to other areas of diversity management.[103]

This year's Top 50 companies for diversity were asked three questions about their Web sites: Whether there was a section of the site labeled diversity; whether diversity was on the homepage and whether there were images of multicultural people. Thirty-nine of the top 50 said yes to the first question; 45 of 50 to the second; and 37 of 50 to the third.

4. Community Outreach

Companies that want to make serious inroads into communities must reach out to the people in those communities where they live, shop, worship and are educated. And they must involve community leaders. This is the best way to develop trust, brand reputation and long-term customers.

For example, the Rev. Johnny Miller of Chicago's Mount Vernon Baptist Church is one of a growing number of African-American clergy who view the church as vital to spreading the message of economic empowerment in communities of color. Last year, Miller's church of approximately 1,000 parishioners joined forces with One Thousand Churches Connected. Launched by the Rev. Jesse Jackson under the umbrella of the Rainbow/PUSH coalition in 2001, the One Thousand Churches Connected is designed to bring the message of economic responsibility to families through churches across the country.

Another example of commitment to a community occurred this year, when the nation's No. 2 bank, JPMorgan Chase, announced plans to make a $500 billion commitment to the minority and underserved home-mortgage markets over the next seven years. The company hopes the large lending commitment will double its presence in these markets and it intends to seek advice from community leaders on the most successful ways to reach out to their constituencies. JPMorgan Chase said this is the largest initiative to date for single-family mortgages to these segments of the market.

The $500 billion will double the amount of capital JPMorgan Chase currently lends to the minority and underserved home-mortgage markets. In 2002, the company floated about $35 billion of capital to these markets. According to the newly announced plan, this amount should be more than $70 million a year by 2010.

Chase currently is the No. 4 mortgage originator in the United States, with a market share of about 5 percent. Although these numbers change quarterly, the company tends to range between No. 2 and No. 4. With this announcement, the company hopes to achieve about 10 percent of the market share by 2010.

The company hopes to overturn the traditional barriers mainstream corporations have faced entering emerging and underserved markets by gaining the help of community leaders and organizations. Chase has created the National Housing Advisory Council to assist and deal with relevant issues. The council is comprised of real-estate professionals and influential leaders in the African-American, Latino, Asian-American and gay and lesbian communities.

Currently, about 30 percent of JPMorgan Chase's mortgage business stems from the minority or underserved market. With this initiative, Chase expects this market to represent between 35 percent and 40 percent of its total home-mortgage business. This initiative increases single-family home loans to people of color of various economic backgrounds, low-to-moderate income borrowers, and new immigrant families.

Chase has made an effort to reach these customers over the past two years, including low closing costs, low down payments, down payments for those with limited credit, and multi-language documents. The company also plans to offer a wider range of services to customers and potential customers, including expanded language capabilities, referrals to credit-counseling agencies and programs to increase financial literacy. Chase also intends to address predatory-lending practices through community and marketing information. Predatory-lending refers to subprime lenders that lend to high-risk individuals at an increased and often-unfair interest rate.

Chase also has doubled the number of salespersons in these markets, increasing their racial and ethnic diversity, the company said. The company also plans to increase its physical presence in urban markets in New York, California, Texas, Washington, D.C., Illinois, Georgia and Pennsylvania.[104]

5. Public Relations

The ill-timed words of one incompetent employee quickly can render meaningless the CEO's eloquence on diversity issues, the popularity of an employee-affinity network or the latest "Best Company for Everyone to Work" award.

Similarly, a customer-service representative who doesn't speak the customer's language or understand cultural issues can destroy the best of marketing campaigns.

"As companies begin to deal with emerging markets and emerging majorities, it becomes very important, as a working item, for them to ensure their people have that degree of cultural competency," says Matlock & Associates' Rutland. "It doesn't necessarily have to be a person of color in the position, but the person definitely has to have a certain sensitivity."

Smart companies have averted potential embarrassment in the press by making sure they put people knowledgeable about diversity on the phone with reporters who have questions about diversity-related issues. While this sounds like common sense, it's surprisingly rare in corporate America.

Sometimes even a CEO is unprepared to answer a question in a culturally intelligent way. Think of how African-American employees of Georgia Power felt after CEO David Ratcliffe concluded that nooses found at the plant could be explained away as just some of the dozens of knots employees tie as part of their daily work. Ratcliffe later recanted and admitted he hadn't thought of nooses "in a racial context" until a bias lawsuit was filed.

It's no surprise, then, that only a few well-run companies have diversity specialists in their media-relations departments.[105]

"Most companies in the Fortune 1000 do assign knowledgeable people to be spokespeople on various issues," Rutland says.

"The best companies will have people who really understand exactly where the company stands on diversity … [However,] it's like everything else with diversity management: Some are a lot more 'diversity mature' than others. Only a few companies are mature enough to practice strategic diversity management, the kind that permeates every facet of the organization."

IBM is such a company — at least when it comes to making sure the right people are answering diversity-related questions. With some 300,000 employees nationwide, local media people handle many media requests. But should a call touch on a core diversity issue at IBM, reporters are referred to Jim Sinocchi, director of diversity communications.

Sinocchi does not have a background in diversity. He hasn't undergone any special training outside of the mandatory diversity training all managers at IBM receive and are required to teach to their teams.

Rather, because of his broad range of experience, Sinocchi has been put in a position where his job is to know everything that's going on at IBM that relates to diversity — whether it falls under the director of diversity's purview or not.

"My 'beat' is diversity," Sinocchi says, using the journalist's slang for an area of expertise. "I need to be knowledgeable about our corporate diversity strategy and its [unofficial] linkage to each of the business units."

"This is the first time IBM has put an executive in this job," he adds. "We used to have managers or media people. But [the company] wanted someone who could come in with experience from other areas."[106]

Perhaps as vital as having a positive diversity story to tell corporate constituents is the importance of delivering that message in a consistent and unified manner. Consider that the average Fortune 500 company spends millions per year on advertising and millions more on recruitment efforts. Then there are the added expenditures on corporate giving, public relations and employee relations. Each expense represents an important area of focus and each a cost center necessary to generate the hundreds — if not thousands — of communications messages companies aim at consumers, investors, communities and other essential stakeholders.

But what if those hundreds of messages were inconsistent or, worse yet, contradictory? In multicultural markets, for example, contradictory messages lead to distrust, and that can lead to loss of business. For example, years of diversity efforts on Coca-Cola's part were undermined by a class-action racial-bias lawsuit. Why? One reason was that employees clearly weren't getting the "we value diversity" message.

"The point of integrating is to create a consistent voice, a voice that will support your brand message and brand image," says Rutland. "This can only happen if you have everybody on the same page. Those organizations that appoint a diversity czar stand a much better chance of ending up with one overall and consistent voice." To prevent breakdowns in communications, more companies are embracing a strategy of integration that encompasses all areas of diversity — from internal communications to external marketing.

A byproduct of a well-planned and integrated communications strategy is greater efficiency. This is particularly important in a down economy when budgetary resources are scarce.

"It isn't necessarily about reducing staff or cutting costs: It's helping leverage a very small staff with a small budget to really produce some good results," says Sheryl Battles, vice president of external affairs for Stamford, Conn.,-based Pitney Bowes. "Everybody today is trying to be smart relative to operational efficiency and value. When you think about it, the value equation skyrockets when you can take a single set of resources and dollars and leverage them across multiple channels and multiple functional areas."

B. Internal

1. Benefits & Costs

The benefits of successfully communicating diversity initiatives to employees are multiple and have a minimal cost. If employees buy in to the importance of diversity, retention, recruitment and sales increase. If they don't, most of the money spent on these initiatives will be wasted.

2. Affinity Groups

Affinity groups are an important way for companies to gain employee support, test products and ideas in various communities, and recruit new workers.

Ford, for example, has 10 employee-resource groups – the Ford African-Ancestry Network, the Ford Asian-Indian Association, the Ford Chinese Association, GLOBE for its gay, lesbian and bisexual employees, the Ford Hispanic-Network Group, the Ford Interfaith Network, Ford Parenting Network, the Middle Eastern Community, the Professional Women's Network, and the Ford Employees Dealing with Disabilities Network.

Ford, as the economy has faltered, attempted to jump start revenue by providing discounts to the friends and family of employees. Members of the company's Interfaith Network group met with the different churches to encourage people to take advantage of Ford's friends and family deal, says Rosalind Cox, diversity & work-life planning manager for Ford.

The Detroit-based auto company also asked employee members of its Parenting Network to test its Windstar minivan to see if the automobile truly was family-friendly.

Affinity groups are called upon more frequently by corporate brass to weigh in on such marketing campaigns, help with recruitment efforts and represent the company in the community.

The groups provide support to business objectives through participation at job fairs and organizing in-house educational activities, as well as working as liaisons between a company's executive offices and the community at large.

Verizon, which has 12 groups called Employee Resource Groups (ERG) that together account for 20,000 employee members, sponsors resume-writing and public-speaking programs to further develop the skills of the company's employees. ERGs also go out and represent the company at recruitment fairs, says Tracy Edwards, executive director of workforce diversity and business relations for Verizon.

Verizon's groups include the Association of Career Employees – for employees more than 50 years old, the Asian-Focus Group, the Consortium of Information and Telecommunications Executives, Black Professionals in Communications, Disabilities Issues Awareness leaders, Gay, Lesbian, Bisexual, and Transgender Employees of Verizon and their Allies, Hispanic-Support Organization, National Jewish Cultural Resource Group, Native American People of Verizon, Pacific-Asian Cultural Employee Resource Society, South-Asian Professionals Inspiring Cultural Enrichment, Veterans Advisory Board of Verizon and Women's Association of Verizon Employees.

Companies that proactively use their affinity groups usually link them to executive leaders either by placing a senior vice president with a certain group or by holding regular meetings between the groups' leaders and executives.

Verizon also budgets for each of its 12 groups, as do many companies. Ford sets aside $8,000 annually for each of its 10 groups. Edwards says many of Verizon's affinity groups are not-for-profit organizations, while others raise money through membership dues.

Some companies shy away from a monetary relationship with their affinity groups for fear it would take away the group's autonomy. Edwards adds that Verizon management doesn't tell the ERGs where to spend their money.

To stay in touch with their ERGs and provide them with a voice on the executive level, however, Verizon ties senior executive champions to each group. The ERGs choose the executive leader they want as their ombudsman, which is a volunteer effort by the executive.

Ford also provides its affinity groups with an executive champion, who is a senior executive of a Ford business, Cox says.

PepsiCo. is a company for which affinity groups are not new – they've been organized within the company for the past 15 years – but utilizing their expertise for marketing, recruitment and community outreach is a new aspect of the company's relationship with its groups.

PepsiCo, which includes Frito Lay, Quaker Foods and Tropicana, calls them employee networks and is in the midst of streamlining and linking the groups at its first companies, says Ron Harrison, senior vice president for diversity and community affairs.

Since Pepsi is a combination of the four companies, each has its own set of affinity groups, which Harrison's department is attempting to link through satellite organizations at each company. So, for example, the Hispanic Employees Network at Frito Lay would have a representative group at the other three Pepsi companies.

The groups include Frito Lay's Women's Network, Hispanic Employee Network, the Black Employees Network and the Asian Employees Network; Tropicana's groups include the Multicultural Network and the Woman's Network; Pepsi Co.'s groups include the Black Professional's Association, the Hispanic Association, the Women's Network and an Asian Employee Network; and Quaker's groups include the Hispanic Employees Network, the Asian Employee Network, the Gay and Lesbian Employee Network, the Women's Network, and the People of Color in Marketing Network.

American Express (AmEx) credits its gay-and-lesbian employee network, which now is called the Pride Network, with spearheading the idea of domestic-partner benefits at the company, says Bet Franzone, media-relations specialist for the company.

The group, in the late 1990s, developed a cost-benefit analysis and presented that to the company's chairman, who asked for more information to make an informed decision, Franzone says.

AmEx now offers and markets products that, while not geared specifically for gays and lesbians, suits their perceived needs. Products such as the "Travelers Cheque for Two," which allows two people traveling together to co-sign the check, was marketed directly to gays and lesbians in gay publications.

AmEx has 10 national networks based on various affinities.

The objectives include supporting recruitment-and-retention initiatives, participating in educational activities, acting as a liaison between management and the community, participating in outreach and volunteer programs and enhancing marketing efforts in targeted communities.

The company's Asian Employees Network, for example, solved a problem AmEx had with reaching a segment of the Asian population as a result of the many different languages, dialects and cultures under the umbrella of "Asian."[107]

3. Best Practices: Successful Leadership Strategies from Top Companies

This year's Top 50 Companies for Diversity almost all (48 of 50) reported their Intranets were used to communicate their diversity message. Here are summaries of some of the best internal diversity-communications policies:

Altria: Diversity messages are included in virtually all formal communications, starting with the CEO, senior management and middle management. Other vehicles include diversity training, regular presentations to employee groups and entire function groups at each operating company.

BellSouth: [Diversity is communicated internally through] electronic and printed newsletters, classroom and online training, and face-to-face meetings/employee sessions.

Citigroup: Information on diversity initiatives and events is communicated through our corporate diversity Intranet site, which employees can access globally. The content is tied to our four-point diversity strategy around employees, customers, community and suppliers and is updated on a monthly basis. Each year, a report of the prior year's diversity accomplishments and initiatives is published in conjunction with the corporate annual report. Diversity liaisons for each business are responsible for communicating diversity news within their businesses.

FleetBoston: There is a diversity site on the corporate Intranet. We produce brochures. There are dozens and dozens of diversity-awareness events, such as brown-bag lunches, presentations and performances throughout our footprint. Of course, there are several training options, including a diversity-learning map. Lastly, an annual forum is held for diversity leadership, during which training is offered and awards are distributed.

International Truck and Engine: [Diversity is communicated internally through] Diversity Wheel – a set of diversity values and guiding behaviors that exemplify how we live diversity at International. We have brochures available in English and Spanish to all employees. [We have] Inside International, a quarterly newsletter; InBrief, a weekly newsletter; Site Diversity Council newsletters; monthly Truck Diversity conference calls; Site Diversity Council sponsors Diversity Day; community events; monthly awareness programs.

KPMG: [Diversity is communicated internally through] internal newsletters; e-mails from executive leadership; monthly column on diversity Web site; bulletin-board postings; internal promotions of diversity months (Black History Month, Women's History Month, etc.); Web-based diversity calendar.

Marriott: [Diversity is communicated internally through] special messages from the chairman and CEO and the president and COO; training sessions, particularly new-hire orientation sessions; multicultural events and programming; frequent internal updates through regular Intranet mechanisms; brochures and pamphlets; networking conferences; special sessions at regularly scheduled meetings.

Prudential: Internal communications include: communications from the senior leadership team with diversity messages imbedded; communications from the chairman regarding diversity-related issues, such as supplier diversity; regular announcements of our diversity-recognition events; monthly articles in the newly released company-wide daily newspaper; periodic articles in the company magazine, The Leader; company-division and corporate-center Web sites. Diversity communications are monitored and each senior leader's annual diversity leadership progress report includes examples of how he or she has demonstrated commitment to diversity communications.

SBC Communications: Diversity is communicated internally through a number of programs and tools including: diversity Intranet site; informers via company Intranet; diversity collateral, including a brochure and an information sheet; diversity video library; employee-training programs, including orientation; stories on SBC's programs and recognitions in internal newsletters; employee-initiated organizations and events; recognition of employees for increasing opportunities for minority-, women- and disabled-veteran-owned businesses through SBC's annual Supplier Diversity Achievement Awards.

Verizon: Diversity is communicated internally through voicemails/e-mails from the CEO and senior leadership and via internal newsletters. Diversity also is communicated internally through our diversity consultants, who meet with the diversity councils and [it also is communicated] through publications, such as a human-resources newsletter that addresses diversity messages as well as an employee newspaper, VZ News, that covers topics of diversity, such as awards and recognition. Oscar Gomez, [vice president, office of Diversity and Business Compliance] also sends messages directly to the business leaders and to our HR business partners, who are located within each line of business. Diversity is incorporated into executive speeches and TV broadcast messages and is communicated continuously through events and activities sponsored by our affinity groups. The Verizon Intranet site also contains numerous diversity information links for employees.

ADDITIONAL RESOURCES

PART III: CORPORATE COMMUNICATIONS

Association of Hispanic Advertising Agencies (AHAA), 8201 Greensboro Drive, Suite 300, McLean, Virginia 22102 (703) 610-9014. *http://www.ahaa.org/*

Association of National Advertisers (ANA), 708 Third Avenue, New York, New York 10017-4270. *http://www.ana.net/*

Cole, Yoji. "Employee-Affinity Groups: In Lean Times, Smart Companies Use Them As Business Tools." DiversityInc, 30 September 2002. *http://www.diversityinc.com/members/3598.cfm*

Lopez, Elena Maria. " Chase Plans $500B in Home Loans to Diverse Markets; Community Leaders to Help." DiversityInc, 5 February 2003. *http://www.diversityinc.com/members/4406.cfm*

Pine, Jordan T. " How to Market Diversity on Your Corporate Site." DiversityInc, 19 November 2001. *http://www.diversityinc.com/members/1769.cfm.*

Pine, Jordan T. "Malignant Neglect: Managing Corporate Communications, Customer Service and Web Sites.' DiversityInc, 13 February 2002. *http://www.diversityinc.com/members/2361.cfm.*

Pine, Jordan T. " Make the Mission Statement Count: Building Real Trust in Corporate Leadership." DiversityInc, 13 March 2002. *http://www.diversityinc.com/members/2566.cfm.*

Pine, Jordan T. " Special Report: Best Web Sites for Diversity." DiversityInc, 15 November 2001. *http://www.diversityinc.com/members/1747.cfm.*

Make the Mission Statement Count: Building Real Trust in Corporate Leadership

By Jordan T. Pine

© 2003 DiversityInc.com

March 13, 2002

The average corporate mission statement is short, to the point and usually speaks primarily of increasing shareholder value. But after weathering a recession, a terrorist attack on the nation's financial center and the collapse of two book-cooking Wall Street darlings, corporate America needs to be thinking about more than shareholder value. After all, Enron and Global Crossing were also after increasing shareholder value, if by shareholder they meant a select few stockholders in the know.

As DiversityInc.com established in the first part of its ongoing series on Building Trust in Corporate America, corporations must now be focused on developing trust among employees, customers and investors. In short, they need to be communicating with all stakeholders, not just shareholders.

This task falls to the corporate-communications professionals, who are responsible for crafting the company mission statements as well as most other forms of external and internal communications, including press releases, Web-site content and the company newsletters. But what can these professionals possibly say to differentiate their company's business practices from the business practices that have been getting so much press?

They can start with subtle shifts in language, said Laura Moseley, vice president at Caponigro Public Relations in Detroit. "After the Enron debacle, I think all people are looking for words like 'integrity' and 'accountability' within any statement," she said. "Generally, the trust factor was low before Sept. 11. Following the mini-layoffs of last year, folks were not able to articulate it, but they were not as comfortable with their corporate governance as during the 1990s.

"Add to that Sept. 11 and the actual declaration of a recession, although they say it's over now, and we have the beginnings of a major public-relations problem that could grow into a crisis in corporate leadership the likes of which we haven't seen in 20 years. We need to do work now to lay the foundation to restore and enhance trust."

Moseley started her career as one of the first two African Americans on the editorial staff of Time magazine, and, in the 1970s, started one of the first female

Make the Mission Statement Count:
Building Real Trust in Corporate Leadership (cont'd.)

African- American-owned public-relations agencies. As a result of this experience, one of her specialties today is what she calls "special diversity projects" - that is, helping corporate-communications professionals add the diversity dimension to their work. At Caponigro, Moseley has done work along these lines with grocery-store chain Kroger, Home Depot and Comerica bank, among others. She holds up the latter two companies' mission statements as examples of what stakeholders of color will be looking for in the current climate of distrust.

Home Depot, for example, emphasizes "creating shareholder value" in its corporate mission statement. But that value is fourth in a list of "eight core values" that include "taking care of our people," "giving back" and demonstrating "respect for all people." Other values include "doing the 'right' thing" and "building strong relationships."

Comerica bank is even more specific, getting right to the point and using the "T" word. "We are committed to delivering the highest quality financial services by ... [c]reating a positive environment for our colleagues built on trust, teamwork and respect," its official "vision statement" reads. Also emphasized are "building enduring customer relationships" and "demonstrating leadership in our community." Only at the very end is there mention of "ensuring a consistent, superior return for our owners."

Comerica's awareness of the need to communicate these priorities can be traced to a "community-generated urban banking protest" in Detroit in the early 1990s, Moseley said. Following this event, the bank "aggressively met the challenges" that had been set before it and approached Caponigro with the goal of reaching new customers in Detroit's communities of color - namely African Americans, Latinos and Arab Americans. It was then that the bank received a wake-up call.

"I was retained to profile the market they were after, and I found the market wasn't interested in them because of a history of rejection," Moseley said. "This is always quite a surprise to a corporation. It's always a shock to find out that just because you've decided you want these customers doesn't mean they're going to come onboard. It's usually quite a lesson in the history of the consumer relationship for them that can be surprising and painful."

"The flip side is that once they get over it, they realize that going after the market requires diversity strategies and approaches - the kind of strategies that become paradigms for other markets," she added. "This is when they experience what I call pleasant amazement, when they learn that whatever is working for the niche can work somewhere else as well and yield profits."

Make the Mission Statement Count:
Building Real Trust in Corporate Leadership (cont'd.)

A case in point is the relationship Comerica now enjoys with the Arab-American and Chaldean (Christians mostly from Iraq) community in southeast Michigan, the largest such community of its kind nationwide. That relationship began three years ago with a small budget geared toward marketing and outreach. Today, Comerica is the dominant bank in that community, which is roughly 300,000 strong, and it accomplished this at the same it was decreasing the marketing budget it had dedicated to targeting the community.

The strategy that paid off for Comerica was "sending a lot of people into the community to get to know them and to try to become part of their daily lives," said Dave Huiskens, a first vice president at Comerica who is deeply involved with the bank's Arab-American outreach efforts. Initially, that meant attending formal community events externally while educating employees about the cultural aspects of doing business in the community, he said. Comerica also started looking to hire more people from the community to accelerate the learning process.

What the bank discovered is something Moseley has also identified as a truism of which corporate communications professionals should be aware: When it comes to building trust in communities of color, words aren't enough. You have to be visible in the community first.

"People won't believe your line until they've seen what you've done," she said. For example, "a press release has to go further than saying, 'We're interested in you.' What you really want to do is tie the press release to a unique product or service placement, and then say what you perceive the relationship to be."

For example, if a company were looking to sell clothes detergent in a new community, the best way to gain traction would be to sponsor "a how-to class for young teen mothers at a central place in the community," she said. "Social responsibility is often the key tied to getting the attention of target market."

For Comerica, this meant getting involved with the prominent local organizations supporting Arab Americans and their businesses, Huiskens said. These include the Arab Community Center for Economic and Social Services (ACCESS), which serves low-income Arab Americans and Muslims, the American Arab Heritage Campaign and the American Arab Chamber of Commerce. Comerica underwrites their activities, sits on their boards and helps manage their capital campaigns.

The relationship between Comerica and the Arab-American community is so good that the bank's response to Sept. 11 - and the threats of violence directed at

Make the Mission Statement Count:
Building Real Trust in Corporate Leadership (cont'd.)

Arab Americans that followed - didn't need to include any special marketing campaigns or press statements, Huiskens said. Instead, the bank's chairman and vice chairman picked up the phone to community leaders to say, simply, "We know this is a difficult time for you and, if you need our support, we're there for you," he said.

Huiskens added he and the company's diversity chief also drove into the heart of the community in the days that followed just to talk with local businesspeople and address any concerns face to face.

"We received so many positive comments (about that), publicly made in an unsolicited fashion, from people who saw us and knew we hadn't changed the way approach the community," he said. "I don't think we could've bought our way into that kind of acceptance with any amount of money."

The same type of strategies should be applied internally, Moseley said. Employees of color are constantly looking for "language, symbols and messages that indicate whether there's support and understanding" at their place of employment, she said.

"What a corporation says in its newsletter, for example, is just as important as what is say in its mission statement," she said. "It's the continuity of the message and its frequency that helps people meet the daily challenges of working for the company."

Malignant Neglect: Managing Corporate Communications, Customer Service and Web Sites

By Jordan T. Pine

© 2003 DiversityInc.com

February 13, 2002

The ill-timed words of one incompetent PR professional can quickly render meaningless the CEO's eloquence on diversity issues, the popularity of an employee affinity network or the latest "Best Company for Everyone to Work" award.

Similarly, a customer-service representative who doesn't speak the customer's language or understand cultural issues can destroy the best of marketing campaigns.

"As companies begin to deal with emerging markets and emerging majorities, it becomes very important, as a working item, for them to ensure their people have that degree of cultural competency," said Ed Rutland, executive vice president at diversity and PR-consulting firm Matlock & Associates. "It doesn't necessarily have to be a person of color in the position, but the person definitely has to have a certain sensitivity."

In October, DiversityInc.com published an article titled, "Seven Things You Just Shouldn't Tell a Diversity Reporter." The article was born of a staff reporter's recent frustration in dealing with media-relations professionals who demonstrated a distinct lack of "diversity competence."

The article included paraphrases of some typical comments, along with a translation by the reporter. For example:

Company: "It is difficult to recruit people of color. You hire them but then they just don't stay."

Reporter Interpretation: And, of course, white employees never leave.

The point of the article was not to ridicule, but to illustrate how an otherwise tightly wound diversity plan can unravel. This Tuesday, DiversityInc.com identified another diversity-strategy breaker: giving Web-filtering software too much control over what online content employees can access. Below is a closer look at the importance of diversity-savvy corporate communications and two other critical areas that are often neglected but equally important to a sound diversity strategy.

Malignant Neglect: Managing Corporate Communications, Customer Service and Web Sites (cont'd.)

Corporate Communications

Smart companies have averted potential embarrassment in the press by making sure they put people knowledgeable about diversity on the phone with reporters who have questions about diversity-related issues. While this sounds like common sense, it's surprisingly rare in corporate America.

Sometimes even a CEO is unprepared to answer a question in a culturally intelligent way. Think of how African-American employees of Georgia Power - which is being sued for racial discrimination - felt after CEO David Ratcliffe concluded that nooses found at the plant could be explained away as just some of the dozens of knots employees tie as part of their daily work. Ratcliffe later recanted and admitted he hadn't thought of nooses "in a racial context" until the bias lawsuit was filed.

It's no surprise, then, that only a few well-run companies have diversity specialists in their media-relations departments.

"Most companies in the Fortune 1000 do assign knowledgeable people to be spokespeople on various issues," Rutland said. "The best companies will have people who really understand exactly where the company stands on diversity ... (However,) it's like everything else with diversity management: Some are a lot more 'diversity mature' than others. Only a few companies are mature enough to practice strategic diversity management, the kind that permeates every facet of the organization."

IBM is such a company - at least when it comes to making sure the right people are answering diversity-related questions. With some 300,000 employees nationwide, local media people handle many media requests. But should a call touch on a core diversity issue at IBM, reporters are referred to Jim Sinocchi, director of diversity communications.

Sinocchi does not have a background in diversity. He hasn't undergone any special training outside of the mandatory diversity training all managers at IBM receive and are required to teach to their teams. Rather, because of his broad range of experience, Sinocchi has been put in a position where his job is to know everything that's going on at IBM that relates to diversity - whether it falls under the director of diversity's purview or not.

Sinocchi bulleted at least half a dozen diversity-related issues IBM was tackling recently: from National Black Family Technology Awareness Week and the so-called Digital Divide (an official IBM diversity issue) to how accessibility issues for people with disabilities will affect the release of IBM's next generation voice-

Malignant Neglect: Managing Corporate Communications, Customer Service and Web Sites (cont'd.)

activation software.

"My 'beat' is diversity," Sinocchi said, using the journalist's slang for an area of expertise. "I need to be knowledgeable about our corporate diversity strategy and its (unofficial) linkage to each of the business units."

"This is the first time IBM has put an executive in this job," he added. "We used to have managers or media people. But (the company) wanted someone who could come in with experience from other areas." Sinocchi's last posting was with the personal computer division of IBM. He has also worked with the company's sales group and in other key units at IBM.

Much like the ideal marketing executive, Sinnochi is supposed to have his nose in every aspect of the business. That's why even though the diversity group he works for consists of less than 100 people, the "extended team" numbers in the hundreds, he said. For example, if Sinnochi is asked detailed questions about the digital divide this week, he already has a senior African-American executive lined up to provide the best perspective on that issue.

"I could tell you about the digital divide myself, but I'd rather have Rod Adkins (of IBM Software and co-chair of Black Family Technology Awareness Week) tell you about it," he said. "It just makes sense for us to use people who are experts in the subject area. IBM is so big, and there are a lot of things that touch diversity that might get lost in the mix if we didn't utilize this approach."

Customer Service

Even when the most competent professionals are the ones communicating a company's diversity message, that message is still at the mercy of the reporter who writes the story. Not so with customer service, one of the few areas where a corporation has complete control over what messages it sends. And one of the most basic messages a company can send, based on the quality of the service it delivers, is "we care about you."

Consultants at Boston-based Patricia Seybold Group call this "quality of customer experience," or QCE. Principal Patricia Seybold has written several books on the subject, the latest of which is called "The Customer Revolution."

"QCE is basically a discipline whereby executives and managers measure and monitor the quality of the customer experience," said Ronni Marshak, a co-author of Seybold's book and a senior vice president with the firm. "For example, as opposed to measuring how many calls were taken by a call center within an hour, QCE says 'the customers don't care' ... But they would care very much what

Malignant Neglect: Managing Corporate Communications, Customer Service and Web Sites (cont'd.)

native language was spoken."

Marshak used two examples to stress the bottom-line benefits of having a customer focus. Tesco is the most successful supermarket chain in the United Kingdom. One of the keys to its success is a chart in the back of every store that keeps track of customer-satisfaction levels and is updated daily, she said. In the United States, Cisco Systems is another success story built on customer service. Cisco employees wear customer-satisfaction levels and goals on their badges, Marshak said. And CEO John Chambers reportedly spends 80 percent of his time with customers while requiring all executives to spend 50 percent of their time "face to face with customers" as well, she said.

Cisco is far from a model of diversity management, partially because the switch-and-router supplier serves one of worst-ranked industries in terms of employment diversity. In 2000, DiversityInc.com took a look at the biggest names on the Fortune e-50 (a ranking of the biggest players in the Internet economy) and found that while Asian Americans consists of anywhere from 15 percent to 20 percent of the average tech-company workforce, African-American and Latino representation is consistently 3 percent to 7 percent.

But Cisco's strategy can be applied as a part of diversity management strategy as well. After all, if customer satisfaction is king - and census 2000 has shown that one-third of all customers under 40 are not white - then culturally competent service should also be king. Verizon Communications is one company that understands this well.

Verizon headquarters is in New York, one of the most diverse cities in the nation. Queens and Kings counties in New York City occupy the No. 1 and No. 3 spots on the list of most diverse counties in the nation with populations over 100,000, according to San Diego-based market-research firm Claritas. "Select a person from Queens and almost three out of four times, the second person selected will be of a different race/ethnic category," Ken Hodges, director of demography at Claritas, told DiversityInc.com last summer.

Recognizing the increasing diversity of New York, Verizon predecessor AT&T established a Spanish-language call center there in 1969. It was staffed with eight customer-service representatives and one manager. Today, Verizon's Multilingual Center has 783 representatives and 75 managers that cater to customers speaking half a dozen languages, including two dialects of Chinese.

There's also a call center staffed and managed by people with disabilities who can relate to the customer-service issues experienced by people with disabilities,

Malignant Neglect: Managing Corporate Communications, Customer Service and Web Sites (cont'd.)

said Gabriela Ulloa, a facilitation manager for the Multilingual Center. "It's a very interesting place to go and visit," Ulloa said. "There is one person who is blind, and one person who is deaf. They have state of the art equipment available to them, so there are no limitations as far as their work. It's amazing to see the things they accomplish there."

Multicultural Center staffers come from, and remain close to, the communities they serve. They also do double and triple duty, attending ethnic events, such as New York's Lunar New Year celebration, and providing the marketing department with input on the cultural accuracy of its advertisements. Ulloa said she was once asked to view the shooting of a Verizon commercial to make sure it was adequately representing the Latino community.

The payoff for Verizon has been undeniable. Like all call centers, the Multicultural Center competes for sales awards and customer-satisfaction ratings. "Our customers are very pleased, and we always get the highest numbers as far as customer satisfaction," Ulloa said. "In 2001, we were also rated the top team in sales for the major metropolitan area, which includes New York and Pennsylvania."

A strategy as highly developed as Verizon's is ideal, but not every company can afford to match the diversity of its customers - particularly if it is global in scope, Marshak said. In lieu of this, she proposed developing ways to automate cultural competency at call centers.

For example, many call centers have staff read from scripts when handling certain kinds of calls. Such scripts are most often used for telemarketing purposes, she said, but why not use them for cultural purposes? Moreover, caller ID is a sophisticated technology that could allow a company to associate known phone numbers with client profiles. Such technology is already used to help distinguish "gold-level customers" from regular customers, she said. But it could be used for so much more.

Marshak envisions technological solutions so sophisticated that a customer-service representative could tell "that a Japanese wife likes to be addressed informally while the husband prefers you use 'san' (Japanese courtesy title) after his name."

"Ultimately, most companies are dealing with a limited number of cultures, demographics or psychographics," she said. "So they can focus and really understand what makes for an excellent customer experience."

Malignant Neglect: Managing Corporate Communications, Customer Service and Web Sites (cont'd.)

Web Sites

DiversityInc.com has already covered in detail the inadvertent messages corporate Web sites can send about a company's diversity commitment. In a comprehensive two-part report on the subject, AT&T's supplier diversity Web site was highlighted as a prime example of bad content management. Looking at its "milestones" page, one would think AT&T stopped caring about minority- and women-owned businesses in 1998, because that's the date of the last entry shown.

DiversityInc.com reported this embarrassing fact in November, shortly after AT&T Supplier Diversity Director G. Winston Smith took home a major National Minority Supplier Development Council (NMSDC) award. Thus, another message was sent: Smith's award is not a noteworthy milestone. Moreover, AT&T hasn't updated the site in the three months since the story ran, sending yet another message - and so on.

Like the person who answers the phone when reporters or customers call, those who create and manage Web sites need proper training in order to effectively communicate diversity messages. As the Websense example illustrates, technology requires the same degree of vigilance applied to other areas of diversity management.

Reaching Latinos Requires Greater Marketing Budgets, Study Finds

By Ruth Zeilberger

© 2003 DiversityInc.com

April 07, 2003

Corporations are missing a big chunk of the Latino market as a result of inadequate advertising budgets, claims the Association of Hispanic Advertising Agencies (AHAA), and a new report aims to serve as a guide toward maximizing the potential of the Latino buying power.

"Corporate America is severely under-spending against our [Latino] buying power," said Ingrid Otero-Smart, president of AHAA. "You have a market that is significantly affecting corporations' bottom line, and yet they are not speaking to them."

Last year, AHAA released "Missed Opportunities: Vast Corporate Underspending in the U.S. Hispanic Market." The study concluded that for maximum effectiveness, corporations should be allocating a minimum of 8 percent of their total national marketing budgets to the Spanish-dominant and bilingual markets. It also revealed that among the top 50 leading Latino advertisers, current spending targeting Latinos across all categories is approximately 3.2 percent of national budgets – well below the 8 percent recommended threshold.

The AHAA released recommendations Friday on how to set appropriate spending targets based on media usage, consumption data and population data. Latinos, for example, over-index in consumption of most food categories, requiring resource allocations well above their actual representation of Spanish-dominant and bilingual households. To reach Spanish-dominant and bilingual households across top Latino markets commensurate with existing household food consumption budgets, the AHAA concluded that instant coffee and yogurt companies, for example, should direct about $1 out of every $3 in marketing resources.

"The biggest under-spenders are the health-care companies, financial services, electronic companies and travel industry," said Otero-Smart.

"There is a big misconception about Hispanic spending power," she said. "Most of the companies understand the demographics by now. But what they don't understand is the real economic power of the market. They say to me, 'Yes, there are a significant number of Hispanics, but can they really afford our products?'

Reaching Latinos Requires Greater Marketing Budgets, Study Finds (cont'd.)

We're hoping that this study helps shatter some of those misconceptions."

Significant findings in the study include:

- Latino households use more health and beauty care products than non-Latino households and require resource allocations for sales, marketing, advertising, promotions, public-relations, events and sponsorships 50 percent to 100 percent higher than their actual representation of Spanish and bilingual households in those markets.

- Latinos' consumption of children's products is driven by the higher presence of young children in Latino homes. Just to stay in the game with equal share of market and to deliver continued volume growth, children's products urgently call for allocations much higher (100 percent to 350 percent) than the actual representation of Spanish and bilingual households, or up to $1 out over every $2 spent on marketing.

- Categories such as athletic shoes and jeans require allocations 50 percent above their representation of Spanish and bilingual households. To reach the level spending should be close to $1 in every $4 of marketing resources.

- Until the recent upswing in Latino homeownership (already on par with African Americans), insurance has been an under-developed category relative to Spanish-dominant and bilingual households. While investment rates are slightly below household totals, these investments require significant increases over current rates.

- Family-friendly minivans, pick-up trucks and entry-level compacts warrant 25 percent to50 percent higher allocations than the household share of Spanish/bilingual households.

The Latino market's current size, formation of larger households, heavy concentration in the top, youngest, trendsetting markets in the United States, accompanied by their speedy wealth creation, and high consumerism are at odds with the neglect of investment in most categories, concluded the AHAA.

"Corporations need to redefine their allocation paradigm," said Otero-Smart. "They cannot just take it for granted that they are reaching the Hispanic market."

Part III: Corporate Communications

Is Spanish-Language TV Still Best Way to Reach Latino Viewers?

By Angela D. Johnson

© 2003 DiversityInc.com

March 14, 2003

Based on Nielsen Ratings, it can be easy to assume that the U.S. Latino population is only watching Spanish-language television. The top 20 shows on the National Hispanic Television Index, a service Nielsen Media Research started in 1992 to monitor Latino viewing patterns, most often are telenovelas on Univision.

An analysis of Nielsen data from the 2001-2002 programming season released in August by Initiative Media, a New York-based media-services company, finds that the highest-rated English-language network program (UPN's "WWE Smackdown!") appeared at number 44 on the list of programs Latinos watched that season. However, when Latino ratings of prime-time programming from just the top six networks (ABC, CBS, NBC, FOX, UPN and WB) were evaluated, general-market programs such as "Friends" and "E.R." held places in the top 10.

So Latinos are watching general-market primetime programming, but when it comes to developing media plans to reach Latino viewers, general-market shows rarely are included in the mix.

"[Advertising] agencies are saying if you want to reach the Latino market, they can be reached through Spanish-speaking networks," said Alex Nogales, president and CEO of the National Hispanic Media Coalition. "The evidence doesn't show that."

209

Is Spanish-Language TV Still Best Way to Reach Latino Viewers? (cont'd.)

Top 20 Primetime Programs Among Latinos (October 2001-May 2002)	
1	Amigas Y Rivales-Tue
2	Amigas Y Rivales-Mon
3	Amigas Y Rivales-Wed
4	Amigas Y Rivales-Thurs
5	Por Un Beso-Wed
6	Por Un Beso-Thu
7	Amigas Y Rivales-Fri
8	Por Un Beso-Tue
9	Por Un Beso-Fri
10	Por Un Beso-Mon
11	Derecho De Nacer-Mon
12	Derecho De Nacer-Tues
13	Derecho De Nacer-Wed
14	Salome-Wed
15	Derecho De Nacer-Fri
16	Salome-Tues
17	Salome-Thurs
18	Salome-Mon
19	Derecho De Nacer-Thu
20	Salome-Fri

* All shows are Univision programs

Source: IM Futures analysis of Nielsen Media Research data

Nogales said Latino youth are driving the viewing habits of their families. "When you have a TV set in the house and you have children, at a certain point it will be the kids monopolizing the television," he said.

Nogales contended that Nielsen needs to factor in acculturation levels in its Latino pool, because as this population acculturates, its language preferences will lean more toward English. Given the recent census data that stated that roughly 43 percent of the Latino population (about 16 million of the 37 million U.S. Latinos) is foreign-born, Nogales believes a lower percentage of Latinos are watching Spanish-language programming.

The coalition has meet with Nielsen executives several times, but it's still not satisfied with the company's research methods, Nogales said. Karen Gyimesi, vice president of marketing for Nielsen, said the methodology is solid, and added that the company has provided adequate information to the coalition about how it conducts research.

The National Hispanic Television Index surveys 800 Latino households made up of a population that has self-identified as Latino. Each participating household agrees to have a people meter, a device which sends viewing data to Nielsen on a daily basis, attached to its televisions. Nielsen wouldn't provide statistics on language preference of its Latino participants, but the company said the pool mirrors census language-preference data (51 percent Spanish-dominant, 35 percent

Is Spanish-Language TV Still Best Way to Reach Latino Viewers? (cont'd.)

English dominant, and 13 percent preferring Spanish and English equally).

However, studies by other organizations offer different findings. According to the Pew Hispanic Center, just 38 percent of Latinos watch or listen to predominantly Spanish-language programming, while 36 percent of Latinos watch or listen to predominantly English-language programming, and 26 percent of Latinos watch or listen to Spanish and English-language programming equally.

But despite this research, many marketers maintain that the Latino population still is Spanish-dominant.

"The assimilation model has not worked in the Hispanic market," said Raul Lopez, chief operating officer of the Cultural Access Group, a market-research and consulting firm in Los Angeles. "My parents, who have been here 40-plus years, still depend on Spanish-language TV."

Adriana Waterston, director of marketing for Horowitz Associates, a company in Larchmont, N.Y. that studies the Latino market and media usage, agreed that the Latino population often is seen as homogeneous, but she challenged Nogales' theory about youth influence on household television viewing. Because many Latino homes are multigenerational, many young Latinos are living with immigrant and first-generation parents and grandparents who are more likely to prefer Spanish-language programming.

"It's not an either or situation," said Waterston. "There's opportunity for all types of programming."

"There is no one answer (to the best way to reach Latinos)," said Lopez. "Part of the population needs to be addressed in English and a large part needs to be addressed in Spanish." But ultimately, Lopez said, both groups need to be addressed in a culturally competent manner.

Tony Ruiz, partner of the New York-based Latino advertising agency The Vidal Partnership, agreed that both English- and Spanish-language programming should be used to reach Latinos; however, he offered a caveat. "Hispanic viewing of general market TV is highly fragmented over the many broadcast and cable viewing choices they have. In the past we have taken our clients' general-market TV schedules and posted them with Hispanic Nielsen data and found the schedules delivered between 19 percent and 34 percent of their grp [gross ratings point] goal against Hispanics."

Roy Cosme, president of New York-based Latino-marketing firm Arcos Communications, agreed. "Latinos do watch some of the highly-rated shows ....

Is Spanish-Language TV Still Best Way to Reach Latino Viewers? (cont'd.)

They're watching 'Friends' and 'Bernie Mac', but if [advertisers use general-market TV] exclusively, they would not be reaching the Latino market."

Most Latino advertising budgets aren't large enough to afford ad time during general-market prime-time programming, said John Doscher, executive vice president and director of strategic planning for New Perspectives Media, the Miami-based media-planning and buying unit of advertising giant GlobalHue. Nielsen ratings are used to determine how much networks can charge for advertising time during their shows. The higher the rating, the more it costs to advertise during the program because the commercials have the potential to reach more consumers.

According to Advertising Age's survey of prime-time ad pricing during fall 2002, a 30-second spot during "CSI," a top CBS program, cost $280,043. The cost of ad time on Spanish-language shows, which have lower Nielsen ratings than network primetime programming, is considerably lower.

But what about the young Latino population that's positioned to become the next generation of adult consumers? Will their preference for English-language television prompt advertisers to shift from a Spanish-language to an English-language strategy?

Top 20 Primetime Programs by Demographic (October 2001-May 2002)	
Latino Households	**Non-Latino Households**
WWE Smackdown! (UPN)	**CSI** (CBS)
Friends (NBC)	**Friends** (NBC)
Simpsons (FOX)	**E.R.** (NBC)
Monday Night Football (ABC)	Everybody Loves Raymond (CBS)
Malcolm in the Middle (FOX)	**Law and Order** (NBC)
E.R. (NBC)	Survivor: Marquesas (CBS)
George Lopez (ABC)	Survivor: Africa (CBS)
Fear Factor (NBC)	West Wing (NBC)
Wonderful World of Disney (ABC)	**Monday Night Football** (ABC)
Bernie Mac (FOX)	*Leap of Faith* (NBC)
CSI (CBS)	Becker (CBS)
Will & Grace (NBC)	**Will & Grace** (NBC)
The Bachelor (ABC)	Law And Order: SVU (NBC)
Leap of Faith (NBC)	60 Minutes (CBS)
Titus (FOX)	Jag (CBS)
Law and Order (NBC)	Judging Amy (CBS)
That '70s Show (FOX)	Just Shoot Me (NBC)
Love Cruise (FOX)	*Inside Schwartz* (NBC)
Futurama (FOX)	King of Queens (CBS)
Inside Schwartz (NBC)	Frasier (NBC)

Bold: Top 20 program for Latinos and Non-Latinos
Italicized: Cancelled

Source: IM Futures analysis of Nielsen Media Research data

Is Spanish-Language TV Still Best Way to Reach Latino Viewers? (cont'd.)

Latino market specialists predicted that Spanish will remain relevant to younger Latinos.

"Hispanic ethnicity is an important cultural cue," said Alisse Waterston, president of Surveys Unlimited, the social, cultural and ethnic market research division of Horowitz Associates. "Politics and society influences whether Spanish-language interest continues as young Latinos age …. The importance of ethnic politics has given rise to the importance of maintaining one's culture."

Lopez said the ongoing impact of Latino immigration will keep advertisers from making a shift to only using English-language programming to reach the Latino market.

"If that happens, it would happen very slowly," said Lopez. "There will always be a young immigrant population. The pool of Spanish-dependent young people is constantly being replenished."

Part III: Corporate Communications

Mixed Messages: How 'Ethnic' Ads Succeed With, Then Transcend Niche Markets

By Kipp Cheng

B y now, every executive has seen the research data that shows the changing face of the American consumer. However, it's the smart suit that has figured out how to leverage the demographic information and deliver a vital message or value proposition to an underserved market, and then take that message to the masses.

A handful of companies – H&R Block, Gateway, Lincoln-Mercury and the U.S. Postal Service – are examples of companies that have successfully launched multicultural-marketing initiatives over the past year.

The results of their targeted campaigns were revealed on Tuesday during a panel discussion, "The Changing Face of Advertising," held at the Time/Life Building in New York City. Developed by marketing and advertising agencies that specialize in targeting multicultural consumers, the multicultural efforts highlight a growing trend of companies working to integrate niche campaigns with general-market programs.

The panelists included Carlos Ayala, manager of multicultural marketing at H&R Block; Hector Placencia, director of growth markets at Gateway; Mark Robertson, group account director for Lincoln/Mercury at UniWorld Group; and Jeannie Yuen, president and CEO of A-Partnership for the USPS.

The discussion was sponsored by trade groups The Ad Club of New York and Multicultural Marketing Resources and moderated by Laurel Wentz, international and multicultural editor at Advertising Age.

Emphasizing the changing demographic of consumers in this country, panelists expressed concern that mainstream agencies frequently ignore the spending power and cultural impact of diverse consumers, leading multicultural agencies to perform advocacy work about the importance of reaching out to diverse markets.

"The only way there can be progress is if marketers are committed to multicultural marketing," said Robertson.

According to Robertson, who oversees marketing initiatives for the Lincoln-Mercury brand of cars, the highest level of growth for the auto industry will be in

Mixed Messages: How 'Ethnic' Ads Succeed With, Then Transcend Niche Markets (cont'd.)

ethnic markets in the coming years. Automakers who do not initiate programs that address these groups will lose out on a booming market opportunity, he said

In 2001, U.S. marketers spent $2.1 billion to target the Latino market; $1.5 billion on the African-American market; and $254 million on Asian-American initiatives.

Proving that tapping diverse consumers is critical to a company's business strategy is difficult at times because of the dearth of data. However, as evidenced by the four case studies presented during the panel discussion, the speakers said major marketers are seeing the positive results of multicultural-marketing programs and slowly are starting to increase their spending on emerging, ethnic markets.

Familiar Brands for Unfamiliar Markets

For marketers looking to reach out to ethnic consumers who had been previously underserved, the notion that all brands are universal is wrong.

"There's an assumption that brands with strong general market awareness and appeal will translate equally well in ethnic segments," said Gateway's Placencia. "But that's simply not true."

Since 1999, Gateway – one of the first PC makers to address Latinos – has developed marketing initiatives aimed at the Latino market. Placencia said market research showed that Latino households purchase PCs for their homes at twice the rate of the general market. But when it came time to create TV commercials for the Latino market, Placencia said it was not merely a case of translating English spots into Spanish. The look, feel and messaging were altered to better appeal to Latino consumers.

Placencia noted that Gateway's success in marketing to Latino consumers was directly tied to the company's commitment to integrating Spanish-language into all layers of the purchasing cycle, including bilingual customer service, tech support and sales.

Meanwhile, brands that boast high recognition among consumers in the general market, such as H&R Block, may not necessarily have the same level of brand awareness or recognition among diverse markets. H&R Block's Ayala said the financial-services company learned this the hard way.

"The Hispanic market was new [for H&R Block]," Ayala said. "It's been slow steps into the market. We were willing to learn from our mistakes."

Ayala said there have been "some bumps in the road" as H&R Block made a concerted effort to reach out to Latino consumers. Because of H&R Block's high

Mixed Messages: How 'Ethnic' Ads Succeed With, Then Transcend Niche Markets (cont'd.)

brand awareness in the general market – it is the fourth largest retail network and the ninth most recognized brand in the United States – there was an assumption that Latino consumers would also have the same brand awareness.

However, after an initial commercial aired and received a lukewarm reception, new TV spots were developed to better connect with Latino consumers, emphasizing the service's relevance and value. H&R Block has seen 5 percent growth in the Latino market in 2001, but Ayala said it's too soon to say how the new commercials will impact the growth in business.

But Will It Play in Peoria?

One of the benefits of developing advertising campaigns for segment markets is that creative work can sometimes transcend the intended niche and graduate to general market appeal.

A-Partnership's Yuen said that's precisely what happened with a TV commercial for the U.S. Postal Service aimed at Asian-American, small-business owners. The spot, which featured humorous scenes from a day in the life of a small business operated by Asian-Americans, was so successful with its target audience that the USPS moved the campaign into the general market. The commercial has since picked up numerous creative awards.

The key to developing creative work that translates between language and culture, according to Yuen, is to focus on the mindset of a consumer, rather than filling an ad with cultural cues. Yuen cited the difference between Asian-American advertising and Asian Advertising. The former is often filled with cultural cues, such as chopsticks and Chinese restaurants, while the latter does not consider race but focuses instead on the client's product or service.

"In China, there's no such thing as a Chinese restaurant," Yuen joked.

Indeed, Yuen said the success of the TV commercial for the USPS was that it didn't linger on ethnicity or language (there's a fleeting shot of the office door with Chinese characters), but instead sold the value proposition of the USPS to small-business owners.

Robertson said in some cities, an ethnic market is the general market, and to ignore this fact is shortsighted for companies.

"Thirty-seven percent of the U.S. is ethnic," Robertson said. "Diversity [in marketing] is not just about segmenting an audience, it's also about understanding and translating language and culture."

The Perfect Pulpit for Financial Education: One Thousand Churches Connected

By Eric L. Hinton

© 2003 DiversityInc.com

December 17, 2002

When the Rev. Johnny Miller of Chicago's Mount Vernon Baptist Church calls his parishioners together for worship, he has more than spiritual enlightenment on the agenda. Miller is one of a growing number of African-American clergy who view the church as vital to spreading the message of economic empowerment in communities of color.

"When the churches participate in matters of finance, it gives it a different flavor and brings about a different level of trust with people who otherwise wouldn't be present," said Miller.

Last year, Miller's church of approximately 1,000 parishioners joined forces with One Thousand Churches Connected. Launched by the Rev. Jesse Jackson under the umbrella of the Rainbow/PUSH coalition in 2001, the One Thousand Churches Connected is designed to bring the message of economic responsibility to families through churches across the country.

"I saw it as a source of unity that can be transforming," said Miller. "Every church that I've met that is part of One Thousand Churches is involved in some type of economic-empowerment program on an ongoing basis."

The idea is that the ongoing fight for equality is being staged on different battlefields. The First Movement was the struggle to end slavery; the Second Movement was the battle to end segregation; the Third Movement was the march to obtain full voting rights; the Fourth Movement is the quest for equal opportunity through shared economic security and empowerment.

"Rev. Jackson had the vision of creating One Thousand Churches Connected to complete the four stages of our symphony as a people," said Bonita Parker, national director of One Thousand Churches. "The fourth movement is to level the economic playing field. That's what we're working on right now. As part of that, one of the initiatives that play into that is the effort to engage churches to teach financial stewardship from the pulpit as an opportunity to educate our people."

Currently, there are 245 churches signed up in the program, said Parker. Once a church joins, the head of the church is invited to join Jackson and New York

The Perfect Pulpit for Financial Education: One Thousand Churches Connected (cont'd.)

Stock Exchange (NYSE) Chairman Richard Grasso at a quarterly meeting at the NYSE. At that meeting, each religious leader is given a crash course in different areas of financial services to take back to his or her parish.

"In order for them to be able to comfortably demystify financial markets when they return home, they need to have a working knowledge of these things themselves," said Parker. "So the ministers get a trip down to the NYSE where they spend two and half days getting training on the science of capital. Next, every church that joins receives access to all the materials we have on the four modules."

Those four modules are:

- Understanding credit and debt elimination: This encompasses establishing credit, understanding credit scoring and restoring credit.

- Mortgage and home ownership, which covers qualifying for a mortgage, understanding the loan-application process and avoiding predatory lenders.

- Understanding financial services: This includes a review of financial markets, brokerage services and investment clubs.

- Technology as an educational resource: This covers issues of the Internet and privacy as well as electronic-bill payment and transfers.

"We decided to join because the program already was stipulating many of the things that we were already doing by focusing on financial empowerment, but it consolidated many things instead of dealing with fragmented pieces as we had been doing," said Miller. "I saw this as a source of unity that is transforming. Every church that I've met that is part of One Thousand Churches is involved in some type of economic empowerment program on an ongoing basis."

The push to harness the collective economic might of African Americans is bearing some fruit.

In June, the 2002 Ariel/Schwab Black Investor Survey reported African Americans earning in excess of $50,000 annually are investing in the stock market in rapidly growing numbers. Seventy-four percent of "high-income" African Americans today own stocks or stock funds, 30 percent more than those first surveyed in 1998. Among non-investors, twice as many African Americans as whites (42 percent vs. 21 percent) say they are "somewhat" or "very" likely to begin investing next year.

"It's good news all the way around," said Carla A. Foster, vice president of

The Perfect Pulpit for Financial Education: One Thousand Churches Connected (cont'd.)

Specialized Segments Marketing for Charles Schwab & Co. Foster, an African American, has ongoing responsibility for African-American investor services at Schwab. "The biggest piece of news for us is that black participation in the stock market has increased significantly over the last five years. There's a greater attention to overall financial health because people are taking a big-picture view and getting their financial houses in order."

Parker believes the pulpit is the perfect perch from which to preach the importance of financial empowerment.

"The black church is the greatest learning institution for African Americans as a people. There are over 43,000 predominantly black churches in this country. Every Sunday, approximately 21 million African Americans come together so you have a captive audience. And financial stewardship is the single most talked about subject in the Bible, so it makes sense to be taught in the church. "

Miller agreed. In the time since his parish has joined One Thousand Churches, he has instituted a weekly "credit smart" class that provides parishioners with a needed crash course on the subject.

"About 12 people go to this class every Sunday instead of going to Sunday school. It talks about housing, economics and other areas of finance. It's like stepping outside of the box," said Miller. "Having this information is power."

The New Covenant Baptist Church of Orlando, Fla. will be hosting the Third Annual Small Church Conference, Jan. 30 and Feb. 1. Jeremiah Wright, the pastor of Trinity United Church of Christ in Chicago, is scheduled to be the keynote speaker at the event. Among the topics to be discussed is "Operating a Faith-Based, Not-for-Profit Corporation.

The New Trend in Marketing? In-Language Advertising Works Best for Latino Market

By Angela D. Johnson

© 2003 DiversityInc.com

April 03, 2003

Cincinnati, Ohio-based Procter & Gamble (P&G) made news earlier this year when it aired a Spanish-language commercial for its Crest Whitening Plus Scope toothpaste on the CBS broadcast of the Grammy Awards. The effort was designed to tap into the $580 billion in buying power in the Latino market, but it wasn't the only foreign-language commercial getting airtime on English-language networks.

Harbrew Imports, the Freeport, N.Y.-based U.S. distributor for Beijing's Yanjing Beer, began airing a Cantonese ad on the Madison Square Garden Network (MSG) in October. The spot features a man at a karaoke bar belting out a poor rendition of a song. As the audience begins to chant, "Encore, encore," the man thinks the audience wants him to sing another tune. In reality, they're asking for more Yanjing beer. The cast is entirely Asian, the jingle is in Cantonese and the ad closes with the Cantonese phrase, "Yanjing Pijiu (Yanjing Beer)."

Harbrew initially hired New York-based L3 Advertising to create advertising to capture a portion of what the Selig Center at the University of Georgia estimates as $296.4 billion in buying power in the Asian-American market. This spending power is expected to grow to $454.9 billion by 2007.

While Yanjing had an established reputation in the Asian-American market, Richard DeCicco, president of Harbrew Imports, said the general market had no preconceived notions about the brew. Harbrew decided to use the Asian-language ad to promote Yanjing to mainstream consumers, a market that Impact, an alcoholic beverage industry publication, reports spent more than $66 billion on beer between 2000 and 2001.

"The karaoke lifestyle is not out of range [with the general market]," said Joe Lam, president of L3 Advertising. He said the creative was designed to speak to the lifestyle and psychology of the Chinese-American market, but it expresses the universal element of having a good time that can appeal to a variety of consumers regardless of race or ethnicity.

Yanjing Beer currently is sold in roughly 30 markets including San Francisco,

The New Trend in Marketing? In-Language Advertising Works Best for Latino Market (cont'd.)

Los Angeles, Houston, Chicago, and Florida. The television ad airs mainly in the New York tri-state area, but also reaches viewers across the country who access the network through EchoStar's satellite Dish Network. Harbrew hopes that American consumers will embrace Yanjing in the same manner that they have adopted other import beers, such as Corona.

Lam said much of the success of the Yanjing ad with the mainstream audience stems from the beer's relationship with the Houston Rockets, home of Chinese basketball player Yao Ming. Yanjing is the team's official import beer.

For Chinese-American viewers of MSG, Lam said seeing the commercial "is a pleasant surprise for them …. It's a reinforcement of the brand."

P&G's spot, created by San Antonio, Texas-based Bromley Communications, featured a young Latino couple starting their day. As the husband is rushing out the door for work he stops to give his wife, who is dressed in a bathrobe with a tube of Crest sticking out of the pocket, a kiss. The husband leaves, but quickly returns for additional kisses. The dialogue is in Spanish except for the closing tag line: "White teeth. Fresh Breath. In Any Language."

"The spot was pretty universal as far as people being able to understand the spot visually," said Ernest Bromley, president of Bromley Communications.

Daisy Exposito, president of New York-based Latino marketing agency the Bravo Group, said the Crest spot that aired in February was not the first example of a Spanish-language ad on mainstream television. In 1978, Pepsi-Cola aired its first Spanish-language commercial during the Grammy's and in the early 1990s, AT&T ran an in-language spot featuring Latino singer Jon Secada during the same awards show.

Lam said he wasn't aware of any other companies that have aired Asian-language advertising on general market television and he doesn't see it as an effective overall strategy to reach Asian or mainstream markets. With just a portion of the Latino market viewing mainstream television in significant numbers, most marketers find using targeted advertising on general market television to be ineffective as well.

However, Cesar Melgoza, president of Geoscape International in Miami, sees some value in P&G's strategy. "It's going to seem expensive but what they're getting in return may be long term and quite intangible. I think a return on investment from a mathematical or dollars and cents point of view is probably missing the point. It's more of an investment in brand loyalty and awareness."

The New Trend in Marketing? In-Language Advertising Works Best for Latino Market (cont'd.)

And while some see running a Spanish-language ad on a general-market station as an effective strategy to reach some Latinos, Exposito cautions against expecting to see more Spanish-language ads in the mainstream. "I think that we are seeing more and more in-culture, not in-language (advertising). I do think, however, that as more and more programming opportunities arrive and if the percentage of the Hispanic audience is significant within certain programs, yeah, you might begin to see more of that happening."

Bromley sees the potential for more in-language ads "on a spot basis than a national network basis. It's been true for quite some time along the border broadcast markets. But as you move more into the urban centers, Los Angeles and Houston and San Antonio, you may see it happening a little more often than you would now."

Bromley also predicts that as television broadcast moves further in to digital broadcast multicasting it won't be unusual to see CBS affiliates running television commercials and programs in Spanish. "That's a few years away though, but that's a trend we'll be seeing more and more as traditional English-language stations in markets like Los Angeles are going to be grappling with market share."

Chase Plans $500B in Home Loans to Diverse Markets; Community Leaders to Help

By Elena Maria Lopez

© *2003 DiversityInc.com*

February 05, 2003

The nation's No. 2 bank, JPMorgan Chase, has announced plans to make a $500-billion commitment to the minority and underserved home-mortgage markets over the next seven years. The company hopes the large lending commitment will double its presence in these markets and it intends to seek advice from community leaders on the most successful ways to reach out to their constituencies. JPMorgan Chase said this is the largest initiative to date for single-family mortgages to these segments of the market. It will be offered through its Chase Manhattan Mortgage Corporation subsidiary.

The $500 billion will double the amount of capital JPMorgan Chase currently lends to the minority and underserved home-mortgage markets. In 2002, the company floated about $35 billion of capital to these markets. According to the newly announced plan, this amount should be more than $70 million a year by 2010.

Chase currently is the No. 4 mortgage originator in the United States, with a market share of about 5 percent. Although these numbers change quarterly, the company tends to range between No. 2 and No. 4. With this announcement, the company hopes to achieve about 10 percent of the market share by 2010.

The company hopes to overturn the traditional barriers mainstream corporations have faced entering emerging and underserved markets by gaining the help of community leaders and organizations. Chase has created the National Housing Advisory Council to assist and deal with relevant issues. The council is comprised of real-estate professionals and influential leaders in the African-American, Latino, Asian-American and gay and lesbian communities.

In creating the Chase Dream Maker Commitment, JPMorgan Chase said it is responding to President Bush's call to make homeownership available to all members of society but economics and the need for new customers clearly drives this decision as well.

The president wants to increase minority homeownership by 5.5 million households by the end of the decade. This commitment includes single-family home

Chase Plans $500B in Home Loans to Diverse Markets; Community Leaders to Help (cont'd.)

mortgages, refinancing and home-equity loans and lines of credit.

Why have these markets traditionally been underserved? "There is not a lack of 'available money,'" said JPMorgan Chase spokesperson Kristen Batteria. "There is a shortage of lenders who are serving these markets with the appropriate products, services, staff and commitment."

Minority and other underserved markets offer the highest growth opportunities, said Batteria.

Regardless of tough economic times for the corporation, JPMorgan Chase's mortgage division had a record volume of $155 billion in mortgages and home loans in 2002. In the past several months, the company announced anticipated layoffs worldwide, which may be up to 10,000 by the year's end. Mostly investment-bank and technology-support positions lost money.

"They've been beat up pretty, pretty badly," said Kurt Kendis, managing director of The Banking Group in Kimberton, Pa. and a former economics professor at the Wharton School of Business at the University of Pennsylvania. "Their bread-and-butter business at JPMorgan Chase was on the commercial side." With the deterioration of the commercial-credit market, it appears that Chase is moving into the consumer market "to make a buck," continued Kendis.

"It's a very smart business move in addition to being the right thing to do," said Steve Cook, vice president of public relations at the National Association of Realtors. "The simple fact that minority homeownership remains below 50 percent in this country suggests that there's a need." Cook said 2002 was the largest year to date in terms of the amount of homes sold in the United States.

The 2000 U.S. Census reports that 68.3 percent of the 104.7 million U.S. households own their own homes. For white households, 74.8 percent of the 78.8 million households own their own homes. But only 49.5 percent of the 9.3 million Latino households and 47.5 percent of 12.5 million African-American households own their own homes.

Despite the economy, home sales continue to be strong. According to the Federal Reserve, the first three quarters of 2002 experienced double-digit increases in home-mortgage debt by Americans, with increases ranging from 10.3 percent to 12.8 percent. The Fed also reported that Americans had $5.85 trillion in outstanding home-mortgage debt over that same period. This debt includes traditional home mortgages, as well as refinancing, home-improvement and home-equity loans.

Chase Plans $500B in Home Loans to Diverse Markets; Community Leaders to Help (cont'd.)

About 69 percent of white home-loan applicants secured loans in 2001, according to a Federal Financial Institutions Examination Council (FFIEC) report. Only 57 percent of Latino applicants and 43 percent of African-American applicants secured loans at the end of the mortgage process, according to the report.

The FFIEC reported that African Americans accounted for 6 percent of all home-loan applications in 2001, but only 4.2 percent of the home loans secured. Latinos accounted for 7 percent of all home-loan applications and 6.5 percent of all home loans. White households accounted for 61 percent of the home-loan applications in 2001 and 68 percent of all home loans.

The FFIEC is an interagency body reporting to the Federal Reserve System, the Federal Deposit Insurance Corporation (FDIC), the National Credit Union Administration, the Office of the Comptroller of the Currency and the Office of Thrift Supervision.

Currently about 30 percent of JPMorgan Chase's mortgage business stems from the minority or underserved market. With this initiative, Chase expects this market to represent between 35 percent and 40 percent of its total home-mortgage business. This initiative increases single-family home loans to people of color of various economic backgrounds, low-to-moderate income borrowers, and new immigrant families.

Chase has made an effort to reach these customers over the last two years, including low closing costs, low downpayments, downpayments for those with limited credit, and multilanguage documents. The company also plans to offer a wider range of services to customers and potential customers, including expanded language capabilities, referrals to credit-counseling agencies and programs to increase financial literacy. Chase also intends to address predatory-lending practices through community and marketing information. Predatory-lending refers to subprime lenders that lend to high-risk individuals at an increased and often unfair lending rate.

Chase also has doubled the number of salespersons in these markets, increasing their racial and ethnic diversity, the company said. The company also plans to increase its physical presence in urban markets in New York, California, Texas, Washington, D.C., Illinois, Georgia and Pennsylvania.

The Right Clicks: Top Corporate Web Sites for Diversity for 2002

By Kipp Cheng

© 2003 DiversityInc.com

October 16, 2002

Since the fall of 2001, DiversityInc.com has critiqued the corporate Web sites of the nation's largest corporations. Some Web sites have done top-notch jobs at conveying the importance and bottom-line benefits of fostering workplace- and supplier-diversity initiatives, while others have faltered.

The mixed results serve as an accurate reflection of the state of diversity programs and initiatives in U.S. business today. Although communicating a commitment to diversity may or may not represent actual follow-through on diversity programs, it's clear that companies that care about diversity also herald their achievements via their communications and marketing programs. And there's no denying that a corporate Web site is a vital communications platform for any business, disseminating information to a wide and varied constituency.

In revisiting the dozens of Web sites reviewed over the past year, as well as some new entries – this time around paying special attention to the ease of locating a company's diversity message – we have selected the best from the rest.

Here are the companies that made it on to this year's all-star list of the top corporate Web sites for diversity. It's an eclectic roundup of players: the companies come from a variety of industries, are globally and locally based, and range in revenue from several million to several billion of dollars annually. Although the approaches to communicating diversity differ, what each has in common is clarity and consistency of conveying companywide commitments to diversity, as well as focused and appealing approaches to site layout and design.

When it comes to effectively communicating a commitment to diversity, the following corporate Web sites set the standard within their respective industries.

And now, this year's All-Star Web Sites for Diversity:

PSEG (Based in Newark, N.J.) Grade: A+

Simplicity and focus are the keywords for the corporate Web site of Public Service Enterprise Group, the Newark, N.J.-based energy-utility company known as PSEG. Site visitors seeking information about workplace- and supplier-diversity programs can access relevant links directly from the homepage, through the

231

The Right Clicks: Top Corporate Web Sites for Diversity for 2002 (cont'd.)

site's useful search engine, via pull-down menus or from the site map. This multioption navigation design allows for maximum exposure of topics of interest and relevance. It also conveys the sense that PSEG has done its homework when it comes to understanding how different people navigate through sites differently.

The Web site's overall design is clean but also incredibly detailed. A persistent top-level navigation bar helps to orient visitors as they click through pages, while pull-down menus throughout the site make for easier backtracking or flipping between subjects within a given section. Because diversity appears in numerous links – from the homepage and deeper into the site – it's virtually impossible to miss the numerous links to diversity information.

Beginning with an in-depth supplier-diversity section, PSEG effectively outlines its business case for working with diverse suppliers. The language is clear and not cluttered with corporate jargon. What's presented is a well-articulated invitation to minority- and women-owned business enterprises (WMBEs) to participate in PSEG's procurement programs.

"PSEG believes that Supplier Diversity makes good business sense," the site reads. "Developing a value-added, diverse-supplier base encourages job creation, enables purchasing power and builds shareholder equity." The words are plainly spoken and to the point, which is much appreciated when you consider the amount of diversity double-speak that saturates so many corporate Web sites.

Success stories and case studies about diverse suppliers supplement the supplier-diversity section of PSEG's site, giving interested MWBEs real-life examples of how the process works – and succeeds.

In the "Diversity at PSEG" section, diversity is defined as the "mutual respect and appreciation of the similarities and differences" between all PSEG stakeholders, including customers, employees and vendors. In addition to recognizing diversity of age, culture, education, ethnicity, experience, race, religion and sexual orientation, PSEG's diversity statement includes gender identity, an addition that only the most progressive companies include.

There are diversity statements from about a dozen top PSEG executives, but a minor quibble here is that no executives of color are represented and there is only a single woman at the president level. Still, the site effectively showcases PSEG's seemingly unwavering commitment to diversity. From myriad images of people color (and people with disabilities) throughout the site to the elegant design and clearly written language, PSEG's corporate Web site easily emerges as this year's MVP for Web site diversity.

The Right Clicks: Top Corporate Web Sites for Diversity for 2002 (cont'd.)

State Farm Insurance (2002 Fortune 500 Rank: 25) Grade: A

State Farm's engaging and easy-to-navigate corporate Web site puts diversity front and center. A link from the corporate homepage takes visitors to an in-depth series of links that effectively communicate the Bloomington, Ill.-based insurer's genuine interest and commitment to diversity.

A statement from Ed Rust Jr., State Farm's chairman and CEO, says, "we do more than acknowledge differences, we embrace them because they make us a stronger organization. They help us understand the marketplace, how we can do a better job of serving our customers." This focus on customers from diverse backgrounds is reinforced by the company's commitment to "bring diverse talents and experiences to our work of serving the State Farm customer."

Additionally, a statement on the site from Annette Martinez, assistant vice president, diversity, drives home the bottom-line benefits of diversity for State Farm. "At State Farm, diversity is not considered a program," Martinez says. "It's a way of doing business. By creating an inclusive environment where people are able to do their best work, we help to ensure our customers receive the top-quality products and services they deserve."

There's an entire section of the consumer site that's in Spanish, a reminder that State Farm encourages and recognizes Latino consumers to get more information. Awards include recognition by the Association of National Advertisers for State Farm's advertising campaign aimed at Asian-American customers, with one campaign targeting the Chinese-American community in Chinese language.

As for supplier diversity, State Farm's Web site gives detailed information for minority-, women- and people-with-disabilities-owned business enterprises, along with a Frequently Asked Questions and contact information for diverse suppliers interested in participating in State Farm's procurement programs.

Perhaps what's most impressive about State Farm's Web site is its ability to integrate images featuring diverse customers and employees throughout. This inclusive practice gives site visitors a sense that multiculturalism isn't just lip service for the company, it's a holistic part of the company's overall business strategy.

With $46.7 billion in revenue in 2001, State Farm is one of the nation's largest consumer property and casualty insurance companies, and its recognition of the importance of reaching out to emerging markets gives the company a marked advantage over insurers that have not yet communicated the same message of diversity and inclusion.

The Right Clicks: Top Corporate Web Sites for Diversity for 2002 (cont'd.)

Dell (2002 Fortune 500 Rank: 53) Grade: A

Technology companies are notorious for giving diversity programs short shrift, and PC makers, in particular, have acquired a reputation among those working in the diversity field as being especially negligence of addressing emerging markets.

But Round Rock, Texas-based Dell Computer is a happy exception to this unfortunate rule. The corporate Web site for Dell is a shining example of how a company can effectively address the issue of diversity with straightforward and compelling details about their diversity programs.

From the homepage, a direct link to "Diversity at Dell" leads visitors to a message from Michael Dell, the company's chairman and CEO. "At Dell, recruiting and retaining highly skilled men and women with diverse backgrounds is a business performance strategy," Dell says. "Diversity enhances our competitiveness in today's global marketplace. It fosters innovation, creativity and solutions. In a nutshell, it helps the bottom line."

The founder credits diversity as "one of the reasons Dell is the world's leading direct compute-systems company and the fastest growing among all major computer companies." Having buy-in for diversity from the top gives Dell Computers an edge over other companies that relegate diversity to "programs" rather than as an integrated business imperative.

With prominent, top-page links to sections on the company's diversity programs and supplier-diversity initiatives, it's clear that Dell (both the company and the chief executive) takes these issues seriously. From the corporate homepage, visitors can click on one of two links to sections of the Web site featuring diversity-related topics.

The spare design makes the Web site inviting and simple to navigate, and the entire site is written in language that's appealing without being patronizing. A search function located in the top navigation bar will help visitors who are searching for specific keywords. However, the left-hand navigation is well-designed and easy to use, making the search function an unnecessary but appreciated bonus.

Terms about supplier diversity are defined throughout the Web site, so a diverse supplier can understand what it takes to participate in Dell's supplier programs. A "roadmap" to procurement opportunities for diverse suppliers further simplifies the process of gathering information from the site.

Overall, Dell's communication of its commitment to diversity on its site puts it ahead of the pack of other technology companies that lag in the diversity sphere.

The Right Clicks: Top Corporate Web Sites for Diversity for 2002 (cont'd.)

McDonald's (2001 Fortune 500 Rank: 139) Grade: A

Perhaps the most impressive part of McDonald's corporate Web site is its knack of conveying a true commitment to diversity without appearing arrogant. Indeed, the numbers speak for themselves: "Minorities and women represent approximately 37 percent of all McDonald's franchisees in the United States. Minority franchisees operate more than 1,900 restaurants and women operate more than 2,000 McDonald's restaurants in the United States."

This understated approach suits the Oak Brook, Ill.-based fast-food giant. With more than $14 billion in revenue in 2001, McDonald's outpaces its nearest competitor by more than double in annual revenue.

In addition to having a well-thought-out corporate Web site, McDonald's also does a good job at integrating its communications messages. Not only does the site declare a commitment to supporting diverse employees and suppliers, as well as serving diverse customers, this message is reinforced by numerous consumer ads that showcase multicultural people.

McDonald's is the largest spender in the food-service sector in advertising aimed at African Americans, according to research firm CMR, which tracks national advertising. Numerous awards include being named one of the Top 25 Companies for People with Disabilities; Best Employer for Asians; Top 50 Places for Hispanic Women to Work, and Hispanic Magazine – Top 50 Corporate Women in America.

McDonald's corporate Web site delivers its message about diversity in an elegant and compelling manner, and is one example of consistency of message between a company's public and private facades.

Part IV - Emerging Markets

A. Buying Power

The present and future monetary power of emerging or multicultural markets is more apparent each year. With a projected decrease in the overall white-market share and the increase in each of the following emerging markets – Latinos, African Americans, Asian Americans, gay, lesbian, bisexual, transgender, and people with disabilities-smart businesses make increasing efforts to reach these customers.

Exactly what numbers are convincing marketers throughout corporate American to seek these demographics? And why is buying power important?

Buying power, also called spending power, is the amount of disposable personal income spent (after taxes) on personal consumption items.[108]

White consumer-market share is expected to decline from 87.4 percent in 1990 to 80.1 percent in 2007, market share for ethnic markets should see increases across the board, according to the Selig Center for Economic Growth at the University of Georgia. African-American

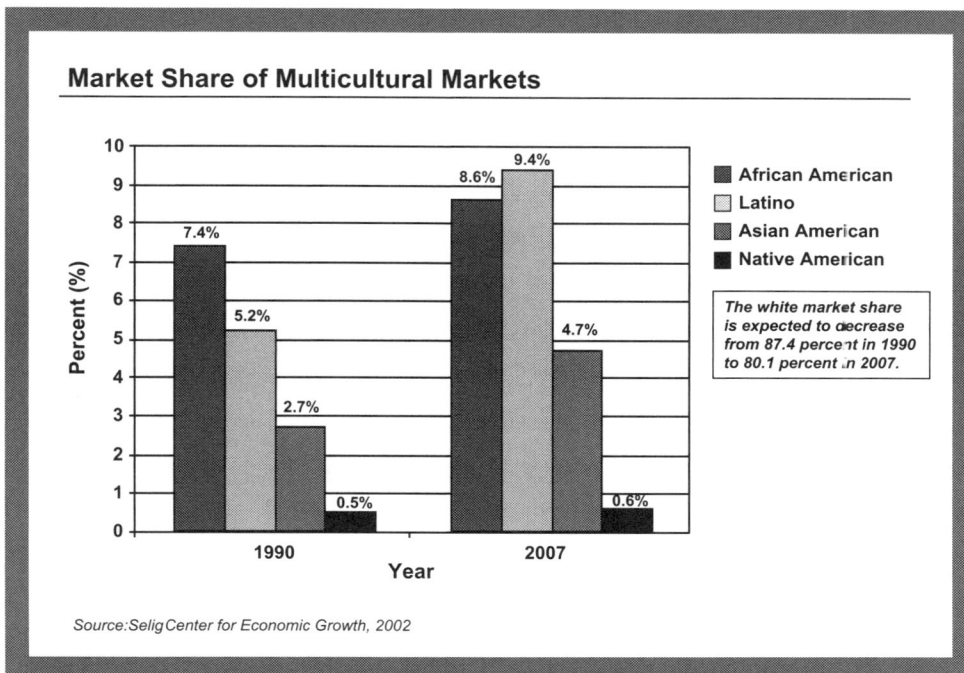

Market Share of Multicultural Markets

Legend:
- African American
- Latino
- Asian American
- Native American

The white market share is expected to decrease from 87.4 percent in 1990 to 80.1 percent in 2007.

Data (1990): African American 7.4%, Latino 5.2%, Asian American 2.7%, Native American 0.5%

Data (2007): African American 8.6%, Latino 9.4%, Asian American 4.7%, Native American 0.6%

Y-axis: Percent (%)
X-axis: Year (1990, 2007)

Source: Selig Center for Economic Growth, 2002

market share is expected to rise from 7.4 percent in 1990 to 8.6 percent in 2007; Latino market share should increase from 5.2 percent in 1990 to 9.4 percent in 2007; Asian-American market share should grow from 2.7 percent to 4.7 percent between 1990 and 2007.

The combined buying power of African Americans, Asian Americans and Native Americans in 2007, according to the Selig Center findings, should be more than triple its 1990 level of $453 billion, totaling almost $1.4 trillion. That represents an increase of more than 200 percent over the 17-year period. (Latinos as a group were excluded from this calculation because they can be of any race.)

Asian-American buying power is projected to reach $454.9 billion in 2007 (from $296.4 billion in 2002). African-American buying power is projected to reach $853 billion in 2007, up from $645.9 billion in 2002.

Total buying power for all U.S. consumers should rise from $4.3 trillion in 1990 to $9.9 trillion in 2007, according to the Selig Center data. Total U.S. buying power in 2002 was $7.6 trillion, according to Selig figures.

Growth of Multicultural Markets

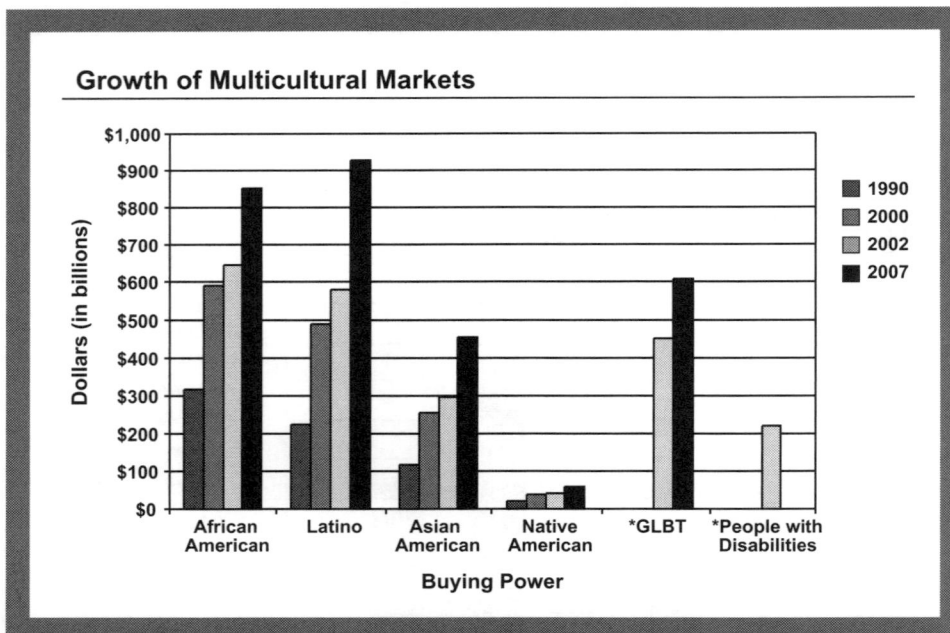

According to the Selig Center, buying power of the white market should increase by 112 percent between 1990 and 2007. In comparison, Asian-American buying power should increase by 287 percent, Native-American buying power should increase by 197 percent and African-American buying power should increase by 170 percent increase over that time.[109]

The combined buying power for these three groups will be 13.8 percent of the country's total buying power by 2007. This is an increase of 10.6 percent since 1990.[110]

The growing buying power for various multicultural groups is evident in increasing homeownership rates for these groups. From 1990 to 2000, homeownership rate for all U.S. households rose from 64.1 percent to 67.2 percent.[111]

1. African Americans

African-American buying power is projected to reach $852.8 billion in 2007 (from $645.9 billion in 2002). While African-American buying power was 7.4 percent of the market in 1990, it is expected to encompass 8.6 percent of the consumer buying market in 2007.[112]

In 2001, 33 percent of all African-American families had incomes of $50,000 or more, according to 2003 Census Bureau figures, and 52 percent of all African-American married-couple families had incomes of $50,000 or more. Twenty-seven percent of married African-American households earned more than $75,000 annually in 2001.[113]

When surveyed, 44 percent of African-American respondents reported household earnings below $30,000 annually, according to the 2002 Pew Hispanic Center study. The study also showed that while 30 percent of African-American households earned between $30,000 and $50,000 annually and 22 percent earned about $50,000 annually, 4 percent did not know their household incomes.[114]

By comparison, in 2001, 57 percent of white families had incomes of $50,000 or greater.[115] When surveyed, 29 percent of white respondents reported household earnings below $30,000 annually, according to a 2002 study conducted by the Pew Hispanic Center. The study also showed that while 27 percent of white households earned between $30,000 and $50,000 annually and 42 percent earned about $50,000 annually, 3 percent did not know their household incomes.[116]

The African-American population also is younger on average than the white population. In March 2002, 33 percent of African Americans were younger than 18, compared with 23 percent of whites, according to Census Bureau figures. And African-American families tended to be larger than white families in 2002, with 20 percent of African-American households consisting of five or more members, compared with 12 percent of white households of that size.[117]

In 2002, the five largest African-American markets accounted for 37.5 percent of African-American buying power, and the 10 largest African-American markets accounted for 61.4 percent of African-American buying power.[118]

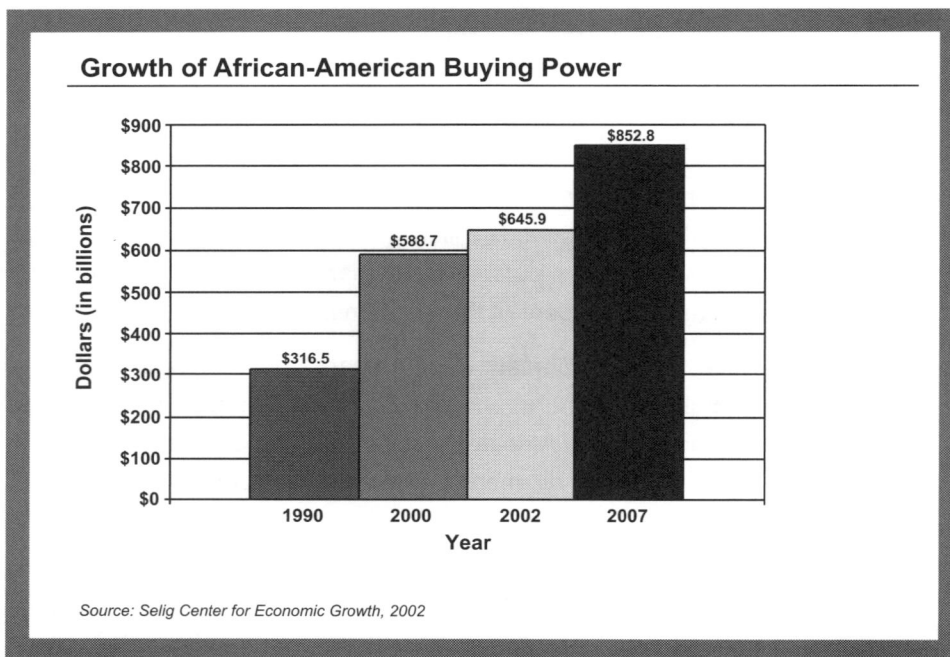

Growth of African-American Buying Power

Dollars (in billions)

Year	Value
1990	$316.5
2000	$588.7
2002	$645.9
2007	$852.8

Source: Selig Center for Economic Growth, 2002

The affluent African-American population is located increasingly in several key areas of the country. This particularly is true of those new to prosperity and the middle class. Instead of assimilating into white communities, they are setting up enclaves with tremendous buying power, a potential boon for smart marketers.

There are 66 communities in the United States that represent the greatest areas of affluence for African Americans,[119] according to research by DiversityInc. These communities have at least 40 percent African-American residents, and those living there have a median, annual household income of at least $50,000. In the No. 1 African-American community in the country, a ZIP code in Bowie, Md., African Americans comprise 66.7 percent of all residents and their median annual household income was $85,240 in 2000.

From 1990 to 2000, African-American homeownership rose from 42.6 percent to 47.6 percent.[120]

African Americans spend more on telephone services, personal care products, electricity and natural gas, children's apparel, and footwear, according to the Selig Center.[121]

2. Latinos

Latinos controlled about $580 billion in buying power in 2002, according to the Selig Center. And from 1990 to 2007, Latinos are expected to experience an increase in buying power of 315 percent, to reach $926.1 billion in 2007. Additionally, the Selig Center projects that Latino buying power should outpace African-American buying power in 2005. Latino buying power was 5.2 percent of the market in 1990, and is expected to encompass 9.4 percent of the consumer-buying market in 2007.[122]

Growth of Latino Buying Power

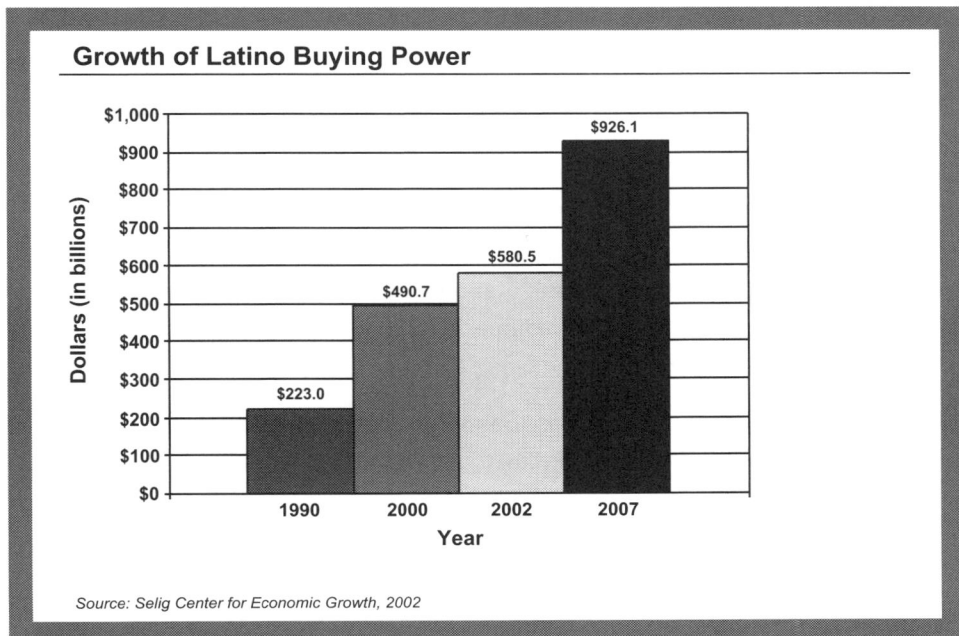

Source: Selig Center for Economic Growth, 2002

The percentage increase from 1990 to 2007 is greater than the 121 percent of non-Latino buying power and 131 percent increase in the buying power for all U.S. consumers. In 2007, Latinos are expected to account for 9.4 percent of all U.S. buying power, compared with to 5.2 percent in 1990.[123]

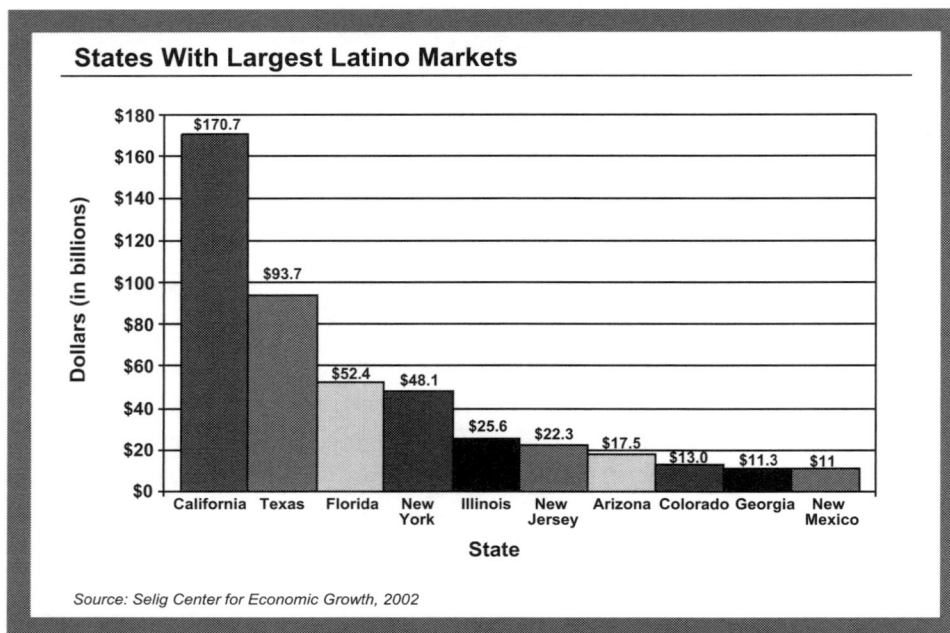

States With Largest Latino Markets

State	Dollars (in billions)
California	$170.7
Texas	$93.7
Florida	$52.4
New York	$48.1
Illinois	$25.6
New Jersey	$22.3
Arizona	$17.5
Colorado	$13.0
Georgia	$11.3
New Mexico	$11

Source: Selig Center for Economic Growth, 2002

As the Latino population increases, so has its economic clout. These new figures impact how businesses market their products and services to this market, which now is estimated to have $580.5 billion in spending power in 2002, projected to reach $927.1 billion in 2007, according to the Selig Center for Economic Growth at the University of Georgia. Latino disposable-income nationwide has grown 160 percent since 1990, and is projected to outpace African-American spending power in 2005, according to the Selig Center.

When surveyed, half of Latino respondents reported household earnings below $30,000 annually, according to a 2002 study conducted by the Pew Hispanic Center. The study also showed that while 23 percent of Latino households earned between $30,000 and $50,000 annually and 17 percent earned about $50,000 annually, 11 percent did not know their household incomes.[124]

While the average disposable income for Latinos ($56,431) was just

77 percent of the total U.S. average for households in 2002, the annual growth rate for Latino household income is expected to rise at 4.8 percent annually, compared with projected growth of 0.4 percent annually for non-Latino households. Researchers attribute this projected growth to the improving educational attainment and employment opportunities for Latinos.[125]

From 1990 to 2000, Latino homeownership rose from 41.2 percent to 45.5 percent.[126]

While the average disposable income for Latino households is 77 percent of the U.S. average, Latino household consumer spending was 81 percent ($51,208 per household) of the U.S. household average. While the national growth rate for consumption spending is projected to be 6 percent from 2002 to 2020, the Latino consumption-spending rate is expected to grow at 9.1 percent annually over this period.[127]

A strong Latino consumer market explains why NBC and parent company General Electric acquired the second-largest U.S. Spanish-language television network, Telemundo, in April 2002. Telemundo says it reaches 91 percent of the U.S. Latino market through 14 stations and more than 30 affiliates, with a distribution to more than 425 cable systems in 115 television markets.

States With Largest Share of Latino Buying Power

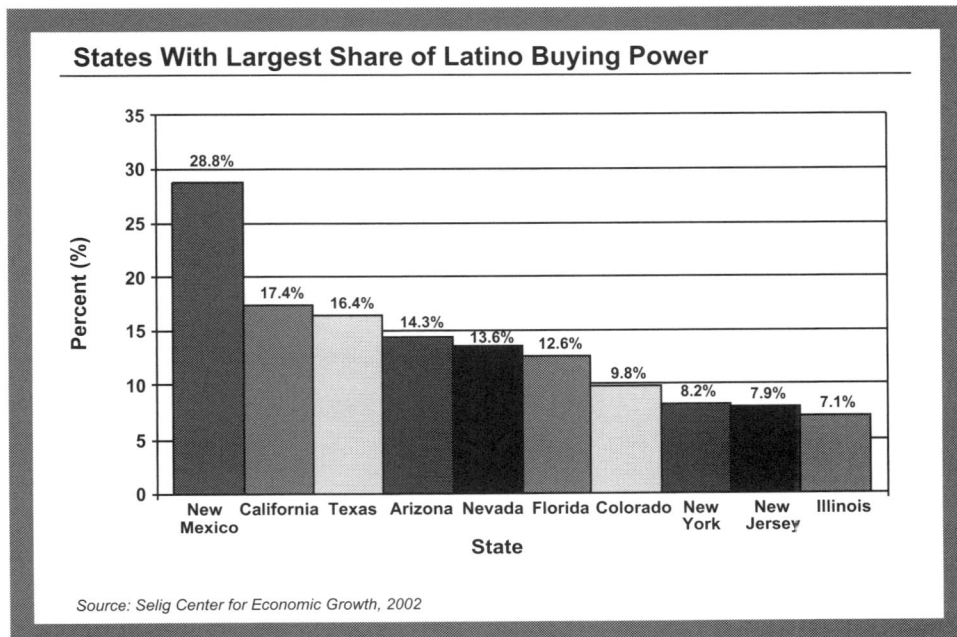

Bar chart. Y-axis: Percent (%), 0 to 35. X-axis: State.

State	Percent
New Mexico	28.8%
California	17.4%
Texas	16.4%
Arizona	14.3%
Nevada	13.6%
Florida	12.6%
Colorado	9.8%
New York	8.2%
New Jersey	7.9%
Illinois	7.1%

Source: Selig Center for Economic Growth, 2002

The per-capita income for Latinos is lower than that of the overall U.S. population. They spend a higher proportion of their income on housing, transportation, goods and services. Although they earn less on average, they spend more on groceries, telephone services, furniture, men's and boys clothing, children's clothing and footwear.[128]

They spend about the same portions of their income, as compared to the total population, on restaurants, alcohol, utilities and fuels, housekeeping supplies, household textiles and supplies, floor coverings, appliances, televisions, radios, sound equipment, and women's and girls' clothing.

Latinos spent less proportionately and monetarily on health care, education, life and other personal insurance, pensions and Social Security, and tobacco products. Latinos also are less likely to own their own home than non-Latinos. While 68 percent of non-Latinos own their own homes, only 47 percent of Latinos own their own homes.[129]

California accounts for 29.4 percent of Latino of buying power. The top five states with the largest Latino markets account for 67.3 percent of Latino buying power. The top 10 states account for 80.2 percent of the total Latino buying power.[128]

California, which already has an established Latino market, is expected to see its overall Latino market increase 4 percent in the next five years, from 13.4 percent to 17.4 percent.[130]

3. Asian Americans

By 2007, 14.2 million Americans, or 4.6 percent, of the nation's population, will be of Asian and Pacific Islander ancestry. This is up from 2.9 percent in 1990 and 3.8 percent in 2000.[131] The Selig Center expects Asian-American buying power to have quadrupled by 2007 from its 1990 numbers.

Asian-American buying power is projected to reach $454.9 billion in 2007 (from $296.4 billion in 2002).[132] This is a 287 percent gain from 1990 to 2007, compared with 112 percent for whites and 131 percent for the United States as a whole. Only Latinos exceed this growth percentage, which is 315 percent.[133]

Asian Americans have increased buying power in the consumer marketplace from 2.7 percent in 1990 to 3.9 percent in 2002. Asian-American buying power is expected to encompass 4.7 percent of the consumer buying market in 2007.

From 1990 to 2000, Asian-American homeownership rose from 49.1 percent to 52.9 percent.[134]

In 2002, the five states with the largest Asian-American consumer markets were California ($104.1 billion), New York ($31.9 billion), New Jersey ($18 billion), Texas ($16.6 billion) and Hawaii ($15.3 billion).[135]

Asian-American buying power has increased at greater rates because of the high-level of education for Asian-Americans, compared with the overall American population.

States With Largest Asian-American Markets

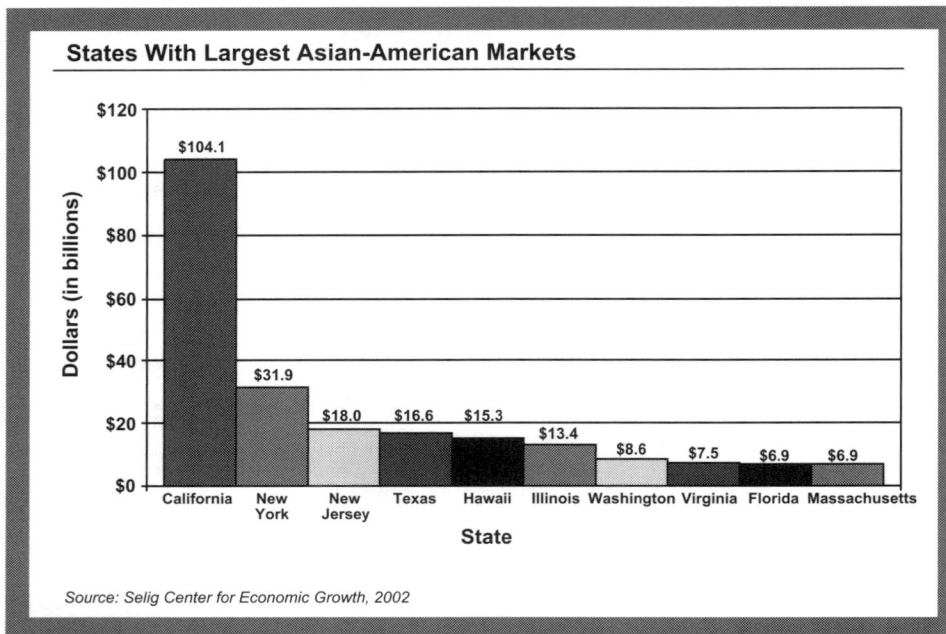

Source: Selig Center for Economic Growth, 2002

States with the largest shares of total buying power for Asian Americans in 2002 were Hawaii at 49 percent, California at 10.6 percent, New Jersey at 6.3 percent, New York at 5.4 percent, Washington at 5.2 percent, Nevada at 4.6 percent, Maryland at 4.1 percent, Alaska at 3.8 percent, Virginia at 3.7 percent, and Illinois had 3.7 percent. These numbers only are expected to increase, with the exception of Hawaii, where the Selig Center projects Asian-American buying power will drop by 8.4 percent in the next five years. Asian Americans' share of the total consumer market in New Jersey is expected to rise to 3 percent by 2007, with a 2.6 percent increase in California, and a 2.1 percent increase in New Mexico and Nevada over the same time.[136]

Of the Asian-American groups, Asian Indians are among the most affluent and opportune to new marketing opportunities. A recent survey conducted by Simmons Market Research for India Abroad — a 32-year-old, U.S.-based English-language newspaper with an audited weekly circulation of 65,000 — found that Asian Indians are the most affluent ethnic group in the country, with the highest level of education and highest level of home ownership.[137]

The India Abroad study found that its readers have an average annual household income of more than $170,000 (compared to a median annual household income of $41,000 in the general population, according to the U.S. Census Bureau). Additionally, India Abroad readers reported an average net worth of $1.3 million. With more than $88 billion in combined spending power, Asian Indians are a highly desirable market.

States With Largest Share of Asian-American Buying Power

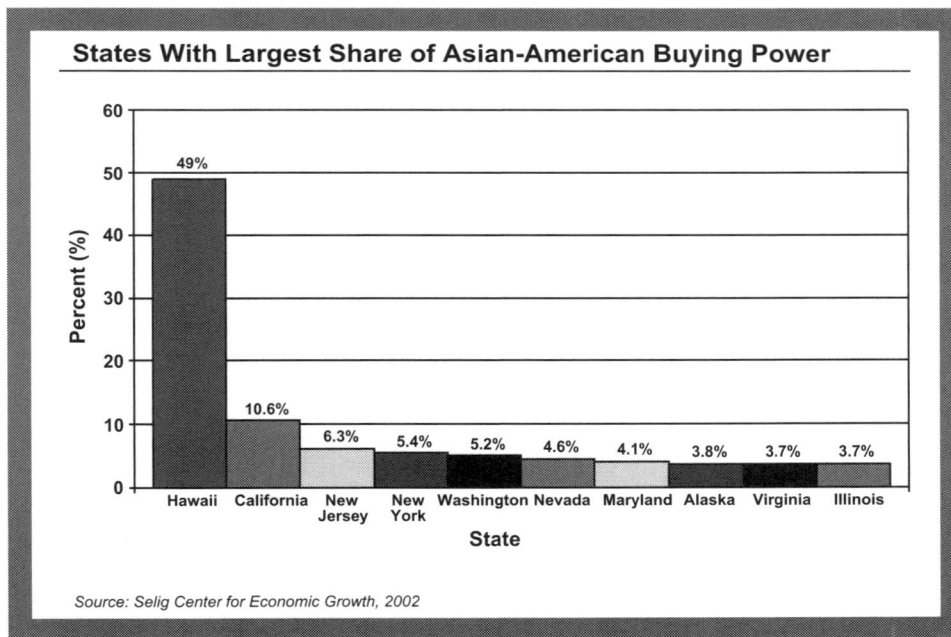

Source: Selig Center for Economic Growth, 2002

4. Gay, Lesbian, Bisexual and Transgender People

According to Professor M. V. Lee Badgett's 1998 study, "Income Inflation: The Myth of Affluence Among Gay, Lesbian and Bisexual Americans," data from the General Social Survey, the 1990 census and Yankelovich Monitor, gay and lesbian people have lower individual incomes than heterosexual people.[138]

Buying power for the gay, lesbian, bisexual and transgender (GLBT) market in 2002 is estimated at $451 billion and projected to reach $608 billion by 2007, a cumulative increase of more than 34 percent from 2002 figures, according to a report from Witeck-Combs Communications and Packaged Facts, a unit of New York-based MarketResearch.com.[139] GLBT buying power is expected to increase to 6.1 percent of the consumer buying-power market in 2007, up from 5.9 percent in 2002.

The Witeck-Combs/Packaged Facts reports shed some light on the formidable buying power of GLBT consumers in the United States. Buying power for the GLBT market in 2002 is estimated at $451 billion and projected to reach $608 billion by 2007, a cumulative increase of more than 34 percent from 2002 figures, according to "The Gay & Lesbian Market: New Trends, New Opportunities" report.

While there is a persistent myth that gay and lesbian consumers are wealthier than consumers from other emerging markets, the report found that GLBT consumers had incomes and spending capacities that are slightly less or in proportion with the general population.

The report revealed that the mean income of gay men and lesbians in 2002 is $38,431 and is projected to reach $46,757 by 2007.

The challenge, says Bob Witeck, president and CEO of Washington, D.C.,-based Witeck Combs, is to avoid taking the buying-power numbers at face value as a way to say how much or how little a market group possesses. "Behavior patterns are much more important," Witeck says, "and using the numbers without insight into behavior trivializes the segment."

The relatively high buying-power numbers of the GLBT market are not surprising since the group is estimated to comprise nearly 15 million people, according to Witeck. He adds that the impact of GLBT consumers on the U.S. economy frequently is undercounted, and the data in the report offers a conservative estimate of GLBT buying power. Unlike ethnic markets, the GLBT market requires members to identify themselves as part of the group. Therefore, pa nting an accurate portrait of how much spending power the GLBT market possesses is difficult, though not impossible.

Witeck says Witeck-Combs derived the GLBT buying power numbers by benchmarking 6 percent to 7 percent of the total U.S. market as GLBT. According to studies conducted by Witeck-Combs in conjunction with research-firm Harris Interactive, approximately 13 million to 14.5 million U.S. residents consistently self-identity as gay, lesbian, bisexual and transgender.

5. People With Disabilities

Fifty-eight percent of respondents had an annual household income below $40,000, while 12 percent of households earned between $40,000 and $54,000 annually, 23 percent of households earned more than $55,000 annually, and 8 percent of households earned more than $100,000 a year, according to the Spring 2002 Heidi van Arnem Disability Consumer Research Report, published by iCan.[140]

Twenty-five percent of respondents in a survey conducted by iCan, the Birmingham, Mich.,-based Internet disability community, reported having household incomes more than $50,000 annually.[141]

In 2002, the aggregate spending (total spending) for people with disabilities was almost $1.1 trillion and discretionary spending (money "left over" after taking care of necessities) was more than $175 billion, according to iCan.[142]

The spending power of the disability community is estimated to be more than $220 billion, according to the National Organization on Disability.

6. Other Groups

Native-American buying power has increased from $19.3 billion in 1990 to $36.4 billion in 2000, $40.8 billion in 2002. Native-American buying power is projected to be $57.3 billion in 2007, an increase of 197 percent since 1990. (White buying power increased by 112 percent over that time period, while the entire population's buying power increased 131 percent and African-American buying power increased 170 percent.)

Native Americans represent only a small percentage of buying power,

Growth of Native-American Buying Power

Dollars (in billions)

- $70
- $60 — $57.3
- $50
- $40.8
- $40 — $36.4
- $30
- $20 — $19.3
- $10
- $0

Year: 1990 | 2000 | 2002 | 2007

Source: Selig Center for Economic Growth, 2002

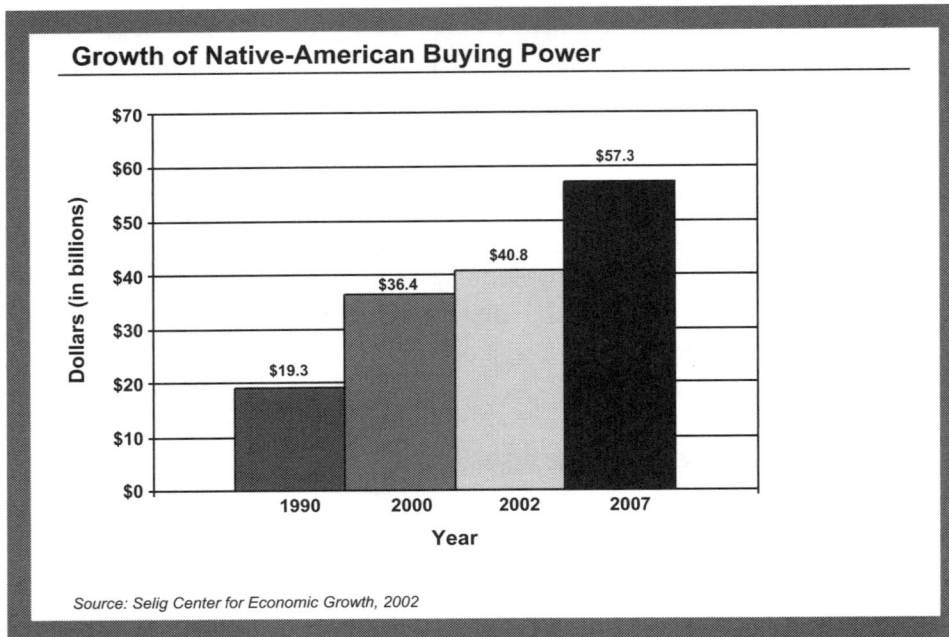

up from 0.5 percent to 0.6 percent from 1990 to 2007. Native-American buying power was 0.5 percent of the market in 1990, and is expected to encompass 0.6 percent of the consumer buying market in 2007.[143]

The Native-American population is expected to grow by 50.3 percent from 1990 to 2007, faster than African Americans (28.6 percent increase), whites (10.6 percent increase) and the overall population (23.2 percent increase).[144]

Although they are less than 1 percent of the overall U.S. population with 2.6 million people, Native Americans have $40.8 billion in disposable income.[145]

Alaska-Native and Native-American-owned businesses made up 1 percent of all U.S. firms in 1997, the last date for which data is available. American-Indian and Alaska-Native owned businesses increased by 83.7 percent by 1997 from the 1992 data. This compares to a 6.8 percent increase in all U.S. businesses from 1992 to 1997.[146]

The five largest Native-American markets account for 45.1 percent of Native American buying power. The 10 largest markets for Native American buying power account for 63.2 percent of total Native-American buying power.

States With Largest Native-American Markets

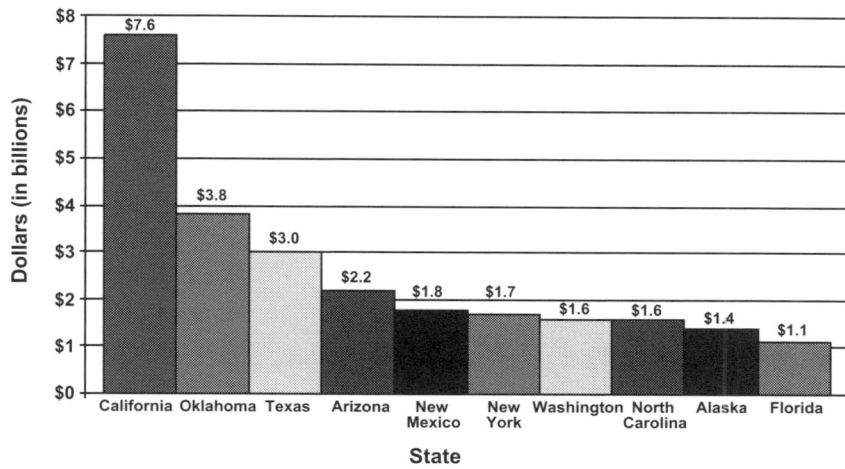

Source: Selig Center for Economic Growth, 2002

States With Largest Share of Native-American Buying Power

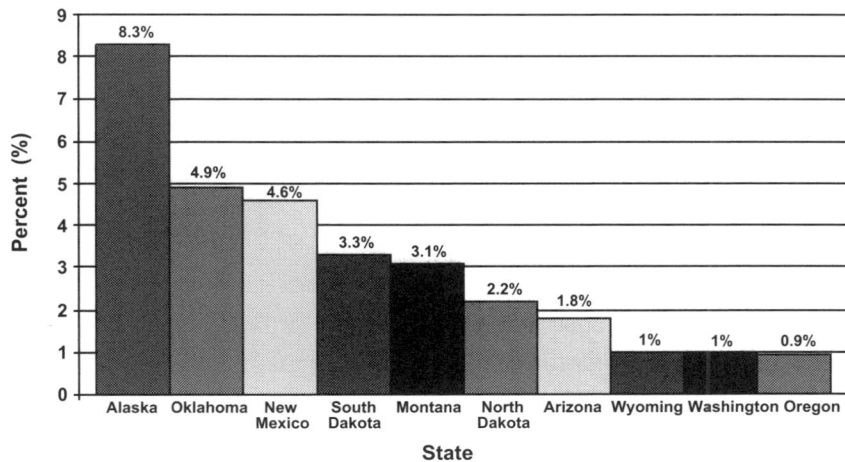

Source: Selig Center for Economic Growth, 2002

B. Attracting New Customers: Finding the Right Markets

"It's a big mistake to rely only on population size," says Pepper Miller, president of The Hunter-Miller Group, a Chicago-based market-research company. "Psychographics – the motivations for the quantitative things that happen in the market – play a key role in understanding emerging markets. And not understanding that is an enormous opportunity lost for corporate America."

Miller tells her clients to consider the psychographic profile of African-American consumers, regardless of what census data shows. "The census is useful, don't get me wrong, but it's also a double-edge sword. It's critical to look beyond the basic numbers of these emerging markets to really understand what makes these consumers tick."

"African Americans outspend other groups in 'badge value' items such as cars, jewelry and fashion, despite being smaller than the overall general market," says Miller. Yet, Miller adds, marketers of high-end products and services often don't understand why they should target African-American consumers over other groups. "These marketers have a limited view of African Americans based on what they see in the media."[147]

Research experts argue that companies aren't interested in paying for the in-depth insights into African-American consumers. Company representatives complain that research firms have, to date, provided faulty research models. Meanwhile, there are lingering misconceptions about the size and strength of the African-American market, despite demographic data.

But in the end, research either is going to drive or halt marketing initiatives aimed at African Americans. Corporate leaders who don't get the business case and can't pinpoint the return on investment aren't going to put money toward the market.[148]

Let's look at the automobile industry, probably the most mature in its diversity efforts. It is at a crossroads. Most automakers are long past believing that diverse markets can be ignored; some of the nation's largest makers of cars and trucks go out of their way to stress in public statements and marketing materials that any increase in market share they eke out in 2003 will come only from African Americans, gays and lesbians, Latinos and Asian Americans.

At the same time, the auto industry is trying to determine when race, ethnicity or sexual orientation – traditional cues to market segmentation – are driving buying decisions and when other factors, such as life-stage or a passion for technology, for example, influence a purchase.

The quandary for automakers, then, is deciding when and how to segment diverse markets. How narrowly should a market be divided? When does market segmentation boost the bottom line? What does research say?

But General Motors, Ford and the Chrysler unit of DaimlerChrysler posted lower sales in 2002, a trend all three companies want to reverse. Meanwhile, according to Autodata, which tracks auto-industry numbers, Honda, Toyota and Nissan all posted market-share gains that they want to extend.

Overall, North American auto sales are projected to fall by nearly 3 percent in 2003, as consumers grapple with economic hardship at home and uncertainty abroad. According to J.D. Power and Associates, U.S. auto sales are expected to drop this year to 16.4 million new cars and light trucks from 16.8 million in 2002. The consumer-research giant is predicting a decline, despite continued sales incentives from U.S.-based automakers.

If there ever was a time to become fluent in the language of segmented marketing, it is now, says Marc Strachan, the African-American chairman of the diversity council for the American Association of Advertising Agencies and co-founder of the New York-based advertising firm, S/R Communications Alliance.

Hispanic Business magazine reported last year that automakers, package-goods marketers and telecommunications companies were spending more to reach Latinos. Ford, GM, Procter & Gamble and AT&T all increased their multicultural-marketing budgets by more than 20 percent, the magazine reported.

As markets become more diverse, corporate America will need to address subgroups of increasing specificity.

While there has been some effort in certain markets, such as the gay, lesbian, bisexual and transgender (GLBT) community, for example, to consider multiple factors (i.e. trying to identify what a lesbian Latina who lives in a rural area might want to buy), when it comes to race, marketers continue to view the markets through the lens of black or white.

But to ignore the growing number of multiethnic consumers in this country is to ignore the reality of America's melting pot. A look at a small but complex ethnic subgroup, Asian Latinos, can offer corporate America a snapshot of what the face of American consumers could look like in a few decades.

The phenomenon of Asian Latinos is based on the history of migration of Chinese, Japanese and Korean people to Central and South America over the past century whose descendents have migrated to the United States, according to Saul Gitlin, vice president of strategic marketing services at Kang & Lee, a New York-based advertising agency specializing in the Asian-American market.

"A not inconsequential number of Koreans migrated to Argentina, while there are a large number of ethnic Japanese in Brazil," Gitlin says. "When they come to the United States, their primary language is Spanish or Portuguese, not Korean or Japanese."

"Asian Americans and U.S. Latinos are very similar in the sense that we both have immigrant cultures in this country and, as a group, both experience a lot of differences within our own groups," says Edmund Lee, site manager at Community Connect, which hosts the community sites AsianAvenue.com, BlackPlanet.com and MiGente.com. "Being from New York and living here, the whole multicultural thing is everywhere. It's just a matter of corporate America catching up to this reality."

Thus far, there has yet to be a definitive count of the number of people who identify as both Asian and Latino in this country. With 6.8 million identifying as two or more races in the 2000 census, the number of Asian Latinos is likely to be very small. However, the combination of Asians and Latinos as a distinct subgroup is notable because it combines the two fastest-growing ethnic populations in the United States that also happen to be the largest ethnic group (Latinos) and the smallest ethnic group (Asians). Additionally, the commonalties shared by Asians and Latinos make for a demographically attractive target market.[149]

ADDITIONAL RESOURCES

PART IV: EMERGING MARKETS

"66 Top Markets for Affluent Black Households." DiversityInc.com, May 14, 2001.

Bean, Linda. "Lack of Data? Lack of Interest? Why Don't We Know More About African-American Auto Consumers." DiversityInc, 7 March 2003. *http://www.diversityinc.com/members/4559.cfm*.

Cheng, Kipp. "Asian Latinos: Do Two Fast-Growing Groups Add Up to an Attractive Niche Market?" DiversityInc, 1 November 2002. *http://www.diversityinc.com/members/3758.cfm*.

Cheng, Kipp. "Beyond Just the Numbers, What Counts As an Emerging Market?" DiversityInc, 1 July 2002. *http://www.diversityinc.com/members/3191.cfm*.

Cheng, Kipp. "Fast-Growing Asian-Indian Population is Affluent, Educated and Ignored." DiversityInc, 14 March 2002. *http://www.diversityinc.com/members/2573.cfm*.

Cheng, Kipp. "Finally the Truth: How Many Gay Americans Are There and What Will They Buy." DiversityInc, 11 April 2002. *http://www.diversityinc.com/members/2737.cfm*.

Cheng, Kipp. "Numbers Make the Case: Ethnic Spending Power Continues Rapid Rise." 6 December 2002. *http://www.diversityinc.com/members/3926.cfm*.

Global Insight. Snapshots of the U.S. Hispanic Market, Lexington, Mass., April 2003.

"The Heidi van Arnem Disability Consumer Research Report." iCan, Inc. Birmingham, MI., Spring 2002.

Humphreys, Jeffrey M. The Multicultural Economy 2002. Selig Center for Economic Growth (Terry College of Business, University of Georgia). Athens, Ga., May 2002.

Pew Hispanic Center and Kaiser Family Foundation. 2002 National Survey of Latinos. Washington, D.C., December 2002.

U.S. Census Bureau. "American Indians and Alaska Natives." Survey of Minority-Owned Business Enterprises, 1997 Economic Census. Washington, D.C., 2001.

ADDITIONAL RESOURCES

PART IV: EMERGING MARKETS

U.S. Census Bureau, The Black Population in the United States: March 2002 (Current Population Reports, Series P20-541). Washington, D.C., March 2003.

U.S. Bureau of the Census, Current Population Survey, March Supplement and Current Population Survey/Housing Vacancy Survey.

Witeck-Combs Communications, Inc. and Packaged Facts. The Gay and Lesbian Market, New Trends, New Opportunities, 3rd edition. New York, October 2002.

256

Asian Latinos: Do Two Fast-Growing Groups Add Up to an Attractive Niche Market?

By Kipp Cheng

© 2003 DiversityInc.com

November 01, 2002

Despite the roller coaster that Wall Street has become, most economists are confident that U.S. consumers – in the long run – will continue to experience significant (though varying) gains in annual net income, thereby fueling growth in consumer spending power. According to projections from the Selig Center for Economic Growth at the University of Georgia, African-American, Asian and Latino consumers together will wield "formidable economic clout" in the coming years as their numbers continue to rise.

As markets become more diverse, corporate America will need to address subgroups of increasing specificity.

While there has been some effort in certain markets, such as the gay, lesbian, bisexual and transgender (GLBT) community, for example, to consider multiple factors (i.e. trying to identify what a lesbian Latina who lives in a rural area might want to buy), when it comes to race, marketers continue to view the markets through the lens of black or white.

But to ignore the growing number of multiethnic consumers in this country is to ignore the reality of America's melting pot. A look at a small but complex ethnic subgroup, Asian Latinos, can offer corporate America a snapshot of what the face of American consumers could look like in a few decades.

The phenomenon of Asian Latinos is based on the history of migration of Chinese, Japanese and Korean people to Central and South America over the past century whose descendents have migrated to the United States, according to Saul Gitlin, vice president of strategic marketing services at Kang & Lee, a New York-based advertising agency specializing in the Asian-American market.

"A not inconsequential number of Koreans migrated to Argentina, while there are a large number of ethnic Japanese in Brazil," Gitlin said. "When they come to the United States, their primary language is Spanish or Portuguese, not Korean or Japanese."

"Asian Americans and U.S. Latinos are very similar in the sense that we both

257

Asian Latinos: Do Two Fast-Growing Groups Add Up to an Attractive Niche Market? (cont'd.)

have immigrant cultures in this country and as a group both experience a lot of differences within our own groups," said Edmund Lee, site manager at Community Connect, which hosts the community sites AsianAvenue.com, BlackPlanet.com and MiGente.com. "Being from New York and living here, the whole multicultural thing is everywhere. It's just a matter of corporate America catching up to this reality."

Thus far, there has yet to be a definitive count of the number of people who identify as both Asian and Latino in this country. With 6.8 million identifying as two or more races in the 2000 census, the number of Asian Latinos is likely to be very small. However, the combination of Asians and Latinos as a distinct subgroup is notable because it combines the two fastest-growing ethnic populations in the United States that happen to also be the largest ethnic group (Latinos) and the smallest ethnic group (Asians). Additionally, the commonalties shared by Asians and Latinos make for a demographically attractive target market.

In addition to having immigrant cultures – albeit different ones – in common, Lee said Asians and Latinos, especially those who are young, do not see race in the same way as older Americans. "These kids aren't seeing each other for their racial background as much as they are seeing the similarities of their lives in America."

Lee said the Asian and Latino members who are active on AsianAvenue.com or MiGente.com, respectively, tend to share cultural interests, such as Hip-Hop music and sports. He added that the pop-culture touchstones, which were born out of African-American culture, are common to African-American, Asian-American and Latino members of the Community Connect sites.

"The new pop culture necessarily includes people of color," said Lee. "It has to because it's about the urban landscape, it's about Hip-Hop, it's about the whole culture of being a person of color."

For those who live in urban centers, such as New York or Los Angeles, the presence of Asian Latinos is nothing new. Indeed, restaurants serving so-called "Chino Latino" cuisine have been fixtures in some cities for years. In New York City's Upper West Side neighborhood, La Caridad restaurant has been serving a fusion of Cuban and Chinese food for more than a decade.

Over the past decade and a half, the tremendous increase in the number of Asian and Latino immigrants has fueled the growth of both Asians and Latinos throughout the country, not just in urban areas. According to updated census data, there are 11.9 million Asian Americans and 35 million Latinos. (Those who identified

Asian Latinos: Do Two Fast-Growing Groups Add Up to an Attractive Niche Market? (cont'd.)

themselves as African Americans number 34.6 million, or 12.3 percent of the overall population, according to updated census data.) By comparison, there were 7.3 million Asians and 22.4 Latinos in the United States, according to 1990 census data. (In 1990, there were 30 million African Americans.)

The U.S. Asian and Latino populations each grew by nearly 50 percent between 1990 and 2000, while the white and African-American populations had relatively smaller percentage growth.

Many Asians and Latinos also have in common non-English-speaking homes. Lee said there is cultural pride in being bilingual and it's one of the key ties between Asian Americans and Latinos. (According to a poll by the AOLTW Foundation and People En Espanol, 69 of Latinos speak Spanish at home. On the other hand, census data reports that 80 percent of Chinese Americans speak Chinese at home.)

The tremendous growth in Asian and Latinos in this country was fueled, in large part, by the influx of immigrants from Mexico and Latin America, while immigration from China and India helped to boost population figures for Asian Americans over the past decade. The dramatic shift in immigration patterns upended the historical pattern of European immigration to this country. In 1999 more than half – 51 percent – of all immigrants came from Latin America and 27 percent from Asia, while 16 percent came from Europe, according to the Population Reference Bureau.

The primary challenges, according to Gitlin, are determining whether the small numbers of Asian Latinos represent a market group that's worth targeting and finding the right media to reach them.

"There isn't a ready-made media channel to reach multiracial consumers," Gitlin said. "If marketers are interested, they would need to do some research to find out their media consumption behavior."

Gitlin said one possible channel would be an online effort, but it would have to be "highly targeted." Using the Web to reach Asian Latinos might be a useful approach, considering that Latinos and Asians in America are more likely to be online at home than their white or African American counterparts, according to a market research report by Insight Research.

Deciding whether Asian Latinos are a viable market comes down to finding the proper media to reach them and exploring the things that make this group similar and different from Asian and Latino consumers independently.

Asian Latinos: Do Two Fast-Growing Groups Add Up to an Attractive Niche Market? (cont'd.)

"We have a very complex understanding of race and identity in this country," said Lee. "When you see Asians and Latinos in this country being in relationships, it's a reflection of that common experience of being outsiders and also having varied cultures within their own group."

The Perfect Pulpit for Financial Education: One Thousand Churches Connected

By Eric L. Hinton

© 2003 DiversityInc.com

December 17, 2002

When the Rev. Johnny Miller of Chicago's Mount Vernon Baptist Church calls his parishioners together for worship, he has more than spiritual enlightenment on the agenda. Miller is one of a growing number of African-American clergy who view the church as vital to spreading the message of economic empowerment in communities of color.

"When the churches participate in matters of finance, it gives it a different flavor and brings about a different level of trust with people who otherwise wouldn't be present," said Miller.

Last year, Miller's church of approximately 1,000 parishioners joined forces with One Thousand Churches Connected. Launched by the Rev. Jesse Jackson under the umbrella of the Rainbow/PUSH coalition in 2001, the One Thousand Churches Connected is designed to bring the message of economic responsibility to families through churches across the country.

"I saw it as a source of unity that can be transforming," said Miller. "Every church that I've met that is part of One Thousand Churches is involved in some type of economic-empowerment program on an ongoing basis."

The idea is that the ongoing fight for equality is being staged on different battle-fields. The First Movement was the struggle to end slavery; the Second Movement was the battle to end segregation; the Third Movement was the march to obtain full voting rights; the Fourth Movement is the quest for equal opportunity through shared economic security and empowerment.

"Rev. Jackson had the vision of creating One Thousand Churches Connected to complete the four stages of our symphony as a people," said Bonita Parker, national director of One Thousand Churches. "The fourth movement is to level the economic playing field. That's what we're working on right now. As part of that, one of the initiatives that play into that is the effort to engage churches to teach financial stewardship from the pulpit as an opportunity to educate our people."

Currently, there are 245 churches signed up in the program, said Parker. Once a

The Perfect Pulpit for Financial Education: One Thousand Churches Connected (cont'd.)

church joins, the head of the church is invited to join Jackson and New York Stock Exchange (NYSE) Chairman Richard Grasso at a quarterly meeting at the NYSE. At that meeting, each religious leader is given a crash course in different areas of financial services to take back to his or her parish.

"In order for them to be able to comfortably demystify financial markets when they return home, they need to have a working knowledge of these things themselves," said Parker. "So the ministers get a trip down to the NYSE where they spend two and half days getting training on the science of capital. Next, every church that joins receives access to all the materials we have on the four modules."

Those four modules are:

• Understanding credit and debt elimination: This encompasses establishing credit, understanding credit scoring and restoring credit.

• Mortgage and home ownership, which covers qualifying for a mortgage, understanding the loan-application process and avoiding predatory lenders.

• Understanding financial services: This includes a review of financial markets, brokerage services and investment clubs.

• Technology as an educational resource: This covers issues of the Internet and privacy as well as electronic-bill payment and transfers.

"We decided to join because the program already was stipulating many of the things that we were already doing by focusing on financial empowerment, but it consolidated many things instead of dealing with fragmented pieces as we had been doing," said Miller. "I saw this as a source of unity that is transforming. Every church that I've met that is part of One Thousand Churches is involved in some type of economic empowerment program on an ongoing basis."

The push to harness the collective economic might of African Americans is bearing some fruit.

In June, the 2002 Ariel/Schwab Black Investor Survey reported African Americans earning in excess of $50,000 annually are investing in the stock market in rapidly growing numbers. Seventy-four percent of "high-income" African Americans today own stocks or stock funds, 30 percent more than those first surveyed in 1998. Among non-investors, twice as many African Americans as whites (42 percent vs. 21 percent) say they are "somewhat" or "very" likely to begin investing next year.

The Perfect Pulpit for Financial Education: One Thousand Churches Connected (cont'd.)

"It's good news all the way around," said Carla A. Foster, vice president of Specialized Segments Marketing for Charles Schwab & Co. Foster, an African American, has ongoing responsibility for African-American investor services at Schwab. "The biggest piece of news for us is that black participation in the stock market has increased significantly over the last five years. There's a greater attention to overall financial health because people are taking a big-picture view and getting their financial houses in order."

Parker believes the pulpit is the perfect perch from which to preach the importance of financial empowerment.

"The black church is the greatest learning institution for African Americans as a people. There are over 43,000 predominantly black churches in this country. Every Sunday, approximately 21 million African Americans come together so you have a captive audience. And financial stewardship is the single most talked about subject in the Bible, so it makes sense to be taught in the church. "

Miller agreed. In the time since his parish has joined One Thousand Churches, he has instituted a weekly "credit smart" class that provides parishioners with a needed crash course on the subject.

"About 12 people go to this class every Sunday instead of going to Sunday school. It talks about housing, economics and other areas of finance. It's like stepping outside of the box," said Miller. "Having this information is power."

The New Covenant Baptist Church of Orlando, Fla. will be hosting the Third Annual Small Church Conference, Jan. 30 and Feb. 1. Jeremiah Wright, the pastor of Trinity United Church of Christ in Chicago, is scheduled to be the keynote speaker at the event. Among the topics to be discussed is "Operating a Faith-Based, Not-for-Profit Corporation.

Profitable Emerging Market: Grocery Products Aimed at Latinos

By Ruth Zeilberger

© *2003 DiversityInc.com*

July 22, 2002

When Spanish immigrants Prudencio and Carolina Unanue moved to New York City, they missed the olives, the olive oil, the beans, the sardines – all the tastes and the aromas that reminded them of home, and comfort. The couple realized that other Spanish immigrants must have longed for Spanish food as well. This sparked the idea for Goya Foods, Inc., founded more than 67 years ago under the name Unanue Inc., in Brooklyn.

Over the years, Goya expanded to serve a growing and increasingly diverse Latino community, primarily on the East Coast. Now, spurred by the growth of the Latino community in the United States, other major food companies are trying to target the Latino consumer. Latinos are now the largest minority market in the United States with 35 million people, according to the 2000 U.S. Census. And Latinos, with an estimated annual buying power between $273 billion and $445 billion, visit grocery stores an average of 4.7 times a week, compared with 2.2 times for the average American. They also outspend other Americans $117 to $87 per week in grocery shopping, according to a study released in May 2002 by the Cultural Access Group Inc. for the Food Marketing Institute (FMI), based in Washington, D.C. That represents a big opportunity for a savvy food company.

A culturally competent advertising campaign could prove key to capturing the Latino market. "There are certain things that tie all Hispanics together: one is cultural identity; another is the love for food and the importance of family. So, a lot of marketing, especially when you talk about food products, concentrates on bringing home that message that you can make the food for your family," says James Forrest, an account group manager for Miami-based Strategy Research Corporation.

There are other aspects of purchasing behavior that are consistent in the Latino market, researchers say. Forty-four percent of Latino grocery shoppers indicate that advertisements in Spanish-language newspapers frequently influence them, compared with 31 percent of ads in English newspapers, according to the FMI report. This has led many companies to advertise their products in Spanish. Companies including Kraft Foods, The Pillsbury Company and Nestlé have initiated Spanish-language campaigns.

Profitable Emerging Market: Grocery Products Aimed at Latinos (cont'd.)

"Many companies have been successful growing their companies through Latinos. Both companies that are owned or controlled by multicultural executives and those that are the traditional companies that have paid attention to the market and have taken the time and effort to understand and take action on that knowledge," says César Melgoza, president of Geoscape International Inc., a marketing company that specializes in Latino retailing strategy.

Although low prices are rated very important by 92 percent of Latino grocery shoppers, 75 percent say the availability of name brands is very important in deciding where to shop, according to the FMI report. In comparison, approximately 50 percent say the availability of lower-priced private label or store brands is a very important consideration. Overall, Latinos tend to be much more brand-loyal than other consumers, according to the report findings.

But companies need to realize "when you talk about Hispanics, they come from over 20 countries, and yet they get lumped into this group of 'Hispanics.' If you are placed in a large Mexican area or a large Mexican pocket, your retailer is going to target its food to that group. If you have a large population that's Puerto Rican, or Cuban, or Central American you're going to do the same," says Forrest.

For Goya Foods, Latinos have always been the core consumers. Goya began marketing its products to Latinos in bodegas and selected grocery stores before expanding to national distribution through major supermarket chains. Today, Goya, which is now based in Secaucus, N.J., is the fourth largest Latino-owned business in the country with $715 million in revenue in 2001, according to Hispanic Business Inc.

Goya has a particularly savvy approach when it comes to targeting the Latino consumer. Supermarkets, which usually organize their goods by product type, set aside a section specifically for Goya foods. "We find our consumers prefer to shop by destination for Hispanic foods because they can find everything they need in our section," says Andy Unanue, chief operating officer of Goya Foods Inc. and a grandson of company founder Prudencio Unanue, who estimates that about 75 percent of Goya's customers are Latino. Supermarkets gain by allowing Goya its own section because some have less experience than Goya targeting Latinos but know that Latinos are a large segment of their customers, says Forrest.

But even Goya has had to face certain hurdles as it tries to target a broader Latino market. "Goya owns the markets in the East Coast, not so much on the West Coast. They've been perceived as a Caribbean company, and not as a Latino company," says Denyse Selesnick, director of the Expo Comida Latina, a Latino

Profitable Emerging Market: Grocery Products Aimed at Latinos (cont'd.)

food and beverage trade show which will open in Los Angeles in November

Latinos tend to be very loyal to brands, but certain brands in Mexico don't exist in Puerto Rico, says Forrest. Goya doesn't have a huge presence in Mexico, even though it's one of the main brands in Puerto Rico. When people immigrate to the United States from Mexico or Puerto Rico, they are very loyal to the brands they would have bought if they had stayed in their home countries. Convincing people to get past that brand loyalty is one of the challenges facing Goya as it tries to get a foothold in the West Coast market, says Forrest. But he adds that Goya is an example of a company that can cross those barriers if it puts the investment into it, and that it can build up a brand that most Latinos identify with if it targets its product effectively.

"Our product skew is much more Mexican on the West Coast and Texas than it is in on the East Coast. We do carry a full line of Mexican and Central and South American products, but we also advertise and carry a lot more Caribbean food [on the East Coast]," says Unanue.

"We do have national advertising that gets our name in front of all the communities. We try to make our ad a kind of 'Hispanic ad'. Where somebody doesn't say 'oh, that's a Mexican ad' or 'oh, that's a Puerto Rican ad', just 'that's an ad.' And it sells our core products. There are products that all Hispanics eat, like beans and rice. So there are definitely products that go across cultures," says Unanue.

Other companies are also trying to build up a brand name in the Latino community. Many big food companies, such as Néstle and Unilever, already have brands in Latin America. One way of building up their brand names in the United States is to bring in the products they distribute in Latin America. A classic example is Néstle Nescafe, a brand of coffee which was hugely successful in Latin America but only introduced in the United States in the past few years, where it met huge success in the Latino community, according to Forrest. It might also catch on in the general market and become a very successful brand, Forrest says.

"I think you'll find the trend toward Latino foods is permeating everything," Selesnick says. "I like to call it the Latinization of the American taste."

The New Trend in Marketing?
In-Language Advertising Works
Best for Latino Market

By Angela D. Johnson

© 2003 DiversityInc.com

April 03, 2003

Cincinnati, Ohio-based Procter & Gamble (P&G) made news earlier this year when it aired a Spanish-language commercial for its Crest Whitening Plus Scope toothpaste on the CBS broadcast of the Grammy Awards. The effort was designed to tap into the $580 billion in buying power in the Latino market, but it wasn't the only foreign-language commercial getting airtime on English-language networks.

Harbrew Imports, the Freeport, N.Y.-based U.S. distributor for Beijing's Yanjing Beer, began airing a Cantonese ad on the Madison Square Garden Network (MSG) in October. The spot features a man at a karaoke bar belting out a poor rendition of a song. As the audience begins to chant, "Encore, encore," the man thinks the audience wants him to sing another tune. In reality, they're asking for more Yanjing beer. The cast is entirely Asian, the jingle is in Cantonese and the ad closes with the Cantonese phrase, "Yanjing Pijiu (Yanjing Beer)."

Harbrew initially hired New York-based L3 Advertising to create advertising to capture a portion of what the Selig Center at the University of Georgia estimates as $296.4 billion in buying power in the Asian-American market. This spending power is expected to grow to $454.9 billion by 2007.

While Yanjing had an established reputation in the Asian-American market, Richard DeCicco, president of Harbrew Imports, said the general market had no preconceived notions about the brew. Harbrew decided to use the Asian-language ad to promote Yanjing to mainstream consumers, a market that Impact, an alcoholic beverage industry publication, reports spent more than $66 billion on beer between 2000 and 2001.

"The karaoke lifestyle is not out of range [with the general market]," said Joe Lam, president of L3 Advertising. He said the creative was designed to speak to the lifestyle and psychology of the Chinese-American market, but it expresses the universal element of having a good time that can appeal to a variety of consumers regardless of race or ethnicity.

Yanjing Beer currently is sold in roughly 30 markets including San Francisco,

The New Trend in Marketing? In-Language Advertising Works Best for Latino Market (cont'd.)

Los Angeles, Houston, Chicago, and Florida. The television ad airs mainly in the New York tri-state area, but also reaches viewers across the country who access the network through EchoStar's satellite Dish Network. Harbrew hopes that American consumers will embrace Yanjing in the same manner that they have adopted other import beers, such as Corona.

Lam said much of the success of the Yanjing ad with the mainstream audience stems from the beer's relationship with the Houston Rockets, home of Chinese basketball player Yao Ming. Yanjing is the team's official import beer.

For Chinese-American viewers of MSG, Lam said seeing the commercial "is a pleasant surprise for them …. It's a reinforcement of the brand."

P&G's spot, created by San Antonio, Texas-based Bromley Communications, featured a young Latino couple starting their day. As the husband is rushing out the door for work he stops to give his wife, who is dressed in a bathrobe with a tube of Crest sticking out of the pocket, a kiss. The husband leaves, but quickly returns for additional kisses. The dialogue is in Spanish except for the closing tag line: "White teeth. Fresh Breath. In Any Language."

"The spot was pretty universal as far as people being able to understand the spot visually," said Ernest Bromley, president of Bromley Communications.

Daisy Exposito, president of New York-based Latino marketing agency the Bravo Group, said the Crest spot that aired in February was not the first example of a Spanish-language ad on mainstream television. In 1978, Pepsi-Cola aired its first Spanish-language commercial during the Grammy's and in the early 1990s, AT&T ran an in-language spot featuring Latino singer Jon Secada during the same awards show.

Lam said he wasn't aware of any other companies that have aired Asian-language advertising on general market television and he doesn't see it as an effective overall strategy to reach Asian or mainstream markets. With just a portion of the Latino market viewing mainstream television in significant numbers, most marketers find using targeted advertising on general market television to be ineffective as well.

However, Cesar Melgoza, president of Geoscape International in Miami, sees some value in P&G's strategy. "It's going to seem expensive but what they're getting in return may be long term and quite intangible. I think a return on investment from a mathematical or dollars and cents point of view is probably missing the point. It's more of an investment in brand loyalty and awareness."

The New Trend in Marketing? In-Language Advertising
Works Best for Latino Market (cont'd.)

And while some see running a Spanish-language ad on a general-market station as an effective strategy to reach some Latinos, Exposito cautions against expecting to see more Spanish-language ads in the mainstream. "I think that we are seeing more and more in-culture, not in-language (advertising). I do think, however, that as more and more programming opportunities arrive and if the percentage of the Hispanic audience is significant within certain programs, yeah, you might begin to see more of that happening."

Bromley sees the potential for more in-language ads "on a spot basis than a national network basis. It's been true for quite some time along the border broadcast markets. But as you move more into the urban centers, Los Angeles and Houston and San Antonio, you may see it happening a little more often than you would now."

Bromley also predicts that as television broadcast moves further in to digital broadcast multicasting it won't be unusual to see CBS affiliates running television commercials and programs in Spanish. "That's a few years away though, but that's a trend we'll be seeing more and more as traditional English-language stations in markets like Los Angeles are going to be grappling with market share."

Reaching Latinos Requires Greater Marketing Budgets, Study Finds

By Ruth Zeilberger

© 2003 DiversityInc.com

April 07, 2003

Corporations are missing a big chunk of the Latino market as a result of inadequate advertising budgets, claims the Association of Hispanic Advertising Agencies (AHAA), and a new report aims to serve as a guide toward maximizing the potential of the Latino buying power.

"Corporate America is severely under-spending against our [Latino] buying power," said Ingrid Otero-Smart, president of AHAA. "You have a market that is significantly affecting corporations' bottom line, and yet they are not speaking to them."

Last year, AHAA released "Missed Opportunities: Vast Corporate Underspending in the U.S. Hispanic Market." The study concluded that for maximum effectiveness, corporations should be allocating a minimum of 8 percent of their total national marketing budgets to the Spanish-dominant and bilingual markets. It also revealed that among the top 50 leading Latino advertisers, current spending targeting Latinos across all categories is approximately 3.2 percent of national budgets – well below the 8 percent recommended threshold.

The AHAA released recommendations Friday on how to set appropriate spending targets based on media usage, consumption data and population data. Latinos, for example, over-index in consumption of most food categories, requiring resource allocations well above their actual representation of Spanish-dominant and bilingual households. To reach Spanish-dominant and bilingual households across top Latino markets commensurate with existing household food consumption budgets, the AHAA concluded that instant coffee and yogurt companies, for example, should direct about $1 out of every $3 in marketing resources.

"The biggest under-spenders are the health-care companies, financial services, electronic companies and travel industry," said Otero-Smart.

"There is a big misconception about Hispanic spending power," she said. "Most of the companies understand the demographics by now. But what they don't understand is the real economic power of the market. They say to me, 'Yes, there are a significant number of Hispanics, but can they really afford our products?' We're hoping that this study helps shatter some of those misconceptions."

Reaching Latinos Requires Greater Marketing Budgets, Study Finds (cont'd.)

Significant findings in the study include:

- Latino households use more health and beauty care products than non-Latino households and require resource allocations for sales, marketing, advertising, promotions, public-relations, events and sponsorships 50 percent to 100 percent higher than their actual representation of Spanish and bilingual households in those markets.

- Latinos' consumption of children's products is driven by the higher presence of young children in Latino homes. Just to stay in the game with equal share of market and to deliver continued volume growth, children's products urgently call for allocations much higher (100 percent to 350 percent) than the actual representation of Spanish and bilingual households, or up to $1 out over every $2 spent on marketing.

- Categories such as athletic shoes and jeans require allocations 50 percent above their representation of Spanish and bilingual households. To reach the level spending should be close to $1 in every $4 of marketing resources.

- Until the recent upswing in Latino homeownership (already on par with African Americans), insurance has been an under-developed category relative to Spanish-dominant and bilingual households. While investment rates are slightly below household totals, these investments require significant increases over current rates.

- Family-friendly minivans, pick-up trucks and entry-level compacts warrant 25 percent to50 percent higher allocations than the household share of Spanish/ bilingual households.

The Latino market's current size, formation of larger households, heavy concentration in the top, youngest, trendsetting markets in the United States, accompanied by their speedy wealth creation, and high consumerism are at odds with the neglect of investment in most categories, concluded the AHAA.

"Corporations need to redefine their allocation paradigm," said Otero-Smart. "They cannot just take it for granted that they are reaching the Hispanic market."

Direct Marketing Reaches Latinos in the Acculturation Process

By Angela D. Johnson

© 2003 DiversityInc.com

March 05, 2003

America has changed from the days when primarily European immigrants entered through Ellis Island and often hid vestiges of their native cultures to succeed economically and socially in the United States. Today, acculturation is the name of the game, particularly for Latino newcomers, according to Carlos Garcia, president of Garcia Research Associates.

Garcia discussed the impact of acculturation on Latino-targeted direct marketing at the Direct Marketing Association's 10th Annual Directo Days Conference in New York Tuesday and Wednesday.

During a luncheon presentation Tuesday titled "Directo al Corazon: Acculturation for Fun and Profit," Garcia said assimilation essentially involves losing one's language, customs, traditions and ties to one's homeland. He said acculturation – the process of adopting a new culture without denying one's heritage – more accurately describes the experience of recent Latino immigrants.

"Hispanics are more in charge of their acculturation than any other group before," said Garcia. "We are picking the things we like about American culture and discarding the things we don't like."

Garcia said intra-Latino acculturation – learning about other Latino cultures in the United States – is the first step in the overall acculturation process. Economic and media pressure then motivates Latinos to adopt traits from mainstream American culture.

And while recent immigrants are retaining their homeland traditions and values, many second- and third-generation Latinos are experiencing retro-acculturation, the rediscovery of one's heritage while maintaining the ability to function in the mainstream.

This acculturation process influences Latinos' perception of direct marketing. While most consumers in the general market dismiss direct marketing materials that show up in their mailboxes as junk mail, Latinos – particularly recent immigrants – welcome it.

"Latinos read direct mail looking for tricks for survival," said Garcia. "If you can

275

Direct Marketing Reaches Latinos in the Acculturation Process (cont'd.)

give them a chance to provide for their family, they will really appreciate it."

This desire for information creates an opportunity for companies in industries such as financial services and health care, services that are most likely to have policies and procedures that are different from Latinos' countries of origin. However, Garcia said the strongest Latino-targeted direct-marketing activity occurs for products such as fast food, household cleaning supplies, packaged foods, and beer and other alcoholic beverages. The majority are bilingual efforts that cater to both acculturated and unacculturated Latinos.

"At some point, category leaders have to educate consumers about the category," said Garcia. "Hispanics need and want information about how life here works."

Garcia stressed that commitment is key for marketers interested in entering the Latino direct-marketing arena.

"Don't be a dilettante," he said. "You have to make a commitment to continuity and have a willingness to make mistakes and to learn from them."

Garcia cautioned that Latino-targeted direct marketing programs must be coordinated with general market efforts. "[Companies] can not do Hispanic marketing as an afterthought. That approach doesn't work…. Reaching Latinos is not the same as convincing Latinos."

In addition to acculturation issues, direct marketers must contend with a tainted industry image in the Latino community. "Latinos have been burned by some direct mail," Garcia told DiversityInc after his session. "The industry needs to protect themselves." To that end, the conference offered a session on privacy issues that spelled out the laws of direct marketing.

Despite some fraudulent activity and increased saturation of direct mail in the Latino market, Latino consumers are still hungry for the information provided in these campaigns, Garcia said. "That's an inherent advantage that won't be lost."

MetLife Goes After Chinese-American Consumers

By Melanie Austria Farmer

© 2003 DiversityInc.com

February 14, 2003

MetLife is taking up Chinese.

At an event held in New York Thursday, the financial-services veteran unveiled a new television advertising campaign targeted at the Chinese-American community.

MetLife Chairman and Chief Executive Officer Robert Benmosche underscored the importance of a diversified workforce and the value recognized by having an ethnically mixed set of financial advisors, insurers and planners. By having a diverse workforce, the company is able to serve the specific needs of people from different countries and backgrounds, he said.

"We have people here that can support and understand them," Benmosche said to an audience of nearly 250 guests. "What you see here tonight is a celebration of those people."

In the past year, MetLife and other large insurers have been making an effort to expand their crop of agents of color. The industry overall had been criticized in the past for not paying serious enough attention to the level of value recognized by having agents on the floor who are able to understand the varying needs of people of color.

MetLife last February announced plans to take a $250 million earnings charge to cover expenses linked to class-action lawsuits and a regulatory inquiry over allegations of racial discrimination.

During the event Thursday, company executives said they want to deliver a marketing message that reaches multicultural consumers.

The new Chinese-American TV ads, set to launch in March, feature families in real-life situations experiencing the peace of mind that comes with financial security and planning. For example, one spot shows a young couple playing with their children in the park. The voiceover explains that the couple recently met with their financial planner who helped them put a plan in place for future education funding and retirement. The ads, which were produced in Mandarin and

MetLife Goes After Chinese-American Consumers (cont'd.)

Cantonese, end with the company's tag line, "Have you met life today?"

Three new ads were previewed during the program, and will run in major cities including New York, Boston, Chicago and San Francisco, all of which have strong Chinese-American populations. The spots will run on major Chinese television stations and other local cable channels.

MetLife, which serves 33 million households in 13 countries, also has targeted several other ethnic/racial markets in the United States, including African Americans, Latinos, Korea-Americans, South-Asian-Americans and Russian-Americans.

Asian Indians: Upscale Marketers Ignore This Prime Consumer Segment

By Angela D. Johnson

© 2003 DiversityInc.com

April 15, 2003

They love luxury cars, have a penchant for designer clothing, and consider cruises almost a right of passage, yet marketers of these goods and services have failed to take note of Asian Indians and other South-Asian immigrants, including people from Bangladesh, Pakistan, Sri Lanka and Nepal. (Asian Indians make up 88 percent this group, according to the U.S. Census Bureau.)

"There is a very strong business case for the South-Asian market," said Tariq Khan, vice president of multicultural marketing for MetLife, a New York-based insurance company. "They have among the highest income and highest education. Their growth is among the highest, also."

An increasing number of businesses have set their sights on Asian-American consumers. However, MetLife is one of the few companies, most which are limited to the financial-services and telecommunications industries, which specifically target the South-Asian segment of this group.

Dave Banerjee, president of the New York-based South Asian advertising agency 1947 Communications, said South Asians have an average household income of $67,552, considerably higher than the $45,257 national average. He estimates that, as a whole, the group wields $137 billion in buying power. "It's the most affluent group among any ethnicity in America, by far."

U.S. Census data show that between 1990 and 2000, the South-Asian population grew 106 percent to 2.2 million. Much of this growth stemmed from South Asians who came to America in the 1990s on HB-1 visas to work in the technology sector. Banerjee said the dot-com fallout is causing this growth trend to begin to taper off.

Neeta Bhasin, president and chief executive officer of ASB Communications, a full-service communications agency in New York, said the South-Asian population was severely undercounted in the latest census. The 2000 Census didn't offer a specific box for South Asians of Pakistani, Bangladeshi, Sri Lankan or Nepalese decent to acknowledge their race. Some may have selected "Other Asian" without denoting their country of origin. Based on this, Bhasin estimates

Asian Indians: Upscale Marketers Ignore This Prime Consumer Segment (cont'd.)

the South Asian population in the United States to be around 3.5 million.

Despite the small size, South Asians' high household income makes the segment an ideal target for marketers of upscale products such as luxury cars and homes.

"If you're talking about Colgate, I'd say our market is not the market," said Bhasin. "But if you're talking about education, real estate ... we are the one."

"I don't see why brands like Ethan Allen wouldn't advertise or Saks Fifth Avenue," said Banerjee. "Any upscale brand should advertise because the ROI [return on investment] is incredible .... The cost of entry for any brand in this market is probably the lowest because the media cost is miniscule compared to any other market, even compared to the Chinese market or the Korean market."

For example, the cost of a full-page ad in the Chicago edition of the weekly India Tribune is $1,800, significantly lower (and assumedly more effective) than a full-page ad in the Chicago Tribune.

South Asians are prime consumers of luxury cars.

"When we come from India, we have one dream," said Bhasin, "to own a Mercedes-Benz."

Travel also is important to this market. "If you haven't been on cruises then you don't belong in [the South-Asian] society," said Bhasin. She added that Disney World often is the first place South Asians want to take their children.

So what's keeping upscale marketers from courting these consumers?

"I would say lack of knowledge, lack of education," said Bhasin. "[Companies] have to have an open mind to listen and understand about this market."

Bhasin said that before the establishment of agencies specializing in the South-Asian market, little research was available about these consumers. Arti Caprihan, marketing manager of the Montvale, N.J.-based Western Union said the challenge now is getting detailed data about segments within the South Asian population.

Marketers also may be intimidated by the idea of addressing a market that has more than 30 different languages and 300-plus dialects. The realization that most South Asians are fluent in English may ease their apprehension, but experts warn against approaching this group in English.

"That will never ever work in this market," Banerjee said. "In fact it can potentially harm a brand. A lot of things that we see on general network television, some of them are culturally not even acceptable by South Asians."

Asian Indians: Upscale Marketers Ignore This Prime Consumer Segment (cont'd.)

"You do not have to have creative in 10 different languages," said Bhasin.

Advertising featuring English dialogue interspersed with some South Asian words – or what Banerjee calls "Hinglish," a mixture of English and Hindi – is most effective.

For companies looking to enter the Asian-Indian market, experts recommend using cultural touch points such as education, family, and future security. "We believe in family values," said Bhasin. "Anything that has to do with family connects you better."

"South Asians are a little crazy about investments," added Banerjee. "They are in some ways very insecure about the future .... Their lives revolve around financial planning."

MetLife's current television advertising campaign plays into the importance of saving and education. Western Union's latest TV commercial taps into the South Asians love of family and the game of cricket to promote its wire transfer service.

There is no silver bullet for penetrating the South-Asian market. To reach these affluent consumers marketers must use a strategic mix of television, print, and radio advertising, as well as grassroots marketing such as participating in community events including the Indian Independence Day and Divali celebrations.

Banerjee said those who have made an effort to reach the South Asian market have found success. "The most important thing [about the South Asian market] is who ever has advertised in this market has never left this market," said Banerjee. "That says something."

Understand Your Audience: Missteps in Marketing to Asian Americans

By Kipp Cheng

© 2003 DiversityInc.com

November 06, 2002

When it comes to reaching out to multicultural markets, cultural sensitivity is as important as authenticity of message. After all, consumers within market segments can immediately spot insincere messaging, or worse, be completely offended by missteps that reveal how unaware a marketer is to a given market.

Some recent examples of multicultural-marketing missteps in the Asian-American market were discussed during the Tuesday session of the Association of National Advertisers' Multicultural Marketing Conference in San Francisco.

During the panel, titled "Mistakes to Avoid and Lessons Learned in the Asian-American Market," moderator Mark Dubas, vice president of the International Channel, cited several examples of culturally insensitive and offensive ads that appeared in media aimed at Asian Americans. The ill-informed ads and marketing efforts included:

- T-shirts from a popular apparel retailer that featured faux Chinese characters that read: Wong Brothers Laundry, Two Wongs Make It White.

- A print ad written in Chinese for a major national bank placed in a Filipino newspaper.

- A magazine ad for a discount retailer that showed a wok floating in space with a dog being beamed into the pan, implying that Chinese cook and eat dogs.

Dubas said the ads illustrated how marketers want to reach out to Asian-American consumers and yet continue to be insensitive to the nuances of the group.

"From a market perspective, Asian-American consumers are the best kept secret in the United States," Dubas said. "Like Latinos, it's the fastest growing segment today."

With nearly $300 billion in spending power in 2001, Dubas said if Asian Americans were a country, the economy generated by the group would be the 14th largest in the world.

Understand Your Audience: Missteps in Marketing to Asian Americans (cont'd.)

In addition to higher per capita income than all other ethnic groups in the country, Asian Americans, on average, have 23 percent higher income than whites.

Dubas said against the backdrop of being a highly attractive target market, Asian Americans continue to be misunderstood by many companies.

Panelist Vicky Wong, president of Dae Advertising, said the mistake that many markets make when approaching the Asian-American segment is to treat the group as exotic and foreign, appealing to them with stereotypical iconography that rings false.

"You don't need dragons [in ads] to address Chinese people," Wong said wryly.

The proliferation of Asian-American media outlets – which exploded from 200 outlets 15 years ago to more than 600 media outlets today – has helped to bring Asian-American consumers to the fore for markets, said Bill Imada, president and CEO at IW Group, a Los Angeles-based marketing firm.

"The most common mistake," said Imada, "is forgetting about the basic principles of marketing when reaching Asian Americans. Regardless of the audience, it should always start with the basics." Imada added that marketers wishing to reach Asian Americans must be realistic about their goals, budgets and expectations of return on investment.

Wong said because nearly 70 percent of Asian Americans are foreign born, marketing in-language becomes a critical component to an Asian-American marketing plan and working with agencies that understand and are fluent in the language of the campaign is equally important.

Imada said often mass-market agencies will want to take general-market ads and perform straight translations, without respect to cultural and language nuances.

"It's sometimes difficult to convey the concept of a product or service in an Asian language in a 30 second ad," Imada said. "Sometimes it takes a three minute ad [to explain the product], but most mass-market agencies don't understand."

Robert Liu, senior vice president at interTREND, a Torrance, Calif.-based advertising agency, said once marketing programs are in place, it's critical to have established infrastructure to support the message. For example, if a bank is advertising in Chinese-language newspapers, the bank should be prepared to received calls in Mandarin and Cantonese.

"The worst is if the effort is half-hearted," Liu said. "It's important to do it right. If you're a committed marketers, treat [emerging markets] like the legitimate

Volvo Driving Into the GLBT Market

By Ruth Zeilberger

© 2003 DiversityInc.com

May 08, 2003

Volvo is introducing its new SUV with a national car ad picturing happy same-sex couples. A woman holds her partner's pregnant belly in one frame. Two men cuddle an infant in another. A third image shows two women – one African American, the other white – with their legs crossed together and their hands interlocked. Another image shows two men embracing their Yorkie.

The tagline to Volvo's print campaign for the XC90 and the C70 Sedan is: "Whether you're starting a family or creating one as you go."

Below the pictures, the ad reads: "Some families are carefully planned. Others you just meet along the way. Whoever makes up your family, think about making Volvo part of it. From the powerful XC90 to the sleek C70, Volvo combines style with legendary safety engineering for cars that care about the people you care about."

The ad also says Volvo will donate $500 to the Human Rights Campaign, a gay, lesbian, bisexual and transgender (GLBT) political organization, when a vehicle is purchased or leased.

The print effort from May to August in "Out," "Advocacy" and "The Advocate," which also will carry a GLBT family essay contest on advocate.com. It is the second phase of a campaign for the XC90 that began in February – the first time a new car was introduced in GLBT media and mainstream media simultaneously.

This is not the first time Volvo has advertised in GLBT media, but it's the first time the automaker has developed creative ad material specifically for the GLBT market, according to Stephen Bohannon, a spokesperson for Volvo Cars.

The campaign is targeted nationwide, with a specific emphasis on the metropolitan areas of Atlanta and San Francisco.

Volvo is poised to gain handsomely from the new campaign: buying power for the GLBT market in 2002 is estimated at $451 billion and projected to reach $608 billion by 2007, a cumulative increase of more than 34 percent from 2002 figures, according to a report from Witeck-Combs Communications and

Volvo Driving Into the GLBT Market (cont'd.)

Packaged Facts, a unit of New York-based MarketResearch.com.

While Volvo won't release the percentage of its GLBT customers, the automaker is very popular among gay and lesbian consumers, according to Wesley Combs, president of Witeck-Combs Communications in Washington, D.C. which has conducted GLBT market research for Volvo. "How a company treats its employees internally is important to the GLBT community," said Combs. "Volvo is a Swedish company and Sweden is known for some of the most progressive laws and a culture that is very accepting of the GLBT community. Even people who don't know much about the company might just feel that it is the logical place to shop."

The new families campaign from Volvo, which is owned by Ford Motor Company , is the latest result of proprietary Ford gay-market research lead by its agency of record, Witeck-Combs Communications. The research, conducted last fall, already brought Jaguar, also under Ford, into the market with gay-tailored ads launched late last year. Its headline reads, "Life is full of twists and turns. Care for a partner?"

The Volvo campaign – created by Prime Access – was coordinated with Ford Global Marketing. DiversityInc ranked the Ford Motor Company as the number one company for its diversity initiatives. "This marketing program is another example of how Ford strives to be a leader in diversity marketing, which includes gay, lesbian and bisexual consumers," said Jan Valentic, vice president of global marketing at Ford Motor Company.

Ford discovered that the GLBT community is more inclined to SUV's than the general population, 30 percent to 23 percent, according to Valentic, which is why the XC90 is the co-star in Volvo's gay families ad. The popularity of SUV's reflects in part the growing number of same-sex couples with children: there are an estimated 4 million gay and lesbian people with children according to research conducted by And Baby Magazine, a magazine for GLBT parents.

"We felt that the increasing presence of gay and lesbian families wasn't being addressed by markets," said Combs. "The ads also show that you don't have to have children to have a family. Often GLBT people speak about their chosen family, their group of friends. Through these ads Volvo is saying to the GLBT community: 'We are a brand that understands your family.' "

Volvo began testing the GLBT market in June 2001, with a one time mainstream ad for the S60 in Genre, and as a sponsor of the GLAAD Media Awards.

The new Volvo campaign makes Volvo one of few car companies to create tai-

Volvo Driving Into the GLBT Market (cont'd.)

lored GLBT market advertising, following Subaru. But the tone is subdued compared to the racy ads carried for Volvo in Australia.

Volvo is the No. 1 auto brand in the Australian GLBT community, according to Bohannon and the carmaker courted the community extensively. But Bohannon wasn't sure some of the racier Australian ads would translate well to an American audience: "You have to go market by market and that kind of ad would never fly here. America is a more conservative country. It's important to pay attention to different cultural nuances, that's why we handle marketing initiatives on a local level."

The 2003 Sydney Gay & Lesbian Mardis Gras program books carries an image of a phallic-looking parking brake handle in the "erect" position with the headline, "We're just as excited as you." In 2001, in Blue magazine another Volvo ad simply announced, "Volvos are no longer straight."

Advertising to Gay Consumers Bucked Industry Decline in 2001

By Kipp Cheng

© 2003 DiversityInc.com

October 30, 2002

Following several years of tremendous growth in the advertising sector, 2001 was a tumultuous year for many media companies. The first alarm sounded with the burst of the dot-com bubble in 2000, followed by the shock of the Sept. 11 terrorist attacks. While the double-whammy of events fast-tracked the country into economic recession, the media industry still struggles with the aftershocks of the current advertising recession.

Historically, during advertising recessions, the budgets of niche-marketing programs are the first to be cut, as marketers tighten budgets and hope to have the most impact with their dollars by appealing to the broadest audience possible. For the gay, lesbian, bisexual and transgender (GLBT) market, 2001 showed some hopeful, countercyclical trends and offered some encouraging signs of strength, despite modest declines in ad spending in gay media.

According to the "2002 Gay Press Report," while ad spending in overall consumer magazines declined 6.2 percent in 2001, spending in gay print media declined a relatively modest 1.7 percent. Additionally, the lower rate of decline of ad spending in gay print media (compared to overall print media) followed years of rapid growth in the sector. In 1994, $53 million was spent on gay media, and by 2000, spending had peaked at $211 million, the report revealed.

"Generally, niche markets do not fare as well as general markets during tough economic times," said Howard Buford, CEO of the New York-based advertising agency Prime Access, which published the "2002 Gay Press Report" with Rivendell Marketing, a media-representation firm. "In tough economic times, advertisers and marketers tend to focus on their best customers, and I think in the past, niche media has suffered more. But overall, it's probably suffering a little less this time because marketers are feeling that the general message is falling on general ears and [marketers] now want to speak to consumers who, research has shown, are their best customers."

The report revealed that 72 brands from Fortune 500 companies were actively marketed in the gay consumer market in 2001. Over the past year alone, companies such as Chrysler, Ford and Sears have also explored targeting the GLBT

Advertising to Gay Consumers Bucked Industry Decline in 2001 (cont'd.)

segment. Particular gains in spending were seen in categories such as recruiting/jobs, pet care, travel and religious/church organizations, which each experienced more than 200 percent rates of growth in 2001.

Buford said the modest decrease of ad spending in gay print media shows that advertisers have realized the importance of targeting GLBT consumers. He added that, as niche markets have been segmented into increasingly smaller subgroups, media segmentation has reflected this market change.

"There's more segmented media today than ever before," Buford said. "For example, ads on cable TV or in targeted magazines and newspapers let marketers really address the 20 percent of the population that accounts for 80 percent of sales."

One bright spot behind the somewhat gloomy media climate was the increased number of advertising efforts created specifically for the gay and lesbian market. The report found a 34 percent increase of ads tailor-made for GLBT media. According to Todd Evans, CEO of Westfield, N.J.-based Rivendell Marketing, marketers are no longer simply relying on generic ads developed for the mass market to reach GLBT consumers. Additionally, national advertisers are becoming increasingly comfortable with the idea and process of tapping the gay market.

"There's no real shock value in targeting the gay market anymore," said Evans, "not that there ever really was. Marketers are saying, 'We don't have enough money for the greatest number of eyeballs, so we're going to focus in on our consumers within various segments and concentrate there.' "

Evans said no clients have received major negative backlash from pursuing the GLBT market, adding that the decline in spending has more to do with budgetary concerns than philosophic ones. "It seems like now, at this particular time, the declines are a matter of focusing budgets rather than the taboo of the gay market."

Buford said as marketers reassess their budgets, a growing number continue to target GLBT consumers in gay media, because gay consumers have responded positively to gay-friendly marketers.

"One of the really strong messages that's coming out of the issue of the gay market is brand loyalty, and loyalty to companies that support the community," said Cathy Renna, news media director at the Gay and Lesbian Alliance Against Defamation. "So when it's a combination of supporting a gay media outlet, such as PlanetOut or the Advocate, in addition to the inclusive advertising reflecting the market, I think companies understand that sends a strong message and it's something that people within niche markets will respond to."

Advertising to Gay Consumers Bucked Industry Decline in 2001 (cont'd.)

In addition to modest gains in certain advertising categories appearing in gay media, the report also concluded that the representation of GLBT consumers in mainstream media has seen some gains as well.

But has there been a trend of gay representation in advertising in general?

"It hasn't been an overwhelming trend, but there is definitely a trend," said Michael Wilke, executive director of the Commercial Closet, an online repository of ads that feature GLBT representation.

Wilke said marketers are increasingly savvy to the reality that gay consumers like to see themselves portrayed in advertising messages aimed at them.

Buford added that part of the reason why certain industries, such as financial services, have continued to address the gay market is because competitors have already reached out to the market, so there's some catch-up to do.

"This is true of automotive, where foreign automakers, like Subaru, have made inroads with the gay market," said Buford. "It puts the Fords and Chryslers in a defensive mode to gain share within the segment."

Wilke agreed, adding, "There are more advertisers all of the time who are there, in general, and more specifically, for many, also who are there in their own category of business. So if their competitor is already [targeting gay consumers], and is well established, many companies come into the market defensively, so that they don't lose out."

Evans cited the marketing campaign for Bridgestone/Firestone that appeared in magazines such as the Advocate and on Web sites such as PlanetOut as doing a good job at portraying real customers who happen to be gay and lesbian.

The bottom line is that gay media has charted the rocky waters of the advertising recession fairly well, and despite a decrease in spending on gay media, there's resilience in the market as marketers continue to fine-tune messages to reach out to this group.

"It seems that even in hard times, gay media has done relatively well. It shows the continued interest, even if we're still talking modest numbers," said Wilke. "The problem is that while there are many companies that are interested in the gay market, it's like an Olympic-size wading pool. All of these companies are in only about an inch deep. Very few of them are in deeper than that. So there's a lot of interest, but not a lot of spending."

"The report shows that the realm of companies investigating the gay market has stayed strong," said Evans. "And I really think that 2003 will turn out to be a good year for gay media."

New Stock Index Serves as Yardstick for U.S. Latino Economy

By Angela D. Johnson

© 2003 DiversityInc.com

March 06, 2003

In an effort to provide an assessment of the U.S. Latino economy that's on par with barometers used to measure large Latino economies, such as Mexico, Spain and Argentina, Hispanic Business has launched the Hispanic Business Stock Index (HBSI). Developed by HispanTelligence, the research division of Hispanic Business Inc., the index tracks publicly traded companies that are majority Latino-owned or whose main focus is on the U.S. Latino market, regardless of the shareholders' ethnicity.

"Our main objective was to identify and increase the exposure of companies that are in the Hispanic market," Juan Solana, director of market research for HispanTelligence, told DiversityInc.

Only stocks traded in the United States on the New York Stock Exchange, Nasdaq, the American Stock Exchange or over-the-counter were considered for the index. Thirteen companies met the criteria: Univision, Popular Inc. (the holding company of Banco Popular), Hispanic Broadcasting Corp., International Bancshares Corp., Entravision Communications, Spanish Broadcasting System, Gruma Corp., Movado Corp., MasTec Inc., Perry Ellis International, United PanAm Financial, Metrocorp Bancshares Inc., and Radio Unica. Companies in the media industry represent the largest amount of capital on the HBSI; the financial-services category follows closely behind.

Adopting the same methodology used to measure the Standard & Poor's 500 Index, HBSI calculation is based on weighted market capitalization, the price of a company's stock multiplied by the number of outstanding shares. As of December 2002, total market capitalization of the HBSI companies was $15.7 billion; total sales for 2002 amounted to $8.4 billion. Univision, Popular Inc., and Hispanic Broadcasting topped the HBSI, accounting for more than 74 percent of market capitalization.

Over the past decade, the U.S. Latino economy has grown faster than the U.S. economy as a whole. While all indexes experienced a decline in 2002, the HBSI dropped the least. When compared with figures from the Dow Jones Industrial Average, the S&P 500, and the Nasdaq over the last year, the HBSI outperformed

New Stock Index Serves as Yardstick for U.S. Latino Economy (cont'd.)

the Nasdaq by 18.73 points, the S&P by 9.94 points, and the Dow by 3.69 points.

Solana said the strong performance of the U.S. Latino economy can be attributed to the increase in the Latino market, which is driven by a surge in immigration and lower mortality rates. Despite a slow IPO market, he anticipates an increase in the number of companies entering the Latino market.

The HBSI debuted in the March issue of Hispanic Business. Updates, along with information on market developments and industry players, will appear in the magazine each month.

'We Came Out in Our Own Time': Avis Goes After Gay Market

By Melanie Austria Farmer

© 2003 DiversityInc.com

May 23, 2003

Rental-car provider Avis has launched a new advertising campaign geared at the gay, lesbian, bisexual and transgender (GLBT) market. As part of its campaign, Avis is dedicating 5 percent of its total advertising budget in 2003 to the GLBT market.

Avis, based in Parsippany, N.J., is featuring print ads this month with its tagline, "We Try Harder." Full-page ads will be placed in niche magazines including Out, The Advocate and the premiere issue of Out Traveler with additional ads set to run on their respective Web sites.

Avis is part of Cendant's car-rental group, which also owns Budget, another rental-car provider. Avis said this is not the first time it set out to specifically target GLBT consumers. Avis partly is using this ad campaign to promote an existing policy, in which it allows same-sex domestic partners to rent a car without paying an extra fee, usually around $25, to sign on an additional driver. Married couples typically do not get fined an additional charge for multiple drivers while siblings or two friends do pay the fee.

"A very specific and direct benefit like that could be very meaningful and can result in significant loyalty and a shift in volume," said Howard Buford, CEO of the New-York based advertising firm Prime Access. "It's harder than ever to really differentiate your brand and brand loyalty. If you have the opportunity to do that, it's a good idea."

One ad, which shows two men enjoying a drink in a sunny, tropical setting, reads: "At Avis, domestic partners are automatically included as additional drivers. No extra fees charged. No questions asked. That's been our policy for the past 10 years. So, why have we waited so long to tell you? Well, let's just say we came out in our own time."

"We're always looking for different consumer segments ... who are willing to pay a premium for a better product," said Susan McGowan, a spokesperson for Avis. "We think this market is one that cares about service, cares about how they're treated, and is loyal to companies that support this."

'We Came Out in Our Own Time': Avis Goes After Gay Market (cont'd.)

Avis is not the only one coveting that level of customer loyalty.

A growing crop of companies has turned its attention to this profitable market. Big names, such as Chrysler, Ford and Sears, have tapped this segment. Volvo this month introduced its new SUV with a national ad campaign that featured GLBT families. Other rental-car agencies also have made efforts in the past, including Enterprise, Alamo and National Car Rental, through various ways including ads and direct-mail.

And, at the same time, Avis wouldn't mind nabbing a hefty chunk of a very attractive market. The buying power for the GLBT market in 2002 is estimated at $451 billion and projected to reach $608 billion by 2008, a cumulative increase of more than 34 percent from 2002 figures, according to a report from Witeck-Combs Communications and Packaged Facts, a division of New York-based MarketResearch.com.

Wesley Combs, co-founder of Witeck-Combs Communications, a Washington, D.C.-based marketing firm that specializes in the GLBT community, said the travel sector always has been an appealing market for companies to reach GLBT consumers.

The appeal in the travel sector is "largely driven by the fact that only 20 percent of GLBT households have children in them which leaves a lot more discretionary income in 80 percent of the households to be spent on things such as travel and luxury goods," said Combs. "It also allows GLBT people to have the opportunity to pick up and go at a moment's notice because they're not tied down with the responsibility of children."

Despite the downtrodden economy, the travel industry still reports a substantial amount of GLBT customers who dole out cash for vacations. Ninety-seven per-cent of GLBT-identified respondents took a vacation in North America in 2001, according to a survey by Community Marketing, a San Francisco-based market-ing firm. Most notable is the survey response that 56 percent took three or more vacations and 29 percent took four or more vacations during the period.

Buford said it is important for competitors in this industry to meet the needs of GLBT consumers.

"The lesbian and gay men index is very high for travel; it's a market that rental car companies pay attention to," said Buford. "It is not assumed that gay men and lesbians are welcomed, especially in travel, hotels and airlines ... It is important for the travel industry to send a message that says you're not going to have an awkward moment at the hotel registration desk when you're a same-sex couple."

'We Came Out in Our Own Time': Avis Goes After Gay Market (cont'd.)

The basic idea, he said, is that companies relay the message to the community that implies, "Yes, you're welcome here."

As part of its campaign, which will last until the end of the year, Avis also is taking on a stronger sponsorship role in the GLBT market. McGowan said the company will donate $1 per rental to the Gay & Lesbian Alliance Against Defamation (GLAAD).

Other elements of the campaign include sponsorship of gay-and-lesbian film festivals in cities, such as Miami, Los Angeles and San Francisco. The company plans to distribute city guides at each festival that highlight restaurant recommendations, offer rental car upgrades/coupons and other local information.

New Numbers Make the Case: Ethnic Spending Power Continues Rapid Rise

By Kipp Cheng

© 2003 DiversityInc.com

December 06, 2002

Despite the roller-coaster ride that investors have taken on Wall Street, the nation's total buying power remains solid, with projected estimates showing continued growth over the next five years. According to new data from the Selig Center for Economic Growth at the University of Georgia, total buying power for all U.S. consumers should rise from $4.3 trillion in 1990 to $9.9 trillion in 2007.

African-American, Latino and Asian-American consumers – as well as consumers from other emerging markets – play key roles in the expanding U.S. economy. According to the Selig Center's report, "The Multicultural Economy 2002: Minority Buying Power in the New Century," consumers of color "definitely share in [the] success [in economic gains], and together wield formidable economic clout."

The combined buying power of African Americans, Asian Americans and Native Americans in 2007, according to the Selig Center findings, should be more than triple its 1990 level of $453 billion, totaling almost $1.4 trillion. That represents an increase of more than 200 percent over the 17-year period. (Latinos as a group were excluded from this calculation because they can be of any race.)

In 2007, African Americans are expected to account for 62 percent of combined buying power, or $853 billion. While buying power for the white market should increase 112 percent between 1990 and 2007, buying power for Latinos should increase by 315 percent; Asian Americans should increase by 287 percent; and African Americans by 170 percent.

Other findings from the Selig Center report:

- African-American consumers spend more than other groups on products and services such as telephone services, personal-care products, electricity and natural gas, children's apparel, and footwear.

- Latinos spend more than other groups on products and services such as groceries, furniture, men's and boys' apparel, and children's clothing.

- In 2002, the five states with the largest Asian-American consumer markets

New Numbers Make the Case: Ethnic Spending Power Continues Rapid Rise (cont'd.)

were California ($104.1 billion), New York ($31.9 billion), New Jersey ($18 billion), Texas ($16.6 billion), Hawaii ($15.3 billion).

- African-American spending power is projected to reach $852.8 billion in 2007 (from $645.9 billion in 2002).

- Latino spending power projected to reach $927.1 billion in 2007 (from $580.5 billion in 2002). Additionally, the Selig Center projects that Latino spending power should outpace African-American spending power in 2005.

- Asian-American spending power is projected to reach $454.9 billion in 2007 (from $296.4 billion in 2002).

"The buying power data … and differences in spending by race and/or ethnicity suggest that one general advertisement, product or service geared for all consumers increasingly misses many potentially profitable market opportunities," the Selig report said. "As the U.S. consumer market becomes more diverse, advertising, products and media must be tailored to each market segment."

White consumer market share is expected to decline from 87.4 percent in 1990 to 80.1 percent in 2007, while market share for ethnic markets should see increases across the board. African-American market share should rise from 7.4 percent in 1990 to 8.6 percent in 2007; Latino market share should increase from 5.2 percent in 1990 to 9.4 percent in 2007; and Asian-American market share should grow from 2.7 percent to 4.7 percent between 1990 and 2007.

Beyond Just the Numbers, What Counts As an Emerging Market?

By Kipp Cheng

© 2003 DiversityInc.com

July 01, 2002

The tremendous growth of the population of non-white Americans has transformed the ethnic composition of the country over the past decade. Members of the so-called emerging markets – African-American, Latino and Asian-American consumers, as well as gay and lesbian people and people with disabilities – are flexing their collective $1 trillion in spending power, and yet are still frequently ignored by most businesses.

That's because businesses love to play the numbers game. And the number that seems to matter most to business is population size. It's not efficient, many businesses claim, to target small groups of consumers.

But some marketers and researchers believe that raw census numbers don't reveal the entire opportunity that businesses are missing.

"It's a big mistake to rely only on population size," said Pepper Miller, president of The Hunter-Miller Group, a Chicago-based market-research company. "Psychographics – the motivations for the quantitative things that happen in the market – play a key role in understanding emerging markets. And not understanding that is an enormous opportunity lost for corporate America."

The numbers reflecting the growth of ethnic Americans are compelling: According to the 2000 U.S. Census, there are 35.3 million Latinos, 34.7 million African Americans and 11.9 million Asian Americans living in the United States. Ethnic Americans now comprise nearly 25 percent of the total population. Furthermore, there are nearly 600,000 same-sex, unmarried partner households in the country, an increase of more than 300 percent between 1990 and 2000.

While these numbers can be used to describe the volume of certain groups of potential target markets, based on race or sexual orientation for example, they are limited when used to describe other attributes that are necessary to understand how to segment within these emerging markets.

"African Americans outspend other groups in 'badge value' items such as cars, jewelry and fashion, despite being smaller than the overall general market," said Miller. Yet, Miller said, marketers of high-end products and services often don't

Beyond Just the Numbers, What Counts As an Emerging Market? (cont'd.)

understand why they should target African-American consumers over other groups. "These marketers have a limited view of African Americans based on what they see in the media"

Miller tells her clients to consider the psychographic profile of African-American consumers, regardless of what census data shows. "The census is useful, don't get me wrong, but it's also a double-edged sword. It's critical to look beyond the basic numbers of these emerging markets to really understand what makes these consumers tick."

A true investment to research is required, Miller said, if marketers want to break through the excuse of emerging markets being too small.

"When they say it's too small to count, there is some validity to that, I understand what they are saying," said Miller. "But one of the reasons that segments are too small to count is because a lot of times marketers are using data from general market research studies that feature small samples of African Americans. But if you did a study of African Americans alone and looked at the value there, you'd see that the opportunities for companies to increase business share or give them that little push to take them over the top is huge."

Beyond pure numbers, though, the semantics of the phrase "emerging market" can stymie some business marketing programs. Jeff Yang, CEO of Factor, a New York-based marketing agency that specializes in reaching Asian-American consumers, said flagging a group as an "emerging market" often dooms the group to a permanent developmental status.

"It isn't and shouldn't be just a matter of raw population numbers," Yang said. "Attributes such as aggregate disposable income, appropriateness for different product categories, consumer behavior and so forth should factor heavily into the equation."

Yang said there is often a knee-jerk reaction on the part of marketers when it comes to engaging with emerging markets. "They all tend to share common threads in the sense that these emerging markets are not 'ripe' to be dealt with, regardless of what marketing medium, category or brand they're looking at."

Therefore, calling all non-white, non-mainstream target segments "emerging," according to Yang, invokes a kind of "code phrasing" that relegates ethnic, gay and lesbian, and disabled consumers into a marketplace ghetto that allows businesses to avoid the fundamental understanding and sophistication of how to analyze these particular groups.

Beyond Just the Numbers, What Counts As an Emerging Market? (cont'd.)

Emerging markets, then, get short shrift from marketing programs, over more desirable "vertical" markets comprised of consumers with similar consuming patterns and attributes, though not necessarily a shared race.

For example, high-tech marketers spend millions annually to reach narrow target groups such as Linux programmers, Yang said. "It's because this group is perceived as being active listeners to tech branding messages, and because they're often purchasing decision makers, early adopters, etc."

Yet, Asian Americans, a group that's conservatively 10 times as large, and has an equally attractive profile for tech adoption, are generally not targeted in the same way because they are considered an emerging market versus a vertical market.

"[Businesses] sort of dump ethnic groups into a marketplace back lot, and say, 'We'll wait until [the segment] grows to 50 million or 100 million or 80 percent of a certain population,'" Yang said.

The problem, however, is once the consuming patterns of consumers in emerging markets match the general market, then the opportunity to reach out to them is lost.

"By the time a minority group is no longer a minority," said Yang, "any advantage a marketer might have in actually targeting up front is essentially gone with the wind. Generally speaking, businesses try to be safe. If everyone is doing something, for you to do it automatically achieves a certain kind of security. You can't get fired for going along with the herd. At the same time, you're not going to achieve any kind of miraculous results either."

Yang said an investment in researching emerging markets is the first step that a marketer must take to tap into its potential. Whether it's through consumer surveying, sampling or test-product launches and reaching out to key influencers, it's critical for marketers to take the time to understand the niche market it wants to reach.

So what numbers matter most? According to marketing executives and researchers, the answer is a resounding "It depends."

"The number that matters is the one that's the most cost effective," said Bob Witeck, CEO at Witeck Combs, a Washington, D.C.-based marketing and research firm. "One size never fits all for all marketers."

Determining the correct number to characterize an emerging market depends on a variety of factors, including the media channel that the marketer selects to distribute a message to a given target segment, he said.

Beyond Just the Numbers, What Counts As an Emerging Market? (cont'd.)

For example, Witeck said, credit-card and telecommunications companies are industries that rely heavily on direct mail to reach consumers. Given the relatively low response rate of direct mail – which is typically less than 2 percent, according to Iconocast, a company that tracks and analyzes marketing and technology trends – the economies of scale dictate that direct-mail marketers must establish a high set point to be cost effective.

"The mining of the data means that marketers will likely want to do mailings that are in the aggregate of 500,000 to 1 million, in terms of reach," said Witeck. "When you're a credit-card company or a phone company, you're going to have to get a certain number of names in order to do an authentic direct-marketing outreach."

In the case of marketers using direct mail, the answer of how many consumers from a given emerging market they'd like to reach is "going to be pretty high," said Witeck. After all, these marketers are going after the largest reach, and won't be segmenting as much as another marketer.

With the fragmentation of media and the continuing proliferation of technology, especially the Internet, marketers will need to identify smaller and smaller niches within emerging markets to remain competitive.

"There is going to be smaller and smaller segmentation of market groups because you can do it," said Witeck. "Marketers want to talk to their customers as directly and individually as they can."

Still, some marketers are not yet taking advantage of appealing to emerging markets.

"I've been seeing a decline in the perceived value of the African-American market by marketers and business people," said Miller. "There's an important part of the segment that they don't understand. We are still perceived as a homogeneous market versus heterogenous."

"Marketers are spending ever increasing amounts to retain consumers in a slipping mass market," Yang said. "They are not investing in a marginally proportional basis on emerging markets. Anyone looking at census data understands that within a quarter century, within the next decade, 'emerging markets' are going to be the plurality or majority of America."

Want to Attract Consumers of Color? Take A Leadership Lesson From This Industry

By Linda Bean

© 2003 DiversityInc.com

August 26, 2002

Is your company struggling to reach emerging markets? Have you failed to reach consumers of color? Does cross-cultural communication remain a total mystery?

Yes? Then you might take a lesson from representatives of some of the nation's largest museums.

"It is all about the invitation," said Richard Clarke, an African-American trustee at New York City's Metropolitan Museum of Modern Art. "Just because you leave your door open, doesn't necessarily mean you want me to walk in."

Clarke, the owner of Richard Clarke & Associates, a New York City-based executive-recruiting firm, is also known for his collection of African and African-American art. He joined the Met's board six years ago, on the understanding that he would be allowed to initiate a new effort to attract more visitors of color.

"We have a huge population of people who don't feel that a museum is a welcoming institution," Clarke said.

Guided by his belief that museums must do more than open their doors, he led the development of a Multicultural Audience Development Advisory Committee. Committee members are drawn from leading civic organizations for people of color – 100 Black Men, Jack and Jill, and Links Inc., for example.

Links, for example, has 150,000 members nationwide, Clarke noted. "Well-educated, well-heeled young black women."

The committee has been in place for about four years and the "outpouring of interest" from communities of color "has been extraordinary," Clarke said.

But while the Met might be doing a fine job of community outreach, it falls short in terms of metrics. The museum, which reported revenue of $762.8 million last year, doesn't track visitorship by ethnicity, said Donna Sutton, the Met's audience development specialist. "We don't ask that," she added.

Seattle Art Museum, by contrast, does ask – about ethnicity, and much more.

Want to Attract Consumers of Color? Take A Leadership Lesson From This Industry (cont'd.)

Victoria Moreland, director of community affairs at the Seattle Art Museum (SAM), is responsible, in part, for marketing the museum's services to people of color. She gauges her success against Seattle's demographics and has established a series of metrics to track progress.

Moreland doesn't talk about vertical markets or "emerging markets" or even "return on investment." Still, her strategy embodies all the elements that a diversity-deficient company should consider adopting to attract, serve and retain a diverse customer base.

Moreland, a former human-resources executive at Nordstrom, the Seattle-based department store chain, is comfortable with the process of applying the measurable standards in place at the best corporations to the work she does for one of the nation's largest museums.

For example, an extensive outreach program prior to "Long Steps Never Broke a Back" – a recent exhibition of African art – sent African-American attendance at the museum soaring to 12 percent from 2 percent, based on responses to follow-up visitors' surveys, said Moreland, who is African American. Overall, 8.3 percent of Seattle's population is African American.

That outreach system includes identifying key players in each of the city's ethnic communities, issuing open invitations to pre-exhibition planning meetings; building partnerships with community organizations that might have a special interest in a particular exhibition; making top museum officials available to for related programs outside the museum, and attention to follow-up communications.

The museum has in place a program called "Deepening the Dialogue" which aims to "deepen our relationship within communities to increase the frequency of interaction with our current audience," Moreland said.

"We have done audience research, visitors and members surveys – we've interviewed both visitors and non-visitors. We've invited non-visitors in to sit down and talk to them, to ask them what they like and what they don't like," Moreland said. SAM reported total revenue of $67 million last year.

In Kansas City, Mo., meanwhile, the issue of cross-cultural communication is key and it plays itself out in all of the core functions at the Nelson-Atkins Museum.

Only a handful of students graduate each year with a doctorate degrees in art history – the graduate ranks from which museum curators most often emerge. It can take a year or more to hire a curator for a museum collection. The museum,

Want to Attract Consumers of Color? Take A Leadership Lesson From This Industry (cont'd.)

which had revenue of $78.5 million last year, is now seeking a curator for its African collection.

Across the board, museum officials said scholarship – not ethnicity – is the determining factor in the selection of a curator. Still, the question of who is qualified to tell the story behind a certain ethnic group's artifacts "is a very big issue, a very big question," said Gaylord Torrence, curator of the Nelson-Atkins' American Indian collection.

"It's an issue for anyone curating in the art of tribal peoples, and even the word 'tribal' is a political term," Torrence said.

Curators are responsible for the storage and protection of collections; the purchase of new art and the exhibition and interpretation of existing pieces. And it is the responsibility for interpretation that generates the most discussion. Clearly, it is ridiculous to expect the curator of a museum's 16th century Flemish collection to be a resident of 16th century Belgium.

But is it equally ridiculous to demand that the curator of a Chinese or American Indian collection be Chinese or American Indian?

Torrence, 59, is not an American Indian and he doesn't believe that "cultural heritage necessarily translates as cultural knowledge."

But he has been studying their art for most of his adult life. He has studied the creation of parfleche – rawhide containers – an art that died out in 1945. As part of his research, Torrence tracked 1,500 example of parfleche in nearly one hundred public and private collections in the United States, Canada, and Europe – the most extensive examination ever made.

Torrence also invested nearly a decade in the study of the Mesquakie people in central Iowa, "a living community," he said.

"I worked very hard to gain the trust of the traditional people within the community and I felt a tremendous responsibility ... in interpreting the community," he added.

In order to earn that trust, Torrence took the steps that any company desirous of effective cross-cultural communication should take.

He reached out to opinion-makers – traditional elders. He detailed his extensive research so they would recognize the depth of his understanding and interest, and he continued to work closely with them throughout the project.

"I relied upon them for guidance, clarification and support," he said.

Want to Attract Consumers of Color? Take A Leadership Lesson From This Industry (cont'd.)

He also recognized that there were things about the culture "that I will never know," Torrence said. "There are some things I cannot know … there are aspects of their religion that are inappropriate for outsiders to know. It is important for a scholar to recognize that."

Stagnating Insurance Industry Finds New Life with Black, Latino, Asian Customers

By Eric L. Hinton

© 2003 DiversityInc.com

July 15, 2002

Much like the very air we breathe, insurance is an oft-ignored but vital part of the lives of most Americans. If you own a home, then somewhere buried under stacks of dusty papers in the attic is your homeowners' insurance policy. If you're driving anything from a '77 Dodge to a Mercedes convertible SL 500 then, hopefully, tucked away in the glove compartment is your car insurance registration.

And much like oxygen, insurance often goes unappreciated. You won't really miss it until the one afternoon when you need it most.

Whether you have a "Good Neighbor" like State Farm or happen to be in "Good Hands" with Allstate, insurance is a multibillion dollar industry that has proliferated into the lives of nearly all financially educated consumers. Through targeted marketing, advertising and promotion of it various products, the industry had almost done its job too well. While property and casualty, or P&C, insurance – which includes coverage for homes and cars – is estimated to be a $302 billion annual enterprise, over the latter half of the 1990s, P&C carriers found themselves staring apprehensively at annual growth rates barely breaking 3 percent, acording to DataMonitor, a business information company specializing in industry analysis.

By the late 1990s, stagnation threatened to send many of these companies into a tailspin. Their problem was they had already reached most of their existing customer base. And if the insurance companies can't stay in business by finding new customers, consumer options may dwindle and premiums go up.

Then the answer arrived gift-wrapped in 2000, courtesy of the U.S. Census.

The census data showed that the growth rate of the white, non-Hispanic population slowed dramatically in comparison to the growth rates of African-American, Asian-American and Latino populations.

The number of African-American households with annual incomes of at least $50,000 grew to 3.7 million, with 1.4 million African-American households earning annual incomes in excess of $75,000. The Latino population increased by 57

Stagnating Insurance Industry Finds New Life with Black, Latino, Asian Customers (cont'd.)

percent since 1990 with estimates of the buying power ranging anywhere from $273 billion to $445 billion. The Selig Center for Economic Growth at the University of Georgia reported last year that the buying power of Asian-American consumers increased 124 percent over the past decade, topping $255 billion in 2001.

Do the math. Insurance carriers, looking at a tapped-out majority market, were suddenly presented with government-documented proof that ethnic markets were coming of age financially. The era of emerging markets in the insurance industry was born.

Show Me the Money

Let's be clear…insurance carriers' rush to service the emerging markets was not based on altruism, but economics. Consumer-buying power among people of color nearly doubled over the past decade, growing at a much faster rate than overall U.S. buying power, according to the Selig Center for Economic Growth at the University of Georgia. Buying power in the United States is expected to reach $7.1 trillion this year. People of color make up about 18 percent of that figure, or $1.3 trillion a year.

African-American consumers comprise the largest buying-power group at $572.1 billion. And the growth in their spending has outpaced that of white consumers, growing roughly 81 percent since 1990, according to the Selig Center. According to census data, the median household income for Asian Americans was $10,000 above that of white people in 2000.

The implications aren't lost on the larger insurance carriers. "The ethnic groups are the fastest growing and its anticipated that before 2050, those populations will reach 50 percent of the total U.S population, so it's a critical piece for us," said Thania Helen Lozano, director of emerging markets at State Farm, the nation's largest insurance carrier.

At Seattle-based SAFECO, the company recently unveiled a new CD-ROM aimed at helping agents grow new business in the emerging markets. The CD-ROM describes the rapidly diversifying marketplace and the opportunities it represents for new business.

"This CD-ROM is the latest in a series of tools SAFECO has developed to help our agents succeed in writing business in these emerging markets," said Raphael Madison, SAFECO's assistant vice president of diversity marketing. "We also have mentoring programs, translated marketing materials, and translation services. These new resources will help our agents provide meaningful products and

Stagnating Insurance Industry Finds New Life with Black, Latino, Asian Customers (cont'd.)

services to segments of the population that traditionally have been under-represented in the insurance industry."

Brendan Ford, a financial analyst with DataMonitor, said the rising affleunce in the emerging markets is attracting a vast array of insurance industry suitors.

"You're seeing major changes in the behavior of these populations in relation to financial products and services, including insurance," said Ford. "These groups are now actively saving and investing and using insurance to protect their assets." Ford recently authored the report "Ethnic Marketing in Financial Services 2001-2002: Strategies for selling banking, insurance and asset management to the U.S. Hispanic, African-American, and Asian-American communities"

"The market that these insurance carriers traditionally market to, that of the male white-led household, is a shrinking slice of the pie," said Ford. "You have everything from non-traditional families to the different ethnic groups to the gay community. All sorts of communities are being ignored when you focus only on that slice of the pie. If you want to continue to have broad appeal to the market you have to find a way to reach out to these different groups in a way that they respond to."

How to successfully reach out to these communities of color is becoming of paramount importance to heady companies. According to Target Market News, which tracks consumer spending patterns in the African-American community, in 1999 African Americans spent a combined $5.4 billion on various insurance-related products. That amount climbed to $6.1 billion in 2000.

While conducting DataMonitor research, Ford said he found there were companies that were paying mere lip service to targeting the emerging markets and those that took the task to heart. While some companies such as Travelers and Nationwide could be doing more to market to the ethnic markets, insurance carriers like Allstate were setting a path to follow.

"Even when you look at other insurance companies, they will usually compare themselves to Allstate. They'll say they looked at what that company was doing or saw how successful they've been and decided to get into this as well," said Ford. "Allstate is by and far the best, particularly in the Hispanic market."

That's exactly what Raymond Celaya wants to hear. Celaya, the assistant vice president of Emerging Markets with Allstate, joined the company in 1977 as an operations supervisor. Today, he oversees the emerging markets team for the Northbrook, Ill. based concern. The "good hands" company is the second-largest U.S. personal lines insurer, behind State Farm. Auto and homeowners lines

Stagnating Insurance Industry Finds New Life with Black, Latino, Asian Customers (cont'd.)

account for about two-thirds of sales. Even with $28.8 billion in 2001 sales and a firm slot at number 57 on the Fortune 500, Celaya believes Allstate's focus on the emerging markets is simply a matter of corporate survival.

"Among the white markets there is some growth, but it's stagnant growth. And even that growth is just the business that insurance companies are taking away from each other," he said. "However, in the emerging markets you're looking at growth anywhere from five to 10 times faster than the general market. The growth rate for household creation in the Hispanic market was 3.5 percent annually. In the non-ethnic market you were talking about .5 percent. It offers tremendous fertile ground to grow our businesses."

Allstate has gone beyond paying mere lip service to the emerging markets. With dedicated staffs for the Asian American and African-American markets, the company has targeted advertising and marketing strategies aimed at both communities. And the Hispanic market? They own the Hispanic market.

"At end of 2001, we were serving 1.4 million households versus the 850,000 in 1995 with over 2 billion in premium coming from the Hispanic market," said Celaya. "We have roughly 70 percent range in households. We had a clear vision which was that we would become the company of choice for the Hispanic market and that every Hispanic household would think of Allstate first when it comes to insurance."

So what's the winning formula? In Part II of our Insurance series, the largest insurance companies reveal their winning strategies for attracting the emerging markets.

Auto Markets: How Small Can You Slice Them?

By Linda Bean

© 2003 DiversityInc.com

May 20, 2003

The business of marketing automobiles is at a crossroads.

Most automakers are long past believing that diverse markets can be ignored; some of the nation's largest makers of cars and trucks go out of their way to stress in public statements and marketing materials that any increase in market share they eke out in 2003 will come only from African Americans, gays and lesbians, Latinos and Asian Americans.

At the same time, the auto industry is trying to determine when race, ethnicity or sexual orientation – traditional cues to market segmentation – are driving buying decision and when other factors, such as life-stage or a passion for technology, for example, influence a purchase.

The quandary for automakers, then, is deciding when and how to segment diverse markets. How narrowly should a market be divided? When does market segmentation boost the bottom line? What does research say?

The prospect of seeking out the answers to those questions might be enough to dissuade some auto executives from exploring the nuances of segmented marketing – if the stakes weren't so high.

But General Motors, Ford and the Chrysler unit of DaimlerChrysler posted lower sales in 2002, a trend all three companies want to reverse. Meanwhile, according to Autodata, which tracks auto-industry numbers, Honda, Toyota and Nissan all posted market-share gains that they want to extend.

Overall, North American auto sales are projected to fall by nearly 3 percent in 2003, as consumers grapple with economic hardship at home and uncertainty abroad. According to J.D. Power and Associates, U.S. auto sales are expected to drop this year to 16.4 million new cars and light trucks from 16.8 million in 2002. The consumer-research giant is predicting a decline, despite continued sales incentives from U.S.-based automakers.

If there ever was a time to become fluent in the language of segmented market-

Auto Markets: How Small Can You Slice Them? (cont'd.)

ing, it is now, says Marc Strachan, the African-American chairman of the diversity council for the American Association of Advertising Agencies and co-founder of New York-based advertising firm, S/R Communications Alliance.

"And you have got to be in it for the long haul," he says. "We are not talking about goodwill or good public relations. We are talking about moving pallets and increasing shareholder value."

Common Ground

Demographics reveal an emerging trend – Americans age 40 and older may prefer marketing campaigns aimed at specific racial or ethnic groups. But younger Americans view their world as more multiethnic and multicultural and are more likely to respond to advertising that reflects that diverse world view.

And the United States is getting more multiracial. According to the U.S. Census Bureau, there are 284 million people living in America. Among Americans aged 70 and older, there are 5.3 white people for every person of color – a ratio of roughly 5-to-1. For Americans below the age 40, the ratio is 2-to-1. For children under 10, the ratio is 1.5-to-1.

But older Americans of different races may have had "significantly different" experiences in the course of their lifetimes, notes Joe Johnson, who is responsible for corporate development and transformation at Mercedes-Benz USA.

"But when you get down to the younger group, you see people whose experiences may be very similar – music, fashion – there's a greater basis for connection," says Johnson.

Contemporary marketing strategies may dictate campaigns aimed at potential buyers of a specific ethnicity, Johnson adds, but future strategies will focus on "commonality of experience."

Now, says Johnson, who is African American, "there's a clear recognition that diverse consumers need to be appealed to in some way, but I think you are going to see [segmented marketing] approaches become more inclusive, more appealing to a broader group of people."

"The general market is going to become a multicultural market," he adds.

"Our young population is coming from a more diverse background," echoes Greg Dixon, who leads the diversity-marketing group at Volvo, a member of Ford's premier auto group.

"Based upon research, we know that ethnicity has become more and more valu-

Auto Markets: How Small Can You Slice Them? (cont'd.)

able to our marketing strategy," Dixon says, a recognition that guides the company's efforts to build relationships with diverse consumers – via event sponsorships, for example – or the placement of advertisements in diverse media.

But Volvo's advertising focuses firmly on the company's cars, Dixon says, and ads are "almost ethnic-neutral."

"We want to inspire consumers to take a look at the Volvo product," he adds.

Art and Science

The auto industry knows the demographic data, says Gary Berman, founder and CEO of Market Segment Research. And most automakers are "attempting a variety of strategies to get their fair share," he says.

"The challenge," Berman adds, "is who is going to win and how they are going to do it."

This is the latest data they are using: In January, the U.S. Census Bureau published estimated population figures that indicate the United States is home to 37.7 million people who identify themselves as black – either black alone, or in combination with another race; 37 million who identify themselves as Latino; 12.5 million Asians or Asian Americans; and 4.3 million Native Americans or Alaska Natives.

The total number of gay, lesbian, bisexual and transgender (GLBT) people in the United States is estimated to be between 13 million and 17 million, according to major studies. Depending on the source, the percentage of GLBT people in this country ranges from 3 percent and 10 percent of the total U.S. population.

According to the University of Georgia's Selig Center for Economic Growth, African-American spending power is projected to reach $852.8 billion in 2007; Latino spending power is projected to reach $927.1 billion; and Asian-American spending power is projected to reach $454.9 billion.

A recent report prepared by Witeck-Combs Communications, a Washington, D.C.-based marketing and research firm with expertise in the gay and lesbian market, estimated buying power for the GLBT market at $451 billion in 2002 and projected buying power at $608 billion by 2007.

Berman's work deals with the alchemy of art and science – but he believes in science first.

"In broad strokes," Berman says, "the most successful automotive marketers are going to be those that institutionalize the idea of multiculturalism across their

Auto Markets: How Small Can You Slice Them? (cont'd.)

organizations in the following ways: Identifying the most profitable customers, via research; understanding the cultural hot buttons that will motivate someone to the make or model they are trying to target; and finally, spending an equal amount of time and money on the customer experience at the dealer level."

"I cannot overemphasize this enough," he says. "There is no point in spending tens of millions of dollars creating awareness and buzz and then having an unpleasant experience at the dealership level."

"This cuts across new car sales, finance and insurance and ongoing service and maintenance," he adds.

Berman's company uses what he calls a "multicultural took kit" to help guide clients through the decision-making process. Initially, he says, he asks clients to consider five issues:

Whether or not a client should market to a particular segment. How much time and money they should spend against a segment. How the money should be spent. What strategies and tactics should come into play as they implement the spend. Finally, how the client will measure the return on investment and "optimize efforts over time."

Corporations have been producing in-language and multicultural advertising "for quite some time," Berman says. "The difference now is that they are listening to those consumers in new and innovative ways."

"I think another big shift is that major manufacturers are treating those customers with significant resources," he adds.

Rough Spots

Advertising budgets are held closely by automakers, and there's no central clearinghouse for information on how much and where they spend their multicultural marketing dollars. There are, however, some indicators.

Hispanic Business magazine reported last year that automakers, package-goods marketers and telecommunications companies were spending more to reach Latinos.

Ford, GM, Procter & Gamble and AT&T all increased their multicultural-marketing budgets by more than 20 percent, the magazine reported.

Advertising Age, a trade publication for the advertising industry, reported that ad spending across all industries targeted toward Latinos was estimated at $2.1 billion (10 percent of all spending) in 2000, the most recent figures available.

Auto Markets: How Small Can You Slice Them? (cont'd.)

Advertising Age pegged overall spending on the African-American market at $1.5 billion (5.5 percent) and spending on the Asian-American market at $363 million (1.5 percent) in 2000. Overall ad spending in 2000 was $216.4 billion, according to Robert J. Coen's Universal McCann U.S. Volume Report.

"Multicultural marketing and advertising is a key priority for ANA members who have been putting enormous effort into all elements of multicultural marketing. They want and need all the messages they communicate to be comfortably multi-cultural," John J. Sarsen Jr., president and CEO of the Association of National Advertisers, said last year.

In November, the ANA released a survey that offered some indicators of that advertising commitment.

One-hundred companies across a range of industries, including a handful of car-makers, responded to the survey. According to the ANA, 72 of the responding companies had some multicultural marketing effort in place and respondents marketed to distinct ethnic segments using targeted media.

"The predominant segments targeted included Hispanic, 70 percent; African American, 59 percent; and Asian American, 27 percent," the survey stated. The responding companies reached consumers through "targeted television to specific market segments, 76 percent; targeted print, 76 percent; targeted radio, 68 per-cent; sponsorships, 57 percent; grass-roots efforts, 56 percent; running main-stream advertising on 'ethnic' programs 39 percent … ."

The survey also indicated that companies are struggling for tools to measure the return on investment from campaigns. For example, 22 percent of the companies that responded to the ANA study said they did not have a system in place to measure the success of their general-market advertising agency; 29 percent said they lacked a system to measure the success of their minority-owned agency.

Companies that did have metrics in place tended to use sales, market research and performance as the primary indicators of success, according to the survey. Only one company expected its agencies to retain diverse employees.

The survey notes that the advertisers that responded didn't "require diverse account teams from their mainstream agencies."

Account representatives from mainstream agencies primarily were white, 77 per-cent; African American, 36 percent; Latino, 32 percent; and Asian American, 14 percent. Agency representatives from minority-owned firms predominantly were Latino, 91 percent; African American, 56 percent; Asian American, 56 percent; and white, 26 percent.

Auto Markets: How Small Can You Slice Them? (cont'd.)

'Special' or Just Ill-Served?

A generation ago, automakers and their marketing partners divided white males, the perceived "general market," into segments according to age and income – convertibles, sedans and luxury cars. And they generally discounted the purchasing potential of women and people of color, known then as "special markets."

In that historic context, "special" was synonymous with ill-served and poorly researched, notes Charles Morrison, an African-American advertising executive.

"Every company would go out and research the general market to a fare-thee-well – all kinds of studies and measurements. They could tell you what cross-eyed, left-handed, white people in Dubuque, Iowa, were like," Morrison says.

The evolution of demographic tools – including the expansion of U.S. Census categories concerning race and ethnicity in 1980 – reinforced an emerging awareness that the U.S. marketplace was changing and generated shifts in marketing strategy, as well. "Special" markets were superceded by target markets, ethnic markets, youth markets, and the once-revolutionary "vertical markets."

Now, the notion of locking multicultural consumers into rigid vertical silos, experts say, is as appealing as musk-based cologne from the 1970s. Instead, the challenge is divining when race or age or sexual orientation motivates buying behavior and when some other intangible factors into the marketing equation.

"It's art – and science," says Miriam Muley, the African-American executive director for GM's Center for Expertise and Diversity Growth Markets. "You have to think about [consumer variables] as a matrix, not as two-dimensional."

GM posted a 0.4 percent increase in market share in 2002 and the company, the largest U.S.-based automaker, controlled 28.7 percent of the U.S. market in 2002. The company evaluates possible market segments by current size and potential for growth.

In theory – and with an infinite budget – a market segment could be sliced as thin as a single consumer. But in reality, notes Muley, a market segment must be of sufficient "size and scale to warrant the investment."

"Media costs are significant – [advertising] agency resources, all of that costs money. You have to have enough scale … to offset costs," she says.

At the same time, "you want to know that the trends going forward are going to bode more growth – purchasing power, size, a predisposition [to favor] the company. That's the other piece."

Auto Markets: How Small Can You Slice Them? (cont'd.)

Once a market segment has been defined, it's time to determine whether those potential consumers can be reached through existing marketing materials. If the company's core communications reach some newly identified segment, "then it doesn't make sense" to establish a separate marketing effort, Muley adds.

If a company determines, in consultation with its advertising agencies and research partners and internal strategists, that a market segment warrants some sort of tailored communication, then the question become just what sort of message would resonate.

"What are the key messages that are going to make a difference? That's the science. The creative part, the art, is bringing the message to life, the emotional connection," Muley says. "Is the music right? Is the talent right?"

And unless all those elements feel, look and sound right, she says, it's best not to take another step.

"Hopefully, you would never get to a point where you would take that kind of gamble," she says. "I would never want to put a company in that position."

When Does Culture Count?

American Honda has been targeting ethnic markets for 13 years, says Barbara Ponce, Honda's manager, emerging markets national advertising. The company sold 1.25 million vehicles in the United States in 2002, a 3.3 percent gain over 2001.

Honda divides markets by ethnicity, by language and "by culture," says Ponce, focusing on African-American, Latino and Asian-American consumers.

"We sub-segment even further in the Asian category," she says, "with in-language marketing to Chinese and Korean customers." Honda runs ads in both Cantonese and Mandarin.

A decade ago, some marketing experts dismissed efforts aimed at African Americans as unnecessary, contending that "you don't need a concerted effort to reach African Americans because they speak English," Ponce recalls.

But that narrow perspective missed altogether the importance of culture, she adds. African Americans maintain a "distinct culture, a strong culture, and our marketing is very tailored and very targeted not just within language, but within culture."

To assure that the company's dealers understand the importance of diverse markets, Honda this year developed a package of resource materials, including a guide entitled "The Emerging Markets in Your Neighborhood."

Auto Markets: How Small Can You Slice Them? (cont'd.)

The guide provides demographic profiles of 50 Honda markets and shows dealers how to create a demographic profile of their own communities. It offers information on psychographics, identifies multicultural media outlets and describes corporate efforts – scholarship programs, for example – to reach each market segment.

What the guide can't do is define for auto dealers when an individual customer's race is going to trump some other consideration in purchasing a car.

"You can slice and dice it so many ways," says Ponce, but the challenges of segmenting a market become clear "if we think about ourselves as individuals."

"I use myself as an example," she says. "I am Hispanic. I'm a professional. I have two kids. If I am a market, do you appeal to me as a Hispanic or as a mom or as a career woman? They all require very distinct strategies."

Beware Backlash

Meanwhile, there are a whole range of issues inherent in the process of segmenting American consumers into discrete markets that "can be volatile in our society," says Leisa Byars, an African-American diversity-marketing executive with Ford Motor Co.

"Looking at race, cultural differences … sexual orientation. Race and sex have been things in our society that you might want to ignore or not think about," Byars says. "If you don't do it right, you [generate] a backlash from the community you were trying to attract. And, if you are too aggressive, you can alienate your existing customers."

She is a passionate believer in research. "I would never risk doing it wrong," she says.

"I've seen advertising, as an African-American woman, and wondered, 'What were they thinking?'" she says. "I've been offended, and when I'm offended, there is no way I would consider buying the product. If you don't have the money for research, don't do" a segmented-marketing push.

Ford, which reported 2002 sales fell 8.7 percent to 3.6 million cars and light trucks, announced in December that it would launch a campaign for its luxury Jaguar brand aimed at gay men. The nation's No. 2 automaker has estimated the gay market at more than 14 million consumers with a buying power of more than $450 billion.

The simplicity of the inaugural ad belies the complexity of the process that led to its creation, says Byars. "Months. It took months. We asked just about every

Auto Markets: How Small Can You Slice Them? (cont'd.)

question we could ask. We have to make sure that what we say is relevant to the target market and relevant to the brand."

The ad itself is simple: A landscape with a winding road, a close up of a Jaguar 2003 X-Type, and a smaller inset photo of a friendly looking man.

"Some people view Jag as beautiful. They don't take the time to drive the vehicle and find out that Jag is also extremely powerful," Byars says. "That is how a lot of gay and lesbian customers feel – that they are not judged by what is true."

In examining segmented markets, Byars says, it is important to recognize that there are considerations – aside from a potential market's size and buying power – which might make it attractive.

"Perhaps it is that they are influencers and trend-setters…it is not just buying power, but influence that has been overlooked," she adds.

Ford worked with Witeck-Combs Communications, to develop the Jaguar campaign.

Effective market segmentation requires "good data and the same kind of thinking and strategic planning you do in any market," says Bob Witeck, CEO of Witeck-Combs. "When we opened the agency 10 years ago, none of that was out there."

Instead, there were "a lot myths – that all gays were gay white men named Marc who live in New York, that kind of thing."

"That is not," he adds, "who all gay people are."

In the last decade, the agency has examined the gay and lesbian market in sharp detail for clients that include American Airlines, IBM, Sears and MTV.

"All gay people look like something else, reflect other kinds of consumers – there are young males who are straight and young males who are gay who may both spend more on entertainment or alcohol," he adds.

Parenthood, for example, or a disability likely outweighs race or sexual orientation as a motivation for a wide range of purchases, Witeck says.

"You are looking for the attributes of gay consumers that match non-gay consumers so you can have some cross-over," he adds. "I think that is going to be the future of niche marketing – that kind of crossover."

Subaru, which signed tennis great Martina Navratilova in 1996, is among a handful of companies that already understand how to make an ad that resonates across cultures.

Auto Markets: How Small Can You Slice Them? (cont'd.)

"They created a campaign that reaches all women, including lesbians – women who are outdoorsy, independent, strong and very at ease with themselves," Witeck adds.

"I am old enough to remember when black people finally arrived on TV," says Witeck, who is white. "Marketers were terrified about backlash. 'If Diahann Carroll endorses our product, will we lose a white housewife?' "

"When the world didn't end," he adds, "they moved on."

Witeck-Combs also is helping Ford develop internal-communications pieces to accompany the Jaguar campaign, which will be rolled out at select events in target cities through the spring.

Effective market segmentation requires more than just a good ad, Byars stresses. "It's not just getting the first-time buyer. It is a building a relationship so that buyer will come back – loyalty and word-of-mouth."

Further, she adds, segmentation is just a question of identifying markets; a company also has to determine "how deep to go."

"Whenever we talk about one of these markets – African American or Hispanic or gay and lesbian – we are talking about consumers who want to build relationships with companies that are involved in their communities. In order to do that, you have to go deep somewhere."

In truth, Byars says, "budget is a huge dictator" of both breadth and depth and may force a company to make hard choices about which markets will receive attention.

"Some of our brands are grappling with that now," she adds. "It's challenging."

It's Still Not Enough

Regardless of advances, automotive-marketing experts contend that the limitations of existing consumer research hamper their work. Without hard numbers about consumer preferences, buying patterns and motivating influences, it is difficult to justify the commitment of resources.

"Life is full of twists and turns," the text says. "Care for a partner?" "We need to do a better job of substantiating [diverse markets] to the broader industry," says Honda's Ponce. "For emerging markets, we are going to need sharper tools. We don't have good measurement tools in place for measuring even sales to our diverse customers."

"Virtually everyone is guess," echoes Morrison. "As multicultural as this world

Auto Markets: How Small Can You Slice Them? (cont'd.)

has gotten, you cannot know what your efforts will return to you in those market. And you can't bet your job on that if you are a brand manager."

J.D. Power and Associates did its first comprehensive study of the Latino market last year. A decade ago, ingrained intolerance might have prevented a corporate executive from considering the value of diverse market segments.

"But I don't think insensitivity is the primary reason today," Morrison adds. "I just think people make mistakes because they are ill-informed."

"I think companies, as part of their long-term investment in multicultural research, should take a very strong stance in joining with their [advertising] agency partners in co-commissioning good, solid research, or funding some outside arm to do the research," he adds.

"By and large, though, we are still looking at vice presidents of marketing and senior directors who have yet to truly embrace the business opportunities and commit the dollars," Strachan says. "This isn't going to pay out tomorrow. It's going to pay out in year five or year six."

Lack of Data? Lack of Interest? Why Don't We Know More About African-American Auto Consumers

By Linda Bean

© 2003 DiversityInc.com

March 07, 2003

Folks in the auto industry generally agree there's a lack of reliable data about African-American preferences and buying habits – data that should be guiding million-dollar decisions on segmented marketing and advertising.

But they don't necessarily agree on why this gap exists, who is responsible for filling it – or whether auto manufacturers should care.

Research experts argue that companies aren't interested in paying for the in-depth insights into African-American consumers. And company representatives complain that research firms have, to date, provided faulty research models. Meanwhile, there are lingering misconceptions about the size and strength of the African-American market, despite demographic data.

But in the end, research either is going to drive or halt marketing initiatives aimed at African Americans. Corporate leaders who don't get the business case and can't pinpoint the return on investment aren't going to put money toward the market.

"If you are just looking at pure volume, it may not be that impressive of a business case," says Leisa Byars, manager for Global Agency Media Alliance and Events at Ford Motor Co. "But you have to understand its influence. A lot of trends start with this market."

Charles Morrison, an executive at New York City-based Uniworld – an advertising agency that specializes in the African-American community, recently took major research organizations to task.

Those firms have done "in my mind, a horrendous job serving their clients – they have been the last to recognize that the world has changed. They have never seriously studied the African-American market or the Latino market."

But Michael Taliefero, the African-American co-founder and managing director of Washington, D.C.-based CLC Compliance Technologies, lays the responsibility for bridging the gap at the feet of corporations.

To suggest that the lack of information is a failing of the research community "is

Lack of Data? Lack of Interest? Why Don't We Know More About African-American Auto Consumers (cont'd.)

a knee-jerk reaction to the failure (of corporations) to think about it and really do targeted marketing," Taliefero says.

Meanwhile, Marc Strachan, the African-American managing partner of a New York City-based ad agency, contends that there's enough responsibility to go around. "I think there is definitely a gap and the gap (relates to) the psychographic and cultural nuances and how some of those things have changed over the last 40 years," says Strachan, managing partner of S/R Communications Alliance, a New York City-based advertising and marketing agency.

"And I don't think anybody is going to take up the (research) challenge unless they think there's an opportunity for them on the back end," Strachan adds.

"We need more consumer research, more segmentation research," says Byars, who is African American. "How are markets similar? How are they different?"

Automakers, she adds, generally "have the feeling that you don't want to offend anyone, so they play it safe."

Toyota, Byars notes, learned firsthand the consequences of a more risky strategy when it commissioned an advertising postcard that featured an African-American man with a broad grin and a piece of gold-tooth jewelry, shaped like a Toyota RAV4.

The Rev. Jesse Jackson condemned the marketing strategy and then launched a much broader criticism of the company's relationship with African-American consumers, vendors and employees. Toyota has since adopted a number of measures aimed at increasing diversity and diminishing conflict, including the development of an external diversity council.

"I think Toyota was trying to reach out and connect, but they came across as insensitive," Byars says.

"And then," she adds, "there's the issue of not doing it right. When do you treat African Americans differently from other consumers and when do you treat them in a similar way? It is a balancing act and very challenging."

As a result, strong consumer research "is invaluable," Byars says.

Ford has enough quality research "for the most part, to play it safe. We do things that are insightful, that are thoughtful, but we don't take chances. That is what Toyota did," she adds. "If you want to be riskier, you need more research."

In Strachan's view, the responsibility for examining the African-American market lies with those who have a "vested interest" in understanding African-American

Lack of Data? Lack of Interest? Why Don't We Know More About African-American Auto Consumers (cont'd.)

consumers. This might be a good time, he says, for African-American ad and marketing agencies to pool their resources and partner with a large research organization to delve into psychographic and cultural issues.

"Here's an example: The black church has always been a rock-steady component of the African-American community. And the black church has changed and is changing and has become more sophisticated," Strachan says.

African-American churches have a taken a strong interest in economic empowerment. "It is no longer just about faith for faith's sake," he adds. "It's about how you empower a people economically in today's world. It represents a more business-focused environment, but no one has really looked into that. What does that mean today?"

Before a company can be persuaded to invest in detailed research, there has to be a foundation for the business case, Stachan says, built from data provided by the Census Bureau and Bureau of Labor Statistics, and information provided by the Selig Center for Economic Growth at the University of Georgia.

The Selig Center recently reported, for example, that combined buying power of African Americans, Asian Americans and Native Americans should reach almost $1.4 trillion, compared with $453 billion in 1990 – an increase of more than 200 percent in 17 years. In 2007, African Americans are expected to account for 61 percent of that combined buying power, or $853 billion.

In the late 1990s, advertising executive Don Coleman partners with North Carolina-based Yanklovich to prepare a research report on the African-American community entitled "The African-American Monitor."

It was the first time, Strachan says, that he had seen data that went beyond economics and demographics to address the nuances of cultural competency.

"I remember thinking 'Oh, boy. Somebody finally did something.' It talked about where African Americans were making strides in leadership in buying goods and services," he adds. "It began talking about 'urban' and what that meant ... how this young consumer group is spending money and time and attitude."

"I also think there are gaps in understanding the differences among African Americans and the budget you have to spend against this market isn't enough," Byars says. "It's challenging to develop a communication piece that will reach an educated writer, an 18-year-old and a single mother."

"We don't understand the subtleties and the differences – the huge differences," she adds, "and that is where research comes in."

The Faces of Beauty: Cosmetics Giants Go After Women of Color

By Melanie Austria Farmer

© 2003 DiversityInc.com

April 21, 2003

Some women make a day of it, treating themselves to a new lipstick or browsing through aisles of hair-care products and skin-care potions with intense interest. Others run, maybe even sprint, to a local drugstore the moment they are out of their favorite mascara or when a lipstick they swear by is down to its last layer of color. Time and time again, beauty products have served a specific need and provided women an outlet for creativity, individuality and self-expression.

But, for Pepper Miller, who is African American and heads a market-research firm, the search still is on to find a perfect foundation shade that matches her cocoa-color skin. Major drugstore cosmetic giants have yet to prove to her they can deliver the products that suit her particular needs.

"It is 2003 in America, we're still asking for the same [products] over and over again and it's not being met," said Miller, president of Chicago-based The Hunter-Miller Group, which specializes in African-American market research. "I still think there's a need, an opportunity for a line of cosmetics or skin care at a mass retail level targeted to women of color."

To address this need, more and more drugstore cosmetic giants, such as Cover Girl, L'Oréal, Maybelline and Revlon have been busy revamping their advertising strategies and investing heavily in research and development (R&D) to create products that serve all women who have a variety of skin types and tones. Several companies have initiated strong efforts to tap African-American, Latina and Asian-American consumers – a multicultural segment that is poised for steady growth.

The U.S. market for ethnic health and beauty care, which include product categories such as hair care, color cosmetics, skin care and nail care, is on a steady rise. Retail sales of ethnic health- and beauty-care products are expected to reach $1.9 billion in the next three years, according to a report produced by Packaged Facts, a division of consumer researcher MarketResearch.com. Total sales growth from 2001 to 2006 is expected to increase at a healthy clip of 20 percent, compared with 2.4 percent from 1997 to 2001, according to the report.

The Faces of Beauty: Cosmetics Giants Go After Women of Color (cont'd.)

Aiming to grab their share of this market, specialty players, such as Fashion Fair Cosmetics and Black Opal for African-American customers and Zhen Cosmetics for Asian-American customers, also have been attempting to fill the void. A slew of cosmetic companies are on the same path, hoping to nab a large slice of this very lucrative pie.

"The multicultural consumer is and has been a critical component of our overall marketing strategy," said Ed Bullock, vice president of diversity for L'Oréal USA. Bullock said the company has increased its total advertising with an emphasis on boosting ads placed in ethnic magazines such as Essence, Honey and Latina.

"Our spending has grown from $3.5 million to a projected $36 million in 2003 in the ethnic category and the number of ethnic spokesmodels that represent our brands has also increased dramatically over the same time period," said Bullock. Recent spokesmodels for L'Oréal include Latina superstar Jennifer Lopez and African-American pop entertainer Beyonce Knowles.

Cover Girl Cosmetics, a division of Procter & Gamble which also owns cosmetics maker Max Factor, also has been doing its part to gain a foothold. Cover Girl, which prides itself on being among the first mass-market cosmetic brand to feature spokesmodels of color, including high-profile African-American entertainer Queen Latifah, has made a strong commitment to attract a diverse clientele.

The company said it features women of color in nearly 50 percent of its advertising and continues to pay attention to the needs of African-Americans and Latina customers. Revlon as well has developed an ad campaign that features Halle Berry, the first African-American actress to win an Academy Award in a leading role, along with Cuban actress Eva Mendes, who began appearing this year as the new face for Revlon.

Meanwhile, high-end cosmetics maker Estee Lauder, which owns a string of luxury brands including Bobbi Brown, MAC and Prescriptives, recently signed on its first spokesmodel of color. Liya Kebede, who was born and raised in Ethiopia and made a name for herself as a runway model, has joined actress Elizabeth Hurley and model Carolyn Murphy, both of whom are white, as the new face of the cosmetics powerhouse. The move is part of Estee Lauder's ongoing efforts to attract younger customers.

While people who track the sector applaud the industry's direction to better cater to a diverse customer base, they also agree it will take time for the improved strategies to resonate with consumers of color, who for so long did not equate the

The Faces of Beauty: Cosmetics Giants Go After Women of Color (cont'd.)

products with their individual beauty needs.

"For years, the Cover Girl [tag] line has been 'Easy, breezy, beautiful Cover Girl,' and I always associated that with blond hair and blue eyes," said Miller. "Now, they have the same tag line but replaced it with a black face … It's still not talking to me."

Schuyler Brown, who is associate director of strategic intelligence for global-advertising firm Euro RSCG, agreed with Miller that the challenge relies heavily on convincing an audience that previously was not a priority.

"It's not as simple as just putting a [diverse] face to a product," said Brown. "It's a start to put a face in ads or on the [TV] screen that viewers identify with but it's like the Barbie doll issue. You've got a more complicated cultural story that you're not telling."

In the mid-90s, Brown worked for Lancôme, a high-end cosmetics brand owned by L'Oréal and primarily sold in department stores such as Macy's and Bloomingdale's. At the time, Brown said, Lancôme offered only four different shades of foundation and possibly one of the four could have matched African-American or Latina skin tones and none could have served Asian-American women.

For their part, mass cosmetics brands have invested heavily in research and development to better serve the individual needs of all women. Some companies also have been scooping up boutique shops to beef up their offerings.

For one, French cosmetics behemoth L'Oréal this year invested $11 million in a new research and development center based in Chicago dedicated to the scientific research of African-American hair care and skin care. The company recently also acquired Soft Sheen-Carson to better serve the beauty needs of African-American customers and bought Shu Uemura cosmetics for its Asian-American consumers. Uemura is a Japanese make-up artist who launched his self-named product line in the late 1960s.

Verdia Johnson, president of Footsteps, a New York-based ad agency that specializes in the African-American market, said while the acquisitions of product lines are a faster way for companies to better serve a multicultural customer base, the Soft Sheen-Carson deal might only be a temporary fix for L'Oréal.

"Soft Sheen is still Soft Sheen. It's not L'Oréal," said Johnson. "People who love Carson products are still going to buy Carson. The product hasn't changed, it just got a new parent. [The acquisition] didn't rub off at all on L'Oréal. What would

The Faces of Beauty: Cosmetics Giants Go After Women of Color (cont'd.)

rub off on L'Oréal is if they put their name on something and run with it."

Johnson said cosmetic companies are heading in the right direction when they invest more on research and development efforts and making changes to consumer-research practices.

Anne Martin, vice president of global cosmetics and marketing at Cover Girl, said the company continually conducts consumer research to find out what women are looking for in their cosmetics products, including new shades. As an example, Martin said Cover Girl's newly launched Clean Oil-Control Foundation is particularly appealing to women of color as shine control was cited as the second most-desired foundation benefit by African-American and Latina consumers.

"Cover Girl realizes the growing size and influence of Hispanic, African-American and Asian consumers and has addressed the unique beauty needs of ethnic women for many years," said Martin.

The shift cosmetic companies are making clearly is necessary, but obstacles remain in capturing a solid base of loyal customers of color.

"You can put a person [of color] in the ad but if the product doesn't stand up, the method is gong to fall flat," added Brown. "The efforts are definitely being recognized, but companies have a long way to go."

Part V - Supplier Diversity

A. Benefits & Costs

Supplier diversity often is described as an enlightened business decision, based on keen awareness of demographic changes and the competitive marketplace. The historic reality is that motives were somewhat less forward-thinking and more compliance-driven. That doesn't mean companies with strong supplier-diversity initiatives won't benefit from making inroads into emerging markets.

Any company that does business with the federal government has a string of public laws to thank for its core philosophy of doing business with the communities that do business with them.

So is it progressive thinking or outside pressure that drives supplier-diversity programs today? Murray Schooner at Unisys, a veteran supplier-diversity chief, says it's a combination of both. "Government compliance comes first, if applicable, pressure from minority groups second, and recognition of the business case for including diverse suppliers third," he says.

It is increasingly dangerous in a competitive market for any corporation to sully its reputation in communities of color. Reputation is critical and word of mouth is quick. And the same people who buy products own businesses.

The private sector's first foray into supplier diversity in an organized way was a result of the Chicago Business Opportunity Fair of 1968. The event was the work of three organizations: the Chicago Economic Development Corporation (CEDC), the Chicago Urban League and the Western Electric Company. The CEDC later would become the Chicago Minority Business Development Council (CMBDC) and inspire the founding of the National Minority Supplier Diversity Council (NMSDC).

B. Who Is Counted

T he statistics reflect the impact of the changing face of small businesses: Between 1992 and 1997, the most recent year for which the Census Bureau has statistics, the number of women-(WBE) and minority-owned (MBE) business enterprises increased by 150 percent, with WBEs and MBEs generating $495 billion in collective annual revenue as of 1997.[150]

Women-owned businesses grew three times faster than businesses overall in the last decade. Latinos and African Americans now collectively comprise more than a quarter of the total U.S. population. Between 1990 and 2000, Latino-owned businesses grew 30 percent and African-American-owned business grew 22 percent. As the U.S. Small Business Administration (SBA) reports, "minority-owned business share of U.S. firms was 6.8 percent in 1982… grew steadily to 9.3 percent in 1987, 12.5 percent in 1992 and 14.6 percent in 1997."[151]

What defines a diverse supplier varies greatly depending on context. For example, while the federal government considers a minority-owned business an enterprise "owned and at least 51 percent controlled by" one or more people "other than white," the U.S. Small Business Administration and most corporations have specific guidelines for what defines a minority and what defines ownership. At the federal level, women are not considered minorities (although their businesses once were considered "small disadvantaged businesses"). In the private sector, women may be considered minorities. These discrepancies can lead to confusion and its more malignant cousin, obfuscation, when supplier-diversity goals and achievements are being discussed.

In short, supplier diversity isn't always about doing businesses with companies owned by women or people of color. Most companies with a formal supplier-diversity policy include companies owned by service-disabled veterans, HUBZone businesses or the amorphous category "small business" in their reporting.

1. Minority Business Enterprises

People of color owned 3 million of all U.S. non-farm businesses in 1997, the most recent year for which Census Bureau data is available. (The U.S. Census Bureau collects data for minority- and women-owned businesses every five years. Data collected for these businesses in 2002 will be released by the Census Bureau in 2004.) Minority-owned businesses employed 4.5 million people and generated $591.3 billion in business revenues. In 1997, minority-owned businesses accounted for 14.1 percent of the 20.8 million U.S. non-farm businesses, 4.4 percent of employment and 3.2 percent of receipts.[152]

Growth in minority-owned businesses exceeded that of non-minority-owned businesses in both number and gross receipts between 1992-1997,[153] according to the U.S. Department of Commerce's Minority Business Development Agency (MBDA).

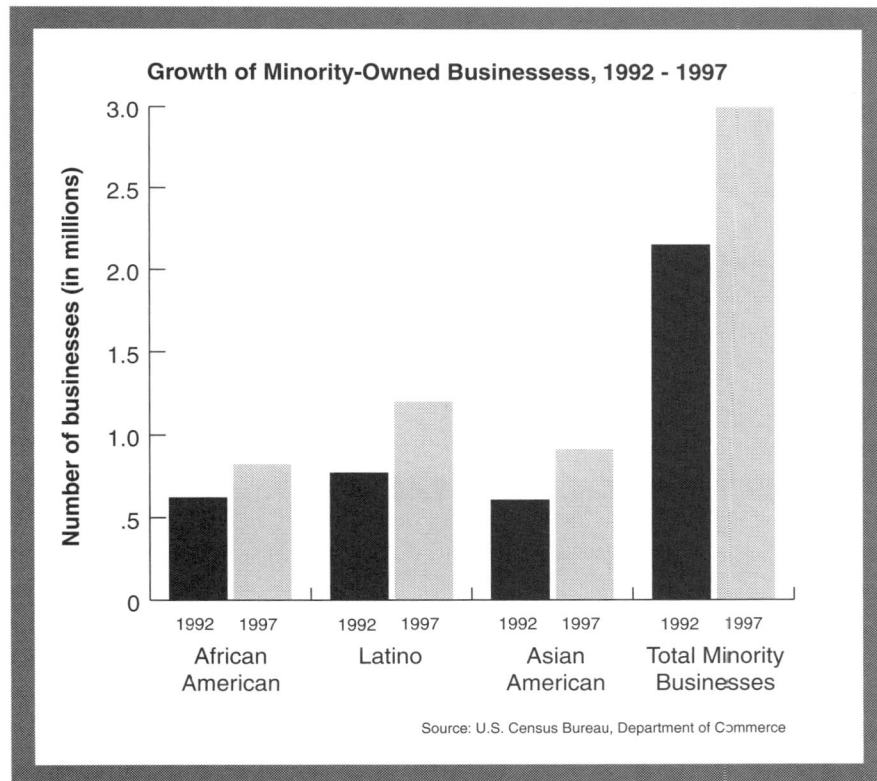

Growth of Minority-Owned Businessess, 1992 - 1997

Source: U.S. Census Bureau, Department of Commerce

The largest group of people of color owning small businesses was Latinos, operating 39.5 percent of minority small businesses. By contrast, Asian Americans owned 30 percent, African Americans owned 27.5 percent, and American Indians and Alaska Natives collectively owned 3 percent.[154]

Asian Americans generated 51.9 percent of the revenue for small businesses owned by people of color, followed by 31.5 percent for Latinos, 12 percent for African Americans and 5.8 percent for American Indians and Alaska Natives.[155]

Minority-Owned Business Share of U.S. Firms

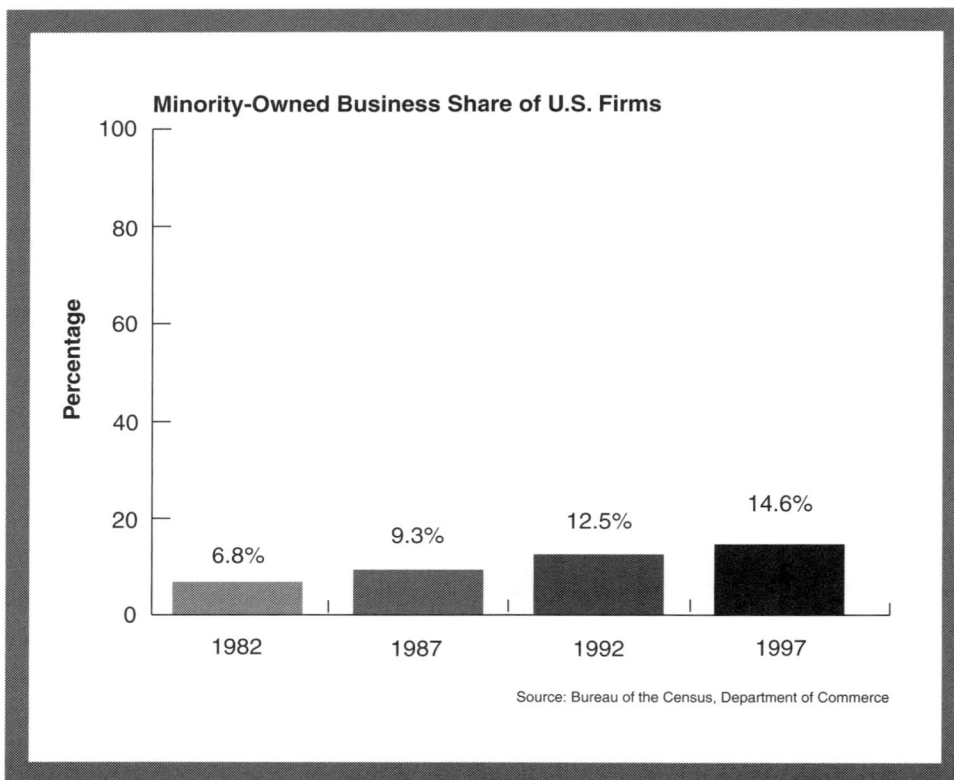

Source: Bureau of the Census, Department of Commerce

a. African-American Business Enterprises

The number of African-American-owned businesses increased almost four times faster than the national average.[156] This is an increase of 25.7 percent between 1992 and 1997, to more than 800,000 businesses. African-American-owned companies employed 718,300 people and generated $71.2 billion in revenue during 1997.

(A sole proprietor is not counted as an employee.) Approximately 8,700 of those businesses had sales of $1 million a year or more.[157]

b. Latino Business Enterprises

The number of Latino-owned businesses increased 30 percent between 1992 and 1997 to more than 1.2 million companies. Latino-owned firms employed 1.3 million people and generated $186.3 billion in revenue in 1997. Despite the rapidly increasing number of Latino-owned business, they still make up only 6 percent of the 20.8 million non-farm businesses in the nation and 1 percent of the $18.6 trillion in receipts for all business. Some 26,700 Latino-owned businesses posted sales of $1 million a year or more.[158]

Based on 1997 Census Bureau numbers, Global Insight, a Lexington, Mass.,-based research and consulting firm, projected there to be more than 1.6 million Latino-owned businesses by 2002, a 33 percent increase over 1997 Census Bureau numbers.[159]

c. Asian-American Business Enterprises

Asian Americans owned approximately 913,000 businesses in 1997, an increase of 30.2 percent from 1992. Of those businesses, 45,300, or 5 percent, had sales of $1 million or more. Asian-American businesses had more than 2.2 million people on the payroll.[160]

2. Women-Owned Business Enterprises

There were an estimated 10.1 million women-owned businesses in 2002, which generated more than $2.3 trillion in sales and 18.2 million jobs.[161]

Between 1997 and 2002, the number of women-owned firms with more than 100 employees rose 44 percent. And the number of women-owned firm posting more than $1 million in revenue climbed by 32 percent – 1.5 times faster than all businesses of comparable size.[162]

In 2002, 20 percent of all women business owners were women of color and their businesses are growing at four times the rate of all firms. Overall, the number of firms owned by women of color increased by 32 percent between 1997 and 2002 – four times faster than all U.S. firms and more than twice the rate of all women-owned firms.[163]

Large corporations are a vital market for women business owners. Six in 10 Fortune 1000 companies report spending $1 billion or more annually with outside suppliers and vendors. Yet this market has not yet been fully tapped by women-owned businesses, who currently receive just 4 percent of all the corporate business.[164]

3. Certification and Recognition

As far as the federal government is concerned, it isn't necessary for a business to acquire third-party certification. Self-certification will do, and no paperwork need be filled out. However, to be eligible for government set-asides or support, companies look to the SBA as the certifying agency for any type of diverse business. Various city and state requirements come in at the lower levels of government.

For example, in 1990, Mayor Richard M. Daley helped institute Chicago's Minority- and Women-Owned Business Procurement Program. Because of this ordinance, when global-bank ABN AMRO wanted to build a $500 million state-of-the-art technology facility in the city's West Loop recently, it had to agree to set aside 25 percent of the construction contract for minority-owned companies and 5 percent for women-owned companies. But only city-certified companies that were at least 51 percent owned and controlled by a minority or a woman were eligible for the set-asides.

Moreover, the city isn't the only certifying agency in Chicago. Each of the city's many agencies has its own rules and guidelines for certification. As the city of Chicago Web site points out: "Certification by the City of Chicago does not in any way ensure certification by any other agency." Metra, Chicago's rail system, must comply with U.S. Department of Transportation (DOT) standards — and so on. Similar fragmentation exists in most major cities.

In the private sector, the NMSDC is the main certifying organization for MBEs, WBENC (Women Business Enterprise National Council) and the National Women Business Owners Corporation (NWBOC) are the main certifying organizations for WBEs, and there currently are no certifying organizations for disabled veterans or other small or disadvantaged business enterprises other than the SBA.

Most certifying agencies generally adhere to the "51 percent ownership" rule indicated above. Here are the major public and private-sector agencies and their requirements:

Small Business Administration (SBA) — As they are defined by legislation, government certification standards are complex and detailed. The SBA currently uses the North American Industrial Classification System (NAICS) to define a "small business," which, as of Oct. 1, 2000, replaced the Standard Industrial Classification (SIC) Codes.[165]

National Minority Supplier Development Council (NMSDC) — "A minority-owned business is a for-profit enterprise, regardless of size, physically located in the United States or its trust territories, which is owned, operated and controlled by minority-group members. 'Minority-group members' are defined as U.S. citizens who are Asian, black, Hispanic and Native American. Ownership by minority individuals means the business is at least 51 percent-owned by such individuals or, in the case of a publicly owned business, at least 51 percent of the stock is owned by one or more such individuals. Further, the management and daily operations are controlled by those minority group members."

U.S. Hispanic Chamber of Commerce (UHCC): Washington, D.C.-based UHCC was organized in 1979 to "advocate, promote and facilitate the success of Hispanic businesses." *www.ushcc.com*

National Women Business Owners Corporation Network (NWBOC) — "There are two basic principles of business, ownership and control, which must apply to your business in order to be eligible for certification by NWBOC. Ownership: A woman or women own(s) one of the following: 100 percent of the assets of a sole proprietorship; at least 51 percent of the equity interests in a partnership; at least 51 percent of each of the classes of outstanding equity securities of a corporation; or at least 51 percent of the membership interests in a limited-liability company. Control: A woman or women control(s) one of the following: 100 percent of the control of a sole proprietorship; at least 51 percent of the control of a general partnership; woman owner is the general partner and, if there s more than one general partner, the managing general partner, of a limited partnership or limited liability partnership; or, the woman owner is entitled to appoint a majority of a corporate board of directors. A woman or women is/are the sole manager, able to appoint unconditionally the majority of managers of a manager-managed LLC or has 51 percent control of a member-managed LLC.

Women's Business Enterprise National Council (WBENC) — "Fifty-one percent ownership by a woman or women... Proof of effective management of the business (operating position, by-laws, hire-fire and other decision-making role)... Control of the business as evidenced by signature role on loans, leases and contracts... U.S. Citizenship or U.S. Resident Alien Status."

As mentioned above, women are not considered a minority as far as the federal government is concerned. Women interested in contracting with the government simply have to say they own the majority of their businesses and control their companies' management and daily business operations. Thus, small, women-owned companies that aren't interested in becoming suppliers to large corporations probably won't benefit from certification.

The reverse is true for companies owned by disabled veterans or people with disabilities. The government will require they meet certain criteria, but there is no national standard in the public sector. Standards vary from company to company.

For example, American Express includes "physically challenged businesses" in its supplier-diversity program. Such businesses are defined as enterprises that are either: a) at least 51 percent owned by one or more physically challenged individuals, b) a subsidiary that is wholly owned by a parent corporation with at least 51 percent of the parent corporation voting stock owned by one or more physically challenged individuals, or c) a joint venture in which at least 51 percent of the management, control and earnings are held by one or more physically challenged individuals."[166]

Apple Computer, on the other hand, includes "small, disabled-owned businesses" in its program, defined as small-business concerns that are "at least 51 percent owned by an individual or individuals who has/have a physical or mental impairment which substantially limits one or more of such persons' major life activities. Individual(s) must be involved in the day-to-day management of the business."[167]

American Express requires veterans who are owners to have day-to-day involvement in their companies. Apple does not. Such seemingly minor discrepancies have led to serious problems. Consider the differences between government and private-sector requirements and the controversy that erupted in 2000 when the NMSDC proposed changing its ownership requirement to less than 51 percent. The idea was to create a loophole in which MBEs could benefit from cash infusions by companies that were not necessarily minority-owned. Put another way, the NMSDC wanted to help MBEs go to the next level by giving them access to venture capital as well as debt capital.

This "growth initiative" fell apart when MBEs realized that while the NMSDC could change standards for the private sector, it couldn't affect the standards for certification in the public sector, which would remain at 51 percent. Thus, for a company to take the plunge and accept venture capital, it would have to cut itself out of any possible subcontracting arrangements with government prime contractors. Foster-Thompson said many MBEs weren't willing to go that route.[168]

That's the public/private problem. But as the American Express vs. Apple example illustrates, things quickly can become inconsistent within corporate America as well. What supplier-certification requirements companies require range from none or self-certification to absolute NMSDC or WBENC compliance. This is significant because it illustrates the lack of consistency in defining supplier diversity for reporting purposes. With leeway, companies are able to appear to be achieving supplier diversity goals by broadening the definition of diverse suppliers.

Across the United States, major corporations have continued to increase their supplier-diversity efforts as an effective way to reach communities of color and emerging markets. The National Minority Supplier Diversity Development Council (NMSDC), which links 39 regional councils, 3,500 corporate members and 15,000 minority-owned businesses, charted 2001 purchasing activity at $63 billion. This is up from $54.3 billion in 2000. Purchasing activity figures for 2002 will be released in October 2003.

Today, there are 39 RMSDCs and 3,500 corporate members in the NMSDC serving approximately 15,000 MBEs.

a. Terminology

Minority-Owned Businesses. Often referred to as an MBE, or "minority business enterprise." This description is applied to a business that is at least 51 percent owned, managed and controlled by one or more SBA-defined minorities. Minority owners can be males or females who are African American, Latino, American Indian, Asian American or Pacific Islander, Native Alaskan and East Indian.

Women-Owned Businesses. Often referred to as a WBE, or "women business enterprise." This description is applied to a business that is at least 51 percent owned, managed and controlled by one or more women.

Disabled Veteran-Owned Businesses. Sometimes referred to as a DVBE, or "disabled veteran business enterprise." May also be called an SDV — "Service Disabled Veteran" — business enterprise. Some companies, such as Apple Computer, also have drawn a distinction between a "disabled-owned business" and a "disabled veteran-owned business." The former is at least 51 percent owned, managed and controlled by "an individual or individuals who has a physical or mental impairment which substantially limits one or more of such persons major life activities." The latter adds, "the physical or mental impairment must have been sustained during active service in one of the United States armed services," according to Apple.[169]

Disadvantaged Businesses. Often referred to as a DBE, or "disadvantaged business enterprise." This description is usually applied to minority-owned businesses, but can include DVBEs, WBEs and businesses in economically depressed areas. May also be called an SDB, or "small disadvantaged business," which combines the definition of a DBE with the SBA's definition of a small business. The SDB certification ensures that small businesses are owned and controlled by socially and economically disadvantaged individuals meeting certain specific criteria, and with good reason. SDB are eligible to receive "a price evaluation credit of up to 10 percent" when bidding on a federal contracts.

Several other combination acronyms exist, such as MWBE for minority- and women- business enterprises and DVMWBE for disabled veteran, minority and women business enterprises exist and may crop up in discussions of supplier diversity.

One of the newest classifications in the disadvantaged business category is the HUBZone business. Such businesses are participants in the SBA's HUBZone Empowerment Contracting Program. To qualify for this program, a company must: a) be a small business by SBA standards; b) have its principal office located within a "Historically Underutilized Business Zone," which are located in urban and rural areas and on federally recognized Indian reservations; c) be owned and controlled by one or more U.S. citizens, a Community Development Corporation or an Indian tribe; and d) have at least 35 percent of its employees living in a HUBZone. The term was coined in 1990 by the President's Commission on Minority Business Development. Its meaning is similar to that of a DBE.[170]

b. Billion-Dollar Roundtable

The Billion Dollar Roundtable (BDR) was founded in 2001 by Shirley Harrison, vice president, diversity management, Altria; Sharon Patterson, the director of supplier diversity at Altria's Kraft Foods unit, and Don McKneely, publisher of Texas-based Minority Business News. BDR's 10 charter members are Altria, parent company to Philip Morris and Kraft Foods; automakers General Motors, Ford and DaimlerChrysler; communications giants AT&T, SBC and Verizon, plus IBM, Lucent and Wal-Mart. The group's two newest members are defense contractor Lockheed Martin and auto-industry supplier Johnson Controls. To qualify for the BDR, companies must spend $1 billion annually with MWBEs.

Taken together, the 12 corporate members of the Billion Dollar Roundtable (BDR) spend more than $20 billion a year with businesses owned by women and people of color. That's more than the annual revenue of 414 of the Fortune 500 corporations, notes Raymond Arroyo, manager for corporate diversity at Altria, and more than the gross domestic product of 72 individual countries.

The BDR was formed with two goals in mind – to provide a top-level forum for BDR members to share strategies and ideas and to leverage the combined knowledge of BDR members for use by others.[171]

C. Government Contracts

Supplier diversity, like affirmative action, started out as a government mandate and has evolved into a huge economic opportunity and competitive advantage for forward-thinking companies. As corporate America comes under increased pressure to cut costs and, simultaneously, make inroads through raised brand awareness and community goodwill with the fast-growing Latino, African-American and Asian-American communities, supplier diversity emerges as one of the most viable and attractive method of accomplishing those goals.

Any company that does business with the federal government has a string of public laws to thank for the core philosophy of doing business with the communities that are its customers. Maye Foster-Thompson is the former executive director of the Chicago Minority Business Development Council and founder of the Chicago-based organization that later formed the National Minority Supplier Development Council (NMSDC). Foster-Thompson said "enlightened self-interest" has driven corporate supplier-diversity efforts — once called "minority-purchasing programs" — from the beginning. She recalled how the civil unrest following the assassination of the Rev. Martin Luther King Jr. led to the first Chicago Business Opportunity Fair in 1968, and how public laws mandating the way prime contractors distribute subcontracts were "a big shot in the arm" for the African-American-owned businesses she represented.[172]

Veteran supplier-diversity chiefs echo her recollections. Some companies with a burgeoning sense of social responsibility already were trying to do business with minority-owned businesses before leaders, such as Foster-Thompson, and government regulators came on the scene. A few major corporations, however, have led the way in a cohesive, organized supplier-diversity program, and the benefits to them have been tangible.

Consider San Antonio, Texas,-based SBC Communications, one of the nation's largest telecommunications companies and possessor of what several "best-of-class" lists rank as the nation's No. 1 supplier-diversity program, including DiversityInc's Top Companies for Supplier Diversity for the past two years. In 2002, SBC spent $1.6 billion with businesses owned by women, minorities and veterans with disabilities — or 19.2 percent of its total procurement budget.[173]

"From the beginning, we were able to understand that a world-class supplier-diversity program was a competitive advantage," Stephen Welch, SBC's president of procurement, told DiversityInc two years ago. "As our industry became more competitive, we saw that we could get good business solutions from small businesses. We also knew that the demographics of our customer base were changing, and that minority communities were among our best customers.

"In 1989, in California, public policy began to focus sharply on the need for public utilities to improve their [diversity-spending] results," Welch said. "With some of that stimulation ... SBC began to accelerate its activity in the supplier-diversity programs."[174]

Lucent Technologies of Murray Hill, N.J., a prime supplier to companies such as SBC, confirmed the impact of federal contracting legislation on the telecommunications industry and the sea change that has occurred. "Twenty-five years ago, supplier diversity was a mandated, regulation-driven activity," Heather Herndon-Wright, Lucent's national director of supply-chain diversity, told DiversityInc. "Over the years, the demographics have shifted and changed it into being a market-driven initiative. It's been a total paradigm shift."[175]

D. Tracking Spending

There is an important difference between supplier-diversity spending and share of spending, which looks at dollars spent with diverse suppliers relative to dollars spent among all suppliers.

Not reporting share-of-spending percentages is a major way companies hype their supplier-diversity numbers while de-emphasizing the bigger picture: namely, how big of a cut they're really giving to diverse businesses. The Big Three automakers are a prime example: Ford, GM and DaimlerChrysler spend several billion dollars apiece with diverse suppliers each year. But these spending figures represent less than 10 percent of what the automakers spend annually on procurement.

Of course, the real dollars spent by the auto industry are significant, and when supplier-diversity spending across all industries is taken together, the auto industry's share of that spending is among the largest of any industry. Few other industries are providing diverse suppliers with as many revenue opportunities.

The worsening economy has made the likelihood of more missed goals likely.

So how close do companies come to their projected spending goals? A KPMG Impact Analysis done for the Rainbow/PUSH Wall Street Project Conference in January 2002 looked at 12 companies using this criterion. Of the nine that responded to questions about supplier diversity, most reported stagnancy and/or a low percentage spent with MBEs and WBEs. The five groups Rainbow/PUSH asked about were African Americans, Asian Americans, Hispanic Americans, Native Americans and non-minority women.

The survey tracked percentage growth in spending with these groups between 1992 and 1997, and 1997 and 2001. Most companies reported flat growth that stayed under 1 percent per group. A few reported specific growth in certain categories, but only non-minority women saw spending in excess of 5 percent.

Certain industries also have set growth goals. The telecommunications industry — through its annual event at SUPERCOMM — has pushed more than 70 companies to sign an agreement to increase their percentage of spending each year until hitting at least 10 percent per year.

E. Subcontracting: Second-Tier Spending

What is referred to as "subcontracting" in government circles is called "second-tier spending" in corporate America. To diagram this analogy, consider the Department of Defense to be the corporation, airplane manufacturer Lockheed Martin to be the first-tier supplier and Joe's Wing Assembly to be the second-tier supplier.

Suppose the Department of Defense needs 85 planes, and it contracts with Lockheed Martin (the first-tier supplier) to manufacture them. At a hypothetical $1 million per plane, that would be $85 million for Lockheed. However, since Lockheed doesn't have all the parts and labor on hand to make the planes from scratch, it must subcontract out some of the work. Thanks to legislation such as Public Law 95-507, to have secured that $85 million contract, Lockheed had to guarantee that some of that subcontracting — at least 5 percent — would go to a diverse supplier. This is where Joe's Wing Assembly comes in. Joe, an African American, is the second-tier in the chain. Because of the public law, he is eligible for a piece of the larger contract. And so a supplier-diversity goal is met.

Recognizing that many minority-owned companies aren't large enough to handle the corporate equivalent of an $85 million contract, large companies and the NMSDC have developed second-tier spending goals to ensure diverse suppliers get a piece of the pie. This has not been without controversy since, unlike in the public sector, private companies cannot be compelled to spend a set amount with diverse suppliers.

A significant issue is how companies report their second-tier spending. The standard practice is to report the spending separately. At the very least, if companies combine the two figures, they should make this clear in their reporting.

Some companies add second-tier spending to their total supplier-diversity spending figure for a year. While some companies reveal this practice, such information is often hard to come by in the public sphere.

Rolling up second-tier spending is another way companies inflate their supplier-diversity spending numbers.

F. Best Practices From the Top Companies for Diversity

Ford Motor Co. has been proactive at fostering a diverse-supplier based in critical roles. In 1998, Ford bought $2.5 billion in goods and services from either minority- or women-owned business enterprises. Two years later, company expenditures on WMBEs increased to $3.5 billion, out of a total $90 billion procurement budget. This figure surpassed the procurement spending on WMBEs of any other U.S. company. And even last year, when procurement was down at Ford and many other companies, Ford spent $3.1 billion with diverse suppliers.

Meanwhile, the company expects its business partners to be mindful of supplier diversity as well. Ford requests that its first-tier, primary suppliers purchase at least 5 percent of all the goods and services they use from federally certified minority companies. The automaker has gone as far as to warn companies that fail to get with the program that they "may place their business relationship with Ford at risk."[176]

According to Ford, the second-tier program "continues to expand each year and now generates approximately $1 billion of minority purchases" by first-tier suppliers.

Another example of a company that has exercised social responsibility through diverse suppliers is automotive-systems specialist Johnson Controls Inc. (JCI). The company just joined the Billion-Dollar Roundtable by spending $1 billion on goods and services from diverse suppliers. The company boasts a network of 1,100 minority and women-owned business enterprises (MWBEs).

Johnson Controls is a $17 billion company headquartered in Milwaukee. A major part of its business is manufacturing car seats, batteries and interior systems. Its main customers are the Big Three automakers: Ford, General Motors and DaimlerChrysler. Roughly 40 percent of its sales are attributed to these three companies alone. The company also is a major manufacturer of environmental-control systems for commercial buildings.[177]

Today, the company is also pushing its non-MWBEs to do business with more diverse suppliers. This is referred to as promoting "second-tier spending" in supplier-diversity circles.

Procter & Gamble (P&G), marketer of Tide, Charmin and dozens of other well-known consumer brands, has committed to spending at least $1.5 billion annually with diverse suppliers by 2005. The company will have to spend an average of about 15 percent more each year between now and then to hit that mark, which would equal about 11 percent of its total procurement budget. P&G increased its supplier diversity spending by more than 20 percent in 2002 and 2003 and expects an increase of about 13 percent by 2004 and 2005. The company expects to increase supplier-diversity efforts by about 15 percent a year through 2010.[178]

The reality for these companies was more outside pressure than corporate benevolence. Coca-Cola owes its latest supplier-diversity focus to a major lawsuit by its African-American employees. Toyota was motivated by recent pressure from the Rev. Jesse Jackson and his Rainbow/PUSH advocacy organization.

Of DiversityInc's top 10 companies for supplier diversity announced in April 2003 – SBC, Ford, Altria (tie for second), International Truck & Engine, Shell Oil, IBM, Freddie Mac, Lucent, Eastman Kodak and Sempra Energy, an average of 10.86 percent of total procurement budgets went to diverse suppliers. And these companies spent an average of $1.4 billion with those suppliers.

Those numbers show a commitment, of both resources and dollars, to diverse suppliers and their communities. All the top 10 companies for supplier diversity encouraged tier-two spending (diverse suppliers hiring diverse suppliers) and all but one had formal supplier-diversity programs.

Companies cited some common best practices:

- Tracking, measuring and reporting diverse supplier spend

- Setting clear goals and targets

- CEO support for supplier-diversity initiatives

- Education and training (both internal and external.

- Participate: e.g. trade fairs and supplier-diversity organizations

Companies also cited some unique best practices:

- Targeted bidding

- Mini-CD and marketing brochure for diverse suppliers

- Provided internal trainees with laminated cards containing business case and customer requirements

Third-party Recommendations

Third-party agencies, such as the NMSDC, WBENC and the Rainbow/PUSH Wall Street Project, have put together best practice recommendations as well. The following best practices are common to all of these agencies:

- Demonstrating a top-down commitment to supplier diversity

- Establishing a public commitment and corporate outreach program

- Providing supplier education and mentoring

- Some third-party agencies have offered more unique recommendations. For example, companies responding to a survey prepared for the Rainbow/PUSH Wall Street Project's annual conference[179] collectively recommended:

- Having a full-time manager who sets goals and monitors progress

- Getting executives involved so suppliers are cut in on "mega-deals and partnering opportunities"

- Posting competitive bids on a special Web site and getting MBEs in the electronic system

- Setting aggressive goals

- Getting employees and executives alike involved in supplier diversity and holding them accountable

- Using cross-functional supplier-diversity teams and
  assigning them managers

- Using a "portfolio-management" strategy

- Coaching and mentoring diverse suppliers

- Doing frequent benchmarking and cost-effectiveness
  analyses

The National Women's Business Council's 1999 Best Practice Guide
recommends:

- Targeted solicitation: Require supplier-diversity coordina-
  tors and purchasing staff to actively seek out new
  diverse suppliers

- Accountability: Hold "individual(s) awarding
  contracts…accountable for meeting the company's or
  agency's goals,"

- Incentives: Tie contractors' or buyers' performance evaluations to the number and degree of opportunities created for diverse suppliers

- The Women's Business Enterprise National Council's
  2001 Executive Report on its Corporate Purchasing
  Benchmarking Survey recommends:

- Corporations should train supplier-diversity personnel to
  meet the specific needs of different types of diverse suppliers, and widely publicize supplier-diversity program
  results

- The Joint Center for Political and Economic Studies'
  Effective Minority Supplier Development Programs recommends:

- Focusing on communication, or "real-time information
  sharing" among all parties in order "to increase speed to
  market, reduce defects and innovate processes"

- Collaborating on e-enablement by "educating and promoting e-commerce capabilities between customers and
  (diverse) suppliers"

- On the other hand, best practices that recommend the kind of mentoring that engenders business growth, or helping suppliers gain e-commerce capabilities, speak to issues that are critical to the future survival of any MBE, WBE or other disadvantaged business enterprise.[180]

ADDITIONAL RESOURCES

PART V: SUPPLIER DIVERSITY

"Anatomy of the Nation's No. 1 Supplier-Diversity Program."
DiversityInc, 27 April 2001.

Bean, Linda. "Real Money: Lockheed Martin, Johnson Controls
Join Billion-Dollar Roundtable." DiversityInc, 15 May 2003.
http://www.diversityinc.com/members/4940.cfm.

"Business Case for Supplier Diversity: Lucent Takes the Industry Lead."
DiversityInc, 1 June 2001.

"Case Study in Supplier-Diversity 91 Renaldo Jensen at Ford."
DiversityInc, 5 December 2001, p. 200.

DiversityInc Top 50 Company Survey, 2002. Results published in
June/July 2003 issue.

Humphreys, Jeffrey M. The Multicultural Economy 2002. Selig Center
for Economic Growth (Terry College of Business, University of Georgia).
Athens, Ga., May 2002.

"Johnson Controls Aims for $1 Billion Spent with Diverse Suppliers by
2003." DiversityInc, 12 July 2001.

Native American Business Alliance (NABA):
www.native-american-bus.org

National Black Chamber of Commerce (NBCC): *www.nationalbcc.org*

National Women Business Owners Corporation (NWBOC):
www.native-american-bus.org

Pine, Jordan T. " Supplier Diversity: What's In, What's Out According to
the NMSDC at Rainbow/PUSH." DiversityInc, 22 January 2002.
http://www.diversityinc.com/members/2231.cfm.

Pitney Bowes Inc., NAWBO, Philadelphia Chapter, and Wells Fargo.
Completing the Picture: Equally-Owned Firms in 2002. April 2003.

U.S. Census Bureau. 1997 Economic Census: Survey of Minority-Owned
Business Enterprises (EC97CS-7). Washington, D.C., July 2001.

U.S. Department of Commerce's Minority Business Development
Agency, Washington, D.C.

U.S. General Service Administration (GSA): *www.gsa.gov*

ADDITIONAL RESOURCES

PART V: SUPPLIER DIVERSITY

U.S. Pan Asian American Chamber of Commerce (USPAAC):
www.uspaacc.org

U.S. Small Business Administration, Office of Advocacy. Minorities in Business, 2001. Washington, D.C., November 2001.
http://www.sba.gov/advo/stats.

[More on HUBZone business is available on the SBA's HubZone Web site at: *https://eweb1.sba.gov/hubzone/internet.*]

Zeilberger, Ruth. "Boom in Women-Owned Businesses, But Financing Still a Barrier." DiversityInc, 1 May 2003.
http://www.diversityinc.com/members/4871.cfm.

NASA Supplier-Diversity Programs Set the Standards for Government

By C. Stone Brown

© 2003 DiversityInc.com

The National Aeronautics and Space Administration (NASA) has become the gold-standard agency for contracting opportunities for people of color and women.

"There has been more than a 300 percent increase in doing business with small disadvantaged businesses (SDBs) over the past decade," says Tony Diamond, NASA's small business adviser for the Office of Small Disadvantaged Business Utilization (OSDBU). NASA's commitment to diverse suppliers now comprises more than 19 percent of its spend with all its vendors, an astonishing percentage byany standard.

NASA's OSDBU was started in 1994 to assist the agency in meeting its mission to ensure that SDBs, women-owned businesses and Historically Black Colleges and Universities (HBCUs) and other institutions of color were provided with prime and subcontracting opportunities with the various NASA agencies.

Companies such as QSS, NASA's 2002 Minority Business of the Year, have experienced the benefits of NASA's supplier-diversity programs. Headquartered in Lanham, Md., QSS is a prime contractor at NASA's Ames Research Center and Glenn Research Center. The company provides a broad range of research and development for the Computational Science Division at Ames, in artificial intelligence, knowledge-based systems, autonomy and robotics, neuro-engineering and flight control, and automated software engineering.

Diamond says about 5 percent of NASA's contracting was with SDBs and women-owned companies before 1990 – until Congress stepped in. NASA developed what he called "an 8 percent plan in 1991." Its goal was to have 8 percent of its vendors be SDBs and women-owned businesses by 1994, but NASA reached an 8.5 percent spend with diverse suppliers by 1993.

"Over the years, NASA, like other agencies, didn't really spend too much time on small business. This is more than 10 to 15 years ago. But in 1990, the Congress of the United States grabbed a hold of NASA and said, 'We want you to get to 8 percent of all your work to small minority businesses and women,'" Diamond says.

NASA Supplier-Diversity Programs Set the Standards for Government (cont'd.)

"There's been a history of activity and positive accomplishments within the agency," says Dorothy Hayden-Watkins, assistant administrator for equal opportunity programs (EOP) at NASA. Watkins became the EOP administrator in January 2003 and has plans to make her own mark on diversity at NASA. "We hope that we will become a model just as I think we are a leader in science and space exploration … a model as it relates to equal opportunity and diversity."

Hayden-Watkins has the credentials to lead NASA's diversity programs. Prior to coming to NASA, Watkins worked in private industry as senior vice president for the Hilton Hotels Corporation.

Hayden-Watkins, who holds a Ph.D. in community and human resources, and a master's degree in education and administration from the University of Nebraska, says the remaining diversity challenges at NASA are complex. "One is to change the culture of the organization to see diversity and equal opportunity as an opportunity rather than a burden," she says.

Although supplier diversity at NASA has had a legislative mandate that doesn't necessarily equate to acceptance across the organizational structure, she says, "It's the spirit of the law … we are trying to influence people to voluntarily and proactively support diversity."

It's easy to get people talking about diversity but it's something entirely different "influencing people to believe it and to understand the business opportunity of diversity," Hayden-Watkins says.

Diamond says NASA's outreach extends to the Small Business Administration, where NASA works to set annual goals for contracting with SDBs and women-owned businesses. Because of the critical nature of the work with which NASA is charged, supplier-diversity opportunities have unique challenges.

"Our difficulty has been that we are dealing with high-technology work. We can't just pick companies off the street. We have to make sure that they are qualified to assist us in a very, very scientific and technical mission," Diamond says. NASA doesn't subscribe to a "build it and they will come" philosophy. NASA officials have processes in place to help people of color and women get their fair share of contract opportunities with the agency.

"We now have training and development programs for small businesses in advance technology. Which means if we bring them together, it's a free course where companies can come and spend three days with us to show them what you need to do to prepare to do business with NASA," Diamond says.

NASA Supplier-Diversity Programs Set the Standards for Government (cont'd.)

A similar program is NASA's Aerospace Technology for Disadvantage Small Business Forums. "We go out and ask small businesses to tell us what they can do to help us," Diamond says. NASA brings in top management and procurement people from each of the NASA centers to present to small businesses. "It's a way of getting them [small businesses] involved with NASA by knowing what we need.

NASA's Mentor-Protégé Program is designed to foster relationships of prime contractors with HBCUs, SDBs and women-owned businesses through mentoring with a twist. "We try to marry large businesses with SDBs and women," says Diamond.

Unlike the Department of Defense mentor programs NASA requires prime contractors to have a hands-on working relationship with SDBs. "We work the other way; we say to large businesses: In order to join our mentor program, we want to make sure that you give a subcontract to that small minority business so he or she learns from the experience," says Diamond.

One Great Idea Isn't Enough: Supplier Success Hinges on Diversifying Business

By Linda Bean

© 2003 DiversityInc.com

The Minority Business Executive (MBE) program at Dartmouth College's Amos Tuck School of Business Administration has been educating entrepreneurs for nearly 25 years.

And in that time, MBE Director Leonard Greenhalgh has identified a key threat to the success of businesses owned by women and people of color – failure to diversify.

"You have to have a portfolio," Greenhalgh says. "If you have a single product or service, you are at the mercy of the market. If you have multiple products and services, then you are in much better shape."

A janitorial company that expands into building management, particularly if the company is providing management services to existing customers, would be following the Tuck credo: Get a larger share of the customer you've already got.

"It costs you about five times as much to secure a brand-new customer than retain an old customer. A new customer doesn't know you; you have to make sales calls and set up accounts and you are on a learning curve with a new customer," Greenhalgh says. "With an old customer, you already know how to manage them."

Tommy Hodinh, CEO of Austin, Texas-based MagRabbit, didn't attend Tuck's MBE program, but the Vietnamese immigrant embraces Greenhalgh's views all the same. "I'm re-engineering my company all the time," Hodinh says.

MagRabbit, which started as a company with two employees in 1989, is now a $10 million company with between 75 and 80 employees. Hodinh is intent on building a business worth $1 billion before he retires.

"What he exhibited is what every small-business person is really required to do if they are going to stay alive," says Harriet Michel, president of the National Minority Supplier Development Council.

Hodinh, 50, came to the United States as an 18-year-old refugee in 1970, earned a degree at the University of Texas, El Paso, and went to work for IBM, where he stayed for 15 years.

One Great Idea Isn't Enough: Supplier Success Hinges on Diversifying Business (cont'd.)

Hodinh, whose English retains the strong accent of his homeland, say IBM was "a very good company."

"But my communication ability was a liability for me. It forced me to feel like I wasn't really going to make it there," he says. At the same time, he knew he possessed the intelligence and drive to build his own business.

"I'm the kind of guy, if somebody else can do it, I can do it, too," he says.

He founded MagRabbit, duplicating software for computer companies to sell to their customers. That process, formally known as magnetic replication, coupled with the speed represented by the rabbits Hodinh admires, gave the company its name.

By 1995, MagRabbit had grown into a full-service software-delivery company – taking orders for its customers, packaging software and shipping it directly to consumers. It was a strong business plan, Hodinh says, but not one that was going to survive the expansion of the Internet.

Customers weren't going to order software if they could purchase it online and download it at their desks, he adds.

"I started thinking about how to service the Internet," Hodinh says. "We had been taking orders by phone; we started taking orders over the Internet."

Hodinh's company began managing businesses such as Dellauction.com, where shoppers bid on Dell computer equipment. MagRabbit employees track the bids, notify the winners, collect the money, and pack and ship the goods.

"We went from very low-tech to very high-tech," he says.

"He's been incredibly smart about it," Michel says.

Some entrepreneurs, "in their eagerness to build their business," attempt to marry incompatible operations, she says.

"But you can't be asbestos remover and then go into auto parts" with any hope of tapping the existing customer base, Michel adds. "You need to expand service to current customers before you go looking for new customers."

Now Hodinh is expanding MagRabbit through joint ventures with overseas transportation firms and a domestic company that provides temporary transportation and logistics employees.

"We complement each other," he says.

Hodinh's business model could be a textbook example: He carved out a niche,

One Great Idea Isn't Enough: Supplier Success Hinges on Diversifying Business (cont'd.)

built a strong customer base and expanded within that niche to serve existing customers. Building on that early success, he's expanding into related areas with established partners.

He also sinks the majority of profits back into the business, eliminating another significant cause of failure – a lack of cash flow.

"That's a key mistake, running out of cash," says Tuck's Greenhalgh. "People don't think through the cash-flow issues. They don't plan for it. But if you put money out in salaries and (other expenses), by the time people pay their bills, you may run out of cash."

At the Tuck MBE program, instructors stress that businesses don't fail "for the lack of great ideas," says Greenhalgh. "They fail for lack of execution."

"There's a lack of customer focus, inefficient processes, a lack of control systems that work," he says. "Maybe they don't have performance appraisals or don't have budgets or don't have good ways of doing" basic functions.

Tuck accepts 180 students into its MBE program each years – 120 into the basic program and 60 into an advanced session.

The program accepts entrepreneurs who have been running businesses with $300,000 or more a year in profits. And it only accepts entrepreneurs who have been running a business for three years or longer.

"These are businesses that are staying alive – a lot of badly run businesses can survive," Greenhalgh says. "But can they prosper? It is one thing to survive in the good times, but what do you do when times turn bad?"

Applicants to the program are required to fill out an assessment of their operations before attending, using a set of standards developed by the university. By the time they show up on campus, Greenhalgh says, they've diagnosed their own problems and are ready to learn to run their businesses well.

"If you look at the rate of failure of (minority-owned) businesses, it is horrendous.

Greenhalgh says. "Not because the idea wasn't good or the person wasn't good, but because the business was run poorly."

"An entrepreneurial mind-set isn't enough," he adds.

Hodinh would agree. Still, he says, that mind-set is important.

"You have to have the character to motivate yourself," says Hodinh. "You have to

One Great Idea Isn't Enough: Supplier Success Hinges on Diversifying Business (cont'd.)

have the desire to be a success. You have to be independent. Entrepreneurs don't want to work for anyone else."

As he's built his business, Hodinh says, he has learned to ask the advice of others – including subordinates. "I hire people who are smarter than I am," he says.

And he's not shy about asking other successful business people to share their insights.

"I say 'I'm a rookie on the block. Please tell me what you know,' " Hodinh says. "And they do."

Meanwhile, "you have to do community service and all that good stuff you should do as a good human being. That is fundamental. There are so many choices in the world … people don't have to do business with me. They have to like me and respect me to want to do business with me," he adds.

The transportation and logistics industry is a $700 billion business, he says. "I just want to take $1 billion of that," Hodinh says.

But in the final analysis, he adds, he measures his success by the strength of his business – including the strength of his relationships with employees, customers and partners.

"I like money," he adds, "but money is just the end game."

Top 3 Trends in Supplier Diversity: Bigger Suppliers, Deeper Databases, More Faces of Color

By Linda Bean

© 2003 DiversityInc.com

Corporate America is under increasing pressure to cut costs and streamline internal operations. At the same time, leading corporations want to leverage every dollar spent with diverse suppliers into heightened brand awareness or community goodwill among increasingly important markets of color.

Now, diverse suppliers need to determine just how they are going to help their corporate customers meet both goals.

"Instead of focusing on the diversity side of supplier diversity, we have to focus on the supply part, and on the supply chain," says Ralph Moore, the African-American CEO of RGMA Consulting, a Chicago-based business-development consulting firm.

Major corporations, including those with a demonstrated commitment to supplier diversity, "have found that it is more difficult to do business with a lot of suppliers … and the majority of opportunities are for larger suppliers," says Chick Lee, an African-American entrepreneur from Horsham, Pa., who specializes in developing strategic alliances and joint ventures.

"That is the kind of emphasis corporate America is putting on supplier diversity," he says.

What does corporate America want? Ask Johnson Controls, based in Milwaukee, which spent at least $955 million with minority-owned businesses in 2002, or roughly 16 percent of the company's total procurement budget.

"We are looking for suppliers that can be competitive in terms of cost, quality and delivery of products and services," says Reginald Layton, JCI's director of supplier diversity.

"We will deal with any size company if they can fulfill a particular need. Some of our needs are huge and global and we need a huge supplier, but other needs are small. We don't need ABC Studios to produce a video. We can hire a videographer, a sole proprietor, for a job like that," he adds.

Top 3 Trends in Supplier Diversity: Bigger Suppliers, Deeper Databases, More Faces of Color (cont'd.)

That said, Layton acknowledges that the company – which builds auto interiors and climate-control systems and runs a facilities-management business – sees clear advantages to working with larger diverse suppliers.

At the same time, JCI believes it has a responsibility to help suppliers grow and develop. "It's easy to say we want bigger suppliers. The question is, 'what do we need to do to help them get bigger?' "

To promote expansion, JCI might bring several suppliers with complementary strengths together and urge a joint venture. Alternatively, JCI might identify a single diverse supplier with strong management skills and encourage that supplier to manage several smaller firms. Those "lead supplier" arrangements allow JCI to include several smaller firms in a single project.

JCI expects suppliers to manage their growth and has put in place a number of programs aimed at aiding expansion.

"We train them on best practices. We have an institute and seminars," Layton says. "We need to look at the minority company's processes. We need to ask whether processes (suppliers) have in place to manage quality, train the workforce, grow the customer base."

Corporate vendor-diversity managers are "getting more sophisticated in how to do these deals and work with diverse suppliers," he adds. "It's not about making the biggest deal. It's about longevity."

"If you do a big deal and a year later the company fails … that is a problem," he adds.

There have been significant changes in supplier diversity in recent years. When Moore, 53, was 25 and a self-described "hot-shot," supplier-diversity efforts focused on creating businesses owned by women and people of color.

Those were the days, he says, when the Small Business Administration (SBA) would provide a $75,000 loan "that was not enough money to develop a retail store that would go out of business in two or three years." Supplier-diversity advocates saw success in the number of new businesses created, regardless of how well those businesses fared.

The federal government, through contract requirements, agency rules and executive orders, encouraged the development of minority-owned business – and helped generate awareness among corporations of supplier diversity.

Moore credits federal initiatives with giving supplier diversity a seat at corporate

Top 3 Trends in Supplier Diversity: Bigger Suppliers, Deeper Databases, More Faces of Color (cont'd.)

America's table. But in the end, Moore says, suppliers and corporations are only well-served when business development meets a market demand.

"We can't develop businesses in a vacuum. They have to serve a purpose. They have to respond to a need in the marketplace," Moore adds. "We have to bring solutions to the marketplace."

The U.S. Census Bureau, as part of its data-collection process, tallies business ownership by ethnicity every five years. In 1997, the last year for which the data is available, there were more than 823,000 African-American-owned businesses in the United States, many of them sole proprietorships, employing 718.300 other people. Approximately 8,700 of those businesses had sales of $1 million a year or more.

Latinos owned 1.2 million businesses in 1997, employing more than 1.3 million people. Some 26,700 Latino-owned businesses posted sales of $1 million a year or more.

Asian Americans owned some 913,000 businesses in 1997, and had more than 2.2 million people on the payroll. Of those, 45,300, or 5 percent, had sales of $1 million or more.

Minority-owned businesses grew more than four times as fast as U.S. firms overall between 1992 and 1997, increasing from 2.1 million to about 2.8 million firms. That compares to an overall increase in business ownership of 7 percent, from 17.3 million in 1992 to 18.4 million in 1997.

Now, says Moore, "we have to start thinking really big ... buying offshore, global relationships."

"It's going to take the next generation of entrepreneurs to go beyond thinking small," he adds.

Lee, 60, is a longtime member of the National Minority Supplier Development Council (NMSDC) and the business of developing diverse suppliers "is so dear to my heart," he says.

Although an increasing number of people of color own medium- to large-size businesses, greater expansion will require cooperation, Lee says.

"It is extremely difficult to grow minority businesses without looking at strategic alliances and joint ventures," Lee says. "You have to look at different ways to grow – but it is tough, extremely challenging. Most (business people) don't want to give up their autonomy; they don't feel comfortable sharing information. How

Top 3 Trends in Supplier Diversity: Bigger Suppliers, Deeper Databases, More Faces of Color (cont'd.)

do you make decisions? Who makes the decision? It's a trauma for most people."

"We need to start focusing on minority CEOs," echoes Moore, "and talking about how to create alliances. I always tell people two things: You have to hire somebody smarter than you are. Until you are ready to hire someone smarter than you are, you aren't going to make it. Two, you have to be prepared to pay someone more than you pay yourself."

Initially, the nation's largest corporations – at least those doing business with the federal government – adopted supplier-diversity practices that allowed them to comply with government regulations.

But as programs have evolved, says Icy Williams, head of supplier diversity for Proctor & Gamble, the emphasis at some of the nation's largest companies has shifted away from compliance toward bottom-line impact.

"You have to think about this in a holistic fashion. It is not just about procurement and procurement spend … it is about your consumers," she says.

Williams, who is African American, is a former line executive who firmly believes that vendor diversity is a strategic issue. "I believe that the companies who get it, who really understand diversity in the broader sense, are those companies that continually reach out there and open doors and make this part of their overall strategy," she says.

But for every leader like Williams, there's an internal procurement chief who hasn't drawn the connection between vendor diversity and the bottom line.

And bringing those players to the table, Lee says, poses a considerable challenge.

Lee particularly is interested in bringing some of the nation's larger companies on board – companies that report anywhere from $500 million to $1 billion in sales each year. In 1992, the last year that the Census Bureau tallied the data, there were some 90,000 companies in the range.

Many of them, Lee says, are primary suppliers to the Fortune 500. Historically, "there's been no hammer, no incentive for them to participate."

"Many of those corporations have not been at the table and there was no one forcing them to be there," he adds.

That's changing, as corporations increasingly demand a greater diversity commitment from their primary, or first-tier suppliers. Now, it is up to supplier-diversity advocates, like the NMSCD, "to deliver to that group the services and programs that will attract and retain them."

Partnerships With Diverse Suppliers Key to Building Corporate Trust

By Yoji Cole

© 2002 DiversityInc.com

Corporations seeking inroads to communities of color and ways to buttress the public's crumbling trust in corporate America, need look no further than their efforts to conduct business with diverse suppliers.

Supplier diversity is the avenue that leads corporations to businesses owned by women and people of color – vendors who can supply goods and services that range from messenger and janitorial services to legal expertise and technology specialists.

Corporations regularly tout their expenditures with businesses owned by women and people of color to show their commitment to inclusion and investment in community, with the highest prize being admittance into the Billion Dollar Roundtable. The roundtable boasts corporate members, such as Philip Morris, Ford, General Motors and Verizon Communications, each of which spends more than $1 billion annually with diverse suppliers.

As CEOs boast of their spends with diverse suppliers, to prove their commitment to inclusion and markets of color, their claims are coming under scrutiny as questions arise of the amount of business they exclude from the equation and whether their relationships with diverse suppliers are direct or a few vendors removed, says Ralph G. Moore, president of RGMA, a Chicago-based consultancy that specializes in developing corporate supplier-diversity programs.

"What they spend and how they figure out what they spend is the hottest discussion today, because in reality they shouldn't exclude anything," says Moore, whose company consults with Major League Baseball, Nike, British Petroleum, IBM and Station Casino in Las Vegas, to name a few clients.

Many corporations exclude spending in areas where they don't believe businesses owned by women or people of color exist. Expenditures in areas such as utilities, hotels and rental cars routinely are excluded from corporations' supplier-diversity percentages.

"There shouldn't be anything that is excluded," Moore says. "There will always be an asterisk next to the supplier-diversity numbers if you start using excludables."

Partnerships With Diverse Suppliers Key to Building Corporate Trust (cont'd.)

To find businesses owned by women and people of color, supplier-diversity executives refer to groups such as the National Minority Supplier Diversity Council (NMSDC), the Women's Business Enterprise National Council or the National Association of Minority and Women Owned Law Firms. Their lists of businesses or firms owned by women and people of color are extensive, but not comprehensive.

Xerox Corp., when figuring its spend among diverse suppliers, does not include what it spends on utilities, international payments or manufacturing facilities, intercompany business, major airlines and hotels, says Dan Robinson, manager of global purchasing and market access for Xerox.

"Until there is evidence – and not the one guy down the street – but pervasive evidence that minority companies do exist [in a certain area], then that's how we decide and define our exclusions," says Robinson.

Robinson says that around the beginning of the year, he asked the NMSDC to produce a list of hotels owned by women or people of color, and he was provided a list of small motels without the amenities that Xerox executives require when traveling.

"When thinking about what and how you measure your performance, you measure it on the basis … of where there is evidence that minority- and women-owned businesses exist," says Robinson. "If there is not existence in utilities and some other things, then you don't include those in your numbers because to do so would distort the performance."

Major League Baseball (MLB) excludes utilities from its calculations of the money it spends with diverse suppliers, says Wendy Lewis, vice president of strategic planning, recruitment and diversity for MLB.

"Anyone accounting to supplier-diversity efforts should benchmark where they do have a choice to spend and where they don't," Lewis says, offering her choices for electricity providers as an example.

Since there is not an electricity provider that is owned by a woman or a person of color, it would be faulty to lump in that expenditure with the amount that's spent on all suppliers, Lewis says.

"I don't have a choice of a minority-owned or female-owned power company so that should not be accounted in my utilization expenditures because I don't have an option there," Lewis says.

The telecommunications industry traditionally excluded expenditures on telecom-

Partnerships With Diverse Suppliers Key to Building Corporate Trust (cont'd.)

munications equipment up until 1997, says Julian Birdsong, director of supplier diversity for Verizon.

Moore contends that to exclude it is to misrepresent the truth. While there might not be a business in a particular area, such as car rentals, that is owned by a woman or person of color today, that doesn't mean that there won't be tomorrow, he says.

"We're just one transaction away from a minority firm buying a company within any area," Moore says. "Companies say they'll exclude their car-rental expenses because there is no minority firm that does that, but we were looking at a situation recently where a minority group came very close to buying Budget Rent-a-Car."

And, for companies that send executives to Miami, The Crowne Plaza Hotels and Resort franchise partnered with R. Donahue Peebles, an African American and president of Peebles Atlantic Development Corp., to build and own the Royal Palm Crowne Plaza Resort in Miami Beach. The 422-room hotel, which sits on South Beach, is the largest African-American-owned hotel-resort in the nation.

Verizon stopped excluding its expenditures on switching equipment from its spends with diverse suppliers after the industry in 1997 decided to invite diverse suppliers that already worked with the technological aspects of the industry to increase their business by manufacturing that equipment.

The industry's largest spend was in switching equipment, which is the computer brains and cabling that allows calls to be processed across the country, Birdsong says.

White-owned vendors manufactured the equipment before but wanted to reduce their costs, so they partnered with companies owned by people of color and women. The white-owned vendors then sold parts to vendors of color and women. Verizon could then buy the total switching package from diverse suppliers.

"The other approach was where the main vendor or supplier subcontracted the work [to a vendor of color or woman]," Birdsong says. "It was their [the white vendors'] decision on how they went about partnering with minority-owned vendors."

The largest percentage of Verizon's supplier-diversity spend comes from the purchase of switching equipment, Birdsong says. Companies can also expect questions about their first-tier and second-tier relationships. Some companies buy goods and services directly from people of color and women – tier-one suppliers.

Partnerships With Diverse Suppliers Key to Building Corporate Trust (cont'd.)

And some companies insist that their tier-one suppliers make an effort to work with smaller businesses owned by people of color and women.

"Those are going to be very sensitive topics in the next 12 to 18 months as accountability issues continue to hit corporate America," Moore says. "It won't take long for that spotlight on accountability to be focused on supplier diversity."

Dell Computer Corp. has had a tough time finding businesses owned by women and people of color that develop microchips or operating systems for computers, says Stephanie Shipp, senior manager of supplier diversity for Dell.

"For our fiscal year 2002, we spent over a billion dollars with small businesses," Shipp says, which included businesses owned by war veterans, women and people of color, in addition to businesses in Housing and Urban Development districts.

"We drive all of our first-tier suppliers to utilize diverse suppliers within their supply chain in their efforts to support us," Shipp says.

The nation's changing demographics means that to thrive, companies will have to understand how to tap directly into communities of color rather than giving lip service, Moore says. "The fastest growing customer base is people of color so supplier diversity can't help but be an issue of the future," Moore says. "In this climate of mistrust, senior executives can't talk of a number [of expenditures] that can't be defended."

P&G's Icy Williams: Moving Supplier-Diversity Focus Beyond Spending

By Linda Bean

© 2003 DiversityInc.com

March 07, 2003

Icy Williams, the supplier-diversity director at Procter & Gamble, went to work for the Cincinnati-based consumer-goods company in 1980, when she identified P&G as a workplace on what she calls "the leading edge" of diversity.

Williams was living in Green Bay, Wis., then – a predominately white community with only a handful of African-American families. Her husband Clarence had retired from his professional football career to run his own business and it was time, she says, to focus on her own career.

"Procter & Gamble had already moved beyond affirmative action – even in Green Bay – into what was called a 'multicultural organization.' That intrigued me," she says.

Williams, who earned a bachelor's degree in education and had food-service manufacturing experience, wasn't entirely sure her qualifications would meet the company's needs. But what she discovered, she says, is that P&G was willing to look beyond traditional credentials to find management talent.

The company "had the ability to look outside the box and to understand that a particular degree does not necessarily dictate what the outcome is going to be," she says.

From 1980 to 1987, the company increased the percentage of African-American managers to 26, or about 8 percent. And that represented a significant commitment to diversity in a community that had a relatively small population of people of color, Williams says.

"When I moved to Green Bay in 1970, there were only 25 African-American families," she says.

During her 22-year career, Williams has moved four times to take advantage of opportunities offered by P&G, but her decision in 2001 – before she accepted the supplier-diversity post – was the toughest, she says.

At that point, Williams was running a perfume plant in Avenel, N.J., had responsibility for global fragrance operations. Given her years of experience, Williams

P&G's Icy Williams: Moving Supplier-Diversity Focus Beyond Spending (cont'd.)

could have accepted a buy-out the company was offering at the time and retired. Instead, Instead, she elected to take on an entirely new challenge.

"I had to ask myself prior to taking on this role whether I wanted to stay with P&G and it was a tough choice," she says. "But I looked at the company's principles, and the way they've acted and behaved in the past … and I fell back on that. It helped me make the decision."

Success in any job is "predicated on the people," Williams says, "but people ebb and flow. You have to have confidence in how a company is going to behave … in its longstanding values."

Williams was preceded in her current post by Howard Elliott, who was well-known and well-respected within the ranks of supplier-diversity experts. And she inherited a program generally regarded as "one of the best in the country," says Ralph Moore, who run a supplier-diversity consulting company in Chicago.

P&G's reputation was built on the company's ability to "sustain meaningful relationships with minority business owners," Moore says. When the company couldn't find a minority-owned bottling company with the capacity it required, for example, it facilitated a partnership between a majority-owned bottling firm and a minority-owned company.

"Other companies would have said, 'Well, we tried … we looked for a minority-owned firm,' and they would have left it right there," Moore says. "Procter & Gamble went the extra mile."

In October 2001, just months before Williams assumed her new role at P&G, the company announced a new supplier-diversity spending target: $1.5 billion with women- and minority-owned companies by 2005.

"We are a consumer organization, thinking about how we can make a difference," she says. The opportunity to work with women business owners and entrepreneurs of color "kind of matched with what I wanted to do in making an impact, helping to close the wealth gap."

Over the next year, Williams expects the company to spend $700 million with businesses owned by people of color and $450 million with women-owned operations – about 8 percent to 10 percent of the company's total U.S. procurement budget.

But hitting the spend mark isn't Williams' primary challenge.

"We have the infrastructure in place," says Williams. "Now, we have time to

P&G's Icy Williams: Moving Supplier-Diversity Focus Beyond Spending (cont'd.)

work on the sustainability of our suppliers. That is the next phase – building sustainable businesses."

Accomplishing that mission requires Williams and her staff to advocate within P&G to assure a continued focus on vendor diversity.

"As you take a mature organization, you need to be putting in place the systems so that becomes part of the organization, integral to your company" she says. "Seeing that it gets put on scorecards and factors into performance reviews."

At P&G, supplier-diversity experts conduct training and development courses for employees at all levels of the company, expanding the understanding of supplier-diversity issues beyond the corps of procurement executives.

"You want to take from an area already doing supplier diversity – like manufacturing and product supply – to new areas like research and development – that's the next phase," she says.

"You want to work the leadership and you also want to start from the bottom up with training and curriculum," Williams adds. "Hopefully, they will meet in the middle."

The supplier-diversity team works directly with vendors, helping them develop strategic business and succession plans.

"We ask them about their business plans and business models. We send them to course at Tufts [University] and the Kellogg School of Business [at Northwestern University]. We've put together a select group of suppliers to serve as an advisory council," Williams said.

"This is exciting," she adds. "This is an exciting time."

Major League Baseball Hits the Long Ball With Supplier Partnerships

By Yoji Cole

© 2003 DiversityInc.com

June 24, 2002

The Houston Astros' Damian Babin scouts prospects for the team – but instead of players, he seeks businesses owned by people of color and women.

Like a player scout, Babin, director of treasury and office services, hunts for businesses that will work best with the team's current stable of companies, but he doesn't inspect organizations as a scout would scrutinize various high schools and colleges for prospective talent. Babin goes straight to the sources: The National Minority Supplier Development Council (NMSDC) and Women's Business Enterprise National Council (WBENC).

"We have to go where the information is and that's where the information is," said Babin.

Major League Baseball (MLB) as a whole is going where the information is in an attempt to team Major League clubs with businesses owned by people of color and women. In what is being touted as the first agreements of their kind with a professional sport, both the NMSDC AND WBENC have signed individual partnership agreements with MLB.

"It's the first sports organization to reach out and create this alliance and if you're going to have an effective supplier-diversity process it takes a number of different strategies," said Ralph G. Moore, president of RGMA, a Chicago-based consultancy that specializes in developing corporate supplier-diversity programs.

RGMA is closely aligned with the NMSDC and Moore considers the partnership with MLB a critical piece to the league's supplier development and sourcing strategy.

Officials at WBENC agree and congratulate MLB for coming to the table with a plan in the works that enabled the partnership to zing from the start.

"MLB had a very well-integrated plan," said Susan Phillips Bari, president WBENC. "Instead of asking what they should do, they had already looked at the landscape, planned and budgeted in terms of what they wanted to accomplish."

377

Major League Baseball Hits the Long Ball With Supplier Partnerships (cont'd.)

The partnerships between MLB, NMSDC and WBENC include memberships for the league's central office, which has a national focus, and the 28 member baseball clubs, which will work with the regional offices of the NMSDC and WBENC. Each team has a representative focused on the relationship and MLB paid the first year of corporate dues for the 28 domestic teams, which for the WBENC equaled $2,500 each or a total of $70,000.

NMSDC struck a similar deal that cost MLB at least $34,500, which is commensurate with the dues paid by the member organizations with sales of $30 billion or more, according to Joseph Benitez, manager of member services at NMSDC.

"MLB was considering the fact that the owners probably had not budgeted for business with NMSDC and WBENC businesses," Bari said and noted that while the dues are not exorbitant, they "can be an impediment if there isn't a budget line."

The partnerships will give MLB access to the databases of national and local member businesses, which are owned by women and people of color, in addition to comprehensive resources such as seminars, training and technical assistance that will supplement the league's supplier-diversity programs and enhance its diverse vendor procurement efforts.

"It's unique for an organization to negotiate affiliate relationships for all their franchises from the corporate level but as we increase our spending levels I will have the integrity and the sophistication of the programs that they bring to the party to ensure that we have certified vendors," said Wendy Lewis, vice president of strategic planning, recruitment and diversity for MLB. "They will also help us market and advertise our message that we have a premier supplier-development program."

Lewis said MLB has already placed ads in magazines that target business owners of color such as Black Enterprise, Asian-American Biz, Caribbean/ Hispanic Business Journal and Hispanic Business.

"Between now and the rest of the year you will see us featured in Ebony and a number of other media and publication sources that we're talking to at this time in addition to our own all-star program booklet," Lewis said.

Since 1998, MLB said it has spent more than $200 million with people of color- and women-owned businesses and has purchased more than $75 million in direct business-to-business goods and services from businesses owned by people of color and women. One of the companies reaping the rewards of MLB's outreach to companies owned by women and people of color is Proftech, a supply compa-

Major League Baseball Hits the Long Ball With Supplier Partnerships (cont'd.)

ny that focuses mainly on providing MLB and its clients with office, computer supplies and office furniture. Every now and then, however, the Elmsford, N.Y.-based company receives an irregular request for a unique item and that's when it truly gets to show its value.

"You can buy supplies from anybody," said Jose Montiel, owner of Proftech. "We compete pricewise [with Office Depot] but we provide more of a service. The other day [the central MLB office] called and was in need of some Cracker Jacks. So we got them all of the Cracker Jacks that they needed ["caseloads"]. It doesn't matter if it's one item or a thousand. What we believe is important is that when the customer calls and says I'm in a jam and I need X, then we get it."

Proftech, which has been in business for 22 years, has worked with MLB for two years and been a member of the NMSDC for 18 years. Montiel, whose company also boasts Johnson & Johnson as a client, suggests that businesses which plan to provide a service for MLB, or a team in their locale, should take time to educate themselves on the particular team, the league and the individual needs of the two as sports companies.

"Every company is different," said Montiel. "When we are afforded the ability to sell to the Minnesota Twins we need to understand that team as a separate entity. It's not Major League Baseball. It's the Twins or the Yankees. You get the entrée, now you must prove you can service the company."

Montiel also credits the NMSDC with providing a smoother avenue to success for his company.

"An association like the NMSDC really opens doors for you," said Montiel. "It's expensive. It might cost us $10,000 to $15,000 [for a booth at the next NMSDC convention] but it takes one account to generate the cost associated with doing the trade show."

And the possibility of partnering with MLB or a particular team isn't a prospect many small companies owned by women or people of color can afford to let slip by, especially when the league is looking for prospects. Individual teams and the central MLB office track their supplier-diversity expenditures by benchmarking their spending in areas where diverse vendors are able to provide a service, Lewis said.

Currently MLB's supplier-diversity efforts are at about 6 percent of discretionary spending, Lewis said.

"Anyone accounting to supplier-diversity efforts should benchmark where they

Major League Baseball Hits the Long Ball With Supplier Partnerships (cont'd.)

do have a choice to spend and where they don't," Lewis said and provided her choices for electricity providers as an example.

Since there is not an electricity provider that is owned by a woman or a person of color, it would be faulty to lump that expenditure in with the amount spent on all suppliers, Lewis said.

"I don't have a choice of a minority-owned or female-owned power company so that should not be accounted in my utilization expenditures because I don't have an option there," Lewis said. "Discretionary spending is where you do have those vendors."

Discretionary spending among vendors can run the gamut of corporate gifts, professional services to general contracting, Lewis said.

"It's a huge range of opportunity to incorporate business-to-business relationships for minority- and female-owned vendors," said Lewis. "The pie is still phenomenally big, it's just that there are things in the universe that so far are not under the ownership of a minority-owned or female-owned company."

MLB's partnership with NMSDC and WBENC is a supplier-diversity model because it brings together companies owned by women and people of color with individual team organizations and their central office, said Moore.

"Part of any effective supplier-diversity strategy is outreach and sourcing minority and women businesses," Moore said. "The best practice in supplier diversity is to have senior-level support. In this case, we have 28 teams with their owners involved and then a measurement process. And all of that has been put in place."

Female Entrepreneurs of Color Lead the Pack of New Business Owners

By Ruth Zeilberger

© 2003 DiversityInc.com

October 24, 2002

Corporate America take note: the number of companies owned by women of color is growing at a rate that's four times faster than any other U.S. business sectors. The tremendous surge in the number of minority-women-owned businesses could signal a sea change for U.S. businesses and is a major factor in future economic growth, according to a new study released Tuesday by the Center for Women's Business Research, a Washington, D.C.-based think tank.

The study concluded that African-American and Latino women business owners are now more likely than ever before to start companies as full-time ventures. That's a sign that female entrepreneurs of color are treating startup businesses as ventures with serious growth potential, and in the process add jobs and make expenditures on business items such as computers and banking services.

"The study highlights the fact that women business owners of color are indeed a strong market that corporations should consider marketing to and reaching out to," said Stephanie Peacock, a spokesperson for the Center for Women's Business Research. "We see more and more financial institutions opening up programs and starting to develop initiatives to reach out to them."

Although women of color own a mere 5 percent of the 22 million U.S. companies, the growth rate among this group is accelerating. The number of companies owned by women of color grew four times the national average in between 1997 and 2002, compared to three times the national average in the preceding decade.

The question for many major U.S. corporations – that may be seeking the products and services from diverse suppliers – is whether women entrepreneurs of color differ from other business owners in how they manage their companies, and whether the drive to start companies against the odds help to better target products and services.

"As business growth is one of the top concerns among Latino women business owners, our 10-year, $3 billion lending goal to Latino small-business owners will continue acting as a vital component of their continued success," said Tim Rios, a

Female Entrepreneurs of Color Lead the Pack of New Business Owners (cont'd.)

spokesperson for the Wells Fargo Latino business services program. The San Francisco-based financial institution underwrote the study to find out how to market their services to women business owners of color, he said.

Across the board, women of color who participated in the study said access to funding capital is a major concern, said Peacock. The study also found that women of color tend to launch businesses on their own more frequently than their white counterparts. The differences are especially pronounced among African-American women, who own more than 365,000 companies. Seventy-two percent of African-American women start or buy their businesses without a partner, compared to 62 percent of white women.

"Gaining access to capital is particularly difficult because women of color, more than ever, are starting their businesses on their own and they're starting them full time," Peacock said. "And that's different from before because it means that they're really committed to growing their business. They are not doing it as a hobby or a part-time thing while they work their day job. "But launching a business by themselves is more challenging because they have to find resources on their own."

Almost 50 percent of African-American women business owners reported encountering obstacles to obtaining financing, compared to 28 percent of white women. They blamed the disparity on less experience with lenders and more overt discrimination from financial institutions. Twenty-two percent of Asian women and 27 percent of Latino women reported similar obstacles. While the Center does not recommend specific actions for corporations to take based on its findings, financial institutions could use the data to develop initiatives to reach out to women of color who are considering starting businesses, said Peacock.

The impact of women business owners of color to the overall U.S. economy can't be overlooked. African-American and Latino women business owners of color are more likely to use higher levels of start-up capital in the past, and that presents financial institutions with a big opportunity – particularly when other businesses, treading carefully in light of the sagging economy, are borrowing less. Just 5 percent of Latino women business owners did not use start-up capital in 2002, compared to 14 percent in 1998. Forty-nine percent of the African-American women business owners surveyed in 2002 used less than $25,000 in start-up capital, compared to 59 percent of those surveyed in the 1998 study. Meanwhile, Asian and white women business owners appear to use lower levels of start-up capital, the study indicated.

An additional sign of the growing maturity of the market for financial services is

Female Entrepreneurs of Color Lead the Pack of New Business Owners (cont'd.)

that significantly more women business owners of color are using commercial bank loans as a source of start-up capital. And as women of color seek to expand their businesses, they will need additional financing.

"More women of color are finding the resources and the assistance and the support to start their own businesses. There are many different programs targeted toward helping them succeed. They're gaining visibility with both the press and financial institutions," said Peacock. "They are really poised for growth."

Boom in Women-Owned Businesses, But Financing Still a Barrier

By Ruth Zeilberger

© 2003 DiversityInc.com

May 01, 2003

One woman in 11 is an entrepreneur. Sound amazing? Perhaps not as amazing as some of the other statistics released Wednesday by the Washington, D.C.-based Center for Women's Business Research.

Between 1997 and 2002, for example, the number of women-owned firms with more than 100 employees rose 44 percent. And the number of women-owned firm posting more than $1 million in revenue climbed by 32 percent – 1.5 times faster than all businesses of comparable size

The new numbers, announced at the Center annual executive roundtable held in New York City, are sending a buzz among financial institutions and corporations. After all, an increase in number of women-owned businesses translates into new clients for the banking industry and a larger pool of potential corporate suppliers.

The numbers have also created a buzz in the White House, according to Cindi Williams, special assistant at the White House Office of Public Liaison.

"Much was made of the fact that 9.4 million Hispanics voted in the last election," said Williams. "There are more women who own their own business than Hispanics who voted in the last election. If women who owned their own businesses got together as a voting bloc they could exercise some real power."

Elaine Chao, U.S. Secretary of Labor and the keynote speaker at the executive roundtable, confirmed the significance of the numbers.

"Women are a force to be reckoned with in our society," Chao said.

"Women entrepreneurs are leading a quiet revolution in today's business world. More of you are starting businesses than ever before; your businesses are growing faster and, most importantly, you are leaders in creating jobs," said Chao. Chao was recognized Wednesday by the Center for her career in public service with the first annual Leading by Example in the Public Sector Award.

But despite their successes, women-owned businesses still have plenty of obstacles to overcome. They receive on average only 4 percent of every $1 billion spent on procurement by the Fortune 1000 companies. Corporations and women

Boom in Women-Owned Businesses, But Financing Still a Barrier (cont'd.)

entrepreneurs agree that the top challenges to supplier diversity are trends toward cost cutting and vendor consolidation.

Among the findings released by Wednesday by the Center for Women's Business Research:

- Women of color are a vital part of the women's entrepreneurship movement. In 2002, 20 percent of all women business owners were women of color and their businesses are growing at four times the rate of all firms. Overall, the number of firms owned by women of color increased by 32 percent between 1997 and 2002 – four times faster than all U.S. firms and more than twice the rate of all women-owned firms. "A top priority for the Center is to give visibility to each segment," said Myra Hart, chair of the Center for Women's Business Research and a professor at Harvard Business School.

- Fast-growing women- and men-owned firms use a wider variety of sources of capital, and are more likely to use bank credit than other firms. Yet, only 29 percent of fast-growth women owners have a commercial bank loan compared to 52 percent of fast-growth men owners.

- Large corporations are a vital market for women business owners. Six in 10 Fortune 1000 companies report spending $1 billion or more annually with outside suppliers and vendors. Yet this market has not yet been fully tapped by women-owned businesses, who currently receive just 4 percent of all the corporate business.

- Growth is the key focus for all women entrepreneurs, regardless of race or ethnic background. In 2002, more than half of the women business owners reported that their businesses had grown over the past three years and business growth is the primary goal for the vast majority (86 percent African American, 84 percent Latina, 80 percent white, 71 percent Asian American).

- The workforce of women-owned firms shows greater gender equity. Women business owners overall employ a roughly gender-balanced workforce (52 percent women and 48 percent men), while men business owners employ, on average, 38 percent women and 63 percent men.

- Women and men business owners have different management styles. Women are less hierarchical, may take more time when making decisions, seek more information, and are more likely to draw upon input from others – including information from fellow business owners, employees and subject-matter experts.

Boom in Women-Owned Businesses, But Financing Still a Barrier (cont'd.)

- Women-owned firms in the United States are more likely than all firms to offer flex-time, tuition reimbursement, and, at a smaller firm size, profit-sharing to their workers.

Real Money: Lockheed Martin, Johnson Controls Join Billion-Dollar Roundtable

By Linda Bean

© 2003 DiversityInc.com

May 15, 2003

"A billion here, a billion there," the late Sen. Everett Dirksen said, "pretty soon it adds up to real money."

Dirksen was taking a wry shot at congressional spending when he uttered that line, but the Illinois Republican had the math right.

Consider this: Taken together, the 12 corporate members of the Billion Dollar Roundtable (BDR) spend more than $20 billion a year with businesses owned by women and people of color.

That's more than the annual revenue of 414 of the Fortune 500 corporations, noted Raymond Arroyo, manager for corporate diversity at Altria, and more than the gross domestic product of 72 individual countries.

"It's huge," said Arroyo. "It's very, very powerful."

The BDR was founded in 2001 by Shirley Harrison, vice president, diversity management, Altria; Sharon Patterson, the director of supplier diversity at Altria's Kraft Foods unit, and Don McKneely, publisher of Texas-based Minority Business News.

BDR's 10 charter members are Altria, parent company to Philip Morris and Kraft Foods; automakers General Motors, Ford and DaimlerChrysler; communications giants AT&T, SBC and Verizon, Lucent, IBM, and Wal-Mart, the nation's leading retailer.

Altria Wednesday hosted the BDR's annual meeting in New York City – a day-long strategy session – and a reception to honor the group's two newest members, defense contractor Lockheed Martin and auto-industry supplier Johnson Controls.

The BDR was formed with two goals in mind – to provide a top-level forum for BDR members to share strategies and ideas and to leverage the combined knowledge of BDR members for use by others.

The first generation of supplier-diversity experts – those who started programs in

Real Money: Lockheed Martin, Johnson Controls Join Billion-Dollar Roundtable (cont'd.)

the late 1970s and early 1980s – had to rely on trial and error. Through the BDR, the next generation "can pull (that knowledge) off the shelf," said Reginald Layton, supplier diversity director for Johnson Controls.

While $1 billion in spending with diverse suppliers represents remarkable success, challenges remain, executives said.

Altria's supplier-diversity program is well-established and mature. Her challenge, Patterson said, "is to make sure we maintain the level of spend and grow even more."

At Johnson Controls, the challenge is assuring that managers in 250 local offices share the corporate focus on supplier diversity, Layton said. "National processes – local delivery," he said.

Johnson Controls works with about 1,100 diverse suppliers in a wide range of service and commodity areas.

"We are growing really rapidly," Layton said.

At Lockheed Martin, Supplier-Diversity Director Michael Bush is focused on expanding the organization's use of diverse suppliers.

"Our drive is to make it a normal part of the business process," Bush said.

Honored separately was Susan Phillips Bari, president of the Women's Business Enterprise National Council (WBENC). WBENC is an advocate for the advancement of women-owned businesses as vendors and suppliers to the nation's corporations.

Bari received the Impact Award, an honor given to "an individual whose work significantly enhances the growth of minority- and/or women-owned business enterprises and positively impacts the ability of MWBEs to meet corporate America's needs."

Part VI - Measurement

A. Work-Force Metrics

Diversity leaders and change agents in corporations must provide a measurement that offers a return on investment and proves to the top management in a corporation that diversity isn't a feel-good initiative but a quantifiable means of bringing in new revenue streams.

Measuring just people of color in an organization is static and doesn't change the organizational status. Equal Employment Opportunity and/or affirmative-action numbers tell a limited portion of the story.

Two key points to remember on metrics – they should be applied to all business units and they must be reported directly to the CEO and top management. And compensation, especially for senior management, should be tied to these metrics.

What are companies measuring? According to a 1998 study by the Conference Board, the most common tools used for measuring diversity are:

- Equal Employment Opportunity and Affirmative Action metrics

- Employee attitude surveys

- Cultural audits

- Focus groups

- Customer surveys

- Management and employee evaluations

- Accountability and incentive assessments

- Training and education evaluations

Those are traditional HR measures, but they may have little impact outside the HR department. The study's author, Michael Wheeler, recognizes the need for a more comprehensive and integrated system of new metrics in six categories:

- Demographics

- Organization culture

- Accountability

- Productivity/profitability

- Benchmarking

For example, he says, to show a measurable return on investment for diversity programs, link diversity efforts with the organization's sales and marketing functions. Minority markets are growing rapidly, and each represents billions of dollars in spending power in the United States in an increasingly competitive market. Linking internal diversity initiatives with external efforts to capture diverse markets not only enhances the credibility of your diversity efforts, it also enhances the credibility of marketing efforts to emerging markets.

B. Marketplace Metrics

Ethnic consumer power is not the only thing being noticed and monitored lately. Two new indices were set up in the last year to track African-American and Latino businesses. In 2002, the ING Gazelle Index surveyed nearly 1,500 African-American-owned businesses with about 10 to 100 employees. The survey tracked economic conditions, business activity, employment and confidence.

In an effort to provide an assessment of the U.S. Latino economy that's on par with barometers used to measure large Latino economies, such as Mexico, Spain and Argentina, Hispanic Business launched the Hispanic Business Stock Index (HBSI). Developed by HispanTelligence, the research division of Hispanic Business Inc., the index tracks publicly traded companies that are majority Latino-owned or whose main focus is on the U.S. Latino market, regardless of the shareholders' ethnicity.

Only stocks traded in the United States on the New York Stock Exchange, NASDAQ, the American Stock Exchange or over-the-counter were considered for the index. Thirteen companies met the criteria: Univision, Popular Inc. (the holding company of Banco Popular), Hispanic Broadcasting Corp., International Bancshares Corp., Entravision Communications, Spanish Broadcasting System, Gruma Corp., Movado Corp., MasTec Inc., Perry Ellis International, United PanAm Financial, Metrocorp Bancshares Inc., and Radio

Unica. Companies in the media industry represent the largest amount of capital on the HBSI; the financial-services category follows closely behind.

As of December 2002, total-market capitalization of the HBSI companies was $15.7 billion; total sales for 2002 amounted to $8.4 billion. Univision, Popular Inc., and Hispanic Broadcasting topped the HBSI, accounting for more than 74 percent of market capitalization.

The HBSI shows the resiliency of the Latino economy. Over the past decade, the U.S. Latino economy has grown faster than the U.S. economy as a whole. While all major indexes experienced a decline in 2002, the HBSI dropped the least. When compared with figures from the Dow Jones Industrial Average, the S&P 500, and the NASDAQ over the last year, the HBSI outperformed the NASDAQ by 18.73 points, the S&P by 9.94 points, and the Dow by 3.69 points.

C. Supplier-Diversity Metrics

Metrics in supplier diversity that are measured readily, such as meeting dollar and percentage goals for spending with diverse suppliers, are easy, provided companies are willing to reveal the data. But establishing standards for the business case for supplier diversity is more difficult.

For those companies that do this, the rewards are tangible. Murray Hill, N.J.-based Lucent Technologies, for example, in 2000 realized savings of $82 million from its supplier-diversity program because of the lower cost structure minority- and women-owned businesses had compared with other vendors. SBC Communications reported similar savings in warehousing costs gained by using diverse supply chains.

To improve supplier-diversity metrics, companies should use procurement software to track their spending with diverse suppliers accurately. They also should adopt a unified standard for reporting supplier-diversity spending that is equitable and transparent, including the creation of a substantive penalty for non-participation.

D. Best Practices From the Top Companies for Diversity

New York-based JPMorgan Chase is an organization that's best in class when it comes to measuring diversity's results.

The second-largest financial-services company in the United States, the firm uses a Diversity Scorecard to ascertain where it stands with demographics, psychographics, diversity-leadership activities and diversity initiatives, says Steve Young, senior vice president of diversity.

Even though JPMorgan Chase operates worldwide – its U.S. retail banking branches are concentrated in the Northeast and Texas – when measuring its demographics, it breaks down the number of employees of color, women and white men in each business unit – a total of 30 key businesses. The Scorecard specifically asks for the number of African Americans, Asian Americans, whites, Latinos and women who are senior vice presidents and managing directors.

JPMorgan Chase focuses on the highest-echelon jobs in measuring diversity, believing that change is most necessary at that level, and that greater representation numbers at lower levels will follow naturally.

The company's CEO, Bill Harrison, personally audits the Scorecards and the diversity business plans of each business leader, whose diversity performance is linked to his or her compensation. Harrison and his diversity team then look at the business units' three-year outlooks.

Here are some other measurements used by companies in the Top Companies for Diversity survey:

- HR metrics/scorecard includes hiring objectives and increased retention/decreased attrition objectives. The employee base should be surveyed regularly. Exit interviews should be compiled and reviewed. Human Resources should provide regular, perhaps quarterly, hiring, promotion and termination reports specifically highlighting gender and race.

- Measure relationships with professional organizations, such as the National Society of Hispanic Engineers, and numbers of recruits, interns coming, and number of meetings attended.

- Diversity training must be measured in terms of attendance, feedback, and, most importantly, results.

- Work/life programs (usage and satisfaction) including child care, elder care, life- care resource and referral programs, adoption reimbursement and leaves of absence.

- Principal Succession Planning, compensation planning and pay equity .

- Track success of interns and pipeline development.

ADDITIONAL RESOURCES

PART VI: MEASUREMENT

U.S. Equal Employment Opportunity Commission (EEOC),
1801 L Street, N.W.Washington, D.C. 20507 (202) 663-4900.
http://www.eeoc.gov/

Part VII - Industries in the Front Line

A. Automotive

Why has the auto industry been so far ahead of other industries in reaching out to emerging markets? Those at the top of this industry long have understood the ability to market to first-time buyers as well as those needing to trade-up or purchase additional cars. They also are increasingly aware that many potential customers exist in the African-American, Latino and Asian-American markets. If CEOs and top managers in the auto industry set the game plan, auto dealers are those who implement it. Making sure they are on the right track is critical to the companies.

1. Dealers

The National Association of Minority Auto Dealers (NAMAD) surveyed auto makers late in 2002 and found that on average, 5.22 percent of their dealerships were owned by people of color.[181] Of the Big Three auto makers, Ford Motor Co. had the most, 7.15 percent, or 369 of 5,164 dealers. General Motors (GM) had 5.40 percent, or 387 of 7,166 dealers, while DaimlerChrysler had 3.29 percent dealers of color, or 140 of 4,259 dealers.

A case study about how to educate dealers to the benefits of diversity has been occurring at Ford.

Ford Motor Co. and the Small Business Administration are giving minority-owned dealerships access to more capital and other resources, such as technical and business-development assistance.

In addition, Ford and the National Association for Minority Automotive Dealers have joined forces to increase the number of minority-owned dealerships.

And in April 2002, Ford and Arizona State University (ASU) announced two programs to prepare ASU business students to become automobile dealers.[182]

Ford announced its Auto Dealership Education Program for Minorities (ADEPM) at ASU – a five-year post-graduate training program that will be managed by the company's Minority Dealer Operations organization.

People of color who graduate from ASU's certificate program are offered an opportunity to participate in ADEPM.

The program represents a first for the auto industry, says George Frame, the automaker's executive director for Dealer Development.

ASU, in Tempe, Ariz., is offering a new certificate in dealership management as part of its undergraduate business degree. The program equips students "with automotive industry-specific knowledge and experience," the university says. As part of a four-year degree program, the certificate demonstrates that graduates have hands-on training in dealership management, preparing them for careers immediately upon graduation.

Through the program, ASU offers students the "long-term knowledge" required for a professional career "and help them in a practical way," says Larry Penley, dean of the ASU College of Business.

ADEPM students train through the National Automotive Dealers Association (NADA) and are eligible for Ford-run dealer-development programs that provide financing, continuing education and consulting services. "There are tools available to help people who have the talent, but don't have the money," Frame says.

Ford is not the only automaker keenly aware of the need for cultural competence at dealerships. GM established a dealer-development initiative for people of color 30 years ago, the first program of its kind in the auto industry. GM retooled its minority dealership program in 1998, following the completion of an in-depth review initially sought by the Rainbow/PUSH organization. The review, performed by Weldon Latham, an attorney who had served with the federal Department of Housing and Urban Development, produced 215 recommendations in 10 broad categories.

DaimlerChrysler started its minority-dealership program in 1983 and has partnered with the Hispanic Association of Corporate Responsibility (HACR), the National Association for the Advancement of Colored People (NAACP) for an additional program called Fair Share Agreement.

2. Employees

This year, Ford was the No. 1 company on DiversityInc's Top 50 Companies for Diversity List. Ford reported that 30 percent of its new hires in 2002 were people of color, with 8 percent African American, 3 percent Latino and 19 percent Asian American. The company said 16 percent of its management employees were people of color, with 7 percent African American, 2 percent Latino and 6 percent Asian American. Ford also said 13 percent of its 50 highest-paid employees were people of color, with 9 percent African American, 2 percent Latino and 2 percent Asian American.

Neither General Motors nor DaimlerChrysler filled out the survey. On its Web site, GM reported that as of 2001, 24 percent of hourly workers and 18 percent of its salaried workers were people of color. Approximately 20 percent of hourly workers and 13 percent of salaried workers were African American; 3 percent of hourly workers and 2 percent of salaried workers were Latino; 1 percent of hourly workers and 3 percent of salaried workers were Asian American. No numbers are available for DaimlerChrysler.

Ford uses its 10 employee-affinity groups to test products and to help market products to emerging-market communities. The Detroit-based auto company asked employee members of its Parenting Network to test its Windstar minivan to see if the automobile was truly family-friendly. Ford calls its affinity groups employee-resource groups and it has 10. They are: the Ford African-Ancestry Network, the Ford Asian-Indian Association, the Ford Chinese Association, GLOBE for its gay, lesbian and bisexual employees, the Ford Hispanic-Network Group, the Ford Interfaith Network, Ford Parenting Network, the Middle Eastern Community, the Professional Women's Network and the Ford Employees Dealing with Disabilities Network.[183]

In late 2001, Ford's diversity and work-planning departments decided to demonstrate diversity's direct impact on the bottom line. Madeline S. Eason, director, diversity and personnel relations, and Rosalind Cox, diversity & work-life planning manager, brainstormed with the employee-resource groups, and the groups decided the company's Friends and Neighbors Program was ideal. The program provides discounts on car purchases to employees' extended family and friends. The plan paid off, with an increase in sales to these groups. The African-Ancestry Network brought in the most revenue, $50 million.[184]

3. Customers & Marketing

The quandary for automakers is deciding when and how to segment diverse markets. How narrowly should a market be divided? When does market segmentation boost the bottom line? What does research say?[185]

The auto industry knows the demographic data of the United States, says Gary Berman, founder and CEO of Market Segment Research. And most automakers are "attempting a variety of strategies to get their fair share," he says.

"The challenge," Berman adds, "is who is going to win and how they are going to do it."

"In broad strokes," Berman says, "the most successful automotive marketers are going to be those that institutionalize the idea of multi-culturalism across their organizations in the following ways: Identifying the most profitable customers, via research; understanding the cultural hot buttons that will motivate someone to the make or model they are trying to target; and finally, spending an equal amount of time and money on the customer experience at the dealer level."

Hispanic Business magazine reported last year that automakers were spending more to reach Latinos. Ford and GM increased their multi-cultural-marketing budgets by more than 20 percent, the magazine reported.

Volvo, which is owned by Ford, in the spring of 2003 announced a national advertising campaign aimed at gays and lesbians.

Volvo is introducing its new SUV with a national car ad picturing happy same-sex couples. A woman holds her partner's pregnant belly in one frame. Two men cuddle an infant in another. A third image shows two women – one African American, the other white – with their legs crossed together and their hands interlocked. Another image shows two men embracing their Yorkie.[186]

The tagline to Volvo's print campaign for the XC90 and the C70 Sedan is: "Whether you're starting a family or creating one as you go."

This is not the first time Volvo has advertised in GLBT media, but it's the first time the automaker has developed creative ad material specifically for the GLBT market, according to Stephen Bohannon, a spokesperson for Volvo Cars.

The campaign is targeted nationwide, with a specific emphasis on the metropolitan areas of Atlanta and San Francisco.

As for GM, it recently unveiled a new Spanish-language advertising campaign aimed at Latinos. The television spot, which aired on Univision and Telemundo, features GM President Gary Cowger, who is fluent in Spanish.[187]

The ad marked the first time a top auto company executive has appeared in a commercial designed specifically for the Latino audience.

"General Motors has recognized that as our consumers become increasingly diverse, we must continue to reflect that diversity in our advertising, as well as in our product offerings," says Sonia Maria Green, GM's director of Hispanic Marketing.

4. Supplier Diversity

Ford Motor Co., which was tied for No. 2 on this year's DiversityInc Top 10 Companies for Supplier Diversity, reported spending $3.2 billion with 306 diverse suppliers, 6 percent of its procurement budget. All three top automakers are members of the Billion-Dollar Roundtable, corporations that have the distinction of spending more than $20 billion a year combined with diverse suppliers.[188]

Ford calculates its number by counting checks the company paid to business owners certified by the National Minority Supplier Development Council. All Ford's Tier-1 suppliers also must conduct a percentage of sales with diverse Tier-2 suppliers. Tier-2 suppliers accounted for $1 billion worth of business in 2002, according to Ford.

"The objective for everything we do culminates in creating wealth in minority communities," says Renaldo Jensen, Ford's director of supplier-diversity development. The company has begun a computer database called M-Tier Program with DaimlerChrysler and Toyota that will trace suppliers from the Tier-1 level to the Tier-5 level and make available information on the products and services they provide.

On its Web site, GM states it spent $6.2 billion with Tier 1 and Tier 2 diverse suppliers in 2002, $3.8 billion with Tier 1 suppliers and $2.4 billion with Tier 2 suppliers, or those who contract with Tier 1 suppliers. GM, which said it was the first auto company to have a supplier-diversity program, said it instituted new policies in 2002 that require its Tier 1 suppliers to source a minimum of 6.5 percent of its Tier 2 GM business to certified minority companies.

Further, GM said it mentors 54 certified minority companies in efforts to grow their strategic capabilities to position them for greater growth potential.

DaimlerChrysler, on its Web site, said it purchased more than $3 billion in goods and services from minority suppliers, representing about 11 percent of its total procurement budget.[189]

Chrysler Group has several supplier-diversity initiatives in place, including a mentoring program in which Chrysler Group Procurement & Supply executives work directly with minority suppliers to assist in their growth and development. The goal of each relationship is to help suppliers cut costs, improve quality and increase new business opportunities outside of Chrysler Group.

The company also has a "Matchmaker" program that pairs minority suppliers with Tier 1 suppliers to increase business opportunities among the two companies. The program is entering its third year. Since its inception, it has generated $30 million in additional business opportunities to minority suppliers, according to Chrysler.

ADDITIONAL RESOURCES

PART VII - INDUSTRIES IN THE FRONT LINE

Bean, Linda. "Auto Industry First: Ford, Arizona State Univ. Announces Programs to Train Dealers." DiversityInc, 5 April 2002.
http://www.diversityinc.com/members/2705.cfm

Bean, Linda. "Auto Markets: How Small Can You Slice Them?" DiversityInc, 20 May 2003.
http://www.diversityinc.com/members/4943.cfm

Bean, Linda. "GM 'Diversity Tour' Aims to Reach Diverse Consumers, Reporters." DiversityInc, 17 April 2003.
http://www.diversityinc.com/members/4798.cfm

Bean, Linda. "Real Money: Lockheed Martin, Johnson Controls Join Billion-Dollar Roundtable." DiversityInc, 15 May 2003.
http://www.diversityinc.com/members/4940.cfm

Cole, Yoji. "Ford Motor Company: This Year's Top Company for Diversity." DiversityInc, June/July 2003.

Hispanic Association of Corporate Responsibility (HACR), 1444 I Street, NW, Suite 850, Washington, D.C. 20005. *http://www.hacr.org/*

National Association of Minority Automobile Dealers (NAMAD), 8401 Corporate Drive, Suite 405, Lanham, MD 20785.
http://namad.org/index.asp

National Automotive Dealers Association (NADA), 8400 Westpark Drive, McLean, VA 22102. *http://www.nada.org/*

Rainbow/PUSH Coalition, 930 East 50th Street, Chicago, IL 60615-2702. *http://www.rainbowpush.org/*

Zeilberger, Ruth. "Volvo Driving Into the GLBT Market." DiversityInc, 8 May 2003. *http://www.diversityinc.com/members/4902.cfm*

Lack of Data? Lack of Interest? Why Don't We Know More About African-American Auto Consumers

By Linda Bean

March 07, 2003

© 2003 DiversityInc.com

Folks in the auto industry generally agree there's a lack of reliable data about African-American preferences and buying habits – data that should be guiding million-dollar decisions on segmented marketing and advertising.

But they don't necessarily agree on why this gap exists, who is responsible for filling it – or whether auto manufacturers should care.

Research experts argue that companies aren't interested in paying for the in-depth insights into African-American consumers. And company representatives complain that research firms have, to date, provided faulty research models. Meanwhile, there are lingering misconceptions about the size and strength of the African-American market, despite demographic data.

But in the end, research either is going to drive or halt marketing initiatives aimed at African Americans. Corporate leaders who don't get the business case and can't pinpoint the return on investment aren't going to put money toward the market.

"If you are just looking at pure volume, it may not be that impressive of a business case," says Leisa Byars, manager for Global Agency Media Alliance and Events at Ford Motor Co. "But you have to understand its influence. A lot of trends start with this market."

Charles Morrison, an executive at New York City-based Uniworld – an advertising agency that specializes in the African-American community, recently took major research organizations to task.

Those firms have done "in my mind, a horrendous job serving their clients – they have been the last to recognize that the world has changed. They have never seriously studied the African-American market or the Latino market."

But Michael Taliefero, the African-American co-founder and managing director of Washington, D.C.-based CLC Compliance Technologies, lays the responsibility for bridging the gap at the feet of corporations.

To suggest that the lack of information is a failing of the research community "is

Lack of Data? Lack of Interest? Why Don't We Know
More About African-American Auto Consumers (cont'd.)

a knee-jerk reaction to the failure (of corporations) to think about it and really do targeted marketing," Taliefero says.

Meanwhile, Marc Strachan, the African-American managing partner of a New York City-based ad agency, contends that there's enough responsibility to go around. "I think there is definitely a gap and the gap (relates to) the psychographic and cultural nuances and how some of those things have changed over the last 40 years," says Strachan, managing partner of S/R Communications Alliance, a New York City-based advertising and marketing agency.

"And I don't think anybody is going to take up the (research) challenge unless they think there's an opportunity for them on the back end," Strachan adds.

"We need more consumer research, more segmentation research," says Byars, who is African American. "How are markets similar? How are they different?"

Automakers, she adds, generally "have the feeling that you don't want to offend anyone, so they play it safe."

Toyota, Byars notes, learned firsthand the consequences of a more risky strategy when it commissioned an advertising postcard that featured an African-American man with a broad grin and a piece of gold-tooth jewelry, shaped like a Toyota RAV4.

The Rev. Jesse Jackson condemned the marketing strategy and then launched a much broader criticism of the company's relationship with African-American consumers, vendors and employees. Toyota has since adopted a number of measures aimed at increasing diversity and diminishing conflict, including the development of an external diversity council.

"I think Toyota was trying to reach out and connect, but they came across as insensitive," Byars says.

"And then," she adds, "there's the issue of not doing it right. When do you treat African Americans differently from other consumers and when do you treat them in a similar way? It is a balancing act and very challenging."

As a result, strong consumer research "is invaluable," Byars says.

Ford has enough quality research "for the most part, to play it safe. We do things that are insightful, that are thoughtful, but we don't take chances. That is what Toyota did," she adds. "If you want to be riskier, you need more research."

In Strachan's view, the responsibility for examining the African-American market lies with those who have a "vested interest" in understanding African-American

Lack of Data? Lack of Interest? Why Don't We Know More About African-American Auto Consumers (cont'd.)

consumers. This might be a good time, he says, for African-American ad and marketing agencies to pool their resources and partner with a large research organization to delve into psychographic and cultural issues.

"Here's an example: The black church has always been a rock-steady component of the African-American community. And the black church has changed and is changing and has become more sophisticated," Strachan says.

African-American churches have a taken a strong interest in economic empowerment. "It is no longer just about faith for faith's sake," he adds. "It's about how you empower a people economically in today's world. It represents a more business-focused environment, but no one has really looked into that. What does that mean today?"

Before a company can be persuaded to invest in detailed research, there has to be a foundation for the business case, Stachan says, built from data provided by the Census Bureau and Bureau of Labor Statistics, and information provided by the Selig Center for Economic Growth at the University of Georgia.

The Selig Center recently reported, for example, that combined buying power of African Americans, Asian Americans and Native Americans should reach almost $1.4 trillion, compared with $453 billion in 1990 – an increase of more than 200 percent in 17 years. In 2007, African Americans are expected to account for 61 percent of that combined buying power, or $853 billion.

In the late 1990s, advertising executive Don Coleman partners with North Carolina-based Yanklovich to prepare a research report on the African-American community entitled "The African-American Monitor."

It was the first time, Strachan says, that he had seen data that went beyond economics and demographics to address the nuances of cultural competency.

"I remember thinking 'Oh, boy. Somebody finally did something.' It talked about where African Americans were making strides in leadership in buying goods and services," he adds. "It began talking about 'urban' and what that meant ... how this young consumer group is spending money and time and attitude."

"I also think there are gaps in understanding the differences among African Americans and the budget you have to spend against this market isn't enough," Byars says. "It's challenging to develop a communication piece that will reach an educated writer, an 18-year-old and a single mother."

"We don't understand the subtleties and the differences – the huge differences," she adds, "and that is where research comes in."

Jesse Jackson Urges Auto Industry to Be More Inclusive

By Linda Bean

© 2003 DiversityInc.com

October 26, 2002

The auto industry has "limited growth by limiting opportunity" for women and people of color, the Rev. Jesse Jackson said Thursday at the opening session of Jackson's Rainbow/PUSH auto summit.

The Detroit summit – "Marketing to a New Agenda for Total Inclusion" – drew some 250 auto executives and suppliers to a series of sessions on advertising, financing and the overall state of diversity in the auto industry.

Jackson opened the summit by reminding U.S. automakers that their failure to attend to diversity cost them dearly a decade ago when they faced the onslaught of competition from European and Japanese manufacturers.

DiversityInc sponsored the summit's first session – "The Business Case for Diversity" – which featured panelists from Ford Motor Co., PepsiCo, SAFECO and the Winters Group, a diversity-consulting firm.

Madeline Sulaiman-Eason, director of diversity and personnel relations for Ford, said sales figures underscored the business case for diversity at the automaker. Between 2000 and 2001, sales to people of color rose 12.7 percent, she said.

Ford ranked 17th on DiversityInc's 2001 list of Top Companies for Diversity.

The automaker has identified emerging markets as a "$3 trillion opportunity," Sulaiman-Eason said. And the consumers that comprise emerging markets are experiencing tremendous population growth, significant increases in income and are "more brand loyal" than their majority counterparts, she added.

But earning that loyalty requires a willingness to re-examine the way a company does business. For example, Sulaiman-Eason said, African Americans tend to replace their new cars every 3.2 years, but the standard auto-design cycle is five years.

Should the automaker retool the design cycle to suit the buying patterns of African Americans? That may be an open question, but what is certain, she said, is that companies need to produce products that are "distinct, relevant and resonate with the cultural values and lifestyles" of emerging markets.

Jesse Jackson Urges Auto Industry to Be More Inclusive (cont'd.)

To that end, Ford has established five broad diversity goals – developing effective diversity leaders in the company's management ranks, developing a diverse workforce, creating a respectful and inclusive environment, supporting work-life balance strategies and building strong external partnerships.

Ronald Harrison, PepsiCo's senior vice president for global diversity and community affairs, said his company's challenge is building a diversity agenda that is relevant worldwide.

PepsiCo is the parent company of divisions that include Pepsi, Frito Lay, Gatorade, Tropicana and Quaker Oats. Although they operate independently, it is the responsibility of the parent company to set the diversity standard.

"One of the things you have to do is make sure that majority managers understand the business imperative" behind diversity strategies, Harrison said.

At PepsiCo, that means recognizing that the retailers who sell the companies' products come from countries around the globe.

In Detroit, Harrison said, retailers include a significant number of Arab Americans, while in New York City, Dominican store owners make up a significant proportion of the retail ranks.

PepsiCo ranked 19th on DiversityInc's list of Top Companies for Diversity. The company has adopted a broad definition of diversity that includes diversity of thought and opinion, as well as race, gender and sexual orientation, and the company has established "inclusion" as a goal.

Harrison likened diversity to the door of a house, open just far enough to let people in. But inclusion, he said, "is making them feel welcome."

PepsiCo, he added, is "starting to document that an inclusive workforce drives productivity."

The company has in place diversity councils, employee networks, systems of measurement, a diversity-communications strategy and a training regimen.

In addition, Harrison added, "every executive's bonus is tied into achieving" diversity goals.

Raphael Madison, assistant vice president of diversity marketing for Seattle-based SAFECO, said his experience following a natural disaster in El Paso, Texas, in 1989, cemented his commitment to diversity as a business imperative.

SAFECO, which concentrates on a property and casualty insurance, had written $11 million in business in El Paso and, in the wake of the violent storm, sent a

Jesse Jackson Urges Auto Industry to Be More Inclusive (cont'd.)

team to Texas to work with its customers. No member of the team, Madison said, spoke Spanish.

Now, the company — the nation's 15th largest insurer — has more than 40 employees who field telephone calls from Spanish-speaking customers. SAFECO ranked 16th on DiversityInc's list of Top Companies for Diversity.

The company recently established a relationship with a group of African-American churches and wrote $60 million in policies for church members. The company's net profit for 2001 was $20 million. In the absence of that partnership, Madison said, the company's financials would have been written in red.

"America is changing, and with that comes a need for us to change," he said.

In New York City, he noted, 60 percent of all residents are people of color. In Chicago, more than 40 percent of the city's residents are people of color, and in Houston, 53 percent are people of color.

"In 48 of the top 100 cities, people of color are the majority," he added. "If you care about being in business in the future, you have to care about diversity."

Mary-Frances Winters, the founder and president of The Winters Group, based in Rochester, N.Y., said she encourages companies to move their diversity efforts out of the human resources office and develop a cohesive strategy that addresses diversity in the company's marketing, procurement and community relations functions, as well as within the workforce.

Winters also noted the widespread failure of companies to "consistently measure the value of diversity."

"What gets measured, get done," she said.

The summit didn't draw top-ranking executives from the nation's largest automakers, but did bring together "functional people — the people who get stuff done, the guys who make things happen," Jackson said later in the day. "And I'm impressed that we have the functional people here."

Overall, he said, Rainbow/PUSH is seeing automakers progress toward a better understanding of diversity. As evidence, the keynote speaker at the summit was Toyota executive Guillermo Hysaw, who was appointed in March to the newly created position of vice president of diversity.

Toyota was taken to task last year by Rainbow/PUSH, following the publication of an advertisement that depicted a smiling African-American man, wearing a piece of gold tooth jewelry shaped like a Toyota RAV 4.

Jesse Jackson Urges Auto Industry to Be More Inclusive (cont'd.)

Jackson charged the ad was insensitive and put the company on notice that Rainbow/PUSH intended to examine the automakers' diversity record.

Toyota, based in Torrance, Calif., apologized and later announced the formation of a high-profile external diversity council.

Jackson's criticism "caused us to recognize that we need to do better. We will do better," Hysaw said.

That council, chaired by former Secretary of Labor Alexis Herman, has been visiting Toyota sites and talking to employees for the past year, Hysaw said.

The council is scheduled to meet with Toyota executives in November and produce its first report by February — a report Hysaw hopes will outline a strong diversity strategy.

"We know what we look like, but we don't know what we should be," he added.

Ford Tries to Capture Elusive African-American Marketing Data

By Linda Bean

© 2003 DiversityInc.com

September 17, 2002

The auto industry doesn't have a very good idea just how many African Americans buy cars and trucks – and that is a troubling information gap at a time when every sale counts and African Americans represent an important demographic.

But that may be changing. Ford Motor Co., in an effort to bridge that gap, has commissioned new custom research from UniWorld Group, the New York-based African-American advertising agency for the Ford and Lincoln-Mercury divisions.

The companies declined to disclose the cost of the new research program or provide technical details, presumably because sharing the methodology would trim the competitive edge the research is expected to provide.

"I will tell you this is big," said Charles Morrison, senior vice president at UniWorld. "You want to be certain you are doing everything you can to attract every single customer you can to the showroom floor ... and it all begins with research."

Barbara Ponce, a national advertising executive at American Honda, recently told DiversityInc.com that tracking African-American sales "is the next challenge for manufacturers and the research community."

"It's a tremendous hole in the research," Ponce said.

Morrison said the major research firms have done "in my mind, a horrendous job serving their clients – they have been the last to recognize that the world has changed. They have never seriously studied the African-American market or the Latino market."

Ford executives commissioned custom research, he said, because "they are very serious about marketing to African Americans and they have been for a long time."

People of color account for 35 percent to 40 percent of the U.S. population, Morrison said. "Ford obviously wants to know the ethnic make-up of its cus-

Ford Tries to Capture Elusive African-American Marketing Data (cont'd.)

tomer base, which customers are spending money, what kind of vehicles Latinos and African Americans are buying."

U.S. companies generally are attempting to find the pulse of multicultural consumers, an effort that has intensified as the economic downturn has continued.

Generally, research firms track purchasing patterns through a combination of surname and ZIP code searches – methods advertised as about 85 percent accurate for the Latino and Asian-American populations. But African Americans present the research community with a unique set of challenges: Surnames don't necessarily reflect ethnic heritage and ZIP code searches capture only those African Americans who live in ethnically segregated neighborhoods.

"A lot of the system put in place to monitoring other ethnic groups doesn't hold true" for African Americans, said Charles Martin, UniWorld's director of research. "Add on top of that the trust issues with the African-American community – they don't like to share ethnicity information. "

Trust is an issue in a community that has experienced decades of systematic discrimination; a number of lawsuits are pending now that accuse auto lenders of charging higher rates to people of color.

Still, Martin said, "there are ways to get around those issues … to get a more accurate picture. It is going to be 100 percent the truth? No."

According to Census 2000 figures, African Americans are now the second largest ethnic group in the nation, with a total population of 34.7 million people. They make up 12.9 percent of the U. S. population. Meanwhile, the number of African Americans living in the nation's biggest cities has increased by 6 percent.

The number of affluent African Americans is rising dramatically.

There are 3.7 million African-American households with annual incomes of at least $50,000 and 1.4 million African-American households with annual incomes in excess of $75,000, according to Census 2000.

Car Show: How are Top Automakers Reaching Consumers of Color?

By Linda Bean

© 2003 DiversityInc.com

September 09, 2002

In a year marked by terror and economic uncertainty, U.S. auto sales have remained strong, bolstered by the 0 percent financing option initially launched by General Motors in the wake of the Sept. 11 attacks.

Auto sales in August alone rose 13 percent and auto industry experts are predicting that 2002 sales will match sales in 2001 – the second-best year in auto sales history. "Consumer fundamentals remain favorable," Jim O'Connor, head of North American sales for Ford Motor Co., said last week. "Low interest rates and inflation, and affordable vehicle prices and terms continue to support strong demand for new cars and trucks."

In fact, consumer demand for autos represents one of the few bright spots in the current economy. David Littman, an economist with Comerica Bank, told The Wall Street Journal last week that consumer demand for autos has added between a quarter and a half a percent to the growth of the U.S. gross domestic product – the total of goods and services produced – over the past year.

It's clear that consumers are willing to keep the auto industry on track. Now, as the automakers continue to roll out 2003 models, it seems only fitting to consider how the industry is reaching its consumers.

DiversityInc.com contacted the top five U.S. and foreign automakers and asked them to provide an overview of the marketing plans or commercial messages that accompany some of their 2003 models.

General Motors: GM, which posted an 18 percent increase in August sales, is hopeful that women, in particular, will respond to the company's marketing campaign for the 2003 GMC Envoy XL, a sports utility vehicle. The Envoy underwent a redesign during the 2002 model year. "It's a wonderful package," said Miriam Muley, who directs marketing and sales efforts aimed at women.

The Envoy XL starts at $28,500, said Muley, and marketing efforts are aimed at "very upscale, white-collar, professional women." A million women who meet that demographic profile will receive $100 gift certificates from the automaker, which can be redeemed for spa treatments after an Envoy test drive. "We are try-

Car Show: How are Top Automakers Reaching Consumers of Color? (cont'd.)

ing to communicate the unexpected comfort and surprising features" of the vehicle, Muley said.

The 2003 model year also marks the debut of GM's Cadillac CTS. At $29,9000, the Cadillac offers an entry point to the luxury market and it is being heavily sold to African American buyers, Muley said. "Again, the target is very upscale and professional."

The Cadillac CTS and the Buick Rendezvous are both being marketed to Asian Americans. Cadillac ads are running in Mandarin, Muley said. And the Rendezvous is the focus of a "very integrated strategy" that includes both print and broadcast advertising.

GM is relying on sports icons Julius Erving and Mohammad Ali to sell the company's SUVs to men – African-American men in particular. Erving and Ali are "professional grade" athletes, Muley said, representing the company's professional grade Envoy and Yukon vehicles.

On the Latino side, GM is "really well entrenched in terms of grassroots events," Muley said. GM advertises a number of its brands specifically to Spanish-speaking consumers and supports its products through broadcast and print advertising and the sponsorship of events important to the Latino community.

Markets of color, in particular, will increase in size going forward, Muley said. "What you will see over the course of the next three to four years are much more aggressive plays in connecting with these audiences."

Ford: The nation's No. 2 automaker posted a 12 percent increase in August sales, driven in large part by the continued strength of the Explorer SUV.

Tim Swies, executive vice-president of Zubi Advertising, said Ford will continue to vigorously market its truck line to Latinos through 2003.

"You can bet we will be extremely aggressive in marketing the F-series pickup trucks and SUVs – from the Escape (the smallest model) to the Excursion."

Ford rolled out a re-engineered Expedition in May, and accompanied that launch with an advertising campaign aimed at Latino men. The ads – print, television and radio – focused on the the key three attributes of the re-engineered vehicle: the powerfold third-row seat, independent rear suspension and the safety canopy. The 2003 Expedition is the only SUV in its class to earn five-star crash ratings from the U.S. government.

On the African-American side, the Expedition was relaunched this year using

Car Show: How are Top Automakers Reaching Consumers of Color? (cont'd.)

Ali's daughter Laila Ali, who is also a boxer.

"For our target of African Americans, 25-49, skewing male, using Laila Ali in national TV and print and regional radio and event appearances announces dramatically that there is something very new, and very special about the 2003 Expedition," said Linda D. Dukette at UniWorld Group, Ford's African-American agency.

The suggested retail price for the 2003 Expedition was announced at the Montreal Auto Show in January. A well-equipped Expedition XLT is priced at $44,760, while the Eddie Bauer model starts at $52,565.

Ford also plans to roll out a new campaign "launching the Focus SVT to the African-American audience," Dukette said. The Focus SVT is a five-door version of the popular three-door entry level car. The Focus starts at about $11,000.

"We're increasing the bandwidth of the target – which had been 75 percent female and younger – to become more inclusive of an older audience with a more even male-female mix," Dukette said.

The new campaign will begin in the first quarter and continue through the year. Ford is anticipating a national TV and print effort, bolstered by regional radio and promotions.

Chrysler: The DaimlerChysler unit last week posted a 25 percent increase U.S. car sales for August. Chrysler also announced last week that it would showcase the new turbocharged version the PT Cruiser at a series of "PT Studios" – multicultural nightlife events in six U.S. cities. That effort is aimed at introducing the new turbocharged PT Cruiser to a younger market.

"The original PT Cruiser became a hit largely because of the Baby Boomer generation," said Bonita K. Coleman, Director, Chrysler Marketing. "The new Chrysler PT Turbo, with its more powerful engine, has the kind of performance that appeals to a younger audience. PT Studios is an innovative way to tell that audience about the Chrysler PT Turbo on their terms and in their environment."

PT Studios kicks off with a high-profile launch events in Los Angeles, Miami, San Francisco, Chicago, New York, and Austin in September and October. PT Studios will create a "lounge environment" where guests will experience the best, new, cutting-edge talent in film, fashion, music and art. The launch and closing events, ranging from 500-800 people, will be news media and celebrity driven and will display a sample collection of all the talent featured during the course of the program, Chrysler said.

Car Show: How are Top Automakers Reaching Consumers of Color? (cont'd.)

American Honda: Honda today will launch the sale of its redesigned Accord, a car the company has been building for 27 years. The company is also preparing to roll out a comprehensive campaign for the Accord, aimed at reaching the African-American, Latino and Asian-American communities.

In the African-American community, the mid-sized Accord will be presented as a stylish and sensuous vehicle, said Barbara Ponce, who oversees the company's advertising communications to communities of color. The ad campaign will run on television, on radio and in print.

On the Asian side, Honda has also approved ads that will run in Chinese and Korean. Meanwhile, advertisements prepared for Latino markets highlight "the surprising attributes of the new Accord," Ponce said. "The focus is on the features and performance."

Honda is also focused on winning Latino buyers for its 2003 Pilot, an all-new SUV.

"That is really driven by the fact that the No. 1 selling vehicle to Hispanics is trucks and we wanted to enter the truck market," Ponce said. The Pilot campaign features a Latino father who uses his SUV to ferry his daughter to soccer, meanwhile dreaming of off-road adventures. The tagline? "The New Honda Pilot: As Big as Your Imagination."

Honda has had been advertising directly to African-American and Latino consumers for 13 years. It launched its first targeted advertising in the Asian-American community in 2001.

Toyota: In the African-American community, the 2003 Camry XLE has been positioned as a vehicle for contemporary, sophisticated consumers, said Garlanda Freeze, who manages the Toyota business for Burrell Communications.

The campaign includes television, radio, magazine and newspaper ads. It revolves around a chess game, played by the hero of the spot and an older man who "is giving him a hard time," Freeze said. The younger man wins the game and his opponent's respect. The 2003 Camry XLE, in the second year of a redesign, starts at around $19,000 and it is aimed at people 25 to 40.

The Corolla, by contrast, is aimed squarely at a young audience and positioned a car that is both practical and fun, Freeze said.

On the Latino side, New York-based Conill has prepared a series of ads for the Camry, Corolla and the new 2003 Matrix.

Car Show: How are Top Automakers Reaching Consumers of Color? (cont'd.)

The Matrix launched in Feburary with a spot that showed a young Latino driver using the crossover utility vehicle for a wide range of activities. The Matrix is designed fro drivers 18 to 34 and starts at about $15,000.

Toyota's big push into the Latino community comes behind it's trucks – the Tacoma and the Tundra. "We wanted to really legitimize the Toyota brand in the truck world," said Neil Baltodano, a Conill executive.

"We are really going against the domestic competition, which has much of the market share among Hispanics," he said. "We are doing a full-line truck campaign, very bold, very aggressive, and that it what it needs to be for us to reach Hispanic males."

The 2002 ad campaign featured Toyota trucks outpacing domestic models. Advertising for the 2003 trucks will roll out in October, Baltodano said. Toyota hopes to reach Latino men, 25 to 49, through ads aired by Telemundo and Univision television stations, as well as ads on Spanish language sports radio stations.

"Especially in Texas, some still believe that Toyota trucks are smaller, weaker, and less tough than their Ford and Chevy counterparts," Baltodano said. "We want to go after that consumer and change that perception."

B. Financial Services

There's a good reason why 13 of this year's Top 50 Companies for Diversity were in the financial-services area. This mature industry has realized for some time that its best chance of growth lies in reaching new customers, and those primarily are in emerging or underserved markets, usually meaning people of color.

Why have these markets traditionally been underserved?

"There is not a lack of 'available money,'" says JPMorgan Chase spokesperson Kristen Batteria. "There is a shortage of lenders who are serving these markets with the appropriate products, services, staff and commitment."[190] Minority and other underserved markets offer the highest growth opportunities, according to Batteria.

The statistics paint a clear picture of ethnic groups that do not understand and, therefore, have not taken full advantage of financial-services offerings. The greatest way to build personal wealth is through homeownership. Yet the 2000 U.S. Census reported that 68.3 percent of the 104.7 million U.S. households own their own homes. For white households, 74.8 percent of the 78.8 million households own their own homes. But only 49.5 percent of the 9.3 million Latino households and 47.5 percent of 12.5 million African-American households own their own homes.[191]

About 69 percent of white home-loan applicants secured loans in 2001, according to a Federal Financial Institutions Examination Council (FFIEC) report. Only 57 percent of Latino applicants and 43 percent of African-American applicants secured loans at the end of the mortgage process, according to the report.

Income clearly is a factor. Forty-four percent of African-American respondents reported household earnings below $30,000 annually, according to a 2002 study conducted by the Pew Hispanic Center. The study also showed that while 30 percent of African-American households earned between $30,000 and $50,000 annually and 22 percent earned about $50,000 annually, 4 percent did not know their household incomes.[192]

The same survey found that half of Latino respondents reported household earnings below $30,000 annually. The study also showed that while 23 percent of Latino households earned between $30,000 and $50,000 annually and 17 percent earned about $50,000 annually, 11 percent did not know their household incomes.[193]

By comparison, 29 percent of white respondents reported household earnings below $30,000 annually. The survey also showed that while 27 percent of white households earned between $30,000 and $50,000 annually and 42 percent earned about $50,000 annually, 3 percent did not know their household incomes.[194]

1. Employees

"I think you would be hard-pressed to find anyone within Deloitte & Touche to say 'You can take your eye off the ball around talent in bad times,' because that would be so incredibly short-sighted," says Redia Anderson, national partner for Diversity & Inclusion Initiative at the giant accounting firm headquartered in New York. "Bad times don't last, and you still need to have that talent."[195]

Deloitte & Touche views diversity staffing as a long-term plan. "What our clients are paying for is really the diversity of our talent, whether they be linguistic, gender-based or ethnic or religious or just thinking styles," says Anderson. "So being able to attract the best talent into the firm is still always a priority for us … regardless of the economic times."

So where to find diverse recruits for the financial-services industry? Top MBA programs would be a good bet but the numbers aren't good.

For students enrolled in the top 50 MBA programs, African Americans, Native Americans and Latinos represented only 6 percent of the total, according to a 2001 research study conducted by the Diversity Pipeline Alliance with the Boston Consulting Group, a management-consulting firm.[196]

In May 2001, the American Institute of Certified Public Accountants (AICPA) told DiversityInc that of the population of CPAs, Latinos represented 1 percent, African Americans represented 1 percent, and Asian Americans comprised 3 percent.

The number of students entering the accounting profession overall at the time was down. According to the AICPA, only 2 percent of college students in 2000 majored in accounting, compared to 4 percent 10 years prior. And the number of high-school students who planned to major in accounting was only 1 percent in 2000, compared with 4 percent in 1999.[197]

So, financial-services companies looking for diverse recruits must make an extra effort to use career Web sites, job fairs at schools with high enrollment of diverse students, internship programs, networking groups and all other means to find talented employees.

2. Customers

People of color, whose numbers quickly are rising, accounted for nearly 40 percent of the growth in homeownership from 1994 to 1999, and are expected to head 30 percent of households by 2010, according to the Mortgage Bankers Association of America. Lower interest rates and specially tailored mortgage-loan programs have given a significant boost to homeownership by low-income households. Between 1993 and 1997, loans to buyers with incomes less than 80 percent of the local median increased by 38 percent, compared with 25 percent for higher-income buyers, according to the Joint Center for Housing Studies at Harvard University's 1999 Housing Trend Report.

Many consumers strapped with debts are refinancing and borrowing their equity, which will impact the amount they can borrow in the years ahead.

Worse still, many new homeowners lack a financial cushion and are beginning to miss payments. As the economy softened over the past two years, and layoffs and energy prices rose, mortgage delinquencies began inching upward.

The solution clearly lies in financial education but the institutions' desires and ability to reach consumers — and to make them understand the pitfalls of credit — are a big question.

Fannie Mae, the nation's largest source of home-mortgage financing, says growth in lending to credit-impaired borrowers is giving rise to two mortgage processes in America – one that leaves borrowers with stronger credit histories feeling more satisfied than ever and a second in which families with credit problems can nevertheless obtain mortgages, but at higher prices, with less confidence and more general dissatisfaction about the mortgage process.

"The ultimate and tragic consequence of these predatory practices is foreclosure," says Martin Eakes, spokesperson for the Coalition for Responsible Lending (CRL), which says these practices costs home-owners and other borrowers an estimated $9.1 billion annually.

Part of the problem is discrimination, both real and perceived. And the real bias, a recent study shows, is quite prevalent. If you were an African American or Latino who looked into purchasing a home or renting an apartment last year, you had a 32 percent chance of facing racial discrimination,[198] according to a 2002 report by the National Fair Housing Alliance (NFHA). Even more disturbing, the NFHA says its numbers represent only about 1 percent of the annual estimated incidents of housing discrimination, as the vast majority of cases go unreported.

The 2002 Fair Housing Trends Report examined 23,500 complaints lodged with NFHA members last year. It indicated race was the most commonly reported basis for housing discrimination in the United States (32 percent of all complaints), followed by disability and familial status (24 percent and 15 percent, respectively).

Complaints based on national-origin discrimination comprise the lowest category of discrimination (10 percent).

Housing discrimination took on various forms, some subtler than others. In some instances, real-estate agents only showed homes to African-American or Latino homebuyers in predominantly minority communities. Other reports included examples in which sellers were unwilling to negotiate the price of a home when offers were made by African Americans or Latinos, but were willing to do so with white buyers. In some cases, sellers took their homes off the market in order to avoid a sale to a person of color.

With apartment rentals, frequent reports of discrimination included denying that rental units were available; refusing to make reasonable accommodations for a person with a disability; quoting higher rents or security deposits; and segregating African-American or Latino families in one part of a building or complex.

Predatory lending, defined as excessive interest charged to certain groups of people (usually those with poor credit histories, mostly people who are African American and Latino), remains prevalent.

Predatory-lending practices, which include charging excessively high interest rates and expensive origination fees, cost Americans an estimated $9.1 billion in lost equity, according to the Coalition for Responsible Lending, a North Carolina-based advocacy group. Financial institutions routinely charge loan applicants with poor credit histories higher interest rates to cover their additional risk, which is not illegal and is considered standard business practice.[199]

A recent study by the Association of Community Organizations for Reform Now found: Low- and moderate-income borrowers, and African-American and Latino borrowers, receive a much smaller share of conventional purchase loans than their percentage of the U.S. population. Low- and moderate-income neighborhoods, including people of all races, comprise 26 percent of the country, but receive just 12 percent of conventional loans. African Americans comprise 12.3 percent of the U.S. population, but receive just 4.9 percent of conventional loans (down from 2000 and from 1996). Latinos are 12.5 percent of the population, but receive only 7.5 percent of conventional loans (up from 2000 and 1996).

3. Financial Education

Communities of color hold great potential for profit for the financial-services industry. The flip side is that predatory practices are more likely to result in foreclosure, and thus could impact industry profits.

The solution is massive financial education to those new or relatively new to the investment process. Consumers need to understand the pitfalls and benefits of stocks, bonds and other financial products.

They need to understand the risks of overextending credit or making late payments. And they need to understand why homeownership is the surest way to financial stability.

But few lenders are willing to aggressively pursue and educate those just beginning to use their services. It's easier and safer to stick with those who already know the system and have good credit. It's also, as all the demographics above demonstrate, a sure way to obsolescence.[200]

4. Marketing

Strategic partnerships, in which global companies align with multiethnic firms, are increasingly popular among corporations that tie their growth potential to these emerging markets.[201]

Minority-owned firms receive various benefits, including an influx of capital, and an ability to expand product lines and customer services.

Global corporations, such as Shell, gain access to cultural experts who know the local markets and are skilled at finding the hidden entrepreneurial gems.

So with potential customers either uneducated about the benefits of homeownership (and the dangers of bad debt) or afraid of discrimination, how does a smart financial-service company make inroads into the African-American and Latino communities?

To catch the eyes and ears of African-American consumers, marketers often enlist a Hip-Hop icon, Hollywood's latest hot or sensual urban prospect, or a superstar athlete. But there's a more direct way to reach African Americans, especially more mature African Americans — go to church.[202]

Church, for many African Americans, is far more than a place of worship. The church may double as a health center, school, bookshop, counseling center, job-placement center, early-childhood development center and more. With that relationship in mind, marketers have hawked everything from investment advice to religious books to shampoo at church, in an attempt to engender brand loyalty with the African-American consumer pool.

"These churches work as many corporations [providing their congregants goods and services] and the trend in church growth is that people don't belong to one church but several, based on the services each provides," says Kim Leathers, associate director of the outreach division of the Howard University School of Divinity.

Leathers fields calls regularly from marketers who request a comprehensive list of African-American churches throughout the nation — a list, she says doesn't exist.

"And pastors generally are very careful about what they pass on to their congregation," Leathers says. "But I know many pastors of all races are caught up with promoting [goods]."

Then again, using celebrities can work as well. In December 2001, talk-show host/actress/rapper Queen Latifah hit the airwaves in commercials nationwide pitching the Freedom Card MasterCard. Issued by Columbus Bank and Trust Co. of Columbus, Ga., Freedom Card was touted as the nation's first minority-owned, unsecured credit card designed specifically to meet the growing demands of the more than 76 million African Americans, Latinos and other underserved consumers nationwide who currently have little or no credit.[203]

The brainchild of Wesley Buford, a former executive producer of "The Montel Williams Show," the card was pitched as a mechanism to bridge the credit divide, and came with high-profile backers such as former Congressman and Housing and Urban Development Secretary Jack Kemp. Among other credit-qualifying criteria, applicants needed to prove they had a job, hadn't filed for bankruptcy within the past six months and had a residence for billing.

What was the catch? Applicants were smacked with interest rates that can run as high as 35 percent depending on credit history. Add on annual fees of $150 on credit lines that run from $300 to $10,000, and suddenly this opportunity doesn't seem quite as golden anymore.

According to Cardweb.com, a leading online publisher of credit-card data, the average rate for a standard credit card is 17 percent. "Those cards don't make any sense because you're paying hundreds in fees the first year and it quickly becomes a very bad deal. But for the credit-card companies, it's a very lucrative market," says Cardweb.com CEO Robert McKinley. "They're often getting even more money from the fees than they are from the high interest rates that are attached."

More recently, Hip-Hop icon Russell Simmons' Rush Communications has forged ties with UniFund, a Cincinnati, Ohio,-based financial-services company that buys and sells bad debt. The debit card, dubbed the "Rush Card," is available now and requires the consumer to pre-deposit his or her own funds into a Visa debit-card account.[204]

The Rush card requires an activation fee of $19.95 as well as the same amount in an annual charge. There is a $1 charge per Visa transaction, which is capped out monthly at $10. For each ATM transaction, the user is charged $1.50. Users who also want to take advantage of the checking service pay $1.95 for each check processed. UniRush offers consumers two checks at no cost per month. Card users, who do not have existing checking accounts, are now able to send checks in lieu of money orders or cash, to pay household bills or mortgages.

There are many other creative partnerships and alliances. For example:

- In May 2003, Seattle-based Washington Mutual confirmed it is hammering out a deal with the Magic Johnson Foundation involving a business agreement with the Johnson Development Corp., which focuses on creating new developments in historically neglected communities of color in both urban and suburban settings.

- San Francisco-based Wells Fargo, as part of the bank's $1 billion Loan Commitment to Latino Small Business Owners Across the Country, partnered with the United States Hispanic Chamber of Commerce to establish a $1 billion, six-year loan program to address the credit needs of Latino-owned businesses. Wells Fargo Houston invested $500,000 in Unity National, and has become a non-voting stockholder for the purpose of promoting community development. Unity National, the only Texas banking institution owned by African Americans, provides a range of financial services to more than 4,800 multi-ethnic groups and businesses in the inner city. "To have another financial-services company ally themselves with a competitor is unusual," says Unity President Larry Hawkins.

- In the Greater Washington, D.C., region, the Collective Banking Group (CBG), a coalition of faith-based organizations assembled to bring financial empowerment to the African-American community, signed a strategic alliance with five area banks. The partnership generated more than $27 million in loans and $34 million in deposits in 2000, bringing the total to $98 million in loans and $132 million in deposits since the partnership began in 1996.

In 2000, Atlanta Life Insurance Co. teamed with The AFLAC Insurance Co. in a strategic partnership. Agents at Atlanta Life Insurance Co., the largest African-American stock-owned life-insurance company in the United States, now can offer clients a full range of AFLAC supplemental insurance products, including: cancer, short-term disability, voluntary indemnity, personal accident and dental.

ADDITIONAL RESOURCES

PART VII - INDUSTRIES IN THE FRONT LINE

Cole, Yoji. "Is An MBA Worth It for People of Color?" DiversityInc, 16 December 2002. *http://www.diversityinc.com/members/3985.cfm*

Farmer, Melanie Austria. "More Latinos Looking at Jobs in Finance, Accounting," DiversityInc, 14 February 2003. *http://www.diversityinc.com/members/4461.cfm*

Farmer, Melanie Austria. "Russell Simmons' Debit Card: Helpful or High Risk?" DiversityInc, 7 May 2003. *http://www.diversityinc.com/members/4896.cfm*

Federal Financial Institutions Examination Council (FFIEC), Washington, D.C. 20006. *http://www.ffiec.gov/about.htm*

Hinton, Eric L. "Pay Now/Pay More Later, The Costly Privilege of High-Interest Credit Cards," DiversityInc, 15 March 2002. *http://www.diversityinc.com/members/2580.cfm*

Hinton, Eric L. "Redlining: Citigroup Steered High-Interest Loans To Minority Neighborhoods, Study Finds," DiversityInc, 21 June 2002. *http://www.diversityinc.com/members/3151.cfm*

Lopez, Elena Maria. "As Jobless Rates Rise for People of Color, Smart Companies Recruit." DiversityInc, 13 March 2003. *http://www.diversityinc.com/members/4599.cfm*

Lopez, Elena Maria. "Chase Plans $500B in Home Loans to Diverse Markets; Community Leaders to Help." DiversityInc, 5 February 2003. http://www.diversityinc.com/members/4406.cfm

National Fair Housing Alliance (NFHA), 1212 New York Ave, Suite 525, Washington, DC 20005. *http://www.nationalfairhousing.org/*

Pew Hispanic Center and Kaiser Family Foundation. 2002 National Survey of Latinos. Washington, D.C., December 2002.

"Predatory Lenders: Are They Draining Future Profits From Buyers Today?" DiversityInc, 31 August 2002.

"To Reach the African-American Consumer – Go To Church," DiversityInc, 17 December 2001.

"Financial Services Look to Multiethnic Partners for Growth," DiversityInc, 15 May 2001. *http://www.diversityinc.com/members/1045.cfm*

Chase Plans $500B in Home Loans to Diverse Markets; Community Leaders to Help

By Elena Maria Lopez

February 05, 2003

© 2003 DiversityInc.com

The nation's No. 2 bank, JPMorgan Chase, has announced plans to make a $500-billion commitment to the minority and underserved home-mortgage markets over the next seven years. The company hopes the large lending commitment will double its presence in these markets and it intends to seek advice from community leaders on the most successful ways to reach out to their constituencies. JPMorgan Chase said this is the largest initiative to date for single-family mortgages to these segments of the market. It will be offered through its Chase Manhattan Mortgage Corporation subsidiary.

The $500 billion will double the amount of capital JPMorgan Chase currently lends to the minority and underserved home-mortgage markets. In 2002, the company floated about $35 billion of capital to these markets. According to the newly announced plan, this amount should be more than $70 million a year by 2010.

Chase currently is the No. 4 mortgage originator in the United States, with a market share of about 5 percent. Although these numbers change quarterly, the company tends to range between No. 2 and No. 4. With this announcement, the company hopes to achieve about 10 percent of the market share by 2010.

The company hopes to overturn the traditional barriers mainstream corporations have faced entering emerging and underserved markets by gaining the help of community leaders and organizations. Chase has created the National Housing Advisory Council to assist and deal with relevant issues. The council is comprised of real-estate professionals and influential leaders in the African-American, Latino, Asian-American and gay and lesbian communities.

In creating the Chase Dream Maker Commitment, JPMorgan Chase said it is responding to President Bush's call to make homeownership available to all members of society but economics and the need for new customers clearly drives this decision as well.

The president wants to increase minority homeownership by 5.5 million households by the end of the decade. This commitment includes single-family home mortgages, refinancing and home-equity loans and lines of credit.

Chase Plans $500B in Home Loans to Diverse Markets; Community Leaders to Help (cont'd.)

Why have these markets traditionally been underserved? "There is not a lack of 'available money,'" said JPMorgan Chase spokesperson Kristen Batteria. "There is a shortage of lenders who are serving these markets with the appropriate products, services, staff and commitment."

Minority and other underserved markets offer the highest growth opportunities, said Batteria.

Regardless of tough economic times for the corporation, JPMorgan Chase's mortgage division had a record volume of $155 billion in mortgages and home loans in 2002. In the past several months, the company announced anticipated layoffs worldwide, which may be up to 10,000 by the year's end. Mostly investment-bank and technology-support positions lost money.

"They've been beat up pretty, pretty badly," said Kurt Kendis, managing director of The Banking Group in Kimberton, Pa. and a former economics professor at the Wharton School of Business at the University of Pennsylvania. "Their bread-and-butter business at JPMorgan Chase was on the commercial side." With the deterioration of the commercial-credit market, it appears that Chase is moving into the consumer market "to make a buck," continued Kendis.

"It's a very smart business move in addition to being the right thing to do," said Steve Cook, vice president of public relations at the National Association of Realtors. "The simple fact that minority homeownership remains below 50 percent in this country suggests that there's a need." Cook said 2002 was the largest year to date in terms of the amount of homes sold in the United States.

The 2000 U.S. Census reports that 68.3 percent of the 104.7 million U.S. households own their own homes. For white households, 74.8 percent of the 78.8 million households own their own homes. But only 49.5 percent of the 9.3 million Latino households and 47.5 percent of 12.5 million African-American households own their own homes.

Despite the economy, home sales continue to be strong. According to the Federal Reserve, the first three quarters of 2002 experienced double-digit increases in home-mortgage debt by Americans, with increases ranging from 10.3 percent to 12.8 percent. The Fed also reported that Americans had $5.85 trillion in outstanding home-mortgage debt over that same period. This debt includes traditional home mortgages, as well as refinancing, home-improvement and home-equity loans.

About 69 percent of white home-loan applicants secured loans in 2001, according to a Federal Financial Institutions Examination Council (FFIEC) report. Only

Chase Plans $500B in Home Loans to Diverse Markets; Community Leaders to Help (cont'd.)

57 percent of Latino applicants and 43 percent of African-American applicants secured loans at the end of the mortgage process, according to the report.

The FFIEC reported that African Americans accounted for 6 percent of all home-loan applications in 2001, but only 4.2 percent of the home loans secured. Latinos accounted for 7 percent of all home-loan applications and 6.5 percent of all home loans. White households accounted for 61 percent of the home-loan applications in 2001 and 68 percent of all home loans.

The FFIEC is an interagency body reporting to the Federal Reserve System, the Federal Deposit Insurance Corporation (FDIC), the National Credit Union Administration, the Office of the Comptroller of the Currency and the Office of Thrift Supervision.

Currently about 30 percent of JPMorgan Chase's mortgage business stems from the minority or underserved market. With this initiative, Chase expects this market to represent between 35 percent and 40 percent of its total home-mortgage business. This initiative increases single-family home loans to people of color of various economic backgrounds, low-to-moderate income borrowers, and new immigrant families.

Chase has made an effort to reach these customers over the last two years, including low closing costs, low downpayments, downpayments for those with limited credit, and multilanguage documents. The company also plans to offer a wider range of services to customers and potential customers, including expanded language capabilities, referrals to credit-counseling agencies and programs to increase financial literacy. Chase also intends to address predatory-lending practices through community and marketing information. Predatory-lending refers to subprime lenders that lend to high-risk individuals at an increased and often unfair lending rate.

Chase also has doubled the number of salespersons in these markets, increasing their racial and ethnic diversity, the company said. The company also plans to increase its physical presence in urban markets in New York, California, Texas, Washington, D.C., Illinois, Georgia and Pennsylvania.

New Index Finds Black-Owned Businesses Down but Hopeful

By Melanie Austria Farmer

© 2003 DiversityInc.com

February 06, 2003

Zeroing in on the growing African-American entrepreneurial sector, financial-services giant ING Thursday unveiled a new index that measures the economic confidence of African-American business owners. Survey results reveal that business leaders continue to experience a negative trend, underlining financial outlooks that have been dampened by increased harsh economic conditions and the possibility of a U.S.-Iraq war.

ING said its new index – the ING Gazelle Index – is helping to serve a rapidly growing sector.

"We really wanted to key into what was going on [in this sector] and understand better the African-American entrepreneurs," said Keith Green, senior vice president of domestic emerging markets at ING U.S. "This is key and a vital piece of the U.S. economy."

In preparation for the launch of the new index, the Dutch banker and insurer began capturing data in early 2002 to gain insight, track history and unveil trends. In the fourth quarter of 2002, the ING Gazelle Index, which surveyed nearly 1,500 African-American-owned businesses with about 10 to 100 employees, showed that executives are facing a more negative outlook. Among the findings, 20.3 percent said economic conditions are better now than they were six months ago, but 51.4 percent revealed that situations have worsened.

The index revealed that business activity slowed in the fourth quarter. Out of 100, the index measured 46.9, down from 52.9 in the previous quarter. Regarding a decrease in employment, the index measured 45.5, showing a slip from 49 in the third quarter.

While current confidence has slipped, a slightly positive upside may be in the wings. One of the four components of the index indicated optimism about the economy six months down the road. Looking ahead, 48.3 percent are more optimistic about the economy while 39.1 percent are more pessimistic.

According to the U.S. Census Bureau the number of African-American businesses jumped 46 percent over a five-year period, from 1992 to 1997. Meanwhile,

New Index Finds Black-Owned Businesses Down
but Hopeful (cont'd.)

white-owned businesses increased 24 percent during the same timeframe. And, a recent study conducted by the Ewing Marion Kauffman Foundation found that African Americans are 50 percent more likely than others to stave off the daily grind and jump into entrepreneurial roles.

Aiming to address an information gap, ING U.S. Chief Executive Tom McInerney said one of the main purposes of the new index is to help small- and middle-sized businesses, particularly African-American-owned businesses, with their own strategies and plans. "By helping those businesses have more know ledge, we can help them make better decisions."

ING's hope is that the index, jointly developed with Atlanta-based Boston Research Group, will serve as a necessary tool for African-American leaders and enable them to thrive even in challenging times.

"This is part of our ongoing effort to assist business owners and entrepreneurs so that they better understand the dynamics and other like-minded businesses," Green added.

ING identified 1,497 African-American owned businesses whose employment increased by a minimum of 5 percent over the last five years and employs between 10 to 100 workers. Each quarter, 350 of these businesses are surveyed randomly. The company conducted its most recent survey during the second week of January.

The index, which is offered online at no-cost, goes live Thursday. Companies that want to be surveyed may participate for free.

Black, Latino Borrowers Pay More for Home Loans

By C. Stone Brown

© 2003 DiversityInc.com

January 23, 2003

One of the most enduring contributions of the Rev. Martin Luther King Jr. is his message of economic equality, echoed in his "I have a dream" speech. On Monday, the day his birthday was commemorated, the California Reinvestment Committee (CRC), a non-profit community development organization, released a study that suggests the "dream" of homeownership – the most common method of building financial independence – is a financial nightmare for African Americans and Latinos.

The CRC study was limited to African Americans and Latinos living in Fresno, Calif., Los Angeles, Oakland, Sacramento and San Diego. The banks used in the study included Citibank, Countrywide, Union Bank, United California Bank and Bank of the West. All failed to meet equal-opportunity standards set by CRC's Equality Benchmark analysis.

"What you look like and where you live should not determine whether you get a loan, or how much you will pay for it," said Kevin Stein, associate director of CRC and author of the study. "Larger financial institutions, such as Citigroup, Washington Mutual and HSBC that own higher cost subprime lenders must ensure that every customer receives the lowest cost loan product for which he or she qualifies."

Some of the major findings in the CRC report, "Who Really Gets Home Loans" determined that African-American and Latino borrowers pay more for home loans and that African Americans, in particular, face the greatest barrier to prime-rate loans. This equated to higher interest rates and loan costs for African Americans in each city. In Oakland, 46.8 percent of subprime loans went to African Americans, compared with 21.8 percent of prime loans. Subprime lenders were more likely to lend to Latinos than their bank counterparts in four of the five survey cities. In Sacramento, 27.9 percent of subprime loans went to Latinos, compared with only 15 percent of prime loans.

Subprime borrowers pay a risk premium for their home loan. In contrast, prime rate borrowers pay interest set by the "prime rate," the rate major banks charges their best customers. Subprime borrowers might pay a rate five to 10 percentage

Black, Latino Borrowers Pay More for Home Loans (cont'd.)

points above prime.

Subprime lenders fill a legitimate void in mortgage loan financing, serving borrowers who otherwise would be rejected by major banks or prime lenders. However, subprime lenders often target people of color, even when they have credit scores for a prime-rate loan.

Citigroup recently acknowledged that more than 17,000 of its subprime borrowers could qualify for a prime loan, yet Citigroup has failed to give these borrowers the lower cost loans they deserve. "This is one of the biggest problems in the banking industry," said Stein.

"Fannie Mae has said 50 percent of subprime loans could be prime rates. Freddie Mac is more conservative, believing the numbers are closer to 35 percent, said Stein, referring to the two government-sponsored entities that are major lenders in this market, competing with the major banks. "Either way, the banking industry isn't serving the interest of community of color."

The CRC included in its study recommendations for banks to implement and move the nation closer to King's dream of economic equality.

The primary recommendation is that in 2003, banks and prime mortgage lenders should double their outreach and marketing efforts to underserved borrowers and neighborhoods. One of the benchmarks that CRC uses in determining discrimination is the percentage of loans banks grant in proportion to the ethnic makeup of the community.

Stein believes if Latinos represent 10 percent of the households in a community, the bank's loan portfolio should reflect at or near 10 percent. "If it doesn't, than they should explain why."

C. Retail

Spurred by the dramatic changes of the U.S. population over the past decade, the face of the American consumer has transformed from a once largely homogenous group into a dynamic mix of people comprised of various races, lifestyles and cultures. Competitive retailers have recognized these dramatic demographic shifts, and moved to manage the needs of current and future customers and employees.[205]

But first, who exactly are these "new" diverse customers? The answer is complicated by more than simply race.

Now more than ever, it's difficult to identify, segment and target customers, in large part because there is little hard data to describe the purchasing behavior of consumers based solely on their race. Therefore, it's critical to understand not only who these customers are, but also what they are like, how they behave and why they purchase what they do.

After all, consumers are major forces in the ever-changing retail landscape. They determine the winners and the losers in retailing, according to a study from Texas A&M University's Center of Retailing Studies (CRS). Authored by David Szymanski and Jay Scansaroli, the study, "Who's Minding the Future?" has identified "megatrends" that will influence the success or failure of a retail establishment in the years ahead.

According to the CRS report, the most compelling trend retailers must heed is the changing ethnic and cultural composition of the American consumer base. In the study, Szymanski cites the transformation of the general perception of the American family as a predominantly white nuclear one to a society that recognizes and accepts multiethnic, diverse households. "America has always been a melting pot," says Szymanski, "and diversity has always been a part of the make-up of our country … [but] its magnitude continues to intensify."

The intensifying magnitude of diversity of consumers also affects the shift in employees as well. After all, consumers are employees at retail companies, and vice versa. The way that consumers respond to poor treatment (or poor customer service) has changed markedly over the years. Rather than simply walking away from a retail establishment and "voting" with their wallets by not patronizing culturally incompetent vendors, today's consumers are going one step further and demanding that retailers, in particular, recognize their needs and provide for them.

1. Employees

There aren't many people of color in the upper ranks of the U.S. department-store industry — such as buyers, vice presidents and beyond.

There are so few, that Jarvis Jefferson, a former department-store executive who now works for executive-search firm Whitehead Mann Pendleton James, says he'd be hard-pressed to come up with 100 names — including Latinos and Asian Americans.[206]

"And the fact I would either know them all or recognize their names says something," he adds.

More than 30 years ago, a handful of African-American department-store executives formed the Black Retail Action Group (BRAG)[207] a support organization for people of color in the retail trade.

The group's original purpose was to give men and women of color an opportunity to socialize, network and commiserate together. Many of the organization's founders were employed at Bloomingdale's.

"We're talking 35 years ago, when it was unheard of for blacks to even shop at Bloomingdale's," says Lawanda Kamara, BRAG's spokesperson. "But Bloomingdale's did have blacks in key positions."

Since then, the organization has expanded its focus to include young people who might be interested in retail careers. BRAG officials host workshops and seminars for high-school and college students, and sponsor an internship program.

According to 2001 data from the Equal Employment Opportunity Commission (EEOC), of the people who work in general merchandise stores, i.e. Wal-Mart, Target and Kmart, 71.3 percent of all retail employees are white and 28.7 percent are people of color. In comparison, 84.3 percent of officials and managers are white and less than 16 percent are people of color. The number of managers of color

(15.7 percent) has gone down from 1999, when the figure was 16.8 percent of officials and managers being people of color.[208]

Ron Edwards, director of research for the EEOC, cautioned that the figures should be used to represent a sample, rather than all retailers in the country. The statistics are derived from retail establishments with 50 or more employees, and therefore, many small stores that employ people of color are excluded from the data set.

"So, for example, an outlet like the Gap may have some stores that have less than 50 employees, so those numbers will not be reported," Edwards says.

2. Customers

Are there different standards of customer service for different groups of consumers?

At least one major retail chain, Macy's, is under fire with a recent lawsuit alleging that it racially profiles its customers.[209]

Sharon Simmons-Thomas, who is African American and works as a legal secretary in Manhattan, filed a lawsuit seeking class-action certification in May against Macy's East and its parent company, Federated Department Stores. The suit alleges that Macy's targets African Americans and other people of color for shoplifting.

The suit seeks $100 million in damages against Macy's East and Federated, which also owns Bloomingdale's department stores, for "targeting African Americans and other non-white shoppers for shoplifting and subjecting such shoppers to false accusations, wrongful detention, searches and confiscation of personal property based on race," according to the suit filed in U.S. District Court in Manhattan.

"Unfortunately, in our society today, people of color are profiled in department stores," says Mary-Frances Winters, president of The Winters Group, a diversity-management consulting firm based in Rochester, N.Y. "Unfortunately, it's so ingrained in our culture that it certainly does happen; there's an assumption made that a person of color has a higher license of being someone with criminal intent, and that's truly unfortunate."

"Many customers are saying, 'So what else is new?' It's old news. [This retailer] just got caught this time. For many customers, this is the story of their life, so what happens is [customers] pick and choose where they feel most welcomed and shop where they do. Retailers need to become aware of this" and need to address it proactively, says Myrna Marofsky, president of ProGroup, a diversity-consulting firm headquartered in Minneapolis.

Marofsky gives an example of one large department store for which she had consulted in the past. This particular store, which she did not want to name, had been faced with a similar incident, but was able to turn itself around.

"[A similar] incident became an impetus for them to start a major diversity initiative and get the attention from top executives," says Marofsky. "They were able to overcome this by the way they handled it. They changed how they viewed diversity as a critical issue for them … They were forced to do some internal soul searching."

She says any time a major company comes across an issue like this, the way in which that company handles the situation going forward is critical. However, most players in the retail sector, she says, have lacked in their efforts to address these issues proactively.

"Many retailing organizations have been very, very lucky," says Marofsky.

Other big companies in the past have managed to reposition themselves in a positive light and slowly gain back consumer confidence. After battling its share of bias lawsuits, Denny's, for example, has enjoyed a comeback of sorts with customers through a number of diversity initiatives, including increasing the number of minority-owned franchises and hiring more people of color at corporate headquarters.

The family-dining chain made headlines when African-American Secret Service agents were treated poorly in one of its restaurants. Other patrons also claimed they were denied service because of their race. The company lost two class-action lawsuits in 1994 and was forced to pay $54 million in damage.

For retailers, respecting varying customer lifestyles is key to penetrating diverse markets. Part of respect lies in the endorsement of community leaders, which greatly enhances consumer loyalty.

Because of the increased access to information and the fragmentation of media outlets, American consumers have become more sophisticated. Diverse consumers, in particular, also recognize when they are being pandered to, rather than being genuinely addressed. Take. for instance. the GLBT market. Based on surveys, most GLBT consumers support marketers who they feel are supportive of the community. "If a company is openly supportive of our community through its advertising, even in a small way, we are so loyal,"[210] says Cathy Renna, news media director at the Gay and Lesbian Alliance Against Defamation (GLAAD).

Similarly, ethnic consumers are better reached and feel more comfortable making purchases from companies that advertise in ethnic media.[211]

In the past, consumers who felt discriminated against might simply walk out of the store and take their business elsewhere, according to Jerome Williams, an associate professor of marketing at Penn State University's Smeal College of Business. But as the Baby Boomer generation has aged and become more affluent, that mind-set has begun to shift, Williams says.[212]

"People today ... are more inclined to say, 'My dollar is a good as anyone else's and I expect to be treated equitably, ' " Williams says.

3. Marketing

Increasing numbers of retail chains, including some of the nation's biggest, found within the last year that in order to grow they have to make a more concerted effort to reach out to customers of color and other emerging-market groups, including the GLBT population and people with disabilities.

Oakbrook, Ill.,-based McDonald's is a prime example. The company is targeting its multiethnic consumers with a growing level of sophistication and vigor, with particular emphasis on Latinos.[213] McDonald's was the No. 5 Latino advertiser overall in terms of dollars spent in 2002, spending $27 million – the No. 1 Latino advertiser was Altria – and the biggest food-product advertiser, according to Hispanic Business. McDonald's also is the largest spender in the food-service sector in advertising aimed at African Americans, according to research firm CMR, which tracks national advertising.

The McDonald's brand is not as powerful as it was in its days of former glory. McDonald's market-leading share of the $47.5 billion fast-food burger industry in the United States lately has flattened out at around 42.7 percent. Wendy's, meanwhile, grew its share to 14.4 percent in 2002, up by 2.5 points since 1998, according to industry-research group Technomic. McDonald's placed behind Wendy's and Burger King in phone surveys of 70,000 Americans who rated fast-food chain's service, quality and value, according to the American Customer Satisfaction Index. Other chains to trump McDonald's included Papa John's, Domino's Pizza, Pizza Hut, Little Caesar, Taco Bell and Kentucky Fried Chicken.

With a drop-off in earnings, McDonald's is coming to the realization that cookie-cutter marketing isn't whetting the appetites of many of its target consumers, so it's trying to improve marketing that has grown a bit tired and frayed at the edges. The efforts have been promising.

McDonald's future may rest in how well it tunes in to its diverse base of owners and operators – as well as giving those operators looser reins. People of color and women represent approximately 34 percent of all McDonald's franchisees in the United States. Franchises owned by people of color operate more than 1,900 restaurants, and women operate more than 2,000 McDonald's restaurants in the United States.

And then there's Kmart, the retail giant that recently emerged from bankruptcy.[214] Kmart didn't neglect people of color in the past, but it didn't especially appeal to them, says Kurt Barnard, president of Barnard's Retail Trend Report, a retail newsletter.[215] If Kmart wants to remain a viable force in the retail marketplace, it will need to woo these consumers, Barnard says.

Kmart is struggling to find a niche between Wal-Mart's low prices and Target's cheap chic, and so it is reaching into a tightened purse to appeal to its strong base of African-American and Latino customers. The Troy, Mich.,-based retailer has launched a new Spanish-language marketing campaign, including a magazine aimed specifically at Latinos, and is acquiring exclusive brands for this market. An insert for African Americans also is gaining steam. In 2002, Kmart also unveiled its unveiled its "Cosas para La Vida" campaign – a Spanish-language offshoot of the "Stuff of Life" campaign – directly targeting its Spanish-speaking customers through television and radio advertising. The "Stuff of Life" campaign was launched in February 2002, and it was tailored specifically for African Americans and Latinos in March 2002 by Michigan-based Global Hue advertising agency.

Forty percent of Kmart's associate base is made up of people of color, says Lyman Locket, Kmart's chief diversity officer. Kmart's management – regional and district managers, directors, divisional vice presidents and higher, was 21 percent female and 8 percent people of color, the company stated in 2002.

"We want to position Kmart as a company that understands the consumer, and that reflects all consumers," says Locket.

ADDITIONAL RESOURCES

PART VII – INDUSTRIES IN THE FRONT LINE

Black Retail Action Group (BRAG), Rockefeller Center Station, PO Box 1192, New York, NY 10185, (212) 319-7751. *http://www.bragusa.org/*

Gay and Lesbian Alliance Against Defamation (GLAAD), 5455 Wilshire Blvd, #1500, Los Angeles, CA 90036 (323) 933-2240 or 248 West 35th Street, 8th Floor, New York, NY 10001 (212) 629-3322. *http://www.glaad.org/*

U.S. Equal Employment Opportunity Commission. 2000 EEO-1 Aggregate Report: SIC 539: Misc. General Merchandise Stores. Washington, D.C., 2002. *http://www.eeoc.gov/stats/jobpat/2000/sic3/539.html*

Does Macy's Racially Profile Customers? Lawsuit Claims It Does, Company Says No

By Melanie Austria Farmer

May 22, 2003

Macy's is under fire after the department store behemoth got hit with a lawsuit, alleging that it racially profiles its customers.

Sharon Simmons-Thomas, who is African American and works as a legal secretary in Manhattan, filed a lawsuit seeking class-action certification Tuesday against Macy's East and its parent company, Federated Department Stores. The suit alleges that Macy's targets African Americans and other people of color for shoplifting.

The suit seeks $100 million in damages against Macy's East and Federated, which also owns Bloomingdale's department stores, for "targeting African Americans and other non-white shoppers for shoplifting and subjecting such shoppers to false accusations, wrongful detention, searches and confiscation of personal property based on race," according to the suit filed in U.S. District Court in Manhattan.

"Unfortunately, in our society today, people of color are profiled in department stores," said Mary-Frances Winters, president of The Winters Group, a diversity-management consulting firm based in Rochester, N.Y. "Unfortunately, it's so ingrained in our culture that it certainly does happen; there's an assumption made that a person of color has a higher license of being someone with criminal intent, and that's truly unfortunate."

Interestingly enough, Federated announced also on Tuesday the appointment of Bill Hawthorne to the newly created position of vice president/diversity and deputy general counsel. Hawthorne will be responsible for corporate wide diversity initiatives including employment, organizational development, work environment, minority vendor relationships, purchasing and business development, the company said.

Federated, based in Cincinnati, did not return phone calls but Macy's reportedly released a statement saying that the store does "not profile, target or discriminate against any minority group or individual," according to The New York Times.

Does Macy's Racially Profile Customers? Lawsuit Claims It Does, Company Says No (cont'd.)

Highlighted in the lawsuit was an incident involving Simmons-Thomas when she was shopping in December at the Macy's located in Herald Square in Manhattan. She alleged that after she exchanged cookware and additional items at the store, plain-clothes security guards detained her, even after she presented her receipts for the new items.

"Without identifying themselves as Macy's security, they accused me of shoplifting," Simmons-Thomas said in a statement released by her lawyer Ken Thompson of New York-based Thompson Wigdor & Gilly. "When I tried to show my receipts, one guard grabbed them from my hand and insisted I come with them. They never said where we were going."

She further described in the lawsuit that Macy's guards conducted a body-search on her, detained her in a holding cell, handcuffed her to a bench, threatened to use physical force and confiscated her purchases.

The lawsuit filing comes on the heels of lukewarm news released from Federated. The company reported quarterly earnings last week ahead of expectations, but said sales fell in the quarter. Like most in the retail sector, Federated has had a challenging time dealing with a sour economy and weakened consumer spending. The company's shares have been fluctuating around $30 per share, down from its 52-week high of $43.15.

It is too early to tell how the lawsuit will impact the company's business overall, or if it will resonate with customers.

Myrna Marofsky, president of ProGroup, a diversity consulting firm headquartered in Minneapolis, said any time a major company comes across an issue like this, the way in which that company handles the situation going forward is critical. However, most players in the retail sector, she said, have lacked in their efforts to address these issues proactively.

"Many retailing organizations have been very, very lucky," said Marofsky, who specializes in the retail industry.

"Many customers are saying, 'So what else is new?' It's old news. [This retailer] just got caught this time. For many customers, this is the story of their life, so what happens is [customers] pick and choose where they feel most welcomed and shop where they do. Retailers need to become aware of this" and need to address it proactively, she said.

Marofsky gives an example of one large department store she had consulted in the past. This particular store, which she did not want to name, had been faced

Does Macy's Racially Profile Customers? Lawsuit Claims It Does, Company Says No (cont'd.)

with a similar incident, but was able to turn itself around.

"[A similar] incident became an impetus for them to start a major diversity initiative and get the attention from top executives," said Marofsky. "They were able to overcome this by the way they handled it. They changed how they viewed diversity as a critical issue for them … They were forced to do some internal soul searching."

Other big companies in the past have managed to reposition themselves in a positive light and slowly gain back consumer confidence. After battling its share of bias lawsuits, Denny's, for example, has enjoyed a comeback of sorts with customers through a number of diversity initiatives, including increasing the number of minority-owned franchises and hiring more people of color at corporate headquarters.

The family dining chain made headlines when African-American Secret Service agents were treated poorly in one of its restaurants. Other patrons also claimed they were denied service because of their race. The company lost two class-action lawsuits in 1994 and was forced to pay $54 million in damage.

Simmons-Thomas appeared with her lawyer in a press conference held Tuesday in front of Macy's in Herald Square. In the suit, Simmons-Thomas and her lawyer called for other shoppers – who may have had a similar experience – to step forward and join the pending class action.

Denny's, Finished Fighting Lawsuits, Reaches Out to Ethnic Customers

By Ruth Zeilberger

© 2003 DiversityInc.com

January 07, 2003

Denny's, America's largest family dining chain, is well known for the bias lawsuits against it and its subsequent efforts to remake itself as a diversity-conscious company. Now, Denny's wants to reposition itself in its customers' eyes – it is launching an advertising campaign to show itself as a friendly place that embraces its diverse clientele. The tagline of the campaign is, "A good place to sit and eat."

"The campaign is designed to reinforce Denny's position as a place for people who just want to relax and enjoy a good, honest meal," said company spokesperson Debbie Atkins. "It's designed to re-establish the company's consumer relevance by embracing and communicating the core values of the basic, unpretentious brand."

Atkins insisted that the new message is not meant to fight any lingering suspicions of bias. Rather, Denny's has positioned itself at the forefront of diversity, she said, and the new ads are a reflection of that.

Still, Denny's was not always a good place to sit and eat for its African-American diners. Denny's made headlines when African-American Secret Service agents were treated poorly in one of its restaurants. Other patrons also claimed they were denied service because of their race. The company lost two class-action lawsuits in 1994 and was forced to pay $54 million in damages.

The effort to reposition the Spartanburg, S.C.-headquartered restaurant chain in the public eye comes after a serious upheaval of diversity practices. The company underwent a major upheaval under the leadership of its former CEO James Adamson. Adamson joined Denny's Corporation, then called Advantica Restaurant Group, after the lawsuits and is credited with turning around the company. He launched several diversity initiatives, including increasing the number of minority-owned franchises and hiring more people of color at corporate headquarters. In 1996, the National Association for the Advancement of Colored People (NAACP) named Adamson, now Kmart CEO, its chief executive of the year. Now, Denny's hopes to deal with a lingering perception problem and improve its financial fortunes through a $37 million campaign. Denny's revenue

Denny's, Finished Fighting Lawsuits, Reaches Out to Ethnic Customers (cont'd.)

for the first three quarters of 2002 fell to $721.7 million, from $792.8 million in the comparable period of 2001. The company posted net income of $67.7 million after a loss of $49.0 million for the period in 2001.

Denny's initial series of ads will run through April, with additional creative input coming in the summer. The company will buy time on programs such as "ER," "King of Queens" and "George Lopez," as well as on national cable and syndicated programs. While none of these programs have a primarily African-American audience, "ER"'s audience runs across racial lines and "George Lopez", which features a Mexican-American family, particularly appeals to Latino audiences. "King of Queens" – featuring the portly Doug – is the chain's nod to those who have the gusto to finish a full Grand Slam breakfast. The campaign is significant for Denny's not only in embracing diversity, but also because it is a national campaign for a chain whose advertising historically has been a collection of haphazard local media buys that missed nearly a quarter of the markets in which the chain operates.

Kicking off the campaign created by Publicis in Mid America Dallas is "Recess," one of four television spots. The ad, which debuted Monday, opens with a multiracial group of dining co-workers laughing as one grabs a cell phone away from another. "Lunch should be like recess," says the voiceover. The camera pans to shots of Denny's "classic lunch" entrees. The work debuts the chain's new tagline, "A good place to sit and eat." There are two versions of the ad – a 15-second spot and a 30-second spot. The 15-second spot features one white male, one African-American male and two white females. The 30-second spot features two white males, two white females and one African-American female.

The company also launched a Latino advertising campaign yesterday, designed to speak directly to Spanish-speaking consumers. The new commercial, which will air in select markets, is the first creative effort of Denny's newly appointed Latino agency of record, cruz/kravetz: IDEAS.

The 30-second spot features Marta, a Latina actress cast as a Denny's waitress. Marta breezily goes about her duties as she encounters a sleepy-eyed security guard who sips his early morning coffee, a young boy mischievously enjoying his whipped cream topped hot chocolate and an animated family sharing stories at the end of the day. The spot concludes with the tagline: "En Denny's, nos ocupamos de ti" (At Denny's, we take care of you).

The company is in the midst of review for its African-American advertising. It hopes to find an agency by the close of 2003. Meanwhile, the company is hoping to regain the loyalty of its African-American customers through charitable contri-

Denny's, Finished Fighting Lawsuits, Reaches Out to Ethnic Customers (cont'd.)

butions. This year, the company has pledged to raise at least $1 million for The King Center, based in Atlanta, as part of a three-year initiative launched in January 2002. As part of the initiative, participating Denny's will donate 20 cents from each All-American Grand Slam breakfast to The King Center. "We see ourselves as a leader in diversity," said Atkins, "and we believe that this is what a leader what do."

Shopping Blitz: Discount Retailers With Cross-Cultural Appeal See Big Payoff

By Ruth Zeilberger

© 2003 DiversityInc.com

December 05, 2002

Deep discounts and special offers helped the Christmas shopping season get off to a surprisingly buoyant start over the Thanksgiving weekend. Discount retailers, particularly popular with multicultural consumers, led the pack – with Wal-Mart Stores and J.C. Penney posting record weekend stores.

But whether stores can leverage strong sales through the rest of the holiday season is an open question, particularly with a week's less shopping time between Thanksgiving and Christmas, compared with last year. While specific details about the demographic breakdown of the enthusiastic holiday shoppers still are anecdotal, some analysts say the key to sustaining strong sales numbers may rest in multicultural appeal.

In spite of a weakened economy, there still are a lot of dollars to go around. U.S. buying power is expected to reach $7.1 trillion this year according to the Selig Center for Economic Growth at the University of Georgia. People of color make up about 18 percent of that figure, or $1.3 trillion a year. African-American consumers comprise the largest buying-power group at $572.1 billion – and that's money they're willing to spend, particularly during the holiday season.

"We want the bling bling," said Pepper Miller, the African-American president of the Hunter-Miller Group, a Chicago-headquartered research firm. "Our buying power is growing and we spend a disproportionate amount of our money on fashion and jewelry.

"Most department stores are still not recognizing blacks as important consumers," said Miller. "But the Wal-Mart approach is to show black shoppers and their lifestyle. Of course, people shop there because they can afford it. But it's also about comfort level and how comfortable you feel in your shopping environment."

Three quarters of American consumers were out shopping over the weekend, according to the Washington, D.C.-based National Retail Federation. ShopperTrak RCT, a Chicago-based company which tracks sales at 22,000 outlets, estimated that sales on Friday were up 12.3 percent over last year's Black Friday to $7.4 billion. It estimated that Saturday sales increased 9 percent to $5.2

Shopping Blitz: Discount Retailers With Cross-Cultural Appeal See Big Payoff (cont'd.)

billion. The day after Thanksgiving has become known as Black Friday since it marks the point when retailers begin making the bulk of their profits for the year.

Bentonville, Ark.-based Wal-Mart set a record for one-day sales on Friday, generating $1.43 billion. Wal-Mart lured savvy bargain hunters with pre-sunrise specials and other tantalizing offers.

"While it's much too early to tell the specific demographic breakdown of the holiday consumers, a company like Wal-Mart is very representative of the composition of the American population," said Kurt Barnard, president of Barnard's Retail Trend Report, an Upper Montclair, N.J.-based retail newsletter.

Online shopping on Black Friday also saw a tremendous surge – rising 61 percent from Black Friday last year, totaling $234.2 million for the day this year, according to BizRate.com, an online retailer, which bases its estimates on feedback from more than 2,000 retailers.

A disproportionate amount of online growth is fueled by Asian Americans, who are more likely than other consumers to shop online. Twenty-seven percent of Asian Americans report making online purchases compared to 11 percent of whites, Latinos and African Americans, according to Market Segment, a Coral Gables, Fla.-headquartered multicultural-consulting firm.

Why the strong sales growth in spite of a flailing economy? Cheap prices may be partially responsible.

"Retailers are discounting earlier than they used to," said Mike Porter, a retail analyst for Morningstar.com, a Chicago-based global-investment research firm. "Yeah, that'll hurt their margins a little bit, but it'll prop up their top line."

And it isn't hurting business that, increasingly, consumers are telling cashiers ringing up their purchases to "put it on the card."

"Good credit terms are easy to come by for pretty much everyone," said Porter. "You can finance pretty much everything over $100. You can go to the Limited and buy a jacket on credit."

"I think that sometimes we forget that even though economic times may not be the greatest right now, cash flows in peoples' households really aren't too bad," said Porter. "With home-equity loans and low, low rates, easy borrowing, no interest/ no payment financing on all kinds of things from TV on up, it's pretty easy to buy.

"And when it's easy to buy," said Porter, "people do it. That's the one thing we can count on."

What Every Retailer Must Know About Emerging Markets

By Kipp Cheng

© 2003 DiversityInc.com

May 08, 2002

Spurred by the dramatic changes of the U.S. population over the past decade, the face of the American consumer has transformed from a once largely homogenous group into a dynamic mix of people comprised of various races, lifestyles and cultures. Competitive retailers have recognized these dramatic demographic shifts, and moved to manage the needs of current and future customers and employees.

But first, who exactly are these "new" diverse customers? The answer is complicated by more than simply race.

Now more than ever, it's difficult to identify, segment and target customers, in large part because there is little hard data to describe the purchasing behavior of consumers based solely on their race. Therefore, it's critical to understand not only who these customers are, but also what they are like, how they behave and why they purchase what they do.

After all, consumers are major forces in the ever-changing retail landscape. They determine the winners and the losers in retailing, according to a study from Texas A&M University's Center of Retailing Studies (CRS). Authored by David Szymanski and Jay Scansaroli, the study, "Who's Minding the Future?," has identified "megatrends" that will influence the success or failure of a retail establishment in the years ahead.

According to the CRS report, the most compelling trend that retailers must heed is the changing ethnic and cultural composition of American consumers. In the study, Szymanski cited the transformation of the general perception of the American family as a predominantly white nuclear one to a society that recognizes and accepts multiethnic, diverse households. "America has always been a melting pot," said Szymanski, "and diversity has always been a part of the make-up of our country … [but] its magnitude continues to intensify."

The intensifying magnitude of diversity of consumers also affects the shift in employees as well. After all, consumers are employees at retail companies, and vice versa. The way that consumers respond to poor treatment (or poor customer service) has changed markedly over the years. Rather than simply walking away

What Every Retailer Must Know About Emerging Markets (cont'd.)

from a retail establishment and "voting" with their wallets by not patronizing culturally incompetent vendors, today's consumers are going one step further and demanding that retailers, in particular, recognize their needs and provide them.

In the past, consumers who felt discriminated against might simply walk out of the store and take their business elsewhere, according to Jerome Williams, an associate professor of marketing at Penn State University's Smeal College of Business. But as the Baby Boomer generation has aged and become more affluent, that mindset has begun to shift, Williams told DiversityInc.com in the article, Are Black Shoppers Treated Unfairly? An Expensive New Reason to Care.

"People today … more inclined to say, 'My dollar is a good as anyone else's and I expect to be treated equitably, ' " Williams said.

The significant shift in the country's ethnic composition has not only redefined the American family, but also the workforce that fuels retail industries. As ethnic diversity continues to rise – with Latino, African-American and Asian-American people representing 33 percent of the total U.S. population – retailers must become sensitive to the needs and expectations of the changing society.

Retail experts agreed that it's hard to ignore the obvious – as emerging markets grow in size, so too does their spending power. "The opportunity is tremendous," said Richard Feinberg, professor of retail management at Indiana's Purdue University. "African Americans, Hispanics, Asian Americans … all those populations are growing at a faster pace than white segments and they have tremendous economic clout."

In addition to race, the new American consumer is also being driven to purchase by other, less tangible factors.

Consider that more younger people control their own discretionary spending, older people are acting younger, 50 percent of the nation's wealth is controlled by women, and nearly 2 million children are now being cared for by fathers, rather than mothers. These findings in the CRS report, Szymanski said, are vivid examples of the mindset shift that retailers must heed or ignore at their peril.

"It's no longer possible to know a customer simply by looking at surface attributes, such as male/female or by ethnic group," Szymanski said in the report. "[Their] lifestyles, opinions and attitudes are much more important."

But while retailers have begun to recognize the changing American consumer, retail corporate parents have been less proactive about placing diverse workers in executive positions.

What Every Retailer Must Know About Emerging Markets (cont'd.)

According to 2000 data from the Equal Employment Opportunity Commission (EEOC), of the more than 2.6 million people who work in general merchandise stores, i.e. Wal-mart, Target and Kmart, 69.3 percent of all retail employees are white and 30.7 percent are people of color. Contrast that with the fact that more than 82 percent of officials and managers are white and less than 18 percent are people of color. While the number of managers of color have edged up slightly from 1999, when the figure was 16.8 percent of officials and managers being people of color, the increase is not in line with the shift of the general population.

Ron Edwards, director of research for the EEOC, cautioned that the figures should be used to represent a sample, rather than all retailers in the country. The data is derived from retail establishments with 50 or more employees, and therefore, many small businesses, which employ people of color, are excluded from the data set.

"So, for example, an outlet like the Gap may have some stores that have less than 50 employees, so those numbers will not be reported," Edwards said.

Edwards added that analyzing the retail sector is more complex than some other industries because of the way retailing is segmented. For example, the EEOC categorizes retail into as many as nine groups, including wholesale trade, building materials and apparel, among others.

Still, when it comes to advancement and hiring of people of color in general merchandise retail, the numbers continue to be lackluster.

Target Corp., for example, this year was sued by The EEOC for bias against job applications of color. The lawsuit, filed in the U.S. District Court for the Southern District of Wisconsin, alleges that Target employees "routinely destroyed the applications of African Americans" and of students who attended minority job fairs at Marquette University and the University of Wisconsin, Milwaukee campus. People of color make up roughly 50 percent of the population of Milwaukee.

Although a decision has not yet been handed down from the court, Target's corporate Web site goes out of its way to communicate a commitment to both supplier and workforce diversity.

So what's the holdup for the retail sector when it comes to reaching out to diverse consumers and employees? Many experts said it's simply a matter of inertia. Retailers often have long-standing relationships with non-diverse suppliers, who may not be as sensitive to the issue of changing demographics. And many retailers are simply waiting for the demographic shift of consumers to

What Every Retailer Must Know About Emerging Markets (cont'd.)

reach a "critical mass" before it becomes efficient – both from the standpoint of economics and reach – to initiate marketing programs addressing diverse consumers.

However, some retailers have decided to be proactive and reach out to emerging markets, for the sake of long-term survival. In March, Kmart hired multicultural marketing and advertising agency GlobalHue to kick off a $25 million campaign aimed at Latino and African-American consumers.

While the new multicultural marketing effort is not a first for Kmart – which has set its sights on niche markets in the past with smaller, targeted campaigns – the initiative represents the most significant monetary investment made by the retailer in marketing to emerging markets.

Retail analysts said Kmart's approach might help the beleaguered retailer to emerge from chapter 11 bankruptcy protection by reconnecting with its traditional constituency of customers of color.

The CRS report concluded that retailers need to respect varying customer lifestyles, and that respect is key to penetrating diverse markets. "[Retailers] can't do business as usual anymore," said Szymanski. "These things have bottom-line implications for all facets of retailing, from customer service, store location, services provided, and relationships with customers."

D. Media/Entertainment

The markets for media are becoming progressively narrower and deeper as more people read and view only what interests them, whether it is about their ethnicity or their personal tastes. Even in special-interest arenas, media that cater to very vertical markets are becoming.

But is the diversity of tastes, backgrounds, race, ethnicity, sexual orientation and viewpoints being lost in the wave of media consolidation, which will be accelerated by the Federal Communications Commission (FCC)'s June 2 decision to loosen the rules on media ownership?[216]

1. Owners/Employees

The new FCC rules allow a single company to own combinations of newspapers and TV and radio stations in the same city, a cross-ownership ban that had been in place since 1975.

The rules also call for lifting cross-ownership restrictions in markets with at least nine or more TV stations, a rule adopted in 1941. Smaller markets would face some restrictions and cross-ownership would be banned in markets with three or fewer TV stations.

Many television-broadcast companies, such as FOX (owned by News Corp.), CBS (owned by Viacom), and NBC (owned by General Electric), have said the old rules had far outlasted their effectiveness and placed the networks at a competitive disadvantage, in a world competing with cable television, satellite broadcasts and the Internet.

In a joint statement by the Tri-Caucus of the U.S Congress, Rep. Elijah Cummings, D-Md., chairman of the Black Caucus, Rep. Ciro Rodriguez, D-Texas, chairman of the Hispanic Caucus, and Rep. David Wu, D-Ore., chairman of the Asian-Pacific-American Caucus, said the FCC decision is "a blow to diversity, competition, and the public having access to multiple sources of information … We are extremely concerned that these new changes will significantly undermine current FCC rules that were intended to promote minority participation, and preserve multiple media voices and opinions in the electronic and print media industries."

The FCC decision was not the only diversity-related issue to impact the nation's media recently. The New York Times' public admission that it had given African-American journalist Jayson Blair less scrutiny than most reporters would receive as he plagiarized and made up information caused ripples in both journalistic and diversity-management circles. Ultimately, most agreed, it was not a failure of either diversity or affirmative-action programs, but, rather, a failure of the Times' management.

The 152-year-old newspaper is confronting its inability to understand and manage diversity – diversity of thought and opinion, as well as race and gender and sexual orientation – and it is stinging from the backlash.[217] Executive Editor Howell Raines and Managing Editor Gerald Boyd have resigned over the scandel.

When Blair's reportorial crimes were uncovered, the newspaper launched an internal probe and produced an exhaustive story that detailed each error. That investigation determined that Blair "committed frequent acts of journalistic fraud while covering significant news events in recent months."

Further, Blair "lifted material from other newspapers and wire services. He selected details from photographs to create the impression he had been somewhere or seen someone, when he had not. And he used these techniques to write falsely about emotionally charged moments in recent history, from the deadly sniper attacks in suburban Washington to the anguish of families grieving for loved ones killed in Iraq."

The New York Times admitted that internal factors – including "a failure of communication among senior editors" – allowed Blair's deceptions to continue unabated. Blair was promoted over the objections of one editor and assigned to one of the most significant stories of the year, the sniper shootings in the Washington, D.C., area.

Blair was recruited to The New York Times through a program, launched in 1995, aimed at "bringing younger and more diverse talent into our newsroom," the company said in an e-mail response to a question from DiversityInc.

But as the newspaper's own reporting reflects, diversity is a murky and ill-defined issue at The New York Times.

When he was asked if Blair was promoted because of his race, Boyd, who is African American, said: "To say now that his promotion was about diversity in my view doesn't begin to capture what was going on. He was a young, promising reporter who had done a job that warranted promotion.

Days later, when he was asked if Blair's race played a role in his assignment to the sniper story, Raines, who is white, said the newspaper "has a commitment to diversity."

"Does that mean I personally favored Jayson?" Raines added. "Not consciously. But you have a right to ask if I, as a white man from Alabama, with those convictions, gave him one chance too many by not stopping his appointment to the sniper team. When I look into my heart for the truth of that, the answer is yes."

Their answers make it clear that neither Boyd nor Raines was prepared to talk about the role of race in the newsroom; Raines left the impression that he believes "diversity" is synonymous with "substandard," according to diversity consultants interviewed.

"They just aren't ready for the question," says Keith Woods, a journalism expert from the St. Petersburg, Fla., Poynter Institute, who is African American.

Woods isn't thrilled with The New York Times' handling of the Blair debacle – primarily because the company has failed to issue a coherent statement on the value that diverse reporters bring to the newsroom.

"Race should have a role," he says. "Now, other people are going to get hurt, not because they did anything, but because the Times was clumsy."

"What often happens in situations like this is that white people, men, straight people – whoever is in the majority – will begin looking at 'those other people' and the other people will start wondering if they have been implicated by the actions of Jayson Blair," Woods adds.

2. Customers/Marketing

Most marketers today realize that going beyond the so-called mainstream and addressing diverse consumers no longer is just about intentions but it is a critical business imperative vital to future success. However, effectively reaching consumers of color, as well as those from multicultural groups such as gays and lesbians and people with disabilities, continues to challenge even the most progressive companies.[218]

As census data continue to illustrate the changing demographics of this country and financial data shows the growing economic clout of ethnic and multicultural consumers, it's clear that marketing to diverse consumers is key to future growth.

For many marketers, marketing to distinct racial and ethnic segments via targeted media has shown success. Research from The Association of National Advertisers (ANA) revealed that the predominant segments targeted by ANA members included Latinos (targeted by 70 percent of those engaged in multicultural marketing), African Americans (targeted by 59 percent) and Asian Americans (targeted by 27 percent of marketers).

Let's look at one of the most vertical and difficult markets to reach – Latinos.

Based on Nielsen Ratings, it can be easy to assume that the U.S. Latino population is watching only Spanish-language television. The top 20 shows on the National Hispanic Television Index, a service Nielsen Media Research started in 1992 to monitor Latino viewing patterns, most often are telenovelas on Univision.[219]

An analysis of Nielsen data from the 2001-2002 programming season released in August by Initiative Media, a New York-based media-services company, finds that the highest-rated English-language network program (UPN's "WWE Smackdown!") appeared at number 44 on the list of programs Latinos watched that season. However, when Latino ratings of prime-time programming from just the top six networks (ABC, CBS, NBC, FOX, UPN and WB) were evaluated, general-market programs such as "Friends" and "ER" held places in the top 10.

So Latinos are watching general-market primetime programming, but when it comes to developing media plans to reach Latino viewers, general-market shows rarely are included in the mix.

"[Advertising] agencies are saying if you want to reach the Latino market, they can be reached through Spanish-speaking networks," says Alex Nogales, president and CEO of the National Hispanic Media Coalition. "The evidence doesn't show that."

The National Hispanic Television Index surveys 800 Latino households made up of a population that has self-identified as Latino. Each participating household agrees to have a people meter, a device which sends viewing data to Nielsen on a daily basis, attached to its televisions. Nielsen wouldn't provide statistics on language preference of its Latino participants, but the company said the pool mirrors census language-preference data (51 percent Spanish-dominant, 35 percent English dominant, and 13 percent preferring Spanish and English equally).

However, studies by other organizations offer different findings. According to the Pew Hispanic Center, just 38 percent of Latinos watch or listen to predominantly Spanish-language programming, while 36 percent of Latinos watch or listen to predominantly English-language programming, and 26 percent of Latinos watch or listen to Spanish and English-language programming equally.

But despite this research, many marketers maintain that the Latino population still is Spanish-dominant.

"The assimilation model has not worked in the Hispanic market," says Raul Lopez, chief operating officer of the Cultural Access Group, a market-research and consulting firm in Los Angeles. "My parents, who have been here 40-plus years, still depend on Spanish-language TV."

Adriana Waterston, director of marketing for Horowitz Associates, a company in Larchmont, N.Y., that studies the Latino market and media usage, agrees that the Latino population often is seen as homogeneous, but she challenged the theory that Latino youth have a major influence on household television viewing. Because many Latino homes are multigenerational, many young Latinos are living with immigrant and first-generation parents and grandparents who are more likely to prefer Spanish-language programming.

"It's not an either-or situation," says Waterston. "There's opportunity for all types of programming."

"There is no one answer (to the best way to reach Latinos)," says Lopez. "Part of the population needs to be addressed in English and a large part needs to be addressed in Spanish." But ultimately, Lopez says, both groups need to be addressed in a culturally competent manner.

Tony Ruiz, partner of the New York-based Latino advertising agency The Vidal Partnership, agrees that both English- and Spanish-language programming should be used to reach Latinos; however, he offers a caveat. "Hispanic viewing of general market TV is highly fragmented over the many broadcast and cable viewing choices they have. In the past, we have taken our clients' general-market TV schedules and posted them with Hispanic Nielsen data and found the schedules delivered between 19 percent and 34 percent of their grp [gross ratings point] goal against Hispanics."

Roy Cosme, president of New York-based Latino-marketing firm Arcos Communications, agrees. "Latinos do watch some of the highly-rated shows. .... They're watching "Friends" and "Bernie Mac", but if [advertisers use general-market TV] exclusively, they would not be reaching the Latino market."

Most Latino advertising budgets aren't large enough to afford ad time during general-market prime-time programming, says John Doscher, executive vice president and director of strategic planning for New Perspectives Media, the Miami-based media-planning and buying unit of advertising giant GlobalHue. Nielsen ratings are used to determine how much networks can charge for advertising time during their shows. The higher the rating, the more it costs to advertise during the program because the commercials have the potential to reach more consumers.

According to Advertising Age's survey of prime-time ad pricing during fall 2002, a 30-second spot during "CSI," a top CBS program, cost $280,043. The cost of ad time on Spanish-language shows, which have lower Nielsen ratings than network prime-time programming, is considerably lower.

ADDITIONAL RESOURCES

PART VII - INDUSTRIES IN THE FRONT LINE

Association of National Advertisers (ANA), 708 Third Avenue, New York, New York 10017-4270. *http://www.ana.net/*

Bean, Linda. "Learn Diversity Lessons From The New York Times' Mistakes." DiversityInc, 19 May 2003. *http://www.diversityinc.com/members/4953.cfm*

Brown, C. Stone. "Are The New FCC Media Rules Anti-Diversity? Trent Lott Says Yes." DiversityInc, 3 June 2003. *http://www.diversityinc.com/members/5033.cfm*

Cheng, Kipp. "Reaching New Customers: Marketers Struggle to Hit Bull's Eye." DiversityInc, 31 January 2003. *http://www.diversityinc.com/members/4388.cfm*

Johnson, Angela D. "Is Spanish-Language TV Still Best Way to Reach Latino Viewers?" DiversityInc, 14 March 2003. *http://www.diversityinc.com/members/4607.cfm*

National Hispanic Media Coalition, 2514 South Grand Avenue, Los Angeles, CA 90007. *http://www.nhmc.org/*

Pew Hispanic Center, USC Annenberg School for Communication, 1919 M Street, NW, Suite 460, Washington, DC 20036. *http://www.pewhispanic.org/index.jsp*

Are The New FCC Media Rules Anti-Diversity? Trent Lott Says Yes

By C. Stone Brown

© 2003 DiversityInc.com

June 03, 2003

In a 3-2 vote, the Federal Communications Commission (FCC) voted Monday to relax media-ownership rules that critics say will further stifle diversity of ownership and viewpoints in print and broadcast media.

The new FCC rules allow a single company to own combinations of newspapers and TV and radio stations in the same city, a cross-ownership ban that had been in place since 1975.

Monday's rules also call for lifting cross-ownership restrictions in markets with at least nine or more TV stations, a rule adopted in 1941. Smaller market towns would face some restrictions and cross-ownership would be banned in markets with three or fewer TV stations.

Many television-broadcast companies such as FOX (owned by News Corp.), CBS (owned by Viacom), and NBC (owned by General Electric), have said the old rules had far outlasted their effectiveness and placed the networks at a competitive disadvantage, in a world competing with cable television, satellite broadcasts and the Internet.

One supporter of the rules change, NBC, said in a written statement, that this is only the beginning. "While today's decision by the FCC to update its media-ownership rules is a first step in the right direction, we have much further to go before there is a level playing field between free and pay TV. The issue will remain a priority to NBC and to all those who value free, over-the-air television. Moving forward, it is also imperative that the broadcast community unite to tackle the regulatory challenges we face in making the transition to digital television."

Opponents, however, say the advent of cable, satellite and Internet sources of news only creates an illusion of diversity of viewpoints because ownership is concentrated.

"People say there is diversity because there are so many new voices. The fact is, the top areas of the Internet where people get their news are owned by the same companies that own the broadcast stations. The top 50 channels on cable televi-

Are The New FCC Media Rules Anti-Diversity? Trent Lott Says Yes (cont'd.)

sion, 90 percent of them, are owned by the same companies that owned the broadcast stations, said Sen. Byron Dorgan, D-S.D., at a Senate Commerce Committee news conference following the FCC vote.

Dorgan who was joined by fellow committee members, Sen. Trent Lott, R-Miss., and Sen. Fritz Hollings, R-S.C., said there were a few winners in the FCC ruling on Monday. "Some interests are celebrating, but they are big interests. Billionaire enterprises won, hometowns of America lost with this decision," said Dorgan.

Surprisingly, critics of the rules change are spread across the political spectrum, ranging from the National Association for the Advancement of Colored People and religious groups to the National Rifle Association. "I think this is a mistake," said Lott, who has a strong conservative voting record and who was under attack by liberals for insensitive comments he made and later apologized for at Sen. Strom Thurmond's 100th birthday party, adding that the FCC has gone too far this time.

"I've been very disappointed in the way the FCC has handled it," said Lott, who said he sometimes favors big business. "I'm not one that has believed always that big is necessarily always bad. I think that sometimes mergers, if they make, you know, good sense in terms of access to the people or businesses, you have to weigh that. That's what we trust an FCC for.

"But when you allow this type of concentration, where you could have a market where one company could own and dominate the print media, could theoretically own one of the dish networks, could own the local cable, could own the local television station or two stations, where is the limit?" he asked.

The outcome of the vote didn't come as a surprise. As early as Sunday, FCC Chairman Michael Powell, a vocal supporter for lifting the ban, said on ABC News the rule changes wouldn't have as severe an impact as critics charged and has said before the rules change would enhance the cause of diversity. "This is not a complete deregulation of the media ... There will be rules and restrictions. Everything that a media company would like to do is not going to be permitted."

"The idea that you're going to get more competition on local TV by having fewer owners is just ridiculous, said Jim Naureckas, editor of Fairness and Accuracy in Reporting (FAIR), a media-watchdog group based in New York.

Naureckas pointed to the example of the 1996 Telecommunication Act. "If you want to see what this is going to do to television news, turn on your radio and listen to what the radio sounds like. Listen to how many commercials are on there; listen to how rarely you see original programming on the radio."

Are The New FCC Media Rules Anti-Diversity? Trent Lott Says Yes (cont'd.)

In a joint statement by the Tri-Caucus of the U.S Congress, Rep. Elijah Cummings, D-Md., chairman of the Black Caucus, Rep. Ciro Rodriguez, D-Texas., chairman of the Hispanic Caucus, and Rep. David Wu, D-Ore., chairman of the AsianPacific-American Caucus, said the FCC decision is "a blow to diversity, competition, and the public having access to multiple sources of information … We are extremely concerned that these new changes will significantly undermine current FCC rules that were intended to promote minority participation, and preserve multiple media voices and opinions in the electronic and print media industries."

The Tri-Caucus cited a study by Santa Clara University and the University of Missouri that determined that diverse ownership encourages diverse content in the media. According to a study by the Department of Commerce, in 2000, people of color owned 248 AM radio stations and 178 FM stations, representing 4 percent of the country's 10,577 commercial AM and FM radio stations. However, since the passage of the 1996 Telecommunications Act, which lifted ownership restrictions on radio ownership, the overall number of radio-station owners has decreased by 30 percent.

Many of the critics opposing the rules change targeted Rupert Murdoch, whose News Corp. owns FOX News Channel, 20th Century FOX TV and film studios, the New York Post and several other media properties. According to the Associated Press, Murdoch told a Senate committee last month he has no plan for a media buying spree after the changes, other than his proposed acquisition of DirecTV, the nation's largest satellite-television provider.

'Boy Meets Boy': Will The Advertisers Go for It?

By Angela D. Johnson

© *2003 DiversityInc.com*

June 04, 2003

Gay, lesbian, bisexual and transgender (GLBT) people have played a role in reality television programs since 1973, when Lance Loud came out to his parents during the filming of PBS's "An American Family." However, with the introduction of two Bravo programs this summer, GLBTs will, for the first time, become the central focus in the current wave of dating and makeover reality shows. In addition to diversifying the genre, Bravo's programming also is contributing to the diversity of media outlets available to advertisers hoping to tap into the GLBT consumer market.

"There are very few effective broadcast vehicles to reach gay consumers," said Howard Buford, founder and CEO of Prime Access, a New York-based advertising agency specializing in the gay and ethnic markets. "This seems to be a kind of pushing the envelope in programming for the gay audience. These programs should be of interest to a number of advertisers."

"Boy Meets Boy," a six-part series that is being touted as the first gay dating series, features a gay leading man who must pick a mate from a pool of bachelors – including a few straight guys. In "A Queer Eye for the Straight Guy," a makeover series that begins airing in July, five gay consultants take on the task of performing a lifestyle transformation on a heterosexual man.

Bob Witeck, founding partner of Witeck-Combs Communications in Washington, D.C., said Bravo has been a leader in the burgeoning area of gay-themed broadcast television programming. In 2000, the network aired "Fire Island," a series which chronicled the summer adventures of one gay and one lesbian couple at the Long Island, N.Y. beach locale. Last fall, the cable network broadcast "Gay Weddings," a documentary-style serial that followed the ups and downs of four GLBT couples as they planned their impending nuptials.

Bravo, founded in 1980, has been part of the NBC family since December 2002. NBC's network has found success incorporating gay issues in shows such as "Will & Grace," a prime-time sitcom featuring two gay lead characters. The company reaches another diverse market, Latinos, through its ownership of Telemundo and mun2. These examples of inclusion make the fact that NBC also

'Boy Meets Boy': Will The Advertisers Go for It? (cont'd.)

supports Michael Savage, a commentator known for espousing racist and homophobic views, troubling.

In March 2003, MSNBC, the cable-news channel run by NBC, began airing Savage's talk show "Savage Nation." GLAAD (the Gay & Lesbian Alliance Against Defamation), launched a campaign asking advertisers to not support Savage's show. In light of the controversy surrounding Savage, companies including Procter & Gamble, Dell Computer Corporation, Casual Male, Idea Village, Cole Media Group and The Sharper Image, pulled their advertising.

"MSNBC does seem to be an anomaly in the NBC family," said Cathy Renna, news media director for GLAAD. "NBC, the network news and the entertainment side in primetime, has been very inclusive. Bravo is an example of attempt to be more fair and accurate.… That's why the continuing support of the Savage program is really disappointing."

Bravo representatives were not available to comment on the channel's new shows or Bravo's role in the NBC family.

Renna said she is intrigued by the "Boy Meets Boy" concept.

"We've certainly advocated for and seen the inclusion of gay and lesbian people but our eyebrows are definitely raised by the fact that half of the bachelors are straight," said Renna. "We want to be included. The place to careful is when people are being exploited because of their sexual orientation."

In the absence of gay-themed television programming, marketers have traditionally turned to print and online vehicles such as Out, The Advocate, and PlanetOut.com to reach GLBT consumers. In the broadcast arena, channels such as Showtime and HBO have been ground-breaking in addressing GLBT issues, but they have not offered the advertising opportunities Bravo's shows provide. The advent of more gay-themed programming will position television as a more effective medium for reaching the GLBT market, which, according to the Selig Center for Economic Growth at the University of Georgia, harnesses roughly $450 billion in buying power.

"If you talk to gay and lesbian consumers in focus groups, they tell you very directly that they have a strong preference for advertising that reflects who they are," Buford said.

However, because there have been very few broadcast vehicles specifically reaching the gay market, there is a dearth of gay-specific television ad creative. Witeck predicts that the Bravo programming will be supported by some gay-vague commercials, but the bulk will be ads designed for the general market.

'Boy Meets Boy': Will The Advertisers Go for It? (cont'd.)

"Advertisers will have to be careful not to air advertising that alienates the market," said Buford. "They definitely want to choose their most gay-friendly executions."

Witeck said, ultimately, it will be the economic climate, not program content, which will dictate whether companies support Bravo's new shows with general market or gay-specific advertising spots.

"With advertising depressed across the board, it's more problematic," said Witeck. "When the economy is more robust, companies will take more chances. Finding the audience is the journey. That's what [advertising] is all about."

Hollywood's Female Powerbrokers: How They're Changing the Game

By Yoji Cole

© 2003 DiversityInc.com

May 05, 2003

Early in her career, Helene Hahn was confronted with the realities of corporate life. In the mid 1970s, Hahn was a young program attorney at the ABC television network. She remembers being one of a few women in the department, putting in long hours at the office and accomplishing the goals that should have assured promotion, but she always was overlooked.

Hahn finally asked her boss why promotions that she should have been granted were given to others and was told she needed to show more of her coquettish side at the office.

"He said I didn't flirt with him so that meant I wasn't interested in this department," says Hahn.

Now, as co-COO of the Los Angeles-based film studio DreamWorks SKG, Hahn is on the industry's "Power 100" list of Hollywood's top female executives, a group which has come a long way in the past 10 years since Sherry Lansing broke through the glass ceiling to become the first woman to chair a film studio when she took the helm at Paramount Pictures in 1992.

By 2000, three other women chaired major motion-picture studios in Hollywood: Laurie MacDonald at DreamWorks, Stacey Snider at Universal and Amy Pascal at Columbia.

Earning the coveted spot of chair of a movie studio is an amazing accomplishment for any woman or man. To become a chair, a person must scratch and claw through the ultra-competitive trenches of the entertainment industry. The women who chair studios, however, bring more than tenacity to their respective organizations and, to a larger extent, the industry as a whole. Overall, they started their climbs up Hollywood's executive ladder from the bottom rung and developed a boot-strap work ethic, a sense of teamwork, and a broad understanding of consumer markets.

"The women getting these top executive jobs are all individuals who have divergent skills – the ability to focus on profits and be effective team-oriented leaders, while dealing with an array of talented and highly unpredictable people, namely

Hollywood's Female Powerbrokers: How They're Changing the Game (cont'd.)

writers, actors and directors," says Denise Mann, chair of the producers program at the University of California – Los Angeles Department of Film and Television.

Their successes, though, should not suggest that women are on par with men in the film industry. Numbers on the amount of women who hold executive positions in the motion-picture industry, and on a larger scale the entertainment industry, range from bleak to promising.

Entertainment-company boards claim only a few women among their members, and women hold just 3 percent of senior media positions, such as chair, CEO or president, according to the Hollywood Reporter, the industry's trade publication. And in 2001, of the leadership of 10 entertainment conglomerates, women comprised only 13 percent of directors and 14 percent of executives – Fox Entertainment and USA Networks did not feature any women in their top executive ranks in their annual reports for that year while Clear Channel and AMC Entertainment had no women on their boards, according to The Annenberg Public Policy Center of the University of Pennsylvania.

When focusing solely on the major motion-picture industry, however, the U.S. Equal Employment Opportunity Commission (EEOC), provides a more promising outlook. The film industry, according to the EEOC, in 2001 employed 36,973 people nationally. Of that number, the EEOC recognized 8,086 as officials and managers or people whose occupations provided them support personnel in addition to setting, "broad policies, exercising overall responsibility for execution of these policies, and directing individual departments or special phases of a firm's operations." Of those positions 3,507, or 43.4 percent, were filled by women, while 4,579 or 56.6 percent were filled by men.

Film-industry experts, such as Martha Lauzen, professor in the School of Communication, San Diego State University, however, believe the EEOC casts a wide net with its category "officials and managers," which inflates the number of women who are in executive managerial positions in the motion-picture industry.

Lauzen, who is regarded in industry circles as the most reliable source on the hiring practices of people behind and before the camera, semiannually releases her own study. In 2001, her study found, men directed more than nine out of 10 films and served as cinematographers on virtually every one, while women comprised 19 percent of executive producers, producers, directors, writers, cinematographers and editors who worked on the top 250 domestic grossing films. As for on-camera talent: Male actors worked twice as many days as female actors in 2001, hoarding 62 percent of the roles. For female parts, the industry tended to opt for younger women, with actresses older than 40 garnering just 27 percent of female

Hollywood's Female Powerbrokers: How They're Changing the Game (cont'd.)

roles and 10 percent of all roles, according to the Screen Actors Guild.

While actresses work less than actors, women are seeing meatier roles and it is more common now for a film to center on a female lead, which lends credence to the argument that comfort with a woman in the role of chair fosters more strong women lead characters or story lines to drive ticket sales. Of the movies that grossed more than $10 million domestically over the past year, the number of films that featured a female lead increased 45 percent, from 20 in 2001 to 29 in 2002, according to The Hollywood Reporter. While the female chairs of Hollywood film studios can't take all the credit for that, a look at the films backed by Pascal, chair of Columbia, and Snider, chair of Universal, may provide evidence that suggests they see opportunity in diverse consumer markets.

Pascal is responsible for overseeing all development and production activities at Columbia, which is a division of Sony Pictures Entertainment, where she doubles as vice chair. Her past and future projects feature a treasure trove of diverse box-office success, both before and behind the camera. Four highly anticipated projects include: Latino director Robert Rodriguez's "Once Upon A Time in Mexico," a sequel to "Desperado," starring the Latino heartthrob Antonio Banderas as the mythic hero El Mariachi; "Charlie's Angels: Full Throttle," which stars actresses Cameron Diaz, Drew Barrymore and Lucy Liu; the third project brings together two African-American male actors, Will Smith and Martin Lawrence, in the sequel "Bad Boys 2"; and "SWAT," starring African-American actor Samuel L. Jackson.

Pascal showed her eye for a blockbuster when she oversaw the production of 2002's "Spider-Man," which grossed $404 million in total domestic box-office sales and more than $800 million worldwide.

Snider is responsible for all production, marketing and domestic distribution activities for Universal. She oversaw or currently supervises the production of films such as "Honey," starring African-American actor Mekhi Pfeiffer of NBC's "ER," "The Guru," starring British actor Jimi Mistry, who is of Indian descent, and 1998's "One True Thing," for which Meryl Streep received an Academy Award nomination as Best Actress.

It is to the credit of Pascal, Snider and the rest of the film industry's top female executives that they learned the business in entry-level positions and worked their way up, says Mann.

"As they developed through the ranks, it was their job to find great writers and directors and other members of creative teams," says Mann. "One socially rein-

Hollywood's Female Powerbrokers: How They're Changing the Game (cont'd.)

forced attribute of women that seems to have assisted these women is the idea that women use teamwork more. Teamwork is absolutely there and I do think that women have a different way of reinforcing teamwork and developing cooperation among members of their team."

Perhaps the team theme is why women have thrived at DreamWorks SKG studios. The company, which was formed in 1994 by its three principal partners – Jeffrey Katzenberg, Steven Spielberg and David Geffen – boasts not only Hahn and MacDonald in its top executive positions, but Terry Press as its head of marketing and Ann Daly as its head of feature animation. The company brass also pride themselves in bringing a more personal and open approach to deal-making in Hollywood, which stands in stark contrast to industry stalwarts Sony Pictures Entertainment, Universal, 20th Century Fox and Paramount. "Being available" not only to directors, actors and writers but employees is a trait, Hahn says, that she and Katzenberg have tried to maintain to provide that personal touch. Another characteristic of a more personal studio is doing away with corporate titles, which both Hahn and Katzenberg decided to implement when DreamWorks was launched.

"I try to see people as individuals and to allow flexibility in their jobs," says Hahn. "It's tough making deals. We should treat people well on the other side, be quick to respond and always available."

Hahn signs off on the financing of all of DreamWorks' movies and partnerships, while MacDonald, in her position as co-head, deals with the creative side. In 2002, MacDonald produced "Men in Black II," which starred Will Smith and Tommy Lee Jones, and "Minority Report," which starred Tom Cruise and was directed by Spielberg.

Partnerships for DreamWorks have proven fruitful in past years. The studio teamed with Columbia on "Men in Black II," with Universal on "Gladiator" (2000) and "A Beautiful Mind" (2001) – both winners of Best Picture awards at their respective Oscar ceremonies – with Paramount on "Deep Impact" (1998) and "Saving Private Ryan" (1998), as well as with 20th Century Fox on "What Lies Beneath" (2001).

"I make every deal," says Hahn, who in 2002 brokered a cash infusion through refinancing from JPMorgan Chase and FleetBoston Financial Corp., which the studio plans to use to expand its animation facilities as well as its live-action film production. She also negotiated a two-year, seven-figure deal with NBC, which provides the network a first look at all TV drama, comedy and reality projects developed by DreamWorks.

Hollywood's Female Powerbrokers: How They're Changing the Game (cont'd.)

After her rocky start at ABC, Hahn moved to Paramount in 1977, where she started as an attorney in the motion-picture legal department and finished as senior vice president of the business-affairs department in 1984. "When I started, there were very few women in this industry," says Hahn. "You'd often be the only woman in the room during a meeting."

Mentors were tough to come by. When Hahn moved to Paramount she had two male supervisors, Jeffrey Katzenberg and Michael Eisner. Katzenberg took a liking to her work ethic. When he moved to Walt Disney Studios with Eisner, he asked that she join him as head of the company's business-affairs department. When she joined DreamWorks, she left Disney as the executive vice president of Walt Disney Studios. Hahn chose to develop the mentor/mentee relationship with Katzenberg because she saw that he valued the business side of the film industry and valued the way she conducted business, she says.

She suggests that women in corporate America who seek a mentor "find somebody who appreciates [your personality], your work and the quality of your work. If you can't find that, then sometimes it's better to move on."

Female executives in Hollywood also are utilizing the tastes of diverse consumer markets to help their movies succeed. As a result, women are featured as strong female protagonists in a variety of movies that also saw box-office success. For example, in 2001 women were the lead characters in comedies such as "The Princess Diaries," starring Julie Andrews and Anne Hathaway, and "Legally Blonde," starring Reese Witherspoon. Female characters were featured in suspense thrillers such as "The Others," starring Nicole Kidman, as well as action films, such as "Lara Croft: Tomb Raider," starring Angelina Jolie. Each of those films grossed close to or more than $100 million.

"Somebody had to take a risk and green-light those movies and the risk paid off so that's why we have more," says Orly Adelson, producer of ESPN's TV movie "The Junction Boys" (2002). "The industry is realizing that there is diversity within the female consumer group."

Adelson concedes that there will always be a group of men who rule the roost because, "women have more complexities in their lives" and that women still must tread between being too assertive and too gracious in Hollywood's corporate offices. But in general, however, it seems the industry is open to women producing more than female-themed motion pictures, which is caused in part by the success of the female chairs, she says. "They opened the doors for us and we're marching through those doors," says Adelson, who also is a member of Women In Film, a group that created the Crystal Awards and Lucy Awards to recognize the accomplishments of women in the film industry.

Hollywood's Female Powerbrokers: How They're Changing the Game (cont'd.)

Adelson, as producer of "The Junction Boys," is an example of a woman who was provided an opportunity that wouldn't have come her way years ago. In addition to her production of the football picture "The Junction Boys," she will produce for the cable-sports network a movie about the Ice Bowl, the 1967 NFL Championship game between the Green Bay Packers and Dallas Cowboys in which the temperature at game time registered a frigid 13 degrees below zero.

"Today, they don't say a woman can't produce a football movie," says Adelson. "Today, they look for someone who can tell a story and that's a telling change because I don't think 10 years ago someone would have thought of a woman doing a football movie."

E. Pharmaceuticals/Health Care

For both the health-care and pharmaceuticals industries, reaching people of color is increasingly critical. Yet in both industries, cultural competency in dealing with customers and effective recruitment of diverse employees are in their infancy.

1. Employees

The pharmaceutical industry is facing a dilemma: Consumers are becoming more diverse but efforts to hire employees who can relate to these consumers often flounder. Some drug companies still haven't realized that they need to make this recruiting effort in the first place.[220]

Pharmaceutical companies sell over-the-counter drugs to consumers as well as prescription medicines to doctors and hospitals. So, if a pharmaceutical company does not employ people who understand how to market products to the Latino mother who buys drug products for her family, for example, or a group of Asian-Indian physicians, then sales revenue clearly will be diminished.

"Most of our diversity recruitment is in the areas of sales and marketing because we need to have salespeople who can respond to doctors and various organizations that are health-care groups," says Janet Portzer, director of U.S. diversity for GlaxoSmithKline (GSK). "The sales and marketing teams are our face to the large buyers, like Wal-Mart and the pharmacies. If they're aiming to look like the world, we need to as well."

To find recruits of color, GSK advertises its employment opportunities with specialty Web sites and attends job fairs at Historically Black Colleges and Universities plus other schools that have a large number of students of color. Of GSK's 24,000 U.S. employees – 100,000 people worldwide – 19 percent are people of color and 51 percent are women, says Portzer. The company spent $30,752 in 2002 on advertising in the magazines Jet, Black Enterprise and The Advocate out of a total spend of $259,274, according to New York-based research firm CMR, which tracks national advertising.

Diversity recruitment also was important to Wyeth Pharmaceuticals, which in 2002 enhanced its quarterly diversity metrics report, making it available to its human-resources department and senior managers. The enhanced report includes placement rates for women and employees of color, their overall representation, as well as the rates at which they resign and are terminated or laid off. Those figures were not made available for this article.

The Collegeville, Pa.,-based Wyeth Pharmaceuticals and Wyeth Corporate have for the past two and six years, respectively, partnered with INROADS, an organization that specializes in placing students of color in corporate internships, says Doug Petkus, spokesperson for Wyeth. Over the years, the company has hosted 30 interns, but only recently made its first full-time hire from the organization. The company also partners with the National Black MBA Association, the National Society of Hispanic MBAs, the National Association of Black Accountants and the Temple MARC Program, which also places diverse candidates in internships.

"Diversity links to creativity, which links to discovery, which leads to development, which links to profitability," says Petkus.

Wyeth lists most of its employment opportunities on a major Internet job board, from which they are linked to smaller job boards that attract diverse job seekers, says Petkus. As for advertising with magazines geared toward diverse readers, the company worked with one in 2002, Ebony, with which it spent $9,788. Its total spend on advertisements in magazines in 2002 was $184,170, according to CMR.

Companies also are focused on developing retention methods and creating a pipeline of future recruits by building interest in the pharmaceutical industry among diverse students who have yet to enter high school.

As a means to retain diverse employees once they're hired, New York-based Pfizer established a global leadership-effectiveness group with the responsibility of identifying and developing future company leaders, says Solade Rowe, manager of university relations and diversity recruitment for Pfizer.

"This group is charged with making sure we have a diverse balance within the various areas of Pfizer," Rowe says.

Wyeth sought to establish incentives for diversity recruitment by including diversity in reviews of senior management and creating development programs for diverse employees. Management is to identify high-potential female employees and employees of color and complete an individual development plan for each such employee. The company's succession-planning procedures, in which employees who can replace managers in key positions are identified, also must include a review of female employees and employees of color, says Petkus.

Diversity-pipeline issues are being addressed by GSK, which is attempting to create diverse employees of the future by tapping into middle schools. The aim is to ensure that students of color are engaged in their math and science courses, which are part-and-parcel of the foundation for future research-and-development scientists. Since pharmaceutical companies tend to hire Ph.D.s over medical doctors, it's important that math and science become a focus for middle-school students who will have to build a strong foundation in those two subjects to eventually earn doctorate degrees. Latinos and African Americans who are interested in the medical field, however, tend to become physicians rather than Ph.D.s, says Portzer.

"Certain groups, such as African Americans, don't traditionally think of our industry, but send students to medical school, but not for their Ph.D.," says Portzer, who adds that the industry must educate diverse communities on the opportunities the pharmaceutical industry provides not only for doctorate employees but also sales and marketing people.

2. Customers

Data from the 2000 U.S. Census revealed that 17.9 percent of those 5 years old and older speak a language other than English at home, with nearly half of those claiming to speak English less than "very well." Percentages are significantly higher in metropolitan areas, such as Miami, Chicago, New York City, and San Francisco. One out of 10 of those speaking a foreign language at home converse in Spanish, while 3.8 percent use other Indo-European languages and 2.7 percent rely on Asian or Pacific Island dialects.[221]

Research has shown that limited English proficiency can have a significant impact on perception and delivery of quality patient care and compliance with treatment plans. A 1999 study published in the Journal of General Internal Medicine found that 52 percent of non-English speaking patients were satisfied with emergency room medical care compared to 71 percent of English speakers. A 2000 study in the same journal revealed that those with language barriers were less likely to be given a follow-up appointment after an emergency room visit.

To ensure that all patients receive culturally and linguistically appropriate health care, several organizations have issued guidelines for health-care providers. In December 2000, the Office of Minority Health published the National Standards for Culturally and Linguistically Appropriate Services with the Federal Register. In addition to guidelines and recommendations for providing culturally competent care and suggestions of structure, policies and procedures to implement these services, the document includes mandates for language services, which are enforced by the Office of Civil Rights (OCR).

Under Title VI of the Civil Rights Act of 1964, any organization or individual that receives federal financial assistance, either directly or indirectly, through a grant, contract or subcontract, must ensure that persons with limited English skills can effectively access critical health and social services. The title is designed to protect against discrimination based on race, ethnicity or national origin.

While hospitals have some flexibility in how they fulfill their language-assistance obligations, the Office of Civil Rights has found that effective programs usually include the following four elements:

- Assessment of the language needs of the population being served.

- Development and implementation of a comprehensive written policy that will ensure meaningful communication.

- Training to increase staff members' understanding of the policy and ability to carry it out.

- A regular monitoring of the language-assistance program to ensure that those with limited English proficiency have access to the program.

Some hospitals rely on untrained interpreters, including family members, to serve their foreign-language-speaking populations, despite federal mandates that call for professional translators. A recent study by the Commonwealth Fund found that just half of Latinos who reported needing an interpreter during a medical visit said they usually or always were provided with one.

Just 1 percent of those who were provided with interpreters had a trained medical interpreter. More than half (55 percent) had a staff member acting as a translator, while 43 percent used a family member or friend.

3. Marketing

For pharmaceutical companies that have acknowledged the market potential in multicultural communities, the challenge is figuring about the best way to reach them. Vehicles, such as neighborhood pharmacists and targeted media, can be effective strategies.

Jim Wilson, president of Wilson Health Information, a research company in New Hope, Pa., says his company's WilsonRx Ethnic Market Report tracks Latino, African-American and Asian-American views of pharmacy issues. While the study, conducted in English, doesn't include Spanish- and Asian-language-dominant consumers, it offers some insight into the multicultural market's perceptions of the pharmaceutical industry.

Wilson says research found that multicultural consumers spend an average of $1,800 to $2,400 a year on prescription drugs, an amount that's probably 60 percent to 70 percent lower than actual figures because it doesn't take into account money contributed by third parties, such as health-insurance providers.

According to the study, 73 percent of Latinos, 66 percent of Asian Americans and 63 percent of African Americans spoke to their pharmacist about their last new prescription. African Americans spent the most time talking to their pharmacist, averaging a six-minute conversation. Latinos and Asian Americans had shorter discussions, five minutes and three minutes, respectively.

Despite relying on pharmacists for information, less than half of Latinos, African Americans and Asian Americans surveyed said they were highly satisfied with the information and counseling they received. Wilson attributes this dissatisfaction to pharmacists' lack of experience in dealing with people of color and the lack of materials available in-language or in-culture.

"There are 55,000 pharmacies and 150,000 pharmacists [in the country], but how many of them are bilingual?" Wilson says. "Pharmacies

491

aren't delivering the high level of satisfaction. ... There's a great opportunity [for pharmaceutical companies] to partner with pharmacies for prescription or over-the-counter medications."

Pharmaceutical companies also are failing to take advantage of targeted media to reach multicultural consumers. Arthur Korant, co-founder and creative director for New York marketing agency Double Platinum, says this especially is true in the gay and lesbian communities. Conditions such as breast cancer, stress and anxiety, substance abuse and hepatitis are prevalent among gay and lesbian consumers. However, pharmaceutical companies are promoting only their HIV and AIDS drugs in publications targeting these communities. Korant says because gays and lesbians may not consume the same media as the general market, they are not getting information about drugs to treat non-AIDS-related illnesses.

"There's a resonance in marketing to people where they live," says Korant. "The resonance of a community that a company speaks to in their own voice is significant."

Latinos and African Americans exhibit a higher incidence of diseases such as diabetes, hypertension and asthma. However, they rarely are included in clinical trials for drugs designed to help manage these illnesses.[222]

White men are not the only people who get sick, says Sarah Harrison, vice president, customer strategy integration and public affairs for AstraZeneca. "We need to have tomorrow's trials represent everyone."

Kimberly France, director, global professional affairs at Wyeth Pharmaceuticals, agrees. "It's embarrassing to include these groups in our ads and not have the medical data about how these drugs work [on ethnic populations]," she said.

When it comes to targeting Latino, African-American and Asian-American consumers, the pharmaceutical industry is in its nascence. Industries such as financial services and packaged goods have been in the multicultural marketplace for more than 15 years. However, pharmaceutical marketers have just started to develop a business case for multicultural marketing over the past few years.

Much of this lag can be attributed to a lack of cultural competence among pharmaceutical companies. There are few people of color in pharmaceutical companies' sales, marketing, and development teams. Because of this, many of these marketers fail to consider the cultural differences that influence how African Americans, Latinos and Asian Americans cope with illness and perceive the health-care industry.

Pharmaceutical companies also have limited insight into what resonates with multicultural consumers. France provides an example of how her company missed the mark. In order to reach African-American consumers, Wyeth placed a general-market ad for a hormone-replacement-therapy drug in Ebony magazine. The ad featured actress Lauren Hutton and was the only one in the magazine to feature a white model or spokesperson. The company thought placing an ad in Ebony showed a commitment to the African-American market. However, France says the ad probably did more harm than good because it illustrated that the company didn't have a true understanding of these consumers.

General-market advertising is not enough to reach multicultural consumers, says Mark Robertson, director of business development for the UniWorld Group. "We need to send a personal invitation that links to cultural traits," he says.

Robertson advises pharmaceutical marketers to pay attention to cultural distinctions, such as the role of the church as a vital source of health-care information for African Americans and the position of the neighborhood pharmacist as a consulting physician for many Latinos.

Once pharmaceutical marketers are up to speed on the nuances of multicultural consumers, they should be encouraged to educate the physicians with whom they work. Most people of color are seen by doctors of a different race or ethnicity, which increases the chance of miscommunication between physician and patient.

Dr. S. Jayashankar, past president of the Association of Physicians of Asian Indian Origin, said that cultural humility is key in successful relationships between physicians and patients of color. He said doctors must stress sincerity without falling into patterns of using stereotypes, being condescending, or exhibiting cultural arrogance.[223]

ADDITIONAL RESOURCES

PART VII - INDUSTRIES IN THE FRONT LINE

Association of Physicians of Asian Indian Origin, 17W300 22nd St, Suite 300A, Oakbrook Terrace, IL 60181-4490 630.530.2277 *http://www.aapiusa.org/aapi.nsf*

Cole, Yoji. "Pharmaceutical Industry: Diversity Recruiting Still in Its Infancy." DiversityInc (Magazine), June/July 2003.

Johnson, Angela D. "Are Doctors Best Way for Drug Companies to Reach Diverse Consumers?" DiversityInc, 20 March 2003. *http://www.diversityinc.com/members/4639.cfm*

Johnson, Angela D. "Cultural Competency Is Rx for Success in Pharmaceutical Marketing," DiversityInc, 19 March 2003. *http://www.diversityinc.com/members/4632.cfm*

Johnson, Angela D. "Is Your Hospital Culturally Competent? Language Barriers Get in the Way," DiversityInc, 2 May 2003. *http://www.diversityinc.com/members/4868.cfm*

INROADS, Inc., 10 South Broadway, Suite 700, St. Louis, Missouri 63102 (314) 241-7488. *http://www.inroads.org/*

National Association of Black Accountants, 7249-A Hanover Parkway, Greenbelt, Maryland 20770 (301) 474-NABA. *http://www.nabainc.org/*

National Black MBA Association, 180 N. Michigan Ave., Suite 1400, Chicago, IL 60601 (312) 236-BMBA (2622). *http://www.nbmbaa.org/*

National Society of Hispanic MBAs, 1303 Walnut Hill Lane, Suite 300, Irving, TX 75038 (877) 467-4622. *http://www.nshmba.org/*

Office of Minority Health Resource Center, P.O. Box 37337, Washington, D.C. 20013-7337 1-800-444-6472. *http://www.omhrc.gov/omhrc/*

Pharmaceutical Research and Manufacturers of America (PhRMA), 1100 Fifteenth Street, NW, Washington, DC 20005 (202)-835-3400. *http://www.phrma.org/*

Pharmaceutical Industry Diversity Recruiting Still in Its Infancy

© 2003 DiversityInc.com

By Yoji Cole

The pharmaceutical industry is facing a dilemma: Consumers are becoming more diverse but efforts to hire employees who can relate to these consumers often flounder. Some drug companies still haven't realized that they need to make this recruiting effort in the first place.

Pharmaceutical companies sell both over-the-counter drugs to consumers as well as prescription medicines to doctors and hospitals. So, if a pharmaceutical company does not employ people who understand how to market products to the Latino mother who buys drug products for her family, for example, or a group of Asian-Indian physicians, then sales revenue clearly will be diminished.

"The sales people in the pharmaceutical industry are waking up," says Rupa Ranganathan, ethnic strategist and senior vice president of Strategic Research Institute, a New York-based organization that creates, produces and manages multicultural conferences.

"We've seen that there is an increase in the number of pharmaceutical companies that are coming to multicultural conferences to learn about different ethnic markets and see how successful they would be marketing to Asian Americans, African Americans and Latinos," Ranganathan says. "Medical marketers want to know how they can market to the African-American Cardiologists Association. If they want to reach more Asian doctors, [they want to know] how they can talk to the American Association of Physicians of Indian Origin."

The industry's foray into emerging markets follows years in which research-and-development costs continually have climbed. The pharmaceutical industry is the most research-intensive industry in the nation and in the past 25 years steadily has increased its investment in research and development, according to the Pharmaceutical Research and Manufacturers of America (PhRMA), the industry's lobbying group.

To keep ahead of costs, bring in new talent and a pipeline of products, the industry has experienced some mega-mergers, such as GlaxoWellcome with SmithKline and Pfizer with Warner-Lambert and Pharmacia. Most consumer revenue is from products for chronic rather than acute diseases and from older con-

Pharmaceutical Industry (cont'd.)

sumers, who consume three times as many drugs as younger people. The Baby-Boomer generation is an important demographic for this industry. Its approximately 77.5 million members range in age from 39 to 57 and, according to the U.S. Census Bureau, have a ratio of one person of color to every 2.8 white people .

Never before has it been so important for drug companies to attract as many consumers as possible to their products. And yet, while Ranganathan and others say drug companies are seeking diverse recruits at their events, many major pharmaceutical companies declined to be interviewed for this article, saying they didn't have any ongoing diversity-recruitment efforts.

For those who are beginning efforts to recruit diverse people, the methods are varied. "One way they reach our members is by placing advertising [in our organization's magazines] that will direct prospects to their Web sites," says Pamela Sharif, magazine publisher for the National Society of Black Engineers.

Advertising in magazines that attract people of color, gays and lesbians, and other diverse groups is an excellent method for attracting diverse prospects. Diverse people pay more attention to advertising efforts that appear in the publications targeted at them than to advertisements in mainstream magazines; it's like receiving a personal invitation to a party rather than getting an invitation through a friend of a friend.

But according to New York-based research firm CMR, which tracks national advertising, from January to December 2002, 79 pharmaceutical companies – a list that included the industry's top 10 – spent $2.2 million with magazines that specifically target diverse consumers, such as Black Enterprise and Jet for African-American consumers, The Advocate and Out for gay and lesbian consumers and Latina and RD Selecciones for Latino consumers. None of NSBE's magazines, which include Career Engineer and NSBE Magazine appeared on CMR's list of media used by pharmaceutical companies. By comparison, that same year General Motors, Ford Motor Company and DaimlerChrysler spent $3.96 million among magazines that specifically target diverse consumers, according to CMR.

"Most of our diversity recruitment is in the areas of sales and marketing because we need to have sales people who can respond to doctors and various organizations that are health-care groups," says Janet Portzer, director U.S. diversity for GlaxoSmithKline. "The sales and marketing teams are our face to the large buyers, like Wal-Mart and the pharmacies. If they're aiming to look like the world we need to as well."

Pharmaceutical Industry (cont'd.)

To find recruits of color, GlaxoSmithKline (GSK) advertises its employment opportunities with specialty Web sites and attends job fairs at Historically Black Colleges and Universities plus other schools that have a large number of students of color. Of GSK's 24,000 U.S. employees – 100,000 people worldwide – 19 percent are people of color and 51 percent are women, says Portzer. The company spent $30,752 in 2002 on advertising in the magazines Jet, Black Enterprise and The Advocate out of a total spend of $259,274, according to CMR.

Diversity recruitment also was important to Wyeth Pharmaceuticals, which in 2002 enhanced its quarterly diversity metrics report, making it available to its human-resources department and senior managers. The enhanced report includes placement rates for women and employees of color, their overall representation as well as the rates at which they resign and are terminated or laid off. Those figures were not made available for this article.

The Collegeville, Pa.-based Wyeth Pharmaceuticals and Wyeth Corporate have for the past two and six years, respectively, partnered with INROADS, an organization that specializes in placing students of color in corporate internships, says Doug Petkus, spokesperson for Wyeth. Over the years, the company has hosted 30 interns, but only recently made its first full-time hire from the organization. The company also partners with the National Black MBA Association, the National Society of Hispanic MBAs, the National Association of Black Accountants and the Temple MARC Program, which also places diverse candidates in internships.

"Diversity links to creativity which links to discovery which leads to development which links to profitability," says Petkus.

Wyeth lists most of its employment opportunities on a major Internet job board and they are then linked to smaller job boards that attract diverse job seekers, says Petkus. As for advertising with magazines geared toward diverse readers, the company worked with one in 2002, Ebony, with which it spent $9,788. Its total spend on advertisements in magazines in 2002 was $184,170, according to CMR.

Petkus sites a combination of factors when saying why diversity recruitment has become a focus.

"[The] factors include government pressures, patent expirations and rising R&D costs that demand a workforce that is highly resilient, able to manage and drive change and able to respond to multiple priorities," says Petkus.

Companies such as Wyeth, GSK and Pfizer have been participating in conferences that attract diverse engineers and scientists as well. Sharif of NSBE says a

Pharmaceutical Industry (cont'd.)

number of companies will host events for recruiting purposes at the organization's conferences.

Pfizer's sales and marketing teams for its consumer and pharmacy sales departments are focused on recruiting for diversity, especially for the Latino consumer market, says Solade Rowe, manager of university relations and diversity recruitment for Pfizer.

Based in New York City, Pfizer's pharmaceutical group established a few years ago its Hispanic Advisory Board, which is comprised of outside members who are Latino. It's charged with providing the company an understanding the nuances of the Latino consumer market, says Rowe.

Pfizer also has increased its involvement with the National Association of Hispanic MBAs to include participation on both the national and local levels. In spite of that focus, however, Pfizer did not purchase in 2002 any advertising in a magazine focused on Latino consumers but bought $3,315 worth of advertising in Black Enterprise, according to CMR. However, through its partnership with the National Association of Hispanic MBAs, Pfizer sponsored three fellows in 2001, eight fellows in 2002, five fellows in 2003 and extended offers for employment to many of them, Rowe says. He would not reveal how many fellows were hired, the company's demographics or goals for recruitment.

Companies also are focused on developing retention methods and creating a pipeline of future recruits by building interest in the pharmaceutical industry among diverse students who have yet to enter high school.

As a means to retain diverse employees once they're hired, Pfizer established a global leadership effectiveness group with the responsibility of identifying and developing future company leaders, Rowe says.

"This group is charged with making sure we have a diverse balance within the various areas of Pfizer," Rowe says.

Wyeth sought to establish incentives for diversity recruitment by including diversity in reviews of senior management and creating development programs for diverse employees. Management is to identify high-potential female employees and employees of color and complete an individual development plan for the employee. The company's succession planning procedures, where employees who can replace managers in key positions are identified, also must include a review of female employees and employees of color, says Petkus.

Diversity pipeline issues are being addressed by GSK, which is attempting to cre-

Pharmaceutical Industry (cont'd.)

ate future diverse employees by tapping into middle schools. The aim is to ensure that students of color are engaged in their math and science courses, which are part-and-parcel of the foundation for future research-and-development scientists. Since pharmaceutical companies tend to hire Ph.D.s over medical doctors, it's important that math and science become a focus for middle-school students who will have to build a strong foundation in those two subjects to eventually earn doctorate degrees. Latinos and African Americans who are interested in the medical field, however, tend to become physicians rather than Ph.D.s, says Portzer.

"Certain groups, such as African Americans, don't traditionally think of our industry, but send students to medical school but not for their Ph.D.," says Portzer, who adds that the industry must educate diverse communities on the opportunities the pharmaceutical industry provides for not only doctorate employees but also sales and marketing people.

GSK, which bases its U.S. operations in Philadelphia and Research Triangle Park, N.C., has developed a program with the University of North Carolina and a number of HBCUs in the area that features a moving science laboratory housed in a bus. The bus drives through lower-income neighborhoods in eastern North Carolina stopping at local high schools so students can get hands-on experience in the laboratory, says Portzer.

The pharmaceutical industry as a whole appears to be in its infancy of diversity recruiting. Of the companies that declined to be interviewed because of their lack of diversity recruiting, all but one were among the industry's top 10, according to the business-information Web site Hoovers.com. Will they take it to the next level in time to reach diverse consumers?

Can Recruiting People of Color End the Nursing Shortage?

© 2003 DiversityInc.com

By Angela D. Johnson

The number of registered nurses of color in the United States is growing at a rate 17 times greater than their white counterparts, according to the U.S. Department of Health and Human Services. Between 1996 and 2000, the population of African-American, Latino, Asian-American, Pacific-Islander and Native-American nurses rose 35 percent, compared with a 2 percent increase among white nurses. Given this growth, tapping into these numbers may be a solution to the country's crisis-level nursing shortage and compromised quality of care for patients of color.

Research by institutions, such as the Vanderbilt University School of Nursing in Nashville, Tenn., finds a relationship between the size of a nursing staff and adverse patient outcomes, including the length of hospital stay. Larger nursing staffs are associated with a 2 percent to 25 percent reduction in adverse outcomes.

And while the quality of health care for all patients is compromised by the shortage, the impact is particularly severe for patients of color. "Because we have identified an issue of access to care for people of color, one worries that the impact [of the nursing shortage] may be felt more severely in that population," says Patricia Grady, director of the National Institute of Nursing Research at the National Institute of Health, in Bethesda, Md.

"Just think of how sick African Americans are in this country," says Alicia Georges, chairman of the Lehman College Department of Nursing in the Bronx, N.Y., and president of the National Black Nurses Foundation. "It's not a question that we have this disparity in health care. We need to at least have an advocate."

Nurses of color exist at percentages lower than their representation in the general population, according to the Bureau of Health Profession within the U.S. Department of Health and Human Services Health Resources and Service Administration (HRSA). African Americans make up about 13 percent of the U.S. population; however, they represent just 5 percent of registered nurses in the work force. Latinos account for another 13 percent of the general population, yet account for only 2 percent of registered nurses.

Can Recruiting People of Color End the Nursing Shortage? (cont'd.)

Having nurses of color on staff is imperative because there tends to be distrust and anxiety about the medical system among patients of color, Grady says. They are more receptive to receiving information, particularly bad news, from someone of their own race or ethnicity. "People have a sense of what the lived experience has been of a patient who looks like them," says Georges.

Nurses of color also are vital in addressing the cultural nuances that influence the way people of color perceive illness, how they describe their ailments and their willingness to seek and compliance with medical care. For example, a Latino man suffering from heartburn may view his symptoms as punishment for eating poorly and could be reluctant to seek treatment or take medication prescribed by his doctor. Some Caribbeans use the term "foot" to describe the entire lower-leg region. Differences such as these can add to confusion in assessing an ailment. In some cultures, daughters take on the responsibility of handling the medical care of their parents, while sons never are involved. "We have to be able to understand these differences and deal with them," says Grady.

For medical facilities servicing immigrant populations, language also presents a challenge in providing quality health care. Patients who aren't English-dominant often have a difficult time understanding the instructions from their caregivers. "It's typically better to have someone who speaks the language, but that's not always possible," says Grady. In the absence of a bilingual nurse, a translator usually is an adequate substitution.

Some in the health-care industry believe cultural competency is not exclusive to those who share the same race. "[Quality patient care] has little to do with ethnicity and more to do with the ability to relate to the patient," says Sheila Thorne, president of Multicultural Healthcare Marketing Group, in Parsippany, N.J.

Thorne notes that women of any race or ethnicity are better at dealing with patients of color. "It's a compassion factor. Women are just better communicators," she says.

"If people are culturally competent, we have no problem [if they're not of color]," agrees Georges. However, she does acknowledge the benefits of a patient being treated by a nurse with a similar cultural background.

HRSA predicts that by 2020, there will be 808,416 unfilled nursing positions in the United States. But despite the job opportunities, people of color aren't choosing the nursing profession in great numbers. In the fall of 2002, 116,099 students were enrolled in nursing programs leading to a baccalaureate degree, a 9 percent increase over the previous year, according to the American Association of

Can Recruiting People of Color End the
Nursing Shortage? (cont'd.)

Colleges of Nursing. Of those students, 22 percent were students of color.

A study of registered nurses by the HRSA reveals that, despite low enrollment in baccalaureate nursing programs, the number of nurses of color in the work force is growing significantly. Between 1996 and 2000, the overall nursing population grew just 5.4 percent, while the number of Latino nurses jumped 25 percent, African-American nurses increased nearly 17 percent and the Asian-Pacific Islander segment grew 8.8 percent. The pool of white nurses declined 3.5 percent during the same time period.

Valley Regional Medical Center in Brownsville, Texas, is just one of the many hospitals in the country affected by the nursing shortage. "We cannot graduate them fast enough," says Ernest Marroquin, the hospital's human-resources recruiter. "There are just too many people needing health care." Marroquin strives to remedy the shortage by maintaining close relationships with local university nursing programs and students. He also visits countries such as the Philippines, England, and Canada to supplement the hospital's nursing pool.

Roughly 85 percent of Valley Regional's patients are Mexican; however, the nursing staff is a diverse group, including Filipinos, Mexicans, and Asian Americans. The nursing staff is not required to be fluent in Spanish, but there are bilingual aides and other employees available to assist those who lack fluency. "Patient care doesn't depend on language," says Marroquin. "It's how you were trained."

The U.S. government, trade organizations and corporations all are working to minimize the nursing shortage. Georges says that part of the challenge in recruiting nurses of diverse backgrounds is the profession's stigma. "Our image has not been attractive, not just to minorities but to anybody. People don't understand that nurses are well-educated. We get master's degrees and doctorates .... You're not a nurse's aide, you're an independent thinker."

In addition to advanced levels of education and responsibility, those in the nursing profession have the potential to earn an attractive salary. According to HRSA, in 2000, registered nurses earned an average of $46,782 a year. The average was higher for specialists, such as nurse practitioners/midwives ($60,534) and nurse anesthetists ($93,787).

Information about average nursing salaries by race or ethnicity is not available; however, given the impact of education levels on income, statistics on educational preparation offer some insight. One in 10 registered nurses in the overall nursing population has a master's or doctorate degree in nursing or a related field.

Can Recruiting People of Color End the Nursing Shortage? (cont'd.)

Native-Hawaiian/Pacific-Islander (16.4 percent) and African-American registered nurses are more likely to have advanced degrees, 16.4 percent and 11.1 percent, respectively. While just 5 percent of Asian-American nurses have master's or doctorate degrees, 55.5 percent have bachelor's degrees, a rate significantly higher than other nurses of color.

For the past several years, the Division of Nursing has participated in the HRSA Bureau of Health Professions' Kids into Health Careers initiative. The program encourages grantees, such as schools, nursing programs, and hospitals, to work with disadvantaged children in kindergarten through 12th grade to inform them about health professions and help them prepare for post-secondary education in the areas including nursing. HRSA's nursing division also has a Nursing Work force Diversity Program designed to assist students in gaining admission to nursing schools.

In February, the Recruitment and Diversity in Nursing Act of 2003, an amendment to the Public Health Service Act, was introduced into the House of Representatives. The bill establishes a program to encourage nontraditional nursing students, including those of color, to serve at least two years at a health-care facility after attending an accredited school of nursing on a federal scholarship. The legislation also supports the promotion of nursing in elementary and secondary schools, with at least half being schools with a large percentage of nontraditional students.

Last year, Fountain Valley, Calif.-based Hyundai Motor America donated $50,000 to the National Association of Hispanic Nurses (NAHN) to fund ongoing education of its members.

In February 2002, Johnson & Johnson, headquartered in New Brunswick, N.J., introduced The Campaign for Nursing's Future, a multi-year initiative to address the nursing shortage. The campaign features a diverse range of actual nursing professionals. "We wanted for everyone to realize they could be a nurse," says Kristen Smith, director of corporate communications for Johnson & Johnson Health Care Systems. "We wanted to appeal to everyone and to show that anyone can do this."

Johnson & Johnson made a concerted effort to have its materials reflect the range of those in the nursing profession–an American-American man, an Asian-American woman, etc. – populations that have an important role in reducing the shortage. "It's expected that we'll need 800,000 nurses by 2020," says Smith. "If we only focused on one ethnicity or background, we wouldn't be able to address the shortage."

Can Recruiting People of Color End the
Nursing Shortage? (cont'd.)

The Campaign for Nursing's Future, estimated to cost more than $20 million for a two-year period, includes recruitment brochures, poster and videos that are distributed to high schools, nursing schools, and other nursing organizations. Two television commercials air on national and local programs such as including network evening news programs and Spanish-language stations. A companion Web site, www.discovernursing.com, serves as a wealth of information about the nursing profession. Scholarships and grants also are provided.

Smith says enrollment in nursing schools has increased 8 percent in the past year. While she doesn't credit Johnson & Johnson alone, she believes the campaign has had a significant impact.

However, the task of diversifying the nation's nursing work force doesn't stop with recruitment. Attention must be paid to retaining current and future nurses of color "People get burned-out very quickly," says Georges."How nurses are treated is critical to getting nurses to stay and encouraging people to come.

"In some places in the country institutional racism [makes it] difficult to move up," she adds. "People leave and never get to leadership positions. People in institutions need to make sure they support their development" through training programs and putting people on the leadership track.

The growth in the population of nurses of color and the need for culturally competent caregivers makes focusing on people of color a viable strategy in addressing the dearth of nursing professionals; however, George cautions that "it's not going to solve the problem overnight. We'll see [progress] in increments. We need to get them in the pipeline and get them through."

Is Your Hospital Culturally Competent? Language Barriers Get in the Way

By Angela D. Johnson

© 2003 DiversityInc.com

May 02, 2003

As a Level 1 trauma center on Chicago's predominantly African-American and Latino West Side, Mount Sinai Hospital is a prime destination for shooting and car-crash victims and other critically injured people. On top of providing top-notch care for these patients, the medical center must contend with language challenges inherent in serving a diverse population.

Rory Lopez, Mount Sinai's director of care management programs, said the hospital has a significant number of Latino, Russian and Polish patients, most of whom have limited proficiency in English. "For the hospital, that's a serious, serious issue," he said.

Debbie Johnson, vice president of administration at Mineola, N.Y.'s Winthrop University Hospital agreed, describing language as "the largest barrier to appropriate health care."

Data from the 2000 U.S. Census revealed that 17.9 percent of those 5 years old and older speak a language other than English at home, with nearly half of those claiming to speak English less than "very well." Percentages are significantly higher in metropolitan areas, such as Miami, Chicago, New York City, and San Francisco. One out of 10 of those speaking a foreign language at home converse in Spanish, while 3.8 percent use other Indo-European languages and 2.7 percent rely on Asian or Pacific Island dialects.

Research has shown that limited English proficiency can have a significant impact on perception and delivery of quality patient care and compliance with treatment plans. A 1999 study published in the Journal of General Internal Medicine found that 52 percent of non-English speaking patients were satisfied with emergency room medical care compared to 71 percent of English speakers. A 2000 study in the same journal revealed that those with language-barriers were less likely to be given a follow-up appointment after an emergency room visit.

To ensure that all patients receive culturally and linguistically appropriate health care, several organizations have issued guidelines for health-care providers. In December 2000, the Office of Minority Health published the National Standards for Culturally and Linguistically Appropriate Services with the Federal Register.

Is Your Hospital Culturally Competent? Language Barriers Get in the Way (cont'd.)

In addition to guidelines and recommendations for providing culturally competent care and suggestions of structure, policies and procedures to implement these services, the document includes mandates for language services, which are enforced by the Office of Civil Rights (OCR).

Under Title VI of the Civil Rights Act of 1964, any organization or individual that receives federal financial assistance, either directly or indirectly, through a grant, contract or subcontract, must ensure that persons with limited English skills can effectively access critical health and social services. The title is designed to protect against discrimination based on race, ethnicity or national origin.

While hospitals have some flexibility in how they fulfill their language-assistance obligations, the Office of Civil Rights has found that effective programs usually include the following four elements:

- Assessment of the language needs of the population being served.

- Development and implementation of a comprehensive written policy that will ensure meaningful communication.

- Training to increase staffs' understanding of the policy and ability to carry it out.

- A regular monitoring of the language-assistance program to ensure that those with limited English proficiency have access to the program.

After 2000 census numbers revealed that the percentage of Latinos in New York's Nassau County had more than doubled, Winthrop University Hospital began investigating ways to serve this growing segment of the community, which includes many with limited English proficiency. In 2002, the hospital launched Diga Si A La Buena Salud (Say Yes to Good Health), an initiative designed to provide community outreach through events such as health fairs. In addition, the program offers Spanish-language classes for hospital staff and bilingual patient navigators in the facility's welcome center.

Winthrop is just one of many hospitals with programs to serve populations with limited English proficiency. Robert Wood Johnson University Hospital in New Brunswick, N.J., relies on its staff and telephone interpreters to serve its patient population. The majority of the hospital's language services assist Latinos; however, the hospital also provides translation serves for a number of Russian, Turkish, Greek, and Chinese patients. The medical center is equipped to handle 37 different languages through onsite personnel. Mount Sinai has 14 interpreters

Is Your Hospital Culturally Competent? Language
Barriers Get in the Way (cont'd.)

on staff: 11 specializing in Spanish, two in Russian and one in Polish. Lopez said "having enough interpreters to cover all areas 24/7" is the hospital's biggest challenge in serving its foreign-language speaking patients.

Many hospitals rely on their surrounding communities as a source of professional interpreters.

"Everyone who interprets here for us is from the community," said Lopez. As part of its recruitment effort, Mount Sinai participates in job fairs and makes visits to local high schools and community colleges to encourage people to become certified interpreters.

Robert Wood Johnson includes recruitment activities in the local Latino community as part of its search of Spanish-speaking employees. The medical center also offers 12-session courses on Latino culture and Spanish for its existing staff. Winthrop includes partnership with community- and faith-based organizations in surrounding Latino neighborhoods as part of its recruitment effort.

Some hospitals rely on untrained interpreters, including family members, to serve their foreign-language speaking populations, despite federal mandates that call for professional translators. A recent study by the Commonwealth Fund found that just half of Latinos who reported needing an interpreter during a medical visit said they usually or always were provided with one.

Just 1 percent of those who were provided with interpreters had a trained medical interpreter. More than half (55 percent) had a staff member acting as a translator, while 43 percent used a family member or friend.

"You just can't grab anyone who speaks another language to interpret," said Denise Stines, a registered nurse at the John Muir Medical Center in Walnut Creek, Calif.

While many ad hoc interpreters aren't familiar with medical terminology, relying on a family member or friend can be particularly problematic. Lopez said instead of giving a true diagnosis a family member or friend may soften the news by telling the patient, "It's OK. We're going to work it out and you'll be fine."

Official medical interpreters are required to go through a certification process that ensures that they are familiar with medical terminology and have been trained in the skills of effective interpreting. Ideally, said Lopez, the interpreter should serve as nothing more than the voice between both parties. "This is a triad conversation, but it's a dialogue between [the doctor] and the patient .... The trust that is being set up is between the doctor and the patient" rather than the

Is Your Hospital Culturally Competent? Language Barriers Get in the Way (cont'd.)

patient and the interpreter.

Stines said financial concerns keep some hospitals from providing adequate interpreter services.

"The health-care industry right now is in crisis," said Stines. "Health care is now a business, where as before we didn't look at the dollars and cents of health …. To the hospital, they're looking at how much it's going to cost to have interpreters on hand and it's not cheap."

Lopez estimated that Mount Sinai spends roughly $500,000 each year on interpretation services, including staff and contract workers. The hospital also provides most of its written materials, from admitting forms to signage throughout the hospital, in English and Spanish and sometimes Russian as well. Translation work is handled by outside agencies which can charge between $15 and $20 a page.

Title VI of the Civil Rights Act of 1964 gives people the right to file complaints against federally-funded organizations that don't provide adequate language services to those with limited English proficiency. Upon receiving a complaint, the OCR will conduct an investigation and issue a letter of findings stating the areas of noncompliance and the steps that must be taken to remedy the problem. If the matter can't be resolved informally, the ORC will seek compliance through the termination of federal assistance or referral to the Department of Justice for injunctive relief or other enforcement proceedings.

Patients have the right to issue a complaint if they are denied adequate health care because of race, ethnicity or national origin, but many are unlikely to do so, said Tawara Goode, director of the National Center for Cultural Competence at Georgetown University in Washington, D.C. "I would say that when you look at people with limited English proficiency, that are not well-educated or affluent, they are probably least likely to complain or seek out a lawyer …. It may not be in the framework of their culture to seek recourse."

Goode added that immigrants from impoverished countries are often just happy to be in the United States and don't want to do anything that would draw attention to themselves.

If patients with limited English skills are less likely to take legal action when they receive inadequate care, what motivates hospitals to provide services to assist those with limited English proficiency?

"One is the changing demographics, that the make up of the United States is

Is Your Hospital Culturally Competent? Language Barriers Get in the Way (cont'd.)

changing significantly," said Goode. "If you can demonstrate that you have the capacity to serve a variety of people well it can't help but increase your market share."

Johnson noted that Winthrop experienced an 18 percent increase in Latino's use of inpatient services and an 83 percent increase in their use of emergency room services following the launch of its Latino program.

Lopez has witnessed similar positive effects in the eight to nine years that Mount Sinai has had a formal language service. Compliance is up and the need for conducting a multitude of costly diagnostic tests has decreased because patients are better able to explain their symptoms.

Cultural Competency Is Rx for Success in Pharmaceutical Marketing

By Angela D. Johnson

© *2003 DiversityInc.com*

March 19, 2003

Latinos and African Americans exhibit a higher incidence of diseases, such as diabetes, hypertension and asthma. However, they rarely are included in clinical trials for drugs designed to help manage these illnesses. The absence of people of color in drug testing was one of several issues marketers grappled with Tuesday during the first day of Strategic Research Institute's Fourth Annual Multicultural Pharmaceutical Marketing and PR conference, held in Princeton, N.J.

White men are not the only people who get sick, said Sarah Harrison, vice president, customer strategy integration and public affairs for AstraZeneca. "We need to have tomorrow's trials represent everyone," she said.

Kimberly France, director, global professional affairs at Wyeth Pharmaceuticals, agreed. "It's embarrassing to include these groups in our ads and not have the medical data about how these drugs work [on ethnic populations]," she said.

When it comes to targeting Latino, African-American and Asian-American consumers, the pharmaceutical industry is in its nascence. Industries such as financial- services and packaged goods have been in the multicultural marketplace for more than 15 years; however, pharmaceutical marketers have just started to develop a business case for multicultural marketing over the past few years.

Much of this lag can be attributed to a lack of cultural competence among pharmaceutical companies. There are few people of color in pharmaceutical companies' sales, marketing, and development teams. Because of this, many of these marketers fail to consider the cultural differences that influence how African Americans, Latinos and Asian Americans cope with illness and perceive the health-care industry.

Pharmaceutical companies also have limited insight into what resonates with multicultural consumers. France provided an example of how her company missed the mark. In order to reach African-American consumers, Wyeth placed a general market ad for a hormone replacement therapy drug in Ebony magazine. The ad featured actress Lauren Hutton and was the only one in the magazine to feature a white model or spokesperson. The company thought placing an ad in

Cultural Competency Is Rx for Success in Pharmaceutical Marketing (cont'd.)

Ebony showed a commitment to the African-American market; however, France said the ad probably did more harm than good because it illustrated that the company didn't have a true understanding of these consumers.

General market advertising is not enough to reach multicultural consumers, said Mark Robertson, director of business development for the UniWorld Group. "We need to send a personal invitation that links to cultural traits," he said.

Robertson advised pharmaceutical marketers to pay attention to cultural distinctions, such as the role of the church as a vital source of healthcare information for African Americans and the position of the neighborhood pharmacist as a consulting physician for many Latinos.

Once pharmaceutical marketers are up to speed on the nuances of multicultural consumers, they should be encouraged to educate the physicians with whom they work, Most people of color are seen by doctors of a different race or ethnicity, which increases the chance of miscommunication between physician and patient.

Dr. S. Jayashankar, past president of the Association of Physicians of Asian Indian Origin, said that cultural humility is key in successful relationships between physicians and patients of color. He said doctors must stress sincerity without falling into patterns of using stereotypes, being condescending, or exhibiting cultural arrogance.

To be truly culturally sensitive, we must add individual variations to the cultural background, Jayashankar said. "Don't put people into stereotype boxes," he said. The second day of the conference will continue to address the importance of building relationships with multicultural consumers with presentations from companies, such as Pepsi, Johnson & Johnson and Wilson Health Information.

Are Doctors Best Way for Drug Companies to Reach Diverse Consumers?

By Angela D. Johnson

© *2003 DiversityInc.com*

March 20, 2003

For pharmaceutical companies that have acknowledged the market potential in multicultural communities, the challenge is figuring about the best way to reach them. Vehicles, such as neighborhood pharmacists and targeted media, were presented as effective strategies during several sessions throughout the second and final day of Strategic Research Institute's Fourth Annual Multicultural Pharmaceutical Marketing and PR conference in Princeton, N.J. Wednesday.

The importance of pharmacists to African-American and Latino consumers was stressed numerous times throughout the conference. During a panel discussion Wednesday on "Zeroing in on Special Market Segments to Accelerate Your Multicultural Growth," Lafayette Jones, president and CEO of Winston-Salem, N.C.-based Segmented Marketing Services, urged pharmaceutical marketers to abandon their traditional notions of promotion and look to neighborhood pharmacists instead of doctors when developing multicultural marketing plans. Jones said African Americans and Latinos, especially men, are reluctant to visit their doctors, but they often will ask their local pharmacists for treatment recommendations.

A presentation by Jim Wilson, president of Wilson Health Information, a research company in New Hope, Pa., provided data to support the status of pharmacists in communities of color. The company's WilsonRx Ethnic Market Report tracked Latino, African-American and Asian-American views of pharmacy issues. While the study, conducted in English, doesn't include Spanish- and Asian-language dominant consumers, it offers some insight into the multicultural market's perceptions of the pharmaceutical industry.

Wilson said research found that multicultural consumers spend an average of $1,800 to $2,400 a year on prescription drugs, an amount that's probably 60 percent to 70 percent lower than actual figures because it doesn't take into account money contributed by third parties such as health insurance providers.

According to the study, 73 percent of Latinos, 66 percent of Asian Americans and 63 percent of African Americans spoke to their pharmacist about their last new

Are Doctors Best Way for Drug Companies to Reach
Diverse Consumers? (cont'd.)

prescription. African Americans spent the most time talking to their pharmacist, averaging a six-minute conversation. Latinos and Asian Americans had shorter discussions, five minutes and three minutes, respectively.

Despite relying on pharmacists for information, less than half of Latinos, African Americans and Asian Americans surveyed said they were highly satisfied with the information and counseling they received. Wilson attributes this dissatisfaction to pharmacists' lack of experience in dealing with people of color and the lack of materials available in-language or in-culture.

"There are 55,000 pharmacies and 150,000 pharmacists [in the country], but how many of them are bilingual?" Wilson remarked. "Pharmacies aren't delivering the high level of satisfaction.... There's a great opportunity [for pharmaceutical companies] to partner with pharmacies for prescription or over-the-counter medications."

Pharmaceutical companies also are failing to take advantage of targeted media to reach multicultural consumers. Arthur Korant, co-founder and creative director for New York marketing agency Double Platinum, said this is especially true in the gay and lesbian communities. Conditions such as breast cancer, stress and anxiety, substance abuse and hepatitis are prevalent among gay and lesbian consumers; however, pharmaceutical companies only are promoting their HIV and AIDS drugs in publications targeting these communities. Korant said because gays and lesbians may not consume the same media as the general market, they are not getting information about drugs to treat these illnesses.

"There's a resonance in marketing to people where they live," said Korant. " The resonance of a community that a company speaks to in their own voice is significant."

Part VII: Industries in the Front Line

Aetna Reportedly Collects Racial Data on Its Members to Probe Gaps

By The Associated Press

© 2003 DiversityInc.com

March 05, 2003

Aetna Inc. has begun collecting data on the racial and ethnic backgrounds of some of its 14 million health plan members in what the insurer calls an effort to narrow the gaps in treatment between whites and minority patients, The Wall Street Journal reported Thursday.

Aetna said it is trying to understand differences in how white and patients of color get medical care, and to develop prevention, education and treatment programs to narrow the gap. But critics say collecting the data raises questions about patient privacy and racial profiling.

One concern is that insurance companies could use such information for underwriting decisions and "make it difficult for the people who need coverage to get coverage," said Clyde Yancy, a cardiologist at the University of Texas Southwestern Medical Center in Dallas, who has studied racial disparities.

"The notion that we would be profiling for health circumstances is something about which we need to be very, very careful."

The Hartford, Conn.-based company rolled out the initiative in 13 states and the District of Columbia in September, asking new members or those changing health plans or beneficiaries to voluntarily list their race or ethnic status on the application.

About 64,000 applicants were asked to provide the information and nearly 52,000, or about 80 percent, did so. The company is adding four more states, including Texas and Florida, by the end of this month and it eventually plans to seek the data from its entire membership.

"There is a disparity under every rock and a disparity behind every tree," Aetna chairman and chief executive John W. Rowe told the paper in a story on its Web site. "We need to do something about it."

The federal Medicare program for the elderly and the federal-state Medicaid program for the poor routinely ask beneficiaries for their race and ethnic background, but asking for such information is rare in the private sector, the newspaper said.

Aetna Reportedly Collects Racial Data on Its Members to Probe Gaps (cont'd.)

Rowe said concerns about gathering the data are valid "but that's not reason enough not to do it."

"We can't provide interventions for people at risk if we don't know who they are," he said. "We came to the view that not doing this was the racist approach."

An Inside Job? Merck's Diversity Chief Says Outside Factors Influence Success

By Linda Bean

© 2003 DiversityInc.com

April 04, 2003

Corporate diversity programs are, by necessity, introspective – examining and exploring the working relationships of people within the organization.

But a diversity director's job requires external vision, too, says Deborah Dagit, executive director of diversity and work environment at Merck & Co., the pharmaceutical manufacturer based in Whitehouse Station, N.J.

"It is really important to understand the environment," says Dagit, both inside and outside the workplace.

Dagit joined Merck in 2002, following a long career in social justice and diversity development on the West Coast. During the Clinton administration, she worked closely with Norman Mineta, Secretary of Commerce, on the development and passage of the Americans with Disabilities Act (ADA) and initiated a California program that placed people with disabilities in jobs.

Her move to New Jersey from California reaffirmed her contention that diversity directors need to be well-schooled in the external nuances that may come into play in the workplace.

The East and West coasts, for example, "are very different."

"You don't hear the term 'minorities' on the East Coast – it is 'people of color.' On the West Coast, no one questions that diversity is important. On the East Coast, [diversity programs] are more compliance-driven."

On the West Coast, Dagit says, there's a strong sense of cultural identity; on the East Coast, there's a strong identification with nation of origin.

"Here, there are communities of Italians and people from Puerto Rico ... people in clusters," she says. "On the West Coast, it's all mixed up – Koreans and Afghanis next to each other."

"If you are a diversity director going from one geography to another – or one industry to another – diversity is approached in very different ways, depending on the context," she says.

An Inside Job? Merck's Diversity Chief Says Outside Factors Influence Success (cont'd.)

Context is critical within the organization, as well. As a diversity director, "you have to look for what is important about diversity to that [individual] business and in that part of the country," Dagit says.

"And it is really important to look at the norms and processes," she adds.

There's a debate among diversity professionals around the most effective placement of corporate diversity executives. Some experts advocate the creation of freestanding offices of diversity, led by an executive who reports directly to the CEO. Others contend that diversity is best incorporated in organizations through well-established human-resource (HR) channels.

The real key, Dagit maintains, is to develop diversity programs in the same way other programs of importance are developed: "What are the symbols the organization uses to approach something important … the symbols we use only when something is really important?" At Merck, the most important projects are led by a cross-functional team, Dagit says. The same model has been used to emphasize the value of diversity at Merck.

On its Web site, for example, Merck features a group photo of top diversity leaders, including Ray Gilmartin, chairman, president and CEO; Ken Frazier, senior vice president and general counsel; Marcia Avedon, senior vice president, Human Resources; Wendy Yarno, executive vice president, Worldwide Human Health Marketing and Dagit – the same sort of cross-functional team that leads other critical activities.

Merck backs up the message by posting a breakdown of the workforce by race, gender and occupational level.

"We are using an existing norm to send the signal that we believe this is important," Dagit says.

According to Merck's breakdown, white males comprise52 percent of the 9,028 officials and managers and white females make up 30 percent. Asian-American men comprise 5 percent of the top officials, followed by African-American males, 4 percent of top officials, African- and Asian-American females, 3 percent; Latinos, 2 percent; Latinas, 1 percent and Native-American men and women, less than 1 percent.

Overall, white women comprise 39 percent of Merck's total U.S. workforce, followed by white men, 35 percent; African-American women, 8 percent; African-American men and Asian-American women, 5 percent; Latinos and Latinas, 2 percent; and Native Americans, less than 1 percent.

An Inside Job? Merck's Diversity Chief Says Outside Factors Influence Success (cont'd.)

While some diversity experts urge the separation of diversity functions from human resources, Dagit firmly believes that the top diversity officer should reside in HR.

"I really feel strongly about that. Otherwise, HR can be the best darn gatekeeper [against] diversity. They have all it takes to be a barrier. If HR doesn't have a buy-in, you are always doing to be up against that," she says.

"Some diversity leaders believe HR is a barrier to diversity and they say 'I'm going to avoid collaboration because it takes me longer ... but I've consistently collaborated with HR and I really feel that is how you move an organization forward quickly."

If the HR staff doesn't have the competencies that a diversity director needs, it is the director's job to "get people up to speed as quickly as possible," Dagit says.

"You need to say 'I need you to be my partner in getting HR to be a leader in diversity. We need to be a model,' " she says. "It's worked extremely well."

The successful implementation of any diversity strategy – trying executive compensation to diversity goals, for example, requires the cooperation and expertise of HR officials, Dagit says.

"When we implemented domestic-partner benefits, the benefits team took the lead. When we do a pay-equity analysis, the compensation team takes the lead," she adds. "I always explain the intersection of diversity, but diversity needed to be embedded in all the other HR core competencies."

Silent Minority: How to Reach Employees and Consumers With Mental-Health Concerns

By Kipp Cheng

May 28, 2003

© 2003 DiversityInc.com

For many companies, reaching out to consumers and employees with disabilities frequently is relegated to the afterthought status of larger diversity initiatives. More often than not, diverse marketing and recruitment efforts focus primarily on race or ethnicity, and neglect to reach out effectively to people with disabilities.

It's a mistake, diversity experts say, to exclude this large and growing segment of the U.S. population. The number of people with disabilities in the United States has risen from 43 million in 1990 to more than 54 million in 2000 (the most recent year when data on the group was collected), according to the U.S. Census Bureau.

As a market segment, people with disabilities wield aggregate income of more than $1 trillion and boast $220 billion in discretionary spending power. More than 30 million people with disabilities are between the ages of 16 and 64, the prime years of employment for most Americans. And with the aging population, the number of people with disabilities only will increase.

When corporations do consider the disability market and work force, most envision people with impairments that are physical and apparent by sight, such as people who require wheelchairs for mobility or workers with repetitive stress injury (better known as Carpal Tunnel syndrome) Thanks, in part, to the Americans with Disabilities Act, which was passed by Congress more than a decade ago, corporate America has an increased understanding of how to make accommodations for consumers and employees with visible impairments.

Lost in the shuffle are consumers and workers with hidden or invisible impairments, such as a person with mental-health issues or HIV-positive status. Advocates for people with disabilities say despite corporate America's better understanding of the disability market, there's a persistent delineation between people with "obvious" disabilities and those with hidden impairments.

"As a society, we have a prioritization of which disabilities are acceptable and which are not acceptable," says Bob Rosner, a retention specialist and syndicated

Silent Minority: How to Reach Employees and Consumers With Mental-Health Concerns (cont'd.)

columnist who writes about workplace issues for ABCNews.com and WorkingWounded.com. "Anything around mental health is like the third rail."

Rosner says employees who have mental-health issues are bound by secrecy or shame because of the biases that even well-educated people have surrounding issues of mental illness. "I think that we all have disabilities," Rosner says, "but when it comes to disclosure about mental-health problems in the workplace, people are reluctant to come out because of their fear of how co-workers and managers would respond. Bias against people with mental-health issues may not be explicit, but it's there."

Post-Sept. 11, Rosner says there was an increased incidence of workers who struggled with depression and yet were unable to voice their problems in the workplace because of fear of stigmatization. As consumers, they also struggled with finding marketing messages that reached out to them, for products and services such as pharmaceuticals and counseling.

"Sept. 11 sort of made it OK to talk about mental-health concerns," Rosner says, "but then the moment passed, and the issue went back into the closet."

The silence of people with mental-health issues feeds off those employees' fears of being passed over for assignments or being perceived as weak or incapable of doing an effective job.

"Many disabilities that are 'silent' are bound by virtue of their associated stigma," says Dr. Richard Wodka, assistant medical director at Raritan, N.J.-based Ortho Biotech, a Johnson & Johnson company. "That's problematic because keeping these impairments in the closet leads to things such as not asking for reasonable accommodations or invalid concerns in hiring practices. We like to think that these things don't happen at most major companies but they do."

Rosner agrees, adding that lack of accommodation sometimes leads employees to lie to get around telling employers what they really need, such as time off during the workday for therapy.

The incorrect image of people with mental-health concerns as "a crazy person" bouncing around a padded room is common, says Beth Clark, president of Allegro Training and Consulting, a Lawrence, Kan., diversity-training firm.

"That's the image when some people first think of mental-health problems," says Clark. "They think of people who are not functioning. But people with chronic mental illness who cannot hold down jobs are a small percentage of the population. There are thousands and thousands of people out there with chronic mental

Silent Minority: How to Reach Employees and Consumers With Mental-Health Concerns (cont'd.)

illness in the work force who are productive and producing."

Indeed, according to the Depression and Bipolar Support Alliance, more than 23 million Americans live with depression and an additional 2.5 million live with bipolar affective disorder (a condition formerly known as manic-depression). Approximately 1 percent to 2 percent of adults and children are afflicted either with bipolar or unipolar mood disorders, and research has shown that mental-health disorders – which include thought, mood, personality and substance-abuse disorders – affect a cross-section of men and women from all races, cultures, and economic and educational classes.

"I think we have to separate out things that would impair reality testing and would not impair reality testing," says Wodka. "[The brain] is just another organ system that has an illness. Mental illness is absolutely genetic, it is absolutely biochemically based and it's 100 percent treatable with medication."

Wodka's perspective on the issue of mental health in the workplace and consumer sector is personal as well as professional.

"I happen to be bipolar," Wodka says. "It's something that I would be very reticent to share with my employer because the concept of someone being bipolar or someone having a mental illness is truly stigmatized at work."

Wodka – who currently is on leave from Ortho Biotech – says open communication with an employer is paramount to giving employees with hidden impairments the opportunity to receive the things they need in the workplace.

Managers will have diminished expectations ...

"Communication is so critical and an important start to breaking down barriers and stereotypes," Wodka says.

From the consumer vantage point, Clark says there's an opportunity to reach an untapped market.

"Even the mental-health community has money and they are buying stuff," says Clark. "The marketing approach may be a little bit different from the general market. But how many companies are going out and actively hiring and pursuing the mental-health community?"

The challenge in the workplace, Clark adds, is getting past preconceived ideas about how a worker with mental-health impairments might function in the workplace. "It's politically incorrect to think that there's anything wrong," Clark says. "But some people really do think that there's something wrong, and rather than

Silent Minority: How to Reach Employees and Consumers With Mental-Health Concerns (cont'd.)

talk about it, they think there's going to be more challenges, more problems for the company, that it's going to cost more money."

Whether it's conscious or not, managers will have diminished expectations about work ability and productivity for people with mental-health impairments, impeding their career-track options, says Wodka, a medical doctor who is board-certified in family practice and behavioral medicine.

"There may be nothing, in a practical sense, to lead a manager or a supervisor to believe a worker with mental illness can't do the work," Wodka says, "except for the pre-established stigma."

"The problem is that it's seen as a weakness or a lack of trustworthiness to do the job," says Rosner.

While the ADA protects disabled employees from blatant discrimination, corporate nondiscrimination policies might not effectively protect employees with mental-health problems.

"I'm not sure all the policies in the world with fix the bias issues," says Rosner.

"We are not protected in most policies," Wodka adds. "Many of the medical concerns are covered by the ADA, but there are not many anti-discriminatory practices for mental health conditions. That's really the issue."

So how can corporations effectively accommodate employees with mental-health concerns that are not necessarily addressed in the ADA or internal nondiscrimination policies?

Notable people with bipolar or unipolar disorders include ...

"I'm a big believer that individual managers can have a tremendous influence," Rosner says. "For a supervisor to lead an honest conversation with people about mental health early on, when a crisis comes up, there's a baseline of support and understanding."

In the case of employees who are HIV positive, for example, Wodka says allowing workers to know that they are supported and not ostracized from opportunities is vital in making room for real conversation. He cites GlaxoSmithKline as an example of a company with a good history of supporting employees who happen to be HIV positive. "It's because they are very involved in the manufacturing, research and development of HIV-related medication," he says.

All agree that Employee Assistance Programs (EAPs) are beneficial, especially when they are implemented promptly and employees are alerted to access before

Silent Minority: How to Reach Employees and Consumers With Mental-Health Concerns (cont'd.)

problems arise.

"Employee Assistance Programs need to be activated early on in the concern," Wodka says. "If things go down poorly with an employee and his or her behavior or acting out as a result of their illness in their work, EAP programs generally cannot provide the kind of advocacy that they need."

More often than not, EAP programs are implemented reactively instead of proactively, Clark adds.

But companies that have successful navigated through the sensitive shoals of mental health with employees can reap enormous benefits, such as loyalty and respect.

"It all comes back to a respect issue," Rosner says. "Loyalty is not a one-way street, and loyalty is not something that can be chipped away at and then expect it to be like there's nothing wrong."

"I can't tell you – as both a physician and as someone with bipolar disease who has spent a lot of time learning about this disorder and individuals whose lives this disorder has touched – I'm continually amazed, working at the state and national level, to see the number of famous and executive-level people who this disease has touched."

Notable people with bipolar or unipolar disorders include media mogul Ted Turner, former first lady Barbara Bush, civil-rights activists James Farmer, and former national security advisor Robert McFarlane, according to Pendulum Resources, an online resource for affective disorders.

"Corporate America needs to include silent impairments as part of their diversity programs," Wodka says. "We need say their names aloud, we need to talk about them and we need to take the fear and the misconceptions away about mental illness."

Part VIII - Business Case Conclusion: What's Next?

When DiversityInc researched and wrote the first Business Case for Diversity three years ago, we weren't sure how quickly supporting information would change. Each year, the Business Case for Diversity has been substantiated and improved by demographic data from the U.S. Census Bureau, buying-power data from the Selig Center for Economic Growth at the University of Georgia, and new hard data from the increasing number of companies making substantial profits by seeking diverse customers through their diverse workforces and suppliers.

This year, the demographics continue the story of the rapidly growing Latino population and a nation undergoing a metamorphosis. Companies that intend to be competitive going forward must understand and actively court emerging-market customers, including people of color, gays/lesbians and people with disabilities. Having a work force representative of those groups is increasingly essential. Involvement in emerging-market communities, from supplier-diversity initiatives to philanthropic endeavors, sends a strong signal of support to potential customers and employees within these communities.

What's next? As the demographics of this nation continue to shift, and as more companies consolidate or fail, those that understand and utilize the Business Case for Diversity become stronger every year.

END NOTES:

INTRODUCTION

[1] Census 2000 data: This number comes from subtracting "non-Hispanic whites" (194.51 million) from the entire U.S. population (281.42 million), which comes to 86.91 million — or 30.9 percent of the U.S. population.

[2] Roberto Ramirez (survey statistician, Ethnic and Hispanic Statistics Branch, U.S. Census Bureau). Interview with DiversityInc, 19 March 2003.

[3] U.S. Census Bureau, *The Black Population in the United States: March 2002* (Current Population Reports, Series P20-541), Washington, D.C., March 2003, 1.

[4] U.S. Census Bureau, *The Asian and Pacific Islander Population in the United States: March 2002* (Current Population Reports, Series P20-540), Washington, D.C., May 2003, 1.

[5] Yoji Cole, "Who's White, Who's Black, Who's Brown, Who's Yellow? Why Do We Care So Much?," DiversityInc, 22 July 2002, *http://www.diversityinc.com/members/3275.cfm*.

[6] "Do the Math, Marketers: Biracial Americans Grow in Numbers," Associated Press, 19 April 2002. [DiversityInc: *http://www.diversityinc.com/members/2772.cfm*]

[7] "Unmarried Couples More Likely to be of Mixed Race," Associated Press, 14 March 2003. [DiversityInc: *http://www.diversityinc.com/members/4605.cfm*]

[8] U.S. Census Bureau, *Black Population*, 1.

[9] Ibid, 2.

[10] Ibid.

[11] C. Stone Brown, "From Negro, Colored, Black to African American – In Search of An Identity," DiversityInc, 3 February 2003, *http://www.diversityinc.com/members/4394.cfm*.

[12] Yoji Cole, "Are You African, Caribbean or African American?" DiversityInc, 19 April 2002, *http://www.diversityinc.com/members/2769.cfm*.

[13] Ibid.

[14] C. Stone Brown, "New Census Numbers: Latino Population Growing Even Faster Than Anticipated," DiversityInc, 22 January 2003, *http://www.diversityinc.com/members/4338.cfm*.

[15] U.S. Census Bureau (mid-2001 population estimates; data released in January 2003); U.S. Census Bureau, "Table 67: Live Births by Race and Type of Hispanic Origin," *Statistical Abstract of the United States: 2002*, Washington,D.C., 2002, p. 59.

[16] Global Insight, *Snapshots of the U.S. Hispanic Market* (Executive Summary), Lexington, Mass., April 2003, 1.

[17] Angela D. Johnson, "Reaching People of Color is the Key to Future Business Success," DiversityInc, 11 April 2003, *http://www.diversityinc.com/members/4771.cfm*.

[18] U.S. Census Bureau, *The Foreign-Born Population in the United States: March 2002* (Current Population Reports, Series P20-539), Washington, D.C., February 2003, 1.

END NOTES:

[19] Ibid, 1-2.

[20] Global Insight, 2.

[21] Pew Hispanic Center and Kaiser Family Foundation, *2002 National Survey of Latinos: Summary of Findings*, Washington, D.C., December 2002, 13.

[22] U.S. Department of Justice, Immigration and Naturalization Service, *2001 Statistical Yearbook of the Immigration and Naturalization Service*, February 2003, 10.

[23] U.S. Census Bureau mid-2001 estimates.

[24] U.S. Dept. of Justice, 10.

[25] Kipp Cheng, "Census Shows Chinese Still Largest Asian Group, Asian Indians on the Rise," DiversityInc, 1 March 2002, *http://www.diversityinc.com/members/2494.cfm*.

[26] Kipp Cheng, "Fast-Growing Asian-Indian Population Is Affluent, Educated and Ignored," DiversityInc, 14 March 2002, *http://www.diversityinc.com/members/2573.cfm*.

[27] Ibid.

[28] Angela D. Johnson, "Asian Indians: Upscale Marketers Ignore This Prime Consumer Segment," DiversityInc, 15 April 2003, *http://www.diversityinc.com/members/4786.cfm*.

[29] Witeck-Combs Communications, Inc. and Packaged Facts, *The Gay and Lesbian Market, New Trends, New Opportunities, 3rd edition*, New York, October 2002, 5.

[30] Ibid.

[31] Kipp Cheng, "Gay-by Boom: Gay Families Emerge as New, Affluent Niche Market," DiversityInc, 28 March 2002, *http://www.diversityinc.com/members/2672.cfm*.

[32] Interview with DiversityInc, 11 April 2002.

[33] Cheng, "Gay-by Boom."

[34] Kipp Cheng, "Gay American Gothic: Rainbow Flag Alongs de Pitchfork," DiversityInc, 22 August 2001.

[35] Kipp Cheng, "What Marketers Should Know About People with Disabilities," DiversityInc, 18 April 2002, *http://www.diversityinc.com/members/2761.cfm*.

[36] U.S. Census Bureau, *Disability Status: 2000* (Census 2000 Brief, C2KBR-17), Washington, D.C., March 2003, 1-2; 5.

[37] Ibid, 1-2.

[38] Ibid.

[39] U.S. Census Bureau, *Foreign-Born*, 1.

[40] Ibid, 1-2.

[41] U.S. Dept. of Justice, 10.

[42] U.S. Census Bureau, *Foreign-Born*, 2.

[43] Ibid.

[44] Ibid, 2-3.

End Notes:

⁴⁵ Ibid, 3.

⁴⁶ Ibid.

⁴⁷ Ibid.

⁴⁸ Center for Immigration Studies, "Census Releases Immigration Numbers for Year 2000," Washington, D.C., 4 June 2002, *http://www.cis.org/articles/2002/censuspr.html*.

⁴⁹ Ibid.

⁵⁰ Steven Camarota, "Immigrants in the United States – 2002: A Snapshot of America's Foreign-Born Population," Center for Immigration Studies, November 2002.

⁵¹ Ibid.

⁵² Ibid.

⁵³ Ibid.

⁵⁴ Ibid.

⁵⁵ Ibid.

⁵⁶ Ibid.

Part II: Corporate Governance

⁵⁷ "Playing the Race Card: For Job Applicants of Color, Racial Network Is An Advantage," DiversityInc, 20 February 2002.

⁵⁸ "How Do Corporations Build Trust? Recruitment and Retention," DiversityInc, 18 March 2002.

⁵⁹ "A Report Card on Diversity," Harvard Business Review, January-February 1999.

⁶⁰ Report from the Society for Human Resource Management (SHRM)

⁶¹ "How Do Corporations Build Trust?"

⁶² "Counting Heads? Measuring Diversity Requires More Than Simple Math," DiversityInc, 30 November 2001.

⁶³ Ibid.

⁶⁴ Employment Management Association/SHRM, 2000.

⁶⁵ U.S. Census Bureau, *Black Population*, 5

⁶⁶ U.S. Census Bureau, *Statistical Abstract*, 561.

⁶⁷ U.S. Census Bureau, *Black Population*, 5

⁶⁸ Ibid.

⁶⁹ Ibid.

⁷⁰ U.S. Census Bureau, *Statistical Abstract*, 561.

⁷¹ U.S. Census Bureau, *The Hispanic Population in the United States: March 2000* (Current Population Reports: P20-535), Washington, D.C., March 2001, 4.

⁷² U.S. Census Bureau, *Asian and Pacific Islander*, 4-5.

END NOTES:

73 Ibid, 5.

74 Ibid, 4.

75 Kipp Cheng, " More Than Numbers: Adequate GLBT Stats Still Elusive, Problematic," DiversityInc, 16 September 2002, *http://www.diversityinc.com/members/3528.cfm*.

76 Witeck-Combs, 60.

77 Ibid, 62.

78 U.S. Census Bureau, *Disability Status*, 2.

79 Ibid, 10.

80 *Heidi van Arnem Disability Consumer Research Report*, iCan, Birmingham, MI, Spring 2002, 2

81 U.S. Census Bureau, *Statistical Abstract*, 561.

82 U.S. Census Bureau, *Women and Men in the United States, March 2002* (Current Population Report, P20-544), Washington, D.C., March 2003, 2.

83 Ibid, 3.

84 *Economic Report of the President*, U.S. Government Printing Office, Washington, D.C., February 2003, 326-327.

85 U.S. Census Bureau, *1997 Economic Census: Survey of Minority-Owned Business Enterprises*,Washington, D.C., July 2001.

86 "Employee Satisfaction Comes First For Big Five Accounting Firm," DiversityInc, 18 January 2001.

87 "Diversity-Savvy Companies Prioritizing Retention," DiversityInc, 28 January 2002.

88 "Occupational Employment in Private Industry by Race/Ethnic Group/Sex, and by Industry, United States, 2001," U.S. Equal Employment Opportunity Commission (EEOC), *http://www.eeoc.gov/stats/jobpat/2001/national.html*

89 "Whole Culture: What Companies Leading in Diversity Are Thinking," DiversityInc, 29 January 2002.

90 *Women of Color in Corporate Management: Three Years Later*, Catalyst, New York, 2002. *http://www.catalystwomen.org*

91 Ibid.

92 Human Rights Campaign (HRC) statistics. www.hrc.org

93 Ibid.

94 "When 'Diversity Director' Means 'Dead End' -- Malignant Neglect: Mistakes You Don't Know You're Making," DiversityInc, 15 January 2002.

95 "How to Make an Impact as a Diversity Director: Affect the Revenue Stream," DiversityInc, 24 January 2002.

96 "Occupational Employment in Private Industry by Race/Ethnic Group/Sex, and by Industry, United States, 2001," EEOC Web Site, *http://www.eeoc.gov/stats/jobpat/2001/national.html*

97 "Benched: Lack of Succession Planning Sidelines Talented People of Color," DiversityInc, 7 January 2002.

END NOTES:

PART III: CORPORATE COMMUNICATIONS

98 "Make the Mission Statement Count: Building Real Trust in Corporate Leadership," DiversityInc, 13 March 2002, *http://www.diversityinc.com/members/2566.cfm*.

99 Ibid.

100 Jordan T. Pine, "How to Market Diversity on Your Corporate Site," DiversityInc, 19 November 2001, *http://www.diversityinc.com/members/1769.cfm*.

101 Jordan T. Pine, "Special Report: Best Web Sites for Diversity," DiversityInc, 15 November 2001, *http://www.diversityinc.com/members/1747.cfm*.

102 Ibid.

103 Jordan T. Pine, "Malignant Neglect: Managing Corporate Communications, Customer Service and Web Sites," DiversityInc, 13 February 2002, *http://www.diversityinc.com/members/2361.cfm*.

104 Elena Maria Lopez, "Chase Plans $500B in Home Loans to Diverse Markets; Community Leaders to Help," DiversityInc, 5 February 2003, *http://www.diversityinc.com/members/4406.cfm*.

105 Pine, "Malignant Neglect."

106 Ibid.

107 Yoji Cole, "Employee-Affinity Groups: In Lean Times, Smart Companies Use Them As Business Tools," DiversityInc, 30 September 2002, *http://www.diversityinc.com/members/3598.cfm*.

PART IV: EMERGING MARKETS

108 *Multicultural Economy, 2002*, Selig Center for Economic Growth, Terry College of Business (University of Georgia), Athens, GA, 2002, 6.

109 Ibid, 7.

110 Ibid.

111 U.S. Bureau of the Census, Current Population Survey, March Supplement (2000) and Current Population Survey/Housing Vacancy Survey.

112 Kipp Cheng, "Numbers Make the Case: Ethnic Spending Power Continues Rapid Rise," 6 December 2002, *http://www.diversityinc.com/members/3926.cfm*.

113 U.S. Census Bureau, *Black Population*, 5-6.

114 Pew, 12.

115 U.S. Census Bureau, *Black Population*, 6.

116 Pew, 12.

117 U.S. Census Bureau, *Black Population*, 2.

118 Selig, 7.

119 "66 Top Markets for Affluent Black Households," DiversityInc, May 14, 2001.

END NOTES:

[120] U.S. Census Bureau, Current Population Survey, March Supplement.

[121] Selig, 7.

[122] Cheng, "Numbers Make the Case."

[123] Selig, 10.

[124] Pew, 12.

[125] Global Insight, 1-2.

[126] U.S. Census Bureau, March Supplement.

[127] Global Insight, 2.

[128] Selig, 11.

[129] Ibid, 10-11.

[130] Ibid, 11.

[131] Ibid, 9.

[132] Cheng, "Numbers Make the Case."

[133] Selig, 9.

[134] U.S. Census Bureau, March Supplement.

[135] Cheng, "Numbers Make the Case."

[136] Selig.

[137] Kipp Cheng, "Fast-Growing Asian-Indian Population is Affluent, Educated and Ignored," DiversityInc, 14 March 2002, *http://www.diversityinc.com/members/2573.cfm*.

[138] Kipp Cheng, "Finally the Truth: How Many Gay Americans Are There and What Will They Buy," DiversityInc, 11 April 2002, *http://www.diversityinc.com/members/2737.cfm*.

[139] Witeck-Combs.

[140] 17

[141] iCan, 3.

[142] Ibid.

[143] Selig, 8

[144] Ibid.

[145] Ibid.

[146] U.S. Census Bureau, "American Indians and Alaska Natives," *1997 Economic Census: Survey of Minority-Owned Business Enterprises* (EC97CS-7), Washington, D.C., July 2001, 12.

[147] Kipp Cheng, "Beyond Just the Numbers, What Counts As an Emerging Market?," DiversityInc, 1 July 2002, *http://www.diversityinc.com/members/3191.cfm*.

[148] Linda Bean, "Lack of Data? Lack of Interest? Why Don't We Know More About African-American Auto Consumers, DiversityInc, 7 March 2003, *http://www.diversityinc.com/members/4559.cfm*.

[149] Kipp Cheng, "Asian Latinos: Do Two Fast-Growing Groups Add Up to an Attractive Niche Market?" DiversityInc, 1 November 2002, *http://www.diversityinc.com/members/3758.cfm*.

END NOTES:

PART V: SUPPLIER DIVERSITY

[150] Small Business Administration; U.S. Census Bureau, *1997 Economic Census*.

[151] U.S. Small Business Administration, Office of Advocacy, *Minorities in Business, 2001*, November 2001, *http://www.sba.gov/advo/stats*; U.S. Census Bureau, *1997 Economic Census*.

[152] U.S. Census Bureau, *1997 Economic Census*.

[153] U.S. Department of Commerce's Minority Business Development Agency, July 12, 2001.

[154] U.S. Census Bureau, *1997 Economic Census*.

[155] Ibid.

[156] Selig, 7; U.S. Census Bureau, *1997 Economic Census*.

[157] U.S. Census Bureau, *1997 Economic Census*.

[158] Ibid.

[159] Global Insight, 2.

[160] U.S. Census Bureau, *1997 Economic Census*.

[161] Pitney Bowes Inc., NAWBO, Philadelphia Chapter, and Wells Fargo, *Completing the Picture: Equally-Owned Firms in 2002,* April 2003.

[162] Ruth Zeilberger, "Boom in Women-Owned Businesses, But Financing Still a Barrier," DiversityInc, 1 May 2003, *http://www.diversityinc.com/members/4871.cfm*. (Citing Pitney Bowes study.)

[163] Ibid.

[164] Ibid.

[165] Information on NAICS standards is available online at *http://www.sba.gov/size*.

[166] "Supplier diversity" section of American Express Web site, *http://amexb2b.disk11.com/completesupplierdiversity.htm*.

[167] Apple's supplier-diversity Web site, http://www.apple.com/supplierdiversity.

[168] Interview with DiversityInc, 23 Jan. 2002.

[169] "Business classifications" section of Apple's supplier-diversity Web site, *http://www.apple.com/supplierdiversity/documents/businessclassifications.html*.

[170] More on HUBZone business is available on the SBA's HubZone Web site at: *https://eweb1.sba.gov/hubzone/internet*.

[171] Linda Bean, "Real Money: Lockheed Martin, Johnson Controls Join Billion-Dollar Roundtable," DiversityInc, 15 May 2003, http://www.diversityinc.com/members/4940.cfm.

[172] Interview with DiversityInc, 23 Jan. 2002.

[173] DiversityInc Top 50 Company Survey, 2002.

[174] "Anatomy of the Nation's No. 1 Supplier-Diversity Program," DiversityInc, 27 April 2001.

END NOTES:

175 "Business Case for Supplier Diversity: Lucent Takes the Industry Lead," DiversityInc, 1 June 2001.

176 "Case Study in Supplier-Diversity 91 Renaldo Jensen at Ford," DiversityInc, 5 December 2001, p. 200.

177 "Johnson Controls Aims for $1 Billion Spent with Diverse Suppliers by 2003," DiversityInc, 12 July 2001.

178 Ibid.

179 From executive summary of KPMG Impact Analysis for Fifth Annual Rainbow/PUSH Wall Street Project Conference, Jan. 15-18, 2002, "A Time to Heal, A Time to Rebuild."

180 Jordan T. Pine, "Supplier Diversity: What's In, What's Out According to the NMSDC at Rainbow/PUSH," DiversityInc, 22 January 2002, *http://www.diversityinc.com/members/2231.cfm*.

PART VII: INDUSTRIES IN THE FRONT LINE

Auto

181 National Association of Minority Automobile Dealers (NAMAD), 8401 Corporate Drive, Suite 405, Lanham, MD 20785. *http://namad.org/index.asp*

182 Linda Bean, "Auto Industry First: Ford, Arizona State Univ. Announce Programs to Train Dealers," 5 April 2002. *http://www.diversityinc.com/members/2705.cfm*

183 Yoji Cole, "Ford Motor Company: This Year's Top Company for Diversity," *DiversityInc*, June/July 2003.

184 Ibid.

185 Linda Bean, "Auto Markets: How Small Can You Slice Them?" DiversityInc, 20 May 2003. *http://www.diversityinc.com/members/4943.cfm*

186 Ruth Zeilberger, "Volvo Driving Into the GLBT Market," DiversityInc, 8 May 2003. *http://www.diversityinc.com/members/4902.cfm*

187 Linda Bean, "GM 'Diversity Tour' Aims to Reach Diverse Consumers, Reporters," DiversityInc, 17 April 2003. *http://www.diversityinc.com/members/4798.cfm*

188 Cole, "Ford."

189 Linda Bean, "Real Money: Lockheed Martin, Johnson Controls Join Billion-Dollar Roundtable," DiversityInc, 15 May 2003. *http://www.diversityinc.com/members/4940.cfm*

Financial Services

190 Elena Maria Lopez, "Chase Plans $500B in Home Loans to Diverse Markets; Community Leaders to Help," DiversityInc, 5 February 2003. *http://www.diversityinc.com/members/4406.cfm*

191 Ibid.

192 Pew, 12

END NOTES:

[193] Ibid.

[194] Ibid.

[195] Elena Maria Lopez, "As Jobless Rates Rise for People of Color, Smart Companies Recruit," DiversityInc, 13 March 2003. *http://www.diversityinc.com/members/4599.cfm*

[196] Yoji Cole, "Is An MBA Worth It for People of Color?" DiversityInc, 16 December 2002. *http://www.diversityinc.com/members/3985.cfm*

[197] Melanie Austria Farmer, " More Latinos Looking at Jobs in Finance, Accounting," DiversityInc, 14 February 2003. *http://www.diversityinc.com/members/4461.cfm*

[198] "One Third of Blacks, Latinos Face Racism in Housing," DiversityInc, 5 April 2002.

[199] Eric L. Hinton, "Redlining: Citigroup Steered High-Interest Loans To Minority Neighborhoods, Study Finds," DiversityInc, 21 June 2002. *http://www.diversityinc.com/members/3151.cfm*

[200] "Predatory Lenders: Are They Draining Future Profits From Buyers Today?" DiversityInc, 31 August 2002.

[201] "Financial Services Look to Multiethnic Partners for Growth," DiversityInc, 15 May 2001.

[202] "To Reach the African-American Consumer — Go To Church," DiversityInc, 17 December 2001.

[203] "Pay Now/Pay More Later, The Costly Privilege of High-Interest Credit Cards," DiversityInc, 15 March 2002.

[204] Melanie Austria Farmer, "Russell Simmons' Debit Card: Helpful or High Risk?" DiversityInc, 7 May 2003. *http://www.diversityinc.com/members/4896.cfm*

Retail

[205] Kipp Cheng, "What Every Retailer Must Know About Emerging Markets," DiversityInc, 8 May 2002. *http://www.diversityinc.com/members/2856.cfm*

[206] "Retail Reality: Recruitment, Retention of People of Color Is Essential," DiversityInc, 19 June 2001.

[207] "Black Action Retail Group Seeks to Mentor Young People of Color," DiversityInc, 15 June 2001.

[208] U.S. Equal Employment Opportunity Commission, *2000 EEO-1 Aggregate Report: SIC 539: Misc. General Merchandise Stores*, Washington, D.C., 2002. *http://www.eeoc.gov/stats/jobpat/2000/sic3/539.html*

[209] Melanie Austria Farmer, "Does Macy's Racially Profile Customers? Lawsuit Claims It Does, Company Says No," DiversityInc, 22 May 2003. *http://www.diversityinc.com/members/4976.cfm*

[210] "Does Diversity-Conscious Advertising Prove a Diversity Commitment?" DiversityInc, 14 May 2002.

[211] "As the Melting Pot Simmers, Ethnic Media Reaches People of Color," DiversityInc, 24 April 2002.

END NOTES:

[212] Cheng, "What Every Retailer."

[213] Ruth Zeilberger, "With Revenues Dropping and Competition Intensifying, McDonald's Goes After Multiethnic Customers," DiversityInc, 18 October 2002. *http://www.diversityinc.com/members/3687.cfm*

[214] Ruth Zeilberger, "Can Kmart's Black, Latino Customers Save It From Bankruptcy?" DiversityInc, 13 September 2002. *http://www.diversityinc.com/members/3517.cfm*

[215] Ruth Zeilberger, "Kmart's Salvation Lies With Customers of Color: Can Joe Boxer Help?" DiversityInc, 8 August 2002. *http://www.diversityinc.com/members/3369.cfm*

Media

[216] C. Stone Brown, "Are The New FCC Media Rules Anti-Diversity? Trent Lott Says Yes," DiversityInc, 3 June 2003. *http://www.diversityinc.com/members/5033.cfm*

[217] Linda Bean, "Learn Diversity Lessons From The New York Times' Mistakes," DiversityInc, 19 May 2003. *http://www.diversityinc.com/members/4953.cfm*

[218] Kipp Cheng, "Reaching New Customers: Marketers Struggle to Hit Bull's Eye," DiversityInc, 31 January 2003. *http://www.diversityinc.com/members/4388.cfm*

[219] Angela D. Johnson, "Is Spanish-Language TV Still Best Way to Reach Latino Viewers?" DiversityInc, 14 March 2003. *http://www.diversityinc.com/members/4607.cfm*

Pharmaceuticals/Health Care

[220] Yoji Cole, "Pharmaceutical Industry: Diversity Recruiting Still in Its Infancy," *DiversityInc*, June/July 2003.

[221] Angela D. Johnson, "Is Your Hospital Culturally Competent? Language Barriers Get in the Way," DiversityInc, 2 May 2003. *http://www.diversityinc.com/members/4868.cfm*

[222] Angela D. Johnson, "Cultural Competency Is Rx for Success in Pharmaceutical Marketing," DiversityInc, 19 March 2003. *http://www.diversityinc.com/members/4632.cfm*

[223] Angela D. Johnson, "Are Doctors Best Way for Drug Companies to Reach Diverse Consumers?" DiversityInc, 20 March 2003. *http://www.diversityinc.com/members/4639.cfm*

NOTES

NOTES

NOTES

NOTES

NOTES